Mastering Sybase SQL
Server 11

Other McGraw-Hill Books of Interest

ALLEN/BAMBARA/BAMBARA • *Informix: Client/Server Application Development* 0-07-913056-9

ANDERSON • *Client/Server Database Design with Sybase* 0-07-001697-6

BAMBARA/ALLEN • *PowerBuilder: A Guide for Developing Client/Server Applications* 0-07-005413-4

BERSON • *Client/Server Architecture 2E* 0-07-005664-1

BERSON/ANDERSON • *Sybase and Client/Server Computing, Featuring System 11, 2E* 0-07-006080-0

CLIFFORD • *Sybase Replication Server Primer* 0-07-011515-X

GREEN/BROWN • *PowerBuilder 5: Object-Oriented Design & Development* 0-07-024469-3

JONES • *Ready-Made PowerBuilder Applications* 0-07-912062-8

JONES • *Developing Client/Server Applications with Microsoft Access* 0-07-912982-X

NEMZOW • *Visual Basic Developer's Toolkit* 0-07-912309-0

ROSEEN • *InfoMaker 5: A Guide to Developing Client/Server Applications* 0-07-053999-5

RIBAR • *The PowerBuilder Construction Kit* 0-07-882079-0

SANDERS • *Developer's Guide to DB2 for Common Servers* 0-07-057725-0

To the memory of my father
and
the living presence of my mother

Contents

Preface   xvii

Chapter 1. System 11 SQL Server 101   1

Introduction   1
SQL Server Command Syntax   1
The SQL Server sa Login Account   2
System 11 SQL Server Roles and Object Owners   2
SQL Server System Administrator Role   4
SQL Server Security Officer Role   4
SQL Server Operator Role   5
The Interfaces File   5
The showserver Command   6
Starting the SQL Server   6
The isql Utility   8
A Word to the Wise   13
Shutting Down the SQL Server   13
Rules for Sybase System 11 SQL Server Identifiers   14
Sybase System 11 SQL Server Reserved Keywords   15
Displaying SQL Server Login Account Information   16
Creating a Login Account   17
Finding Out Who's Using the SQL Server   19
Killing a Process within the SQL Server   20
Chargeback Accounting for the SQL Server   21
SQL Server Kernel Configuration for Chargeback Accounting   21
Reporting Current SQL Server Usage Statistics   24
Initiating a New Chargeback Interval   25
Changing Login Account Defaults   26
SQL Server Kernel Configuration for Password Expiration   27
Changing a Login Account's Password   28
Granting the System Security Officer Role to a Login Account   30
Granting the Operator Role to a Login Account   30
Granting the System Administrator Role to a Login Account   31
Taking on the Identity of a Login Account That Owns a Database   32

Taking on the Identity of a Login Account That Owns Principal Database Objects   32
Revoking the System Security Officer Role from a Login Account   34
Revoking the Operator Role from a Login Account   34
Revoking the System Administrator Role from a Login Account   35
Locking a Login Account   36
Displaying Locked Login Accounts   36
Unlocking a Login Account   37
Dropping a Login Account from the SQL Server   37

Chapter 2. Miscellaneous Stuff   39

Introduction   39
Running the SQL Server on Multiprocessor Platforms   39
SQL Server Kernel Configuration for Multiple Engines   41
SQL Server Kernel Configuration for the Network   44
Remote Servers and Remote Login Accounts   47
SQL Server Kernel Configuration for Remote Servers   47
Reporting on Remote Servers   49
Creating a Remote Server   49
Changing Remote Server Options   50
Dropping a Remote Server   51
SQL Server Kernel Configuration for Remote Login Accounts   52
Reporting on Remote Login Accounts   53
Creating a Remote Login Account   54
Changing Remote Login Account Options   54
Dropping a Remote Login Account   55

Chapter 3. Physical Storage   57

Introduction   57
SQL Server Kernel Configuration for Disk I/O   57
Physical Data Storage Hierarchy   58
Database Devices   59
Creating a Database Device   61
Mirroring a Database Device   64
Unmirroring a Database Device   66
Remirroring a Database Device   67
Dropping a Database Device   68
Reporting on Database Device Usage   69
The d_master Device   70
Default Database Devices   70
Reestablishing a Database Device   72
Disk Fragments   74
Allocation Units   75
Extents   75
SQL Server Kernel Configuration for bcp   75
Pages   76
   Data Page   76
   Index Page   78

Text/Image Page   83
Page Splitting   83
Page Shrinking   84
Run-Time Management of Indexes   84
Overflow Page   84
Allocation and Management of Physical Data Storage   84
Global Allocation Map   85
Allocation Unit Page   86
Object Allocation Map   86
Generic Object Allocation Map Page   87
Extent Object Allocation Map Page   87
Data and Index Page Allocation   88
SQL Server Kernel Configuration for Page Utilization   90
Distribution Page   91

Chapter 4. Memory Resource Management   93

Introduction   93
SQL Server Memory Resource Usage   93
SQL Server Kernel Configuration for Memory   94
The Execution Stack Region   104
Configuring the Execution Stack Region   104
The Audit Queue   107
Cache and Cache Manager Internals   108
The Cache Manager and Reads from Disk   111
The LRU Replacement Strategy   113
The Fetch-And-Discard Replacement Strategy   114
The Cache Manager and Data Modifications   115
The Cache Manager and Writes To Disk   116
Reporting on Fetch-And-Discard Replacement Strategy on an Object Basis   117
Disabling Fetch-And-Discard Replacement Strategy on an Object Basis   118
Enabling Fetch-And-Discard Replacement Strategy on an Object Basis   121
Reporting on Prefetch on an Object Basis   124
Disabling Prefetch on an Object Basis   125
Enabling Prefetch on an Object Basis   127
Disabling and Enabling Prefetch on a Session Basis   131
SQL Server Kernel Configuration for the Cache Manager   131
The HouseKeeper   135
SQL Server Kernel Configuration for the HouseKeeper   136
The Relationship between Procedure Cache and Data Cache   138
Procedure Cache   138
SQL Server Kernel Configuration for Procedure Cache   140
Data Cache   141
Memory Pools   142
Memory Pool Wash Area   145
Creating a Memory Pool   145
Modifying the Size of a Memory Pool   149
Modifying a Memory Pool Wash Area   151
Dropping a Memory Pool   154
Default Data Cache   156

Reporting on Default Data Cache   157
Configuring the Default Data Cache   158
Named Data Caches   159
Reporting on All Named Data Caches   160
Creating a Named Data Cache   161
Configuring a Named Data Cache   164
Dropping a Named Data Cache   166

Chapter 5. Databases   **169**

Introduction   169
Principal SQL Server Database Objects   169
System Databases and User Databases   170
Updating System Tables   170
The *master* System Database   171
System Tables and the *master* System Database   172
The *model* System Database   173
   Modifying the *model* System Database   173
   The *model* System Database and Booting the SQL Server   175
The *tempdb* System Database   176
Temporary Tables   176
Work Tables   177
The *tempdb* Transaction Log   179
Locating the *tempdb* System Database   180
Binding the *tempdb* System Database to Named Data Cache   180
The *sybsystemprocs* System Database   183
The *sybsecurity* System Database   184
SQL Server Kernel Configuration for Databases   185
Creating a User Database   187
User Database System Tables   191
Database Options   193
Setting Database Options   196
Granting Create-Database Permission to a Login Account   197
Determining Database Ownership   198
Changing Database Ownership   198
Functions of the dbo   200
Creating a Database Group   201
Reporting on Users of a Database   202
Adding a User to a Database   203
Adding the "guest" User to a Database   204
Aliasing a User in a Database   205
Removing an Alias from a User in a Database   205
Changing a Database User's Group Membership   206
Reporting on User Permissions in a Database   207
Dropping a User from a Database   207
Dropping the "guest" User from a Database   208
Dropping a Group from a Database   209
Placing a Database in dbo use only Mode   210

Checking Database Consistency   210
Changing the Name of a Database   214
Displaying Information about Principal Database Objects within a Database   217
Determining the Size of a Database   217
Determining the Database Devices Used by a Database   218
Determining the Amount of Space a Database Is Using   218
Changing the Size of a Database   219
SQL Server Kernel Configuration for Database Recovery   223
Dumping a Database   224
Loading a Database   225
Binding a Database to a Named Data Cache   225
Binding System Tables to Named Data Cache   228
Binding System Table Indexes to Named Data Cache   231
Unbinding a System Table from Named Data Cache   232
Unbinding a System Table Index from Named Data Cache   234
Unbinding a Database from a Named Data Cache   235
Unbinding All Databases from a Named Data Cache   237
Dropping an Undamaged Database   238
Dropping a Damaged Database   241

Chapter 6. Transaction Log Subsystem   243

Introduction   243
Write-Ahead Transaction Log   243
SQL Server Failure Events   244
Transaction Log Records   245
Direct Updates   248
Deferred Updates   250
Deferred Index Inserts   252
User Transaction Log Caches   252
Configuring User Transaction Log Caches   254
The Checkpoint Process   256
Configuring the Recovery Interval   256
The SQL Server Transaction Log and Text or Image Data Types   258
Transaction Log Options   259
Setting Transaction Log Options   261
Sizing a Transaction Log   262
Placement of a Database's Transaction Log   262
Determining the Location of a Database's Transaction Log   264
Moving the Transaction Log to another Logical Database Device   264
Increasing the Size of a Transaction Log   267
Dumping a Transaction Log   269
Loading a Transaction Log   271
Configuring "logonly" Type Named Data Cache   271
Binding a Transaction Log to Named Data Cache   273
Determining Transaction Log Buffer Mass Size   275
Configuring Transaction Log Buffer Mass Size   276
Unbinding a Transaction Log from Named Data Cache   278

Determining the Use of Transaction Log Resources   279
The *syslogs* Taboo   280
Misuse of the dbcc log Utility   281
The master..syslogshold Table   282

Chapter 7. User-Defined Data Types, Defaults, and Rules   **287**

Data Types   287
The NULL Value   290
Data-Type Hierarchy   291
User-Defined Data Types   293
Sybase System 11 SQL Server-Provided User-Defined Data Types   293
The IDENTITY Property   293
Database Configuration for the IDENTITY Property   295
SQL Server Kernel Configuration for the IDENTITY Property   297
Creating a User-Defined Data Type   299
Changing the Name of a User-Defined Data Type   302
Dropping User-Defined Data Types   303
Defaults   304
Granting Permission to Create Defaults   304
Creating a Default   305
Changing the Name of a Default   308
Binding Defaults to User-Defined Data Types   308
Binding Defaults to Table Columns   310
Unbinding a Default from a User-Defined Data Type   312
Unbinding a Default from a Table Column   313
Dropping a Default   314
Revoking Permission to Create Defaults   315
Rules   316
Granting Permission to Create Rules   316
Creating a Rule   317
Changing the Name of a Rule   320
Rule and Default Conflicts   321
Binding a Rule to a User-Defined Data Type   321
Binding a Rule to a Table Column   323
Unbinding a Rule from a User-Defined Data Type   324
Unbinding a Rule from a Table Column   325
Dropping a Rule   326
Revoking Permission to Create Rules   328

Chapter 8. Tables and Indexes   **329**

Tables   329
SQL Server Kernel Configuration for Table Partitioning   330
SQL Server Kernel Configuration for Index Fill Factor   333
Displaying Table Information   335
Granting Permission to Create Tables   336
Creating a Table   338

Creating a Schema 351
Table Consistency Checking 352
Determining the Size of a Table 357
Predicting Table Size 358
Altering a Table 360
Changing Maximum Rows per Page of a Table or Index 372
Reporting on Table Constraints 376
Reporting on Primary Key Constraints 376
Reporting on Foreign Key Constraints 377
On-Line Documentation of Table Primary, Foreign, and Common Keys 379
Reporting on Primary, Foreign, and Common Keys 382
Dropping a Primary, Foreign, or Common Key 383
Changing the Name of a Table Column 384
Changing the Name of a Table 385
Granting Access Permission to a Table 387
Reporting on Table Permissions 389
Revoking Access Permission to a Table 391
Truncating an Unpartitioned Table 393
Dropping an Unpartitioned User Table 394
Revoking Permission to Create Tables 395
Indexes 396
Reporting on Table Indexes 400
Creating an Index 400
Maintaining Index Statistics 405
Checking the Consistency of an Index 406
Changing the Name of an Index 408
Dropping an Index 408
Advanced Techniques for Placing Data on User-Defined Segments 409
Binding Objects to Named Data Caches 412
Binding a User Table to a Named Data Cache 417
Binding User Tables with Text/Image Data Types to Named Data Caches 419
Binding a User Table Index to a Named Data Cache 420
Unbinding Database Objects from a Named Data Cache 422
Unbinding User Tables from Named Data Caches 422
Unbinding User Tables with Text/Image Data Types from a Named Data Cache 424
Unbinding a User Table's Indexes from a Named Data Cache 425
Unbinding All Database Objects from a Named Data Cache 426
Bulk Loading Data into Tables 428

Chapter 9. Segments and Thresholds **435**

Segments 435
Segments and System Tables 436
Creating a User-Defined Segment 436
Reporting on Segments within a Database 438
Extending a Segment 438
Unmapping a Segment 439
Dropping a Segment 441

The Database Transaction Log and Segments   441
The Threshold Manager   442
Log Segment Thresholds   443
Data Segment Thresholds   444
Threshold Stored Procedures   446
Examining Segment Thresholds   447
Creating a Segment Threshold   448
Modifying a Database Threshold   449
Enabling Segment Free-Space Accounting   451
Dropping a Database Threshold   452
Threshold Limitations   452

Chapter 10. Stored Procedures, Triggers, and Views   455

Stored Procedures   455
Optimization Stages   456
The Statistical Query Optimizer   457
The Problem of Too Many Data Access Paths   457
Information Examined by the Optimizer   458
Collecting Statistics   460
Query Plan   460
Creating a Show Plan   461
Reresolution of Stored Procedures   462
Granting Permission to Create Stored Procedures   462
Reporting on Stored Procedures   463
Creating a Stored Procedure   464
Granting Permission to Execute a Stored Procedure   466
Executing a Stored Procedure   467
Run-Time Verification of Stored Procedure Permissions   468
Nested Stored Procedures   469
Recompiling a Stored Procedure   470
Changing the Name of a Stored Procedure   471
Creating Threshold Stored Procedures   472
User-Created System Procedures   473
Revoking Permission to Create Stored Procedures   473
Dropping a Stored Procedure   474
Triggers   474
SQL Server Kernel Configuration for Nested Triggers   476
Gathering Information about a Trigger   476
Creating a Trigger   477
Trigger Test Tables   479
Run-Time Verification of Trigger Permissions   479
Changing the Name of a Trigger   480
Dropping a Trigger   482
Views   482
Granting Permission to Create Views   483
Creating Views   484
Run-Time Verification of View Permissions   485

View Resolution   486
Restrictions on Modifying Data through Views   486
Granting Permissions on a View   487
Views versus Stored Procedures   489
Changing the Name of a View   490
Revoking Access Permissions to a View   491
Dropping a View   493
Revoking Permission to Create Views   494

Chapter 11. The Parallel Lock Manager   497

Introduction   497
Lock Granularity   497
Types of Locks   498
    Page Locks   498
    Table Locks   499
Demand Locks   500
ANSI Isolation Levels   500
    Isolation Level 0   500
    Isolation Level 1   501
    Isolation Level 2   501
    Isolation Level 3   502
Choosing Isolation Levels   502
SQL Server Kernel Configuration for Locks   503
SQL Server Kernel Configuration for Lock Manager Spinlocks   504
SQL Server Kernel Configuration for the Lock Manager Freelock Cache   507
Reporting on Blocked Processes   509
Lock Promotion   510
SQL Server Configuration for Lock Promotion   510
Dropping Database Lock Promotion Settings   520
Dropping Table Lock Promotion Settings   520
Simulating Row-Level Locking   521
Deadlocking   521
SQL Server Kernel Configuration Parameters for Deadlocking   522

Glossary   525
Index   533

Preface

With the release of the System 11 SQL Server, Sybase has provided the market with a sophisticated, state-of-the-art, relational database that is well suited for data warehouses, as well as on-line transaction processing.

The purpose of this book is to provide database administrators with the information they need to thoroughly understand, successfully configure, and manage a System 11 SQL Server. In line with this goal, internals of the SQL Server have been provided throughout the book. As a quick review of the Contents reveals, this book has decomposed the SQL Server into its main components and product features. Each chapter is dedicated to a single aspect of the system, and each aspect of the SQL Server is explored in depth.

While this book is geared toward database administrators, it also provides applications developers with a clear insight into how the SQL Server actually operates in support of their queries. While it is not the intention of this book to provide training in Transact-SQL, a large portion was written with application developers in mind.

System 11 SQL Server 101

Introduction

The purpose of this chapter is to provide you with the basic information needed to start up, and use, a System 11 SQL Server. The remaining chapters of the book will explain how to successfully take advantage of the many features of this product, whether you are responsible for administering the SQL Server, designing physical data models that will run on a SQL Server, or developing an application that queries SQL Server databases.

SQL Server Command Syntax

When it comes to basic information, there is nothing more fundamental to using a SQL Server than getting a handle on its command statement syntax. Understanding command statement syntax is System 11 SQL Server 101.

These are the rules for command statement syntax:

1. *SQL Server commands and reserved keywords.* They are both case insensitive.

2. *Mandatory command options.* You must use a mandatory command option; there's no way around them.

3. *Curly braces enclosing vertical bars* (i.e., { option1 | option2 | option3 }). You have to choose one, and only one, of the mandatory command options.

4. *Curly braces enclosing commas and multiple command options* (i.e., { option1 , option2 , option3 }). You have to choose one or more of the mandatory command options. If you choose more than one

mandatory command option, then a comma must separate each option.

5. *Optional command options.* You can choose to use, or not to use, an optional command option.

6. *Square brackets enclosing a single command option* (i.e., [option]). You can choose to use, or not to use, this optional command option.

7. *Square brackets enclosing vertical bars and multiple command options* (i.e., [option1 | option2 | option3]). You can choose to use one, and only one, or none of the optional command options.

8. *Square brackets enclosing commas and multiple command options* (i.e., [option1 , option2 , option3]). You can choose to use one, or more, or none, of the optional command options. If you choose more than one optional command option, then a comma must separate each option.

9. *Ellipsis* (. . .). The three-dot pattern means that you can repeat the preceding section of the command statement syntax.

The SQL Server sa Login Account

Every SQL Server has a login account named sa. This account is analogous to the root account of an operating system. When the SQL Server was installed, the **sa** account was automatically created by the SQL Server installation script, given ownership of all SQL Server system databases, and granted the System Administrator (**sa_role**), the System Security Officer (**sso_role**), and the Operator (**oper_role**) roles.

While all typical login accounts are constrained by the SQL Server's Discretionary Access Control (DAC) protection system, the **sa** login account operates outside these constraints. You might say that the **sa** login account is the "big dog on the porch." For good and bad, the **sa** account is capable of doing everything with and to the SQL Server. Because of this fact, the password for this login must be very tightly guarded, and distributed to as few people as possible; doing anything short of this is complete folly.

System 11 SQL Server Roles and Object Owners

Not all Sybase login accounts are created equally; a definite food chain exists among login accounts. Individual login accounts can be granted roles and object ownership privileges and responsibilities, and conversely, other individual login accounts can be denied such privileges and responsibilities.

Within a System 11 SQL Server, there are three roles:

1. System Administrator (**sa_role**)
2. System Security Officer (**sso_role**)
3. Operator (**oper_role**)

Any login account can be assigned any role, and a role can be assigned to any number of login accounts. However, common sense should tell you to severely limit the assignment of roles to login accounts. Remember, too many cooks can spoil a dish. This is most definitely the case with the **sa_role.** Fortunately, the SQL Server has the capability of auditing the actions of login accounts with roles. From that audit trail, those actions can be traced back to the individual login account. It's really nice to be able to find out who did what, when, and where, particularly if the involved party is not forthcoming with the information you critically need to solve a problem.

In addition to roles, the SQL Server also supports these ownership privileges:

1. Database owner (**dbo**)
2. Principal database object owner

A database can be owned by one and only one login account. A given login account can own zero, one, or more databases. A principal database object (i.e., user-defined data types, defaults, rules, tables, indexes, triggers, stored procedures, and views) can be owned by one, and only one, login account. A given login account can own zero, one, or more principal database objects. In Chap. 5 we will explore database ownership, and in the various chapters covering principal database objects we will explore principal database object ownership.

The **sa** login account and all login accounts that have been granted the privileges of the **sa_role,** can take on the privileges, in all databases, of the login account that has the **dbo** role in relation to a given database. In addition, **sa** login account and all login accounts that have been granted the privileges of the **sa_role,** can create databases that another login account will own, and can create principal database objects that another login account will own. However, because the **sa** login account, and all login accounts that have been granted the privileges of the **sa_role,** operate outside the DAC system, they cannot acquire the permissions of the login account that owns a given principal database object. However, the login account that owns a database can acquire the permissions of the login account that owns a given principal database object.

SQL Server System Administrator Role

The responsibilities of login accounts with the SQL Server System Administrator role, the **sa_role,** are to:

1. Analyze SQL Server problems and undertake the necessary tasks to solve them.
2. Back up and load system and user databases.
3. Change, disable, and drop SQL Server login accounts.
4. Configure the SQL Server to enhance performance.
5. Create databases and, where necessary, transfer ownership of a database to a login account.
6. Create groups in databases and add users to those groups.
7. Grant permissions to SQL Server login accounts.
8. Install the SQL Server.
9. Manage disk devices.
10. Monitor the automatic recovery of system and user databases when the SQL Server is started.

Only the Sybase **sa** login account can designate another login account as having the **sa_role.** As we go forward through this book, when a command requires the **sa_role** command, this fact will be pointed out.

SQL Server Security Officer Role

The responsibilities of login accounts with the SQL Server System Security Officer, the **sso_role,** are all related to security matters. The tasks that the **sso_role** accomplishes are:

1. Administering the (optional) SQL Server Audit System. Only the **sso_role** can access the `sybsecurity.. sysaudits` table.
2. Changing the passwords of login accounts.
3. Creating login accounts.
4. Disabling and enabling the **sa** login account.
5. Disabling and enabling the user login accounts.
6. Granting the **sso_role** and **oper_role** roles to login accounts.
7. Setting the SQL Server's password expiration interval.

Even though the **sso_role** can access any system or user database on the SQL Server, it operates under the constraints of the DAC system.

SQL Server Operator Role

Like the **sso_role,** the Operator role (**oper_role**) basically functions within the constraints of the DAC system. According to the DAC system, only login accounts with either the **dbo** role, or the **sa_role** and the **sa** login account can dump databases and transaction logs. While the **dbo** role is limited to dumping and loading databases and transaction logs it owns, the **sa_role** can dump and load any database or transaction log on a SQL Server. Typically, these tasks are executed through scripts, which implies that the **dbo** or the **sa_role** passwords will be stored in the script. Storing their passwords outside of the SQL Server is a security risk. To avoid this security risk, the **oper_role** has the capability to dump and load any database or transaction log on a SQL Server, and these are the only capabilities of this role. The other benefit of the Operator role is that you can change a **dbo** login account password, the **sa_role** password, or the **sa** account password without having to edit your dump and load scripts.

The Operator role is capable of executing these SQL Server commands against all databases within a SQL Server:

1. `dump database`
2. `dump transaction`
3. `load database`
4. `load transaction`

The Interfaces File

System 11 SQL Servers can potentially interoperate with other SQL Servers, with Open Server-based applications, and with client applications residing on the same host computer, or residing on other host computers in a network. However, before these software components can communicate with one another, they must know the identity of each host computer their target (SQL Server or Open Server-based application) resides on, what communication protocol to use with the target, and what communication ports to use with the target. The information these software components need to interoperate with each other is stored within an interfaces file that has been distributed to them.

When the SQL Server was installed, an interfaces file is automatically created for that SQL Server. It is the responsibility of the SQL Server System Administrator to enter into that file the required information about all other related SQL Servers and Open Server-based applications that need to be accessed by the users, and to work with the operating System Administrator to ensure that the interfaces file is distributed to the users.

The showserver Command

Before you start a SQL Server, or if you are having problems connecting to it, you should verify that the SQL Server is running on its host computer. To verify this for yourself, connect to the SQL Server's host computer and enter the `showserver` command at the operating system prompt.

This command will display the SQL Servers (and Backup Servers) that are currently running on the host computer, as well as the parameters that were passed to the commands that started the SQL Servers. The type of information reported to you depends on the operating system you are using.

Starting the SQL Server

There are two commands, both owned and executable by the *sybase* operating system account, that can be used at the operating system prompt to start (i.e., boot) a SQL Server (and/or a Backup Server):

1. `startserver`

2. `dataserver`

Two distinctly different commands exist to start a SQL Server because you may need to boot the server under distinctly different sets of circumstances.

The simplest way to boot a SQL Server is to enter this command:

```
startserver [[-fNameOfRunServerFile] [-m]] ...
```

where:

f*NameOfRunServerFile*—this optional parameter specifies the relative path name of the SQL Server's (or Backup Server's) run file. If this file is not in your current working directory, then you will have to specify the absolute path name of this file. When you install the SQL Server, the run file is given the name `RUN_`*NameOfSQLServer*. This file contains all the default information the SQL Server (or Backup Server) needs to boot (e.g., the location of the **d_master** device, where to create the error log, etc.). You can start multiple SQL Servers (and Backup Servers) at once when using this command.

m—this optional parameter starts a SQL Server in single-user mode. When a SQL Server is booted in single-user mode, only one System Administrator can connect to the SQL Server. If you do not use this optional parameter, then the SQL Server will boot in multiuser mode, allowing all authorized login accounts to connect to the SQL Server.

If you do not specify the run file, the command will use the run file in the current working directory from which the command was executed. The command will take control of the output terminal, display messages about the process of the boot, and write all boot messages to the SQL Server error log. Once the boot process completes, be certain to read the SQL Server's error log to study the boot report.

The second command provides the Sybase account with far greater flexibility when starting a SQL Server:

```
dataserver -dNameOfMasterDevice [-cNameOfConfigurationFile]
   [-eNameOfErrorFile] [-m]
[-rNameOfMasterDeviceMirror] [-MNameOfSharedMemoryDirectory]
[-iNameOfInterfaceFileDirectory] [-sNameOfSQLServer]
[-pLoginNameOfSystemSecurityOfficer]
```

where:

dNameOfMasterDevice—the absolute path name of the master device (**d_master**). If you do not know the path name of the master device, then you can find it's name by reading the SQL Server's error log. Where device zero is mentioned, the path of the master device is indicated.

cNameOfConfigurationFile—a configuration file found in every System 11 SQL Server. This file instructs the SQL Server to set its configurable parameters to specific values. This optional parameter tells the SQL Server the identity of the configuration file to use when it boots. If this parameter is not provided, the SQL Server will use the configuration parameters stored within the master..sysconfigures system table.

eNameOfErrorFile—an optional parameter that is the absolute path name of the SQL Server's error log. The SQL Server uses this file to record all SQL Server system level error messages that arise when the SQL Server boots and while it is running. If this parameter is not provided, the SQL Server will use the error-log file in the current working directory.

m—this optional parameter starts a SQL Server in single-user mode. When a SQL Server is booted in single-user mode, only one System Administrator can connect to the SQL Server. If you do not use this optional parameter, then the SQL Server will boot in multiuser mode, allowing all authorized login accounts to connect to the SQL Server and execute commands.

rNameOfMasterDeviceMirror—this optional parameter specifies the master device's mirror device. If you are using SQL Server mirroring on the master device, then you must specify the master device's mirror device when you boot the SQL Server.

M*NameOfSharedMemoryDirectory*—this optional parameter tells the SQL Server the operating system directory in which to place its shared memory files, instead of using the directory indicated by the operating system environment variable $SYBASE. If this optional parameter is not used, the SQL Server will use the $SYBASE environment variable.

i*NameOfInterfaceFileDirectory*—this optional parameter tells the `dataserver` command the name of the directory in which to find the interfaces file it will use when connecting to other SQL Servers, or to Open Server-based applications. If this optional parameter is not passed to this command, then the command will use the interfaces file pointed to by the $SYBASE environment variable.

s*NameOfSQLServer*—this optional parameter tells the command which SQL Server to start. If this parameter is not provided, the command will start a SQL Server named SYBASE.

p*LoginNameOfSystemSecurityOfficer*—this optional parameter specifies the login account of the System Security Officer to use when booting the SQL Server. This parameter is used to make the SQL Server randomly generate a new password for that System Security Officer login account. That new password will be displayed on the terminal, then it will be encrypted and saved within the `master..syslogins` system table as that login account's password. Because all login account passwords are encrypted, it is not possible to recover forgotten passwords for System Security Officer login accounts.

The command will take control of the output terminal, display messages about the process of the boot, and write all boot messages to the SQL Server error log. Once the boot process completes, be certain to read the SQL Server's error log to study the boot report.

The isql Utility

When you purchase a SQL Server, you also get a client application, Interactive SQL (**isql**) parser, that enables you to create a session with the SQL Server (i.e., log on to the SQL Server). Throughout this book, where you are instructed to log on to the SQL Server, it is assumed that you will be using the **isql** utility.

To log on to the SQL Server enter this command:

```
isql [-e] [-F] [-p] [-n] [-v] [-X] [-Y] [-A NetworkPacketSize]
  [-H ClientHostName]
[-U loginame] [-P passwd] [-S NameOfSQLServer]
```

[-I *NameOfInterfacesFile*] [-y *SybaseDirectory*]
  [-w *OutputScreenWidth*]
[-c *CommandTerminator*] [-s *ColumnSeparator*]
[-E *CommandLineEditor*] [-h *ColumnHeaders*] [-i *NameOfInputFile*]
  [-o *NameOfOutputFile*]
[-z *AlternateIsqlLanguage*] [-a *NameOfDisplayCharacterSet*] [-q]
[-J *ClientCharacterConversionSet*] [-l *LoginTimeOut*]
[-t *CommandTimeOut*] [-m *ErrorMessageSeverityLevel*]

where:

e—this optional parameter echoes the commands you enter into the SQL Server.

F—this optional parameter turns on the FIPS flagger. With this feature set on, the SQL Server flags any non-SQL standard commands entered into it.

p—this optional parameter instructs the SQL Server to display performance statistics for each command entered into it.

n—normally, the SQL Server displays a number and prompt symbol (>) on each command input line. This optional parameter removes the prompt symbol and the numbering from command input lines.

v—this optional parameter prints the version (and copyright statement) of the **isql** software you are using, and then ends the session by disconnecting from the SQL Server.

X—if the **isql** software crashes while you are using it, a core image of the isql software will be created. In that core image will be your password. To secure your password against this risk exposure, you can pass this optional parameter to the SQL Server. When the SQL Server receives this parameter, it will send an encryption key back to **isql,** which will use this key to encrypt the login password, and the SQL Server will use the encryption key to authenticate the login password when it is sent to it.

Y—this optional parameter instructs the SQL Server to use chained transactions.

A *NetworkPacketSize*—this optional parameter is used to set the network packet size that **isql** and the SQL Server will use to transmit data to one another. When there is a lot of data to move between the two software components, be sure to use this parameter to enhance performance. The value to which you set this parameter must range between the value of the default network packet size and the max network packet size SQL Server configuration parameters, must be one-third the size of the additional network memory SQL Server configuration parameter, and must be a multiple of 512. If there is not enough memory available, then the SQL Server will use the packet size closest to 512.

H *ClientHostName*—this optional parameter sets the name of the host computer on which **isql** runs.

U *loginame*—this optional parameter is the name of the Sybase login account that is logging in to the SQL Server. If this optional parameter is not supplied, then the SQL Server will prompt you for it.

P *passwd*—this optional parameter is the password of the Sybase login account that is logging in to the SQL Server. If this optional parameter is not supplied, then the SQL Server will prompt you for it.

S *NameOfSQLServer*—this optional parameter is the name of the SQL Server you want to log on to. If you use the "-S" parameter and do not specify the name of the SQL Server, **isql** will assume that you want to connect to the SQL Server named SYBASE. If you do not use this optional parameter at all, then the **isql** will connect to the SQL Server specified by the **DSQUERY** operating system environment variable.

I *NameOfInterfacesFile*—this optional parameter specifies the interfaces file that **isql** will use when connecting to the target SQL Server. If you do not specify this optional parameter, then **isql** will use the interfaces file in the directory specified by the SYBASE operating system environment variable.

y *SybaseDirectory*—this optional parameter specifies the SYBASE directory that **isql** will use. If you do not provide this optional parameter, then **isql** will use the SYBASE directory specified by the $SYBASE operating system environment variable.

w *OutputScreenWidth*—the default screen width of displaying **isql** output is 80 characters. As a consequence, most SQL Server system reports are broken into multiple lines, which makes them difficult to read. So unless you want to settle for the limit of 80 characters per displayed line, use this optional parameter (and set it to a much higher value, e.g., 1000).

c *CommandTerminator*—by default, the SQL Server will not act on a command statement until you enter "go" on an input line. If you do not want to type "go" for each command statement, then you can specify the command terminator (e.g., ".") you want to use during your session with the SQL Server. Be certain not to specify reserved words or operating system control character.

s *ColumnSeparator*—by default, the SQL Server uses a blank as a column separator. If you want to specify a different column separator, use this optional parameter. If you elect to use a character as a column separator that has special meaning to the operating system on which the SQL Server runs, then enclose that character in quotes (" "), or precede it with a backslash symbol (/).

E *CommandLineEditor*—the default command line editor that **isql** supports is *vi*. If you want to use another command line editor, then specify it using this optional parameter, or else you can set the EDITOR environment variable to point to the editor.

h *ColumnHeaders*—by default, the SQL Server prints a single heading for a given result set. If you want to have the SQL Server print that heading after a certain count of returned rows, then use this optional parameter to specify how many rows to display between column headings.

i *NameOfInputFile*—use this optional parameter to specify the name of the operating system file you want to pass in when **isql** connects to the SQL Server. This optional parameter is equivalent to using "<NameOfInputFile". If you did not use the optional password parameter, you will be prompted for you password when you use this parameter (or its equivalent).

o *NameOfOutputFile*—use this optional parameter to specify the name of the operating system file to which you want **isql** to write its output. This optional parameter is equivalent to using ">NameOfInput-File".

z *AlternateIsqlLanguage*—if you do not use this optional parameter, then **isql** will display prompts and messages using the SQL Server's default language. If you do not want to use the SQL Server default language, then you can use this optional parameter to specify an alternate language that the SQL Server supports.

a *NameOfDisplayCharacterSet*—this optional parameter is related to the -J and -q optional parameters. You will use this optional parameter when **isql** will display on a terminal whose character set is different from the character set of the host computer on which **isql** is executing. Use this optional parameter with the -J optional parameter to specify the character set translation file that supports the character conversion. Use this optional parameter without using the -J optional parameter only if the **isql** character set is the same as the default SQL Server character set.

q—when you are using **isql** in a Japanese language environment, this optional parameter is used to translate hankaku katakana (half-width characters) into zenkaku katakana (full-width characters). With this optional parameter, use the argument "zenkaku" and the -J flag to indicate **isql**'s Japanese character set (sjis or eucjis). The zenkaku conversion file will only translate from the **isql** terminal display to the SQL Server, and not from the SQL Server to the **isql** terminal display.

J *ClientCharacterConversionSet*—this optional parameter is used to instruct the SQL Server to convert to and from the character set in use on the host computer where **isql** is executing. Use the -J parameter to specify that the host computer, where **isql** is executing, and the SQL Server it is connecting to are using the same Japanese environment character set.

l *LoginTimeOut*—this optional parameter specifies the maximum count of seconds that can pass when attempting to establish a connection between **isql** and a target SQL Server before the login attempt is abandoned. The default is 60 seconds.

t *CommandTimeOut*—this optional parameter specifies the maximum count of seconds that can pass after you enter a command into the SQL Server. If you do not use this parameter, then **isql** will wait, for however long it takes, until the command completes.

m *ErrorMessageSeverityLevel*—you can use this optional parameter to customize the error messages that the SQL Server will display during your **isql** session. For SQL Server errors at the specified severity level, or higher, only the message number, state, and error level are displayed; you will not see any of the text message for that error. For SQL Server errors at levels below the specified severity level, no messages will appear at all.

Here are a few other important facts to know about the **isql** utility:

1. To quit from **isql,** enter either the exit or the quit command.
2. From within **isql,** you can invoke a command line editor by entering the name of the command line editor at the **isql** command line and hitting the enter key. You can use this command line editor to correct command statements, to create new command statements, or to read in files, via the editor, which contains command statements you want the SQL Server to act on. However, do not include the command terminator in the text, because this will result in a failed command execution. When you quit the editor, you automatically return to **isql,** and the command statements you were working with will be stored in the **isql** command line buffer and displayed within **isql.**
3. If you want to execute an operating system command from within **isql,** then enter the !! command. This will bring up the operating system prompt.

4. If you want to clear the **isql** command line buffer, enter the `reset` command.

5. If you are working in a given **isql** command line, then you can enter `Ctrl-c` to cancel the current command and return to the **isql** prompt.

6. The case of the parameters are significant to **isql**.

7. You can include comments within a Transact-SQL statement submitted to the SQL Server when using **isql**.

8. You can direct **isql** to take input from the terminal; it will even use operating system redirection symbols. For example, isql `<<string>`*NameOfOutputFile*, where `string` is any character string (e.g., eof). To terminate input from the terminal, enter the `Ctrl-d` command.

A Word to the Wise

Once you get a handle on the SQL Server syntax and logging on to the SQL Server, it is very tempting to simply enter commands interactively with the SQL Server. This is all well and good for nonpersistent changes to the SQL Server, but do yourself a big favor and do not enter commands interactively with the SQL Server that change the configuration to the SQL Server, alter physical or memory resources, create or alter databases or principal database objects, and so on.

If the commands will permanently change the contents of any system table, then write those commands into a file, use that file as an input file to **isql,** and save those files within some kind of code-change management system. If you adopt this basic discipline, then you will always be able to rebuild any and all parts of the SQL Server whenever the need arises (and believe me, that need will definitely arise, the universe being what it is and all).

If you are not prepared to adopt this discipline, then you are probably in the wrong job. You will definitely spend less time writing and storing your scripts in a safe place then you'll spend polishing your resume and looking for another job.

Shutting Down the SQL Server

To shut down the SQL Server, log on to the SQL Server as an account with **sa_role** privileges and enter these commands:

```
1>shutdown [with {wait | nowait}]
2>go
```

where:

with wait—this is the default parameter to the shutdown command, which shuts the SQL Server down gracefully. When you shut down the SQL Server gracefully (which is the way you want to go unless this course of action is impossible to follow) all logins, except for **sa_role** accounts, will be unable to connect to the SQL Server, a checkpoint will be taken on all databases, and the SQL Server will wait for executing Transact-SQL statements and stored procedures to complete. Shutting down a SQL Server in this way will also decrease the amount of work the SQL Server will have to do when it is started again.

with nowait—when you use this optional parameter, the SQL Server is shut down immediately, without checkpointing all of the databases and without waiting for executing Transact-SQL statements and stored procedures to complete. Use this optional parameter as a last resort. Also, using this optional parameter can increase the likelihood of introducing gaps in the linear-sequential values stored within IDENTITY columns.

Rules for Sybase System 11 SQL Server Identifiers

An *identifier* is nothing more than the name that you assign to SQL Server objects (i.e., login accounts, columns, cursors, databases, defaults, dump devices, indexes, local variables, logical database devices, rules, tables, temporary tables, triggers, stored procedures, stored procedure parameters, and views). The SQL Server has a set of rules to which the identifiers you create must comply:

1. The maximum length of an identifier is 30 bytes long, whether you use single or multibyte character.

2. The first character in the identifier must be either the underscore (_), or an alphabetic character (as defined in the SQL Server's current character set).

   ■ The first character in a temporary table identifier must begin with the "pound" symbol (#).

   ■ The first character in a local variable identifier must begin with the "at" symbol (@).

3. The second through thirtieth characters in the identifier can be alphabetic characters, numeric characters, the underscore, "at", and "pound" symbols, or currency symbols, such as U.S. dollars ($), Japanese yen (¥), or pound sterling (£).

4. Identifiers cannot include embedded spaces.

5. Identifiers cannot include special characters, such as the period (.), !, ^, &, *.

6. A SQL Server reserved keyword cannot be used as an identifier, except when used as a local variable name or as a stored procedure parameter name.

By default, the preceding rules for identifiers apply. However, if you enter the `set quoted_identifier on` command during your session, then your connection can override some of the default rules, and you can create column, table, and view identifiers, by enclosing them in double quotation marks (""), that:

1. Begin with nonalphabetic characters.

2. Include characters that violate the above rules for identifiers, such as the space ( ) symbol.

3. Are SQL Server reserved keywords.

However, the length of such identifiers cannot exceed 28 bytes, and they cannot be used as parameters to SQL Server system procedures. The override stays in effect only for the duration of the connection in which the above `set` command was executed.

Sybase System 11 SQL Server Reserved Keywords

The Sybase System 11 SQL Server has a collection of reserved keywords that cannot be used as identifiers, except when used as a local variable name, or as a stored procedure parameter name. Below is the list of these reserved keywords:

add	char_convert	deallocate	exec
all	check	declare	execute
alter	checkpoint	default	exists
and	close	delete	exit
any	clustered	desc	fetch
arith_overflow	commit	disk	fillfactor
as	compute	distinct	for
asc	confirm	double	foreign
at	constraint	dummy	from
authorization	continue	dump	goto
avg	controlrow	else	grant
begin	convert	end	group
between	count	endtran	having

break	create	errlvl	holdlock
browse	current	errordata	identity_insert
bulk	cursor	errorexit	if
by	database	escape	in
cascade	dbcc	except	index
insert	on	reconfigure	temporary
intersect	once	references	textsize
into	online	replace	to
is	only	return	tran
isolation	open	revoke	transaction
key	option	role	trigger
kill	or	rollback	truncate
level	order	rowcount	tsequal
like	over	rows	union
lineno	partition	rule	unique
load	perm	save	unpartition
max	permanent	schema	update
max_rows_per_page	plan	select	use
min	precision	set	user
mirror	prepare	setuser	user_option
mirrorexit	primary	shared	using
national	print	shutdown	values
noholdlock	privileges	some	varying
nonclustered	proc	statistics	view
not	procedure	stripe	waitfor
null	processexit	sum	where
numeric_transaction	public	syb_identity	while
of	raiserror	syb_restree	with
off	read	table	work
offsets	readtext	temp	writetext

Displaying SQL Server Login Account Information

Every authorized user of a SQL Server has a systemwide unique Sybase login account created for them by an **sso_role** login account. To get the details on login accounts for a SQL Server, log on to the SQL Server as an account with **sa_role,** or as an account with **sso_role,** privileges and enter these commands:

```
1>use master
2>go
1>sp_displaylogin [ loginame]
2>go
```

where:

> master—the name of the master system database. You must be using this database when you enter this command.
>
> loginame—this optional parameter is the name of the Sybase login account for which you want information. If you do not use this optional parameter, then all Sybase login accounts will be reported on.

The displayed report will give you the following information:

1. The systemwide unique ID of the login account.
2. The systemwide unique name of the login account.
3. The full name associated with the login account.
4. All roles granted to the login account (both active and inactive roles).
5. An indication whether or not the login account is locked (i.e., disabled).
6. The date when the login account's password was last changed.

If your account has not been granted either the **sa_role** or the **sso_role** roles, then you can still use the sp_displaylogin command to get this information on you own account. However, you must pass to the sp_displaylogin command your Sybase login account name.

To determine which, if any, roles your login account has, log on to the SQL Server and enter these commands:

```
1>use master
2>go
1>select show_role()
2>go
```

If your login account does not have any roles, then the transaction returns the "null" value. If your login account does have roles, then the transaction will return the role, or roles, your login account has.

Creating a Login Account

Before you can use a SQL Server you must have a systemwide unique Sybase login account created for you by an **sso_role** login account. When your login account is created, a row representing your login account, and its (encrypted) password, is stored within the master..syslogins system table, and a systemwide unique user identifier (`master..syslogins..suid`) is assigned to your login account. Your login account `suid` is the same across all databases you are permitted to use, and all activities you undertake within the server can be related to your `suid`, and can be audited.

To create a Sybase login account, log on to the SQL Server as an account with **sso_role** privileges and enter these commands:

```
1>use master
2>go
1>sp_addlogin loginame, passwd
2>[,defdb[,deflanguage[,fullname]]]
3>go
```

where:

`loginame`—this parameter is the name of the new login account you are creating. The name of a login account must follow the rules for Sybase identifiers, and it must be unique within the SQL Server.

`passwd`—this parameter is the password of the new login account you are creating. A password must be 6 bytes or longer, and can be made of any printable alphanumeric character or symbol. If the login account's password includes characters other than A–Z, a–z, 0–9, _, #, valid single or multibyte alphabetic characters, or accented alphabetic characters, or if the password begins with 0–9, then it must be enclosed within quotation marks (`""`). You cannot specify the character string "null" as a login account password. All login account passwords are stored in encrypted form within the `master..syslogins` table. You can change your own password, and the **sso_role** can change any login account's password.

`defdb`—this optional parameter is the name of the login account's default database. Each time the account logs into the SQL Server, the session could automatically start in this database. However, before the login account can actually start in this database, it must subsequently be added to this database as a user of the database. If users try to use their login account before they are added to their default database, then they will be connected to the *master* system database and the SQL Server will return an error to them. If this optional parameter is not used, then the login account's default database will be the *master* system database. It is advisable to assign a login account to some database other than the *master* system database, particularly if that login account will be granted permission to create any principal database object. The **sa_role** login account can change any login account's default database after the account is created. You can change your own login account's default database, but you will not be able to use it unless the owner of that database has added your login account to their database. If you do not want to specify the login account's default database, but you do want to specify either the login account's default language or full name, then you must enter the string "null" followed by a comma (,) in this location. If the login accounts' default database is subsequently dropped, or the login account is subsequently dropped from their default database, then they will be connected to the *master* system database and the SQL Server will return an error to them.

deflanguage—this optional parameter specifies the login account's default language. All prompts and messages generated by the SQL Server will be displayed in the login account's default language. To determine the alternate languages supported by a given SQL Server, log on to that SQL Server and execute the sp_helplanguage system procedure. If you do not use this optional parameter, then the login account will use the SQL Server's default language, as established by the default language id SQL Server configuration parameter. An **sa_role** login account can change any login account's default language after the account is created. You can change your own login account's default language. If you do not want to specify the login account's default language, but you do want to specify the login account's full name, then you must enter the string "null" followed by a comma (,) in this location. If the login accounts' default language is subsequently dropped from the SQL Server, then they will use the SQL Server's default language, and an error message will be returned to them (so be sure to change the default language property of all affected login accounts).

fullname—this optional parameter is used to document the login account.

Once this command completes successfully, the account is valid within the SQL Server and can be used immediately. This command changes the *master* system database, so to ensure its recovery, be certain to dump the *master* system database. Also, because this command changes the contents of the system tables, it cannot be executed within a transaction.

Finding Out Who's Using the SQL Server

Each process that runs within the SQL Server has its own unique numeric process identifier called spid. To find out which processes are being managed by the SQL Server, log on to the SQL Server and enter this command

```
1>sp_who [loginame | "spid"]
2>go
```

where:

> loginame—this optional parameter is the name of the login account for which you want to display information about the processes the SQL Server is managing on its behalf.

> spid—this is the systemwide unique SQL Server process id. If this optional parameter is passed to this command, then information only about this login will be displayed. Because the command expects a character string, you must enclose this parameter in quotes ("").

The SQL Server will produce a report that shows the spid, its status, the name of the login account that owns the process (if the process is a system process, then this field will contain the "null" string), the name of the host computer from which the process was initiated, and where applicable, the spid of the process that is blocking this process will be shown (or else a zero will be displayed), the name of the database that this process initially connected to (your process could initially connect to your default database, but then switch to another database), and the name of the Transact-SQL command you are currently executing.

Killing a Process within the SQL Server

Every once in a while a process within the SQL Server may need to be killed, that is, removed from the SQL Server. The spid column in the report from the sp_who command contains the sybase process identifier of each process that is present within the current database. To terminate an offending process, log on to the SQL Server as an account with **sa_role** privileges, and enter these commands:

```
1>use master
2>go
1>kill spid
2>go
```

When you issue the kill command, it may take some time before the process is removed from the SQL Server, and you may have to repeat the kill command. Unfortunately, it is still not possible to kill all processes at all times. Killing **dbcc** jobs on system tables is still problematic at times. If you are not able to kill a process that is causing serious problems within the SQL Server, then you may have no other choice but to shut down the SQL Server to destroy the process. While the kill ratio for System 11 is higher than with previous versions of the SQL Server, it is not yet 100 percent.

Chargeback Accounting for the SQL Server

When an account (other than the **sa** account) logs into the SQL Server, the SQL Server starts recording CPU and disk I/O usage for that login account. This usage information is stored within the `master..syslogins` system table. This information can be retrieved by an **sa_role** login account to produce reports for individual login accounts, or for all login accounts.

This information can be used for a couple of purposes. For one, you can use it to differentiate login accounts that consume high amounts of CPU cycles and produce large volumes of disk I/O to assist you in undertaking performance analysis. For another, if your business charges individual accounts for their use of SQL Server CPU and disk I/O use, then this product feature will enable you to accomplish that goal.

As the SQL Server does not collect CPU time and disk I/O use for any process that is owned by the **sa** login account ($suid = 1$), these statistics are not collected for checkpoint, deadlock detection, HouseKeeper, mirror, or network handler process.

SQL Server Kernel Configuration for Chargeback Accounting

The frequency with which CPU and disk I/O usage statistics are updated for a login account by the SQL Server can be configured. The SQL Server has two configuration parameters that control the frequency with which these metrics are collected:

1. `cpu accounting flush interval`
2. `i/o accounting flush interval`

When an account logs off the SQL Server, or when it accumulates more CPU time or disk I/O than the respective configured flushing interval values, the SQL Server automatically writes its new totals to the `master..syslogins` system table.

When a user logs on to the SQL Server, a process is established within the SQL Server, and figures for CPU usage for that process are automatically accumulating within the `master..sysprocess..cpu` system table column, and figures for disk I/O usage for that process are automatically accumulating within the `master..sysprocess..physical_io` system table column. The `cpu accounting flush interval` SQL Server configuration parameter establishes how many machine clock ticks (not SQL Server clock ticks), measured in microseconds, will be accumulated before updating the `master..syslogins..totcpu` system table column with CPU time metrics stored within the `master.. sysprocess..cpu` system table column (this column will be updated when a user logs off the SQL Server as well). The `i/o accounting flush interval` SQL Server configuration parameter establishes how many machine clock ticks, measured in microseconds, will be accumulated before updating the `master..syslogins..totio` system table column with disk I/O time metrics stored within the `master.. sysprocess..physical_io` system table column (this column will be updated when a user logs off the SQL Server as well). When the internal handler flushes the data from the `master..sysprocess` system table to the `master..syslogins` system table, the process's figures for CPU time and for disk I/O usage are initialized, that is, they are set back to zero in the `master..sysprocess` system table. To determine how many microseconds a clock tick is for the machine on which the SQL Server is running, log on to the SQL Server, as any valid login account and enter this command while using any database:

```
1>select @@timeticks
2>go
```

The minimum value of the `cpu accounting flush interval` SQL Server configuration parameter is one (1), and its maximum value is 2,147,483,647. The default value of the `cpu accounting flush interval` SQL Server configuration parameter is 200 machine clock ticks. To determine the current value of the configuration parameter for your SQL Server, log on to the SQL Server as any valid login account and enter these commands:

```
1>use master
2>go
1>sp_configure "cpu accounting flush interval"
2>go
```

Before you go ahead and reset the value of the `cpu accounting flush interval` SQL Server configuration parameter, you need to understand that the SQL Server Lock Manager uses the CPU usage figures collected in the `master..sysprocess..cpu` system table column to resolve detected deadlocks. To resolve the detected deadlock, the Lock Manager will choose the process with the lesser amount of CPU usage time to kill. When you set the value of the `cpu accounting flush interval` SQL Server configuration parameter too low, you create the illusion within the `master..sysprocess..cpu` system table column that long-running processes are consuming less CPU time than they actually are (because you are too frequently reinitializing the `master..sysprocess..cpu` system table column for long-running process). As a consequence, you increase the likelihood that the Lock Manager may choose the wrong process to kill when resolving a detected deadlock.

Determining the value you want to set the `cpu accounting flush interval` SQL Server configuration parameter to depends upon the type of CPU usage reporting you will be doing, or not doing as the case may be. If you never intend to do any CPU usage reporting, then set the value of the `cpu accounting flush interval` SQL Server configuration parameter to its maximum value. If you intend to infrequently report on CPU usage, then set the value of the `cpu accounting flush interval` SQL Server configuration parameter to a relatively high value. If you intend to infrequently report on CPU usage, then set the value of the `cpu accounting flush interval` SQL Server configuration parameter to a relatively low value (but not so low that it starts to kill the wrong process during detected-deadlock resolution). Keep in mind that the more frequently the `master..syslogins` table is updated, the more frequently it will have to be written to disk (i.e., you are increasing SQL Server disk I/O overhead).

To set the value of the `cpu accounting flush interval` SQL Server configuration parameter to 400 machine clock ticks, for example, log on to the SQL Server as an account with **sa_role** privileges and enter these commands:

```
1>use master
2>go
1>sp_configure "cpu accounting flush interval", 400
2>go
```

This change in the SQL Server's configuration takes effect immediately (i.e., you do not have to shut down and restart the SQL Server to have this new configuration value take effect). Also, this command changes the *master* system database, so to ensure its recovery, be certain to dump the *master* system database itself. Also, because this command changes the contents of the system tables, it cannot be executed within a transaction.

The minimum value of the `i/o accounting flush interval` SQL Server configuration parameter is one (1) and its maximum value is 2,147,483,647. The default value of the `i/o accounting flush interval` SQL Server configuration parameter is 200 machine clock ticks. To determine the current value of the configuration parameter for your SQL Server, log on to the SQL Server as any valid login account and enter these commands:

```
1>use master
2>go
1>sp_configure "i/o accounting flush interval"
2>go
```

Determining the value you want to set the i/o accounting flush interval SQL Server configuration parameter to depends upon the type of disk I/O usage reporting you will be doing, or not doing as the case may be. If you never intend to do any disk I/O usage reporting, then set the value of the i/o accounting flush interval SQL Server configuration parameter to its maximum value. If you intend to infrequently report on disk I/O usage, then set the value of the i/o accounting flush interval SQL Server configuration parameter to a relatively high value. If you intend to frequently report on disk I/O usage, then set the value of the i/o accounting flush interval SQL Server configuration parameter to a relatively low value (but not so low that it starts to kill the wrong process during detected-deadlock resolution). Keep in mind that the more frequently the master..syslogins table is updated, the more frequently it will have to be written to disk (i.e., you are increasing SQL Server disk I/O overhead).

To set the value of the i/o accounting flush interval SQL Server configuration parameter to 3000 machine clock ticks, for example, log on to the SQL Server as an account with **sa_role** privileges and enter these commands:

```
1>use master
2>go
1>sp_configure "i/o accounting flush interval", 3000
2>go
```

This change in the SQL Server's configuration takes effect immediately. This command changes the *master* system database, so to ensure its recovery, be certain to dump the *master* system database. Also, because this command changes the contents of the system tables, it cannot be executed within a transaction.

Reporting Current SQL Server Usage Statistics

To produce a report of the current CPU and disk I/O usage on your SQL Server, log on to the SQL Server as a login account that has **sa_role** privileges and enter these commands:

```
1>use master
2>go
```

```
1>sp_reportstats [loginame]
2>go
```

where:

[loginame]—this optional parameter is the name of the login account for which you want to produce a CPU and disk I/O usage report. If you do not use this optional parameter, then a report of CPU and disk I/O usage for all login accounts in the SQL Server will be displayed.

The displayed report will tell you the date on which the current chargeback interval began, the total CPU and disk I/O usage for the current chargeback interval, and, for each login account, the:

1. Name of the login account.
2. Date on which the current chargeback interval began for the login account.
3. Amount of CPU time they used.
4. Percentage of total CPU time consumed by the login account.
5. Amount of disk I/O they used.
6. Percentage of total disk I/O consumed by the login account.

One login account that will always show up in the report is the SQL Server's **probe** login account. The **probe** login account is automatically created, like the **sa** login account, when the SQL Server was installed. The **probe** login account's purpose in life is to support the Two-Phase Commit Probe Process, which uses a challenge and response mechanism to work with the SQL Server in support of two-phase commits.

Initiating a New Chargeback Interval

The SQL Server continues to collect cumulative CPU and disk I/O usage until you reset the usage figures and begin a new chargeback interval. CPU and disk I/O are then accumulated usage from that point in time forward. The cumulative CPU and disk I/O usage can be reset for an individual login account, as well as for all login accounts, in the SQL Server.

To begin a new chargeback interval, and wipe out the existing cumulative CPU and disk I/O usage statistics, log on to the SQL Server as a login account that has **sa_role** privileges and enter these commands:

```
1>use master
2>go
1>sp_clearstats [loginame]
2>go
```

where:

[loginame]—this optional parameter is the name of the login account for which you want to begin a new chargeback interval. If you do not use this optional parameter, then all login accounts will have a new chargeback interval.

This command calls the sp_reportstat command, displays the CPU and disk I/O usage statistics for the previous period, and then resets the CPU and disk I/O usage statistics for the login account, or for all login accounts, whichever the case may be. Also, because this command changes the contents of the system tables, it cannot be executed within a transaction.

Changing Login Account Defaults

It is possible, once a login account is created, to modify the login account's default database, default language, and full name. You can modify these properties of your own login account. A login account that has the **sa_role** privileges can modify these properties of any login account on the SQL Server.

While you can change these properties of your own login account, you will have to be careful when changing your default database and your default language. You will have to make certain that, if you change your default database, the owner of that database will add your login account to that database. Also, if you change your default language you will have to be certain that the language you select is in fact supported by the SQL Server. To determine the alternate languages supported by a given SQL Server, log on to that SQL Server and execute the sp_helplanguage system procedure.

To change login account properties, log on to the SQL Server as the appropriate account and enter these commands:

```
1>use master
2>go
1>sp_modifylogin loginame, column, value
2>go
```

where:

loginame—this parameter is the name of the login account whose properties you want to change.

`column`—this parameter is the name of the login account property you want to change. The legal values for this parameter are `defdb`, `deflanguage`, and `fullname`. Before the login account can actually start in the new default database, the login account must subsequently be added to this database as a user of that database. If the user tries to use the login account before adding it to the new default database, then the user will be connected to the *master* system database and the SQL Server will return an error. If the login account's default database is subsequently dropped, or the login account is subsequently dropped from the default database, then the user will be connected to the *master* system database and the SQL Server will return an error (so be sure to change the default database property of all affected login accounts). If the login account's new default language is subsequently dropped from the SQL Server, then the SQL Server's default language will be used, and an error message will be returned (so be sure to change the default language property of all affected login accounts).

`value`—this is the new setting for the login account property you are changing.

This command changes the *master* system database, so to ensure its recovery, be certain to dump the *master* system database. Also, because this command changes the contents of the system tables, it cannot be executed within a transaction.

SQL Server Kernel Configuration for Password Expiration

A login account with **sso_role** privileges can configure the password expiration period for all login account passwords on the SQL Server. The password expiration period establishes the number of days after the password was created, or changed, that it remains in effect. The SQL Server configuration period that establishes the systemwide password expiration is called *systemwide password expiration*. The default value of the systemwide password expiration SQL Server configuration parameter is zero. When the systemwide password expiration SQL Server configuration parameter is set to zero, the passwords do not expire; they remain in effect forever. The range of legal values for the systemwide password expiration SQL Server configuration parameter is 0 through 32,767, where the expiration period is measured in units of days. When the value of the systemwide password expiration SQL Server configuration parameter is greater than zero, a login account's password expires if a count of days that has passed is greater than the value of the systemwide password expiration SQL Server configuration parameter since the last time the login account's password was created or changed.

At login time, the SQL Server notifies the login account when its password approaches the expiration period. When the count of days remaining before expiration occurs is less than 25 percent of the value of the systemwide password expiration SQL Server configuration parameter, or 7 days, whichever is greater, the SQL Server sends a message to the login account indicating the number of days remaining before password expiration occurs.

Each login account is capable of changing its password at any time before it expires. However, if your password expires, you will still be able to log in to the SQL Server, but the only command you can execute is the `sp_password` system command that enables you to change your password. If you try to execute any other command, then the SQL Server causes the command to fail, and will return an error message to you. Also, the **sso_role** can, while your login account is in the state where it is limited to executing only the `sp_password` command, change your password for you, and as a consequence, your login account will be able to function normally.

To change the systemwide password expiration SQL Server configuration parameter to 30 days, for example, log on to the SQL Server as an account with **sso_role** privileges and enter these commands:

```
1>use master
2>go
1>sp_configure "systemwide password expiration", 30
2>go
```

This change will take effect immediately within the SQL Server. This command changes the *master* system database, so to ensure its recovery, be certain to dump the *master* system database. Also, because this command changes the contents of the system tables, it cannot be executed within a transaction.

Changing a Login Account's Password

In addition to the times when your password has been automatically expired by the SQL Server, for security reasons it is simply good practice to change your account password every once in a while. Every Sybase login account can change its password whenever it wants to. And, the **sso_role** can change any account's password, at any time.

To change your own login account's password, log on to the SQL Server, using any database and enter this command:

```
1>sp_password caller_passwd, new_passwd
2>go
```

where:

> `caller_passwd`—this is your current password. If your current password includes characters other than A–Z, a–z, 0–9, _, #, valid single or multibyte alphabetic characters, or accented alphabetic characters, or if the password begins with 0–9, then it must be enclosed within quotation marks (`""`).
>
> `new_passwd`—this is your new password. A password must be 6 bytes or longer, and can be made of any printable alphanumeric character or symbol. If your new password includes characters other than A–Z, a–z, 0–9, _, #, valid single or multibyte alphabetic characters, or accented alphabetic characters, or if the password begins with 0–9, then it must be enclosed within quotation marks (`""`). You cannot specify the character string "null" as a login account password. All login account passwords are stored in encrypted form within the `master..syslogins` table.

This change takes effect immediately. Because this command changes the contents of the system tables, it cannot be executed within a transaction. To change the password of someone else's login account, log on to the SQL Server as an account with **sso_role** privileges, and, using any database enter this command:

```
1>sp_password caller_passwd, new_passwd, loginame
2>go
```

where:

> `caller_passwd`—this is the login account's current password. If the login account's current password includes characters other than A–Z, a–z, 0–9, _, #, valid single or multibyte alphabetic characters, or accented alphabetic characters, or if the password begins with 0–9, then it must be enclosed within quotation marks (`""`). When the SQL Server is installed, the **sa** login account has the character string "null" as its password. To change the initial password of the **sa** login account, set the value of this parameter to null, but do not enclose this character string in quotes (`""`).
>
> `new_passwd`—this is the login account's new password. A password must be 6 bytes or longer, and can be made of any printable alphanumeric character or symbol. If the login account's new password includes characters other than A–Z, a–z, 0–9, _, #, valid single or multibyte alphabetic characters, or accented alphabetic characters, or if the password begins with 0–9, then it must be enclosed within quotation marks (`""`). You cannot specify the character string "null"

as a login account password. All login account passwords are stored in encrypted form within the `master..syslogins` table.

`loginame`—this parameter is the name of the login account whose password you want to change.

This change takes effect immediately. Because this command changes the contents of the system tables, it cannot be executed within a transaction.

Granting the System Security Officer Role to a Login Account

A login account with **sso_role** privileges can grant the **sso_role** role to other login accounts. To grant the System Security Officer role privileges to another login account, log on to the SQL Server, as an account with **sso_role** privileges and enter these commands:

```
1>use master
2>go
1>sp_role "grant", sso_role, loginame
2>go
```

where:

`loginame`—this parameter is the name of the login account to which you want to grant System Security Officer role privileges.

This command changes the *master* system database, so to ensure its recovery, be certain to dump the *master* system database. Also, because this command changes the contents of the system tables, it cannot be executed within a transaction.

By default, the role granted to a login account takes effect the next time that account logs on to the SQL Server. However, if that account is currently logged on to the SQL Server and wants the new System Security Officer role privileges to take effect immediately, then that login account must enter this command:

```
1>set role sso_role on
2>go
```

Granting the Operator Role to a Login Account

A login account with **sso_role** privileges can grant the **oper_role** role to other login accounts. To grant the Operator role privileges to another login account, log on to the SQL Server as an account with **sso_role** privileges and enter these commands:

```
1>use master
2>go
1>sp_role "grant", oper_role, loginame
2>go
```

where:

loginame—this parameter is the name of the login account to which you want to grant Operator role privileges.

This command changes the *master* system database, so to ensure its recovery, be certain to dump the *master* system database. Also, because this command changes the contents of the system tables, it cannot be executed within a transaction.

By default, the role granted to a login account takes effect the next time that account logs on to the SQL Server. However, if that account is currently logged on to the SQL Server, and wants the new Operator role privileges to take effect immediately, then that login account must enter this command:

```
1>set role oper_role on
2>go
```

Granting the System Administrator Role to a Login Account

A login account with **sa_role** privileges can grant the **sa_role** role to other login accounts. To grant the System Administration role privileges to another login account, log on to the SQL Server as an account with **sa_role** login privileges and enter these commands:

```
1>use master
2>go
1>sp_role "grant", sa_role, loginame
2>go
```

where:

loginame—this parameter is the name of the login account to which you want to grant System Administration role privileges.

This command changes the *master* system database, so to ensure its recovery, be certain to dump the *master* system database. Also, because this command changes the contents of the system tables, it cannot be executed within a transaction.

By default, the role granted to a login account takes effect the next time that account logs in to the SQL Server. However, if that account is currently logged on to the SQL Server, and wants the new System Administration role privileges to take effect immediately, then that login account must enter this command:

```
1>set role sa_role on
2>go
```

Taking on the Identity of a Login Account That Owns a Database

As previously stated, the **sa** login account, and all login accounts that have been granted the privileges of the **sa_role,** can take on the privileges, in all databases, of the login account that owns a given database.

If your login account has been granted the privileges of the **sa_role,** and you want to assume the "real" identity of the login account that has **dbo** privileges in a given database (i.e., the login account that owns the database), then log on to the SQL Server with the login account that has sa_role privileges and enter these commands:

```
1>use NameOfDatabase
2>go
1>set role sa_role off
2>go
```

where:

NameOfDatabase—the name of the database within which you want to assume the "real" identity of the login account that owns the database.

When you take on the identity of a **dbo** login account, you lose the privileges associated with the **sa_role** login account. When you want to resume the privileges of the **sa_role,** then enter this command:

```
1>set role sa_role on
2>go
```

Taking on the Identity of a Login Account That Owns Principal Database Objects

As previously stated, the **dbo** login account can, within the database it owns, acquire the permissions of all login accounts that have principal database object ownership privileges. This capability enables the **dbo** login account to grant permissions on any principal database object to any login account within its database, to create principal database objects that another login account will own, and to manipulate a principal database object owned by another login account.

If your login account is the **dbo,** and you want to assume the "real" identity of the login account that has principal database ownership privileges in a given database (i.e., the login account that owns a given principal database object), then log on to the SQL Server with the login account that has **dbo** privileges and enter these commands:

```
1>use NameOfDatabase
2>go
1>setuser "loginame"
2>go
```

where:

NameOfDatabase—the name of the database you own within which you want to assume the "real" identity of the login account whose permissions you want to acquire.

loginame—this parameter is the name of the login account whose permissions, within the database you own, you want to acquire.

When you take on the identity of another login account, you lose the privileges associated with the **dbo** login account. When you want to reacquire the privileges of the **dbo,** then enter this command while still using the database you own:

```
1>setuser
2>go
```

Also, if after assuming the identity of another login account you were to leave your current database and use another database, the permissions for your login account would be those granted to it in the new database you are using.

Here are a few important points to understand about the use of the setuser command after you have logged on to the SQL Server as an account with **sa_role** privileges:

1. When the **sa_role** uses the name of a Sybase account as a parameter to the setuser command, it temporarily assumes the identity of that Sybase account.

2. To revert back to the **sa_role** account, execute the setuser command without using any parameter.

3. You will retain the identity of this account until either you use another database or you execute `setuser` command without using any parameter.

4. If the account you changed to has permissions to dump the current database, then you will not have to revert back to the **sa_role** account to dump the database.

Revoking the System Security Officer Role from a Login Account

A login account with **sso_role** privileges can revoke the **sso_role** role from other login accounts. But the **sso_role** role cannot be taken away from an account that is currently logged on to the SQL Server. To revoke the System Security Officer role privileges from another login account, log on to the SQL Server as an account with **sso_role** privileges and enter these commands:

```
1>use master
2>go
1>sp_role "revoke", sso_role, loginame
2>go
```

where:

`loginame`—this parameter is the name of the login account from which you want to revoke System Security Officer role privileges.

Revoking a role from a login account takes effect the next time that account logs on to the SQL Server. Also, the SQL Server makes certain that the last login account with **sso_role** privileges does not have its **sso_role** privileges revoked.

This command changes the *master* system database, so to ensure its recovery, be certain to dump the *master* system database. Also, because this command changes the contents of the system tables, it cannot be executed within a transaction.

Revoking the Operator Role from a Login Account

A login account with **sso_role** privileges can revoke the **oper_role** role from other login accounts. But the **oper_role** role cannot be taken away from an account that is currently logged on to the SQL Server. To revoke the System Security Officer role privileges from another login account, log on to the SQL Server as an account with **sso_role** privileges and enter these commands:

```
1>use master
2>go
1>sp_role "revoke", oper_role, loginame
2>go
```

where:

loginame—this parameter is the name of the login account from which you want to revoke Operator role privileges.

Revoking a role from a login account takes effect the next time that account logs on to the SQL Server. Also, the SQL Server does not make certain that the last login account with **oper_role** privileges does not have its **oper_role** privileges revoked.

This command changes the *master* system database, so to ensure its recovery, be certain to dump the *master* system database. Also, because this command changes the contents of the system tables, it cannot be executed within a transaction.

Revoking the System Administrator Role from a Login Account

A login account with **sa_role** privileges can revoke the **sa_role** role from other login accounts. But the **sa_role** role cannot be taken away from an account that is currently logged on to the SQL Server. To revoke the System Administrator role privileges from another login account, log on to the SQL Server as an account with **sa_role** login privileges and enter these commands:

```
1>use master
2>go
1>sp_role "revoke", sa_role, loginame
2>go
```

where:

loginame—this parameter is the name of the login account from which you want to revoke System Administrator role privileges.

Revoking a role from a login account takes effect the next time that account logs on to the SQL Server. Also, the SQL Server makes certain that the last login account with **sa_role** privileges does not have its **sa_role** privileges revoked.

This command changes the *master* system database, so to ensure its recovery, be certain to dump the *master* system database. Also, because this command changes the contents of the system tables, it cannot be executed within a transaction.

Locking a Login Account

Security situations arise for which either the System Administrator or the System Security Officer needs to disable, or lock, a given Sybase login account. When you lock a login account, that account can no longer log on to the SQL Server. While it is possible to lock a login account that is currently logged on to the SQL Server, the lock will not take effect until it logs off the SQL Server. To ensure support of the system, the SQL Server will make sure that the last **sa_role** and the last **sso_role** login account are not locked by mistake. It is possible to lock login accounts that own a database, or that own principal database objects, and to change ownership of databases and objects that are currently owned by a locked login account.

To lock a login account, log on to the SQL Server as an account with **sa_role,** or as an account with **sso_role** privileges, and enter these commands:

```
1>use master
2>go
1>sp_locklogin loginame "lock"
2>go
```

where:

loginame—this parameter is the name of the login account that you want to lock. This can be any and all login accounts, including **sa.**

This command changes the *master* system database, so to ensure its recovery, be certain to dump the *master* system database. Also, because this command changes the contents of the system tables, it cannot be executed within a transaction.

Displaying Locked Login Accounts

To determine which login accounts on the SQL Server are locked, log on to the SQL Server as an account with **sa_role,** or as an account with **sso_role,** privileges, and enter these commands:

```
1>use master
2>go
1>sp_locklogin
2>go
```

The list of locked login accounts will be displayed.

Unlocking a Login Account

To unlock a given login account, log on to the SQL Server as an account with **sa_role,** or as an account with **sso_role,** privileges, and enter these commands:

```
1>use master
2>go
1>sp_locklogin loginame "unlock"
2>go
```

where:

loginame—this parameter is the name of the login account which you want to unlock.

This command changes the *master* system database, so to ensure its recovery, be certain to dump the *master* system database. Also, because this command changes the contents of the system tables, it cannot be executed within a transaction.

Dropping a Login Account from the SQL Server

Just like everything else in this universe, SQL Server login accounts are created, exist for a short while, and are then destroyed. However, login accounts cannot be destroyed if that login account:

1. Is currently logged on to the SQL Server.
2. Is a user in a database (including the **dbo**).
3. Owns a principal database object.
4. Has permissions on principal database objects that are owned by another login account.
5. Has granted permission on principal database objects it owns to other login accounts.
6. Has an alias in a database.
7. Is the last login with **sa_role** privileges.
8. Is the last login with **sso_role** privileges.

So to drop a login account, you must, as required, revoke permissions of database objects, change ownership of principal database objects, change ownership of databases, remove the login account from a database, and possibly grant **sa_role** and **sso_role** privileges to another login account. For these reasons it is often more practical to first lock the login account before you begin the process of dropping the login account from the SQL Server.

To drop a login account, log on to the SQL Server as an account with **sa_role** privileges, and enter these commands:

```
1>use master
2>go
1>sp_droplogin loginame
2>go
```

where:

loginame—this parameter is the name of the login account that you want to drop from the SQL Server.

This command changes the *master* system database, so to ensure its recovery, be certain to dump the *master* system database. Also, because this command changes the contents of the system tables, it cannot be executed within a transaction.

2

Miscellaneous Stuff

Introduction

The purpose of this chapter is to collect in one place a number of features of the SQL Server that are important to understand before we go further with our exploration of the SQL Server but don't really warrant individual chapters of their own.

Running the SQL Server on Multiprocessor Platforms

The System 11 SQL Server has a Virtual Server Architecture (VSA) that allows it to exploit the benefits of *symmetrical multiprocessor* (SMP) platforms by running multiple engines. A SQL Server engine is an executable heavyweight thread scheduled and dispatched by the operating system to run on a CPU. It communicates with other SQL Server engines and shares databases and internal structures, such as memory, disk, and lock resources, through shared memory. In that each SQL Server engine is functionally identical, each can perform any user-of-system task, such as physical and logical I/O or the acquisition of locking resources.

While you can run the System 11 SQL Server on single CPU platforms, it is designed to run on platforms with a symmetric multiprocessing operating system which share memory that is accessed over a common hardware bus, have 1 to 32 CPUs, and do not have a master CPU (this would make them an asymmetrical platform).

Because VSA is symmetrical, a SQL Server engine will be scheduled and dispatched by the operating system to run on any available CPU, processor affinity (binding a given SQL Server engine to a given CPU) is not supported.

If the operating system supports network affinity, then the SQL Server will migrate client connections to the SQL Server engine that is supporting the smallest number of connections. Otherwise, the SQL Server Engine 0 supports all network management tasks. In all other respects, the SQL Server engines are peers. The SQL Server accomplishes load balancing by scheduling and dispatching user and system tasks onto the next available SQL Server engine (i.e., there is no task affinity).

When an application asks to connect to the SQL Server, the SQL Server follows these high-level steps:

1. Engine 0 creates a lightweight thread (that is assigned an internal process identifier), a *task,* to handle the application's request to log on to the SQL Server. Engine 0 determines the application's connection characteristics (e.g., language, character set, sort order, network packet size, is this an authorized login account).

2. Next, Engine 0 determines which SQL Server engine is supporting the least number of client connections. If the chosen SQL Server engine is not Engine 0, then the task is migrated to that target SQL Server engine by passing the task's file descriptor from Engine 0 to the target SQL Server engine, referred to as N_Engine. At this point, the task is put to sleep.

3. Once every clock tick, the N_Engine manages all network reads (incoming commands) for all applications connected to it. When a command (a Transact-SQL statement, a system procedure, etc.) is received, the N_Engine wakes up the tasks, changes its status to runnable, and places it on the bottom of the SQL Server's FIFO run queue. As the SQL Server engines compete with one another, pulling tasks off the run queue and executing them, the task eventually makes its way to the top of the SQL Server's FIFO run queue.

4. When the command hits the top of the FIFO run queue, a SQL Server engine, referred to as the X_Engine, takes the task off the run queue, parses the command, runs it through the statistical query optimizer, and begins to execute the command.

5. The X_Engine runs the task until either it completes (is committed, rolled back, or aborted) or is blocked while waiting for physical or logical I/O or for locking resources. When a task blocks, it is removed from the run queue, its state is saved, and it is placed on the sleep queue. The X_Engine will take another task off of the run queue and execute it. Once the block is resolved, the task is placed back onto the run queue where a SQL Server engine will pick it off and execute it.

6. Once the task blocks for the last time, and completes, the X_Engine fills a Tabular Data Stream (TDS) (this is a proprietary logical net-

work protocol used by Sybase to support client/server communications) buffer with a result set (and message).

7. At this point the task is ready to send a response back to the requesting application, so the N_Engine makes a network send function call on behalf of the task. On the next clock tick, the X_Engine acquires a network I/O structure, stores within it information about pending network I/O (e.g., the task's process identifier, a pointer to the TDS buffer).

8. The X_Engine then links the network I/O structure onto the N_Engine's linked list of pending network I/O structures. And, while waiting for the physical network I/O to be completed, the X_Engine saves the task's state and puts it to sleep by linking it to the sleep queue.

9. Odds are the N_Engine is currently busy executing a task of its own. When that task blocks, the N_Engine's scheduler determines if it must run the next task on the run queue, or if it must process network I/O or completed disk I/O. If it is time to run the next task, then that task is run on N_Engine. Otherwise, if it is time to process network I/O or completed disk I/O, then the I/O Service task is run on N_Engine.

10. The I/O Service task first sends network writes (requests to send the TDS packets) to the underlying operating system. When a given network write completes, the N_Engine purges the network I/O structure from its pending network I/O queue and wakes up the associated task by linking it to the run queue.

11. When all network writes complete, the I/O Service task processes pending network reads and then handles completed disk I/O.

SQL Server Kernel Configuration
for Multiple Engines

To manage multiple SQL Server engines, the SQL Server provides four configuration parameters:

1. `max online engines`
2. `min online engines`
3. `max async i/os per engine`
4. `max async i/os per server`

The first thing you'll need to do before running multiple SQL Server engines is to determine the right number of engines to run. For starters, never configure more engines than there are CPUs on the host computer. In general, having one fewer engine than there are CPUs is a practical number of engines to have on-line because the operating system will need the resources of one CPU to do its thing.

The `max online engines` SQL Server configuration parameter is used to specify the maximum number of engines that will be run on the host computer. By default, when the SQL Server is installed, only one engine is configured to run on the host computer. The default value of the `max online engines` SQL Server configuration parameter is one. The range of values for this configuration parameter is 1 through 32. When you start, or boot, the SQL Server, Engine 0 is fired up. This engine is responsible for completing all initialization tasks, including the recovery of all system and user databases supported by your installation. After the initialization tasks are completed, Engine 0 forks (i.e., creates) the remaining number of on-line engines.

To configure, for example, six on-line engines, log on to the SQL Server as an account with **sa_role** privileges, and enter these commands:

```
1>use master
2>go
1>sp_configure "max online engines", 6
2>go
```

For this change to take effect, the SQL Server will have to be shut down and restarted. As this command changes system tables, it cannot be run from within a transaction. This command changes the *master* system database, so to ensure its recovery, be certain to dump the *master* system database.

The `min online engines` SQL Server configuration parameter is used to specify the minimum number of engines that should be started on the host computer. The default value of the `min online engines` SQL Server configuration parameter is one. The range of values for this configuration parameter is 1 through 32. As the availability of hardware resources can fluctuate over boot cycles, this parameter is used to ensure that at least the minimum number of engines your application needs will be brought on-line.

To configure, for example, three on-line engines at minimum, log on to the SQL Server as an account with **sa_role** privileges, and enter these commands:

```
1>use master
2>go
1>sp_configure "min online engines", 3
2>go
```

For this change to take effect, the SQL Server will have to be shut down and restarted. As this command changes system tables, it cannot be run from within a transaction. This command changes the *master* system database, so to ensure its recovery, be certain to dump the *master* system database.

Because disk I/O requires disk I/O structures resources, some operating systems constrain the number of asynchronous disk I/Os per operating system process, some constrain them per system, and some constrain them for both. Be certain to discuss these (tunable) constraints with your operating System Administrator so that you understand the constraints your SQL Server must be configured to live with. If the limited number of asynchronous disk I/Os is exceeded, the operating system will reject the request and raise an error message. Because operating system calls are expensive (i.e., resource intensive), the SQL Server needs to avoid attempts to carry out asynchronous I/Os that will only be discarded by the operating system.

To avert failed asynchronous disk I/O requests to the operating system, the SQL Server keeps a count of outstanding asynchronous disk I/Os for each engine and for the SQL Server. The SQL Server specifies the maximum number of allowed outstanding asynchronous disk I/O requests for a single engine through the `max async i/o per engine` configuration parameter, and specifies the maximum number of allowed outstanding asynchronous disk I/O requests for the SQL Server through the `max async i/o per server` configuration parameter.

When a SQL Server engine is about to issue an asynchronous disk I/O request to the operating system, the SQL Server determines the count of outstanding asynchronous disk I/Os for that engine. If the count of outstanding asynchronous disk I/Os for that engine equals the value of the `max async i/o per engine` configuration parameter or equals the value of the `max async i/o per server` configuration parameter, then the asynchronous disk I/O request will be delayed until enough outstanding asynchronous disk I/O requests have completed to fall below whichever constraint was exceeded.

The default values of both the `max async i/o per engine` configuration parameter and the `max async i/o per server` configuration parameter is 2,147,483,647. The range of these configuration parameters is 1 through 2,147,483,647. In general, both configuration parameters should be set to the limit allowed by the host computer's operating system for asynchronous disk I/O. At minimum, the value of both configuration parameters should be set to 50, and for servers that perform a lot of disk I/O, a setting of 500 may be more appropriate.

To configure `max async i/o per engine`, for example, to 400, log on to the SQL Server as an account with **sa_role** privileges and enter these commands:

```
1>use master
2>go
1>sp_configure "max async i/o per engine", 400
2>go
```

For this change to take effect, the SQL Server will have to be shut down and restarted. As this command changes system tables, it cannot be run from within a transaction. This command changes the *master* system database, so to ensure its recovery, be certain to dump the *master* system database.

To configure max async i/o per server, for example, to 400, log on to the SQL Server as an account with **sa_role** privileges and enter these commands:

```
1>use master
2>go
1>sp_configure "max async i/o per server", 400
2>go
```

For this change to take effect, the SQL Server will have to be shut down and restarted. As this command changes system tables, it cannot be run from within a transaction. This command changes the *master* system database, so to ensure its recovery, be certain to dump the *master* system database.

SQL Server Kernel Configuration for the Network

SQL Server kernel configuration parameters for the network control communication between the SQL Server and client applications and remote servers. To control network communication, the SQL Server has these four configuration parameters:

1. tcp no delay
2. max number network listeners
3. default network packet size
4. max network packet size

The tcp no delay SQL Server configuration parameter is a toggle switch for Transmission Control Protocol (TCP) packet batching. By default, the tcp no delay SQL Server configuration parameter is set off (i.e., its value is zero). This setting instructs the SQL Server to batch collections of individual TCP packets into single, larger, physical packets. This batching of individual TCP packets results in a slight delay in transmission, but network throughput is improved because the physical network frames are filled with as much data as possible. If the `tcp no delay` SQL Server configuration parameter is set on (i.e., its value is one), then network throughput will degrade as space within physical network frames will be wasted to support individual TCP packets.

To set the `tcp no delay` SQL Server configuration parameter on, log on to the SQL Server as an account with **sa_role** privileges and enter these commands:

```
1>use master
2>go
1>sp_configure "tcp no delay", 1
2>go
```

For this change to take effect, the SQL Server will have to be shut down and restarted. As this command changes system tables, it cannot be run from within a transaction. This command changes the *master* system database, so to ensure its recovery, be certain to dump the *master* system database.

Each SQL Server master port has a single network listener that is used to communicate over one type of network. If the host computer on which the SQL Server runs is connected to heterogeneous network types, and if the SQL Server will communicate with more than one type of network, you may need to tune the `max number network listeners` SQL Server configuration parameter. The `max number network listeners` SQL Server configuration parameter is used to specify the maximum number of network listeners. The default value of this configuration parameter is 15. The range of values for this configuration parameter is 0 through 2,147,483,647.

To set the `max number network listeners` SQL Server configuration parameter to 20, for example, network listeners log on to the SQL Server as an account with **sa_role** privileges and enter these commands:

```
1>use master
2>go
1>sp_configure "max number network listeners", 20
2>go
```

For this change to take effect, the SQL Server will have to be shut down and restarted. As this command changes system tables, it cannot be run from within a transaction. This command changes the *master* system database, so to ensure its recovery, be certain to dump the *master* system database.

You can achieve significant performance gains by configuring the network packet size of data that is being sent to, and returned from, the SQL Server by matching the network packet size to the needs of the applications the SQL Server is supporting. In general, the larger the volumes of data being moved, the larger the network packet size should be (given the available space of the underlying packets on your network).

The `default network packet size` SQL Server configuration parameter is used to specify the default packet size that all connections will use with the SQL Server. By default, the value of this configuration parameter is 512 bytes. This configuration parameter is to be set to any even multiple of 512, up to the maximum value of 524,288 bytes. As explained in detail in Chap. 4, "Memory Resource Management," each connection has a read, a read-overflow, and a write buffer. The size of each of these buffers is established by the value of the `default network packet size` SQL Server configuration parameter. These buffers consume memory resources from the data cache, so when you tune this parameter keep that fact in mind and don't overkill. Also, as there is a direct relationship between the `default network packet size` SQL Server configuration parameter and the `max network packet size` SQL Server configuration parameter, the value of the `default network packet size` SQL Server configuration parameter can never be greater than the `max network packet size` SQL Server configuration parameter.

To set the `default network packet size` SQL Server configuration parameter to 1024 bytes, for example, log on to the SQL Server as an account with **sa_role** privileges and enter these commands:

```
1>use master
2>go
1>sp_configure "default network packet size", 1024
2>go
```

For this change to take effect, the SQL Server will have to be shut down and restarted. As this command changes system tables, it cannot be run from within a transaction. This command changes the *master* system database, so to ensure its recovery, be certain to dump the *master* system database.

The `max network packet size` SQL Server configuration parameter is used to specify the maximum network packet size that a connection can explicitly request. This feature provides a significant benefit to applications, like **bcp,** that move large volumes of data. As there is a direct relationship between the `default network packet size` SQL Server configuration parameter and the `max network packet size` SQL

Server configuration parameter, the value of the `max network packet size` SQL Server configuration parameter can never be less than the `default network packet size` SQL Server configuration parameter, and, for practical purposes, is usually larger.

To set the `max network packet size` SQL Server configuration parameter to 2048 bytes, for example, log on to the SQL Server as an account with **sa_role** privileges and enter these commands:

```
1>use master
2>go
1>sp_configure "max network packet size", 2048
2>go
```

For this change to take effect, the SQL Server will have to be shut down and restarted. As this command changes system tables, it cannot be run from within a transaction. This command changes the *master* system database, so to ensure its recovery, be certain to dump the *master* system database.

Remote Servers and Remote Login Accounts

By default, when the SQL Server is installed, it is configured to communicate with other SQL Server, Open Server–based applications. And, by default, it is configured to allow accounts logged in to other SQL Servers to log on to the SQL Server.

SQL Server Kernel Configuration
for Remote Servers

To manage how your SQL Server will communicate with other SQL Servers or Open Server–based applications, there are three SQL Server configuration parameters:

1. `number of remote sites`

2. `number of remote connections`

3. `remote server pre-read packets`

The `number of remote sites` SQL Server configuration parameter is used to specify the number of internal-site handlers that can be concurrently active. All connections from a remote server are managed by a single internal-site handler. The default value of this configuration parameter is ten. The range of values for this configuration parameter is 0 through 32,767. If you set this configuration parameter to 0, then access by remote servers will be unsupported by your SQL Server.

To set the `number of remote sites` SQL Server configuration parameter to 20, for example, log on to the SQL Server as an account with **sa_role** privileges, and enter these commands:

```
1>use master
2>go
1>sp_configure "number of remote sites", 20
2>go
```

For this change to take effect, the SQL Server will have to be shut down and restarted. As this command changes system tables, it cannot be run from within a transaction. This command changes the *master* system database, so to ensure its recovery, be certain to dump the *master* system database.

The `number of remote connections` SQL Server configuration parameter is used to specify the maximum number of connections that can be concurrently opened to, and from, a single remote server. The default value of this configuration parameter is 20. The range of values for this configuration parameter is 0 through 32,767. If you set this configuration parameter to 0, then access by remote servers will be unsupported by your SQL Server.

To set the `number of remote connections` SQL Server configuration parameter to 40, for example, log on to the SQL Server as an account with **sa_role** privileges and enter these commands:

```
1>use master
2>go
1>sp_configure "number of remote connections", 40
2>go
```

For this change to take effect, the SQL Server will have to be shut down and restarted. As this command changes system tables, it cannot be run from within a transaction. This command changes the *master* system database, so to ensure its recovery, be certain to dump the *master* system database.

Each internal-site handler is capable of prereading and keeping track of data packets from each connection. These data packets are kept in memory and passed onto the receiving process when it is ready to accept them. The `remote server pre-read packets` SQL Server configuration parameter is used to specify the number of packets a site handler can preread. By default, each site handler is configured to support three preread packets. The range of value for this configuration parameter is 0 through 32,767 packets. When you increase the value of this configuration parameter you take memory away from the data cache, so be careful. When you decrease this configuration parameter, you degrade network performance between servers.

To set the `remote server pre-read packets` **SQL Server** configuration parameter to 6, for example, log on to the SQL Server as an account with **sa_role** privileges and enter these commands:

```
1>use master
2>go
1>sp_configure "remote server pre-read packets", 6
2>go
```

For this change to take effect, the SQL Server will have to be shut down and restarted. As this command changes system tables, it cannot be run from within a transaction. This command changes the *master* system database, so to ensure its recovery, be certain to dump the *master* system database.

Reporting on Remote Servers

To produce a report of all remote servers that interoperate with your SQL Server, log on to the SQL Server as any account, and enter these commands:

```
1>use master
2>go
1>sp_helpserver [NameOfRemoteServer]
2>go
```

where:

[*NameOfRemoteServer*]—this optional parameter is the name of the remote server (as shown in the interfaces file) for which you want a report produced. If you do not supply this optional parameter, then a report on all remote servers will be produced.

The report will contain the name of the server, its network name, current status, and identifier.

Creating a Remote Server

Before your SQL Server can interoperate with another server (e.g., execute a remote procedure call on the remote server), a representation of that remote server must be entered into the `master..sysservers` system table. To create a remote server, log on to the SQL Server as an account with **sso_role** privileges and enter these commands:

```
1>use master
2>go
1>sp_addserver lname [, {local | null} [, pname]]
2>go
```

where:

lname—this is the name you will use to address the server. The name of the server must be unique, and it must conform to the SQL Server rules for identifiers. This name for the server need not be the same name of the server as shown in the interfaces file.

{local | null}—the use of the local character string indicates that the server runs on the same host computer as your SQL Server. The "null" character string indicates that the server runs on a different host computer than the one your SQL Server runs on (i.e., it is a remote server). There can be only one local SQL Server.

pname—if the lname you are assigning to this server is not the same name by which it is known in the interfaces file, then you must use this optional parameter. This optional parameter is the name of the server as shown in the interfaces file.

This change will take effect immediately. As this command changes system tables, it cannot be run from within a transaction. This command changes the *master* system database, so to ensure its recovery, be certain to dump the *master* system database.

Changing Remote Server Options

For a given remote server, there are two options you can set:

1. net password encryption—this option is used to indicate whether or not connections with the remote server will use a client-side password encryption handshake. The default setting is false, which avoids the use of password encryption handshakes.

2. timeouts—by default, after one minute with no logical connection, the site handler will drop the physical connection to the remote server. If you don't want such connections to be automatically dropped, then you need to set this option to false.

To enable password encryption handshaking with a remote server, log on to the SQL Server as an account with **sso_role** privileges and enter these commands:

```
1>use master
2>go
```

```
1>sp_serveroption NameOfRemoteServer, "net password
  encryption", true
2>go
```

where:

> *NameOfRemoteServer*—this parameter is the name of the remote server (as shown in the interfaces file) for which you want to enable password encryption handshaking.

This change will take effect immediately. As this command changes system tables, it cannot be run from within a transaction. This command changes the *master* system database, so to ensure its recovery, be certain to dump the *master* system database.

To disable the automatic dropping of physical connections that do not sustain a logical connection, log on to the SQL Server as an account with **sso_role** privileges and enter these commands:

```
1>use master
2>go
1>sp_serveroption NameOfRemoteServer, "timeouts", false
2>go
```

where:

> *NameOfRemoteServer*—this parameter is the name of the remote server (as shown in the interfaces file) for which you want to disable the automatic dropping of physical connections that do not sustain a logical connection.

This change will take effect immediately. As this command changes system tables, it cannot be run from within a transaction. This command changes the *master* system database, so to ensure its recovery, be certain to dump the *master* system database.

Dropping a Remote Server

To drop a server from the `master..sysservers` system table, log on to the SQL Server as an account with **sso_role** privileges and enter these commands:

```
1>use master
2>go
1>sp_dropserver NameOfRemoteServer [, droplogins]
2>go
```

where:

NameOfRemoteServer—this parameter is the name of the remote server (as shown in the interfaces file) that you want to drop.

`[, droplogins]`—if you use this optional parameter, then all remote login accounts associated with the server will also be purged from the `master..sysremotelogins` system table. If you do not use this optional parameter when there are remote logins associated with the server, then the SQL Server will return an error message reminding you to drop these remote login accounts.

This change will take effect immediately. As this command changes system tables, it cannot be run from within a transaction. This command changes the *master* system database, so to ensure its recovery, be certain to dump the *master* system database.

SQL Server Kernel Configuration for Remote Login Accounts

The SQL Server has two configuration parameters that are used to control remote login accounts on your SQL Server:

1. `allow remote access`
2. `number of remote logins`

The `allow remote access` SQL Server configuration parameter is a toggle that control logins from remote servers to the SQL Server. By default, this configuration parameter is turned on (i.e., its value is one), which allows the Backup Server to interoperate with your SQL Server. If you want to prohibit server-to-server remote procedure call, you will have to set this configuration parameter to off (i.e., zero). When you turn this configuration parameter on, the `number of remote logins`, the `number of remote sites`, the `number of remote connections`, and the `remote server pre-read packets` configuration parameters are automatically set to their default values.

To turn off logins remote servers, log on to the SQL Server as an account with **sso_role** privileges and enter these commands:

```
1>use master
2>go
1>sp_configure "allow remote access", 0
2>go
```

This change will take effect immediately. As this command changes system tables, it cannot be run from within a transaction. This command changes the *master* system database, so to ensure its recovery, be certain to dump the *master* system database.

The `number of remote logins` SQL Server configuration parameter is used to specify the number of concurrent remote logins. The default value of this configuration parameter is 20. The range of values for this configuration parameter is 0 through 32,727 remote logins. The value of the `number of remote logins` SQL Server configuration parameter should be set equal to the value of the `number of remote connections` SQL Server configuration parameters.

To set the `number of remote logins` SQL Server configuration parameter to 40, for example, log on to the SQL Server as an account with **sa_role** privileges and enter these commands:

```
1>use master
2>go
1>sp_configure "number of remote logins", 40
2>go
```

For this change to take effect, the SQL Server will have to be shut down and restarted. As this command changes system tables, it cannot be run from within a transaction. This command changes the *master* system database, so to ensure its recovery, be certain to dump the *master* system database.

Reporting on Remote Login Accounts

To produce a report on remote login accounts, log on to the SQL Server as any account and enter these commands:

```
1>use master
2>go
1>sp_helpremotelogin [NameOfRemoteServer[ ,NameOfRemoteLogin
  Account]]
2>go
```

where:

NameOfRemoteServer—this optional parameter is the name of the remote server (as shown in the interfaces file) for which you want a report produced. If you do not provide this optional parameter, then a report covering all remote servers will be produced.

NameOfRemoteLoginAccount—this optional parameter is the name of the remote server login account for which you want a report produced. If you do not provide this optional parameter, then a report covering all remote server login accounts will be produced.

Creating a Remote Login Account

Before a known remote server's login account can establish a connection to your SQL Server, you have to create a representation of that remote server login account within the `master..sysremotelogins` system table. However, before you make this representation, you should create a local login account that the remote server login account will use within your SQL Server. After this step is done, you can proceed.

To create a remote server login account, log on to the SQL Server as an account with **sa_role** privileges and enter these commands:

```
1>use master
2>go
1>sp_addremotelogin NameOfRemoteServer[, loginame [,
  remotename] ]
2>go
```

where:

> *NameOfRemoteServer*—this parameter is the name of the remote server (as shown in the interfaces file) that supports the login account you want to add to your SQL Server.
>
> [, `loginname`—this optional parameter is the name of the account you have created within your SQL Server that maps to the remote server's login account(s). If you do not provide this optional parameter, then the local login account name is the remote name that is used to log on to your server.
>
> [, `remotename`]]—this optional parameter is used to map a given remote server's login account to a given local login account.

This change will take effect immediately. As this command changes system tables, it cannot be run from within a transaction. This command changes the *master* system database, so to ensure its recovery, be certain to dump the *master* system database.

Changing Remote Login Account Options

For a given remote login account, only one option can be set:

1. `trusted`.   If this option is set to `true` then the remote login account's password will not be checked when it logs in to your SQL Server. By default, this option is set to `false`.

To set a remote login account's `trusted` option to `true`, log on to the SQL Server as an account that has **sso_role** privileges and enter these commands:

```
1>use master
2>go
1>sp_remoteoption NameOfRemoteServer, loginame, remotename,
   trusted, true
2>go
```

where:

NameOfRemoteServer—this parameter is the name of the remote server (as shown in the interfaces file) that supports the login account whose option you want to change.

`loginame`—this parameter is the name of the account you have created within your SQL Server that maps to the remote server's login account.

`remotename`—this parameter is the name of the remote server's login account.

This change will take effect immediately. As this command changes system tables, it cannot be run from within a transaction. This command changes the *master* system database, so to ensure its recovery, be certain to dump the *master* system database.

Dropping a Remote Login Account

To drop a remote login account, log on to the SQL Server as an account that has **sa_role** privileges and enter these commands:

```
1>use master
2>go
1>sp_dropremotelogin NameOfRemoteServer[, loginame [,
   remotename] ]
2>go
```

where:

NameOfRemoteServer—this parameter is the name of the remote server (as shown in the interfaces file) that supports the remote login account(s) you want to drop.

`loginame`—this optional parameter is the name of the local login account that maps to the remote server's login account that you want to drop. If you do not provide this optional parameter, then all remote login accounts associated with the remote server will be purged.

`remotename`—this optional parameter is the name of the remote server's login account that maps to the local login account that you want to drop. If you do not provide this optional parameter, then all remote procedures that map to the local login account will be purged.

This change will take effect immediately. As this command changes system tables, it cannot be run from within a transaction. This command changes the *master* system database, so to ensure its recovery, be certain to dump the *master* system database.

3

Physical Storage

Introduction

A solid understanding of how the SQL Server manages physical storage is key to database administration, as well as to successful database (and application) development, testing, and deployment. Misunderstanding the SQL Server's management of physical storage is sure to increase your risk of exposure to unrecoverable databases and severe performance bottlenecks.

SQL Server Kernel Configuration for Disk I/O

To configure disk I/O, the System 11 SQL Server provides you with a couple of parameters:

1. `allow sql server async i/o`
2. `disk i/o structures`

The `allow sql server async i/o` SQL Server configuration parameter enables, or disables, asynchronous disk I/O. For the SQL Server to use asynchronous disk I/O the operating system controlling the host computer it is running on must be configured to support asynchronous disk I/O. When the SQL Server uses asynchronous disk I/O, it does not have to wait for a response from the physical device before issuing additional disk I/O instructions. Because of this feature, asynchronous disk I/O is faster than synchronous disk I/O.

To enable asynchronous disk I/O, log on to the SQL Server as an account with **sa_role** privileges and enter these commands:

```
1>use master
2>go
```

```
1>sp_configure "allow sql server async i/o", on
2>go
```

For this change to take effect, you will have to shut down, and then restart the SQL Server. If you want to disable this feature then substitute `off` for `on` in the preceding command sequence. This command changes the *master* system database, so to ensure its recovery, be certain to dump the *master* system database. As this command changes the contents of system tables, it cannot be executed within a transaction.

The `disk i/o structures` SQL Server configuration parameter controls the number of disk I/O control blocks the SQL Server allocates when it is started. Each user process that wants to launch disk I/O requests must acquire a control block from the SQL Server before proceeding. The default value for the `disk i/o structures` SQL Server configuration parameter is 256. The range of values for the `disk i/o structures` SQL Server configuration parameter is 0 to 2,147,483,647. However, the value you set this configuration parameter to is controlled by the limitation imposed on the SQL Server by the operating system. Basically, to avoid running out of control blocks, which is not a good thing to have happen (this won't crash the SQL Server, but an error message to this effect will be recorded within the SQL Server error log), is to set the value of the `disk i/o structures` SQL Server configuration parameter to as high a value as the operating system will allow.

To set the value of the `disk i/o structures` SQL Server configuration parameter to 1024, for example, log on to the SQL Server as an account with **sa_role** privileges and enter these commands:

```
1>use master
2>go
1>sp_configure "disk i/o structures", 1024
2>go
```

For this change to take effect, you will have to shut down, and then restart the SQL Server. This command changes the *master* system database, so to ensure its recovery, be certain to dump the *master* system database. As this command changes the contents of system tables, it cannot be executed within a transaction.

Physical Data Storage Hierarchy

Within the System 11 SQL Server, physical data storage is structured hierarchically:

1. Logical database devices contain device fragments.

2. Device fragments contain allocation units.

3. Allocation units contain extents.

4. Extents contain pages.

Database Devices

A database device is a logical construct that the SQL Server uses to set aside an entire disk drive, a given section of a disk drive (i.e., a raw partition), and an operating system file for its data storage and data access needs. Sybase also refers to database devices by the handle "logical device."

If your SQL Server is running on a UNIX platform, it is important to avoid using an operating system file-based database device for persistent data storage purposes. Instead, it is best to create your database devices on raw partitions. It takes a little bit more time and effort to take advantage of the benefits of a raw partition, but the time and effort are well spent.

When your database device resides on a raw partition, the SQL Server is in complete control of disk I/O. When the SQL Server Buffer Manager writes a page to a database device residing on a raw partition, it ensures that that page is written directly to the physical disk. In addition, the SQL Server entirely manages the reading of pages from a database device residing on a raw partition.

When your database device resides on an operating system file, the SQL Server is *not* in complete control of disk I/O. When the SQL Server Buffer Manager reads, or writes, a page to a database device residing on an operating system file, it hands off these read and write tasks to the UNIX File Management Subsystem. It is the writing of these pages by the UNIX File Management Subsystem that presents a serious risk to the integrity of stored, or persistent, data.

In accordance with a strategy that aims to minimize disk I/O, instead of writing the pages directly to the physical disk, the UNIX File Management Subsystem places the dirty pages within a volatile (software) buffer cache. The UNIX kernel hopes that processes will find the data they need in the buffer cache, and thereby avoid reads from a disk. To increase the chance of a cache hit, the pages continue to reside in the system buffer cache until the internal periodic process kicks in and flushes the pages in the buffer cache to disk, or the least recently used page algorithm writes certain pages out to disk to make room for new pages.

Also, there is absolutely no assurance that the order in which the SQL Server has written the dirty pages will be the same order in which the UNIX File Management Subsystem will write the pages to disk. UNIX does not treat pages used by the SQL Server any differently from the way it treats pages used by any other process.

Here's the risk: when the UNIX platform experiences a system failure, the contents of its system buffer cache is lost and cannot be rebuilt. In particular, all dirty pages and unwritten transaction log records in use by the SQL Server at the time of the system failure will have disappeared.

In the event of a system failure, the SQL Server will try to recover all databases (except for the *tempdb* system database). If data pages or transaction log records are missing from a database, or if they have been previously written to disk in an incorrect order, the SQL Server cannot recover that database. And, the SQL Server will mark that database as suspect. Marking a database as suspect is the SQL Server's way of telling you that the integrity of your database is highly questionable, and is most likely gone with the wind.

For application-development groups, the use of operating system file-based database devices may be suitable if the risk to the integrity of a development database is acceptable to the business. However, it is rarely the case where such a risk to a production SQL Server database is acceptable to the business. In addition, once you have studied the *master* system database and transaction logs, you will realize the severe risk that is run by placing either of them on an operating system file-based database device.

Now, after having stated all of this, and in that the *tempdb* system database is *never* recovered by the SQL Server, there are significant performance gains that can be achieved by placing the *tempdb* system database, and its transaction log's database device, on an operating system file. In addition, we will explore other alternative uses of operating system file-based database devices when we examine databases.

The `number of devices` SQL Server configuration parameter determines the number of logical database devices that the SQL Server can use. It does not, however, control the number of database or transaction log dump devices the SQL Server can use. The default value for the `number of devices` SQL Server configuration parameter is 10. The range of values for the `number of devices` SQL Server configuration parameter is 0 to 256. Due to internal SQL Server uses, the legal values are 4 through 256, inclusive. However, you must never set the value of the `number of devices` SQL Server configuration parameter lower than the highest existing device number. To find out the highest existing device number, log on to the SQL Server as any valid Sybase account and enter these commands:

```
1>use master
2>go
1>select max(low/power(2,24))+1
2>from master..sysdevices
3>go
```

Also, if you set the value of the `number of devices` SQL Server configuration parameter too low, then the SQL Server, when it reboots, will not be able to recover any database that resides on any logical databases devices whose number is greater than the value of the `number of devices` SQL Server configuration parameter.

At boot time, the SQL Server will allocate 512 bytes of memory to each logical database device, and this memory is allocated before memory resources are allocated to Procedure or Data Cache. Hey, what can I say? There's no free ride on this planet.

To set the value of the `number of devices` SQL Server configuration parameter to 80, for example, log on to the SQL Server as an account with **sa_role** privileges and enter these commands:

```
1>use master
2>go
1>sp_configure "number of devices", 80
2>go
```

For this change to take effect, you will have to shut down, and then restart the SQL Server. This command changes the *master* system database, so to ensure its recovery, be certain to dump the *master* system database. As this command changes the contents of system tables, it cannot be executed within a transaction.

Creating a Database Device

Before a disk, a partition, or an operating system file can be used by the SQL Server for data access, or data storage, it must be readied and assigned a name, that is, it must be initialized. If you have chosen a raw partition, there are three things you must do before initializing the physical device:

1. Be certain to add the operating system name of that raw partition to the UNIX /etc/fstab file, and indicate that it should not be mounted by the operating system (i.e., enter ignore in the third field of the record). To accomplish this edit of the /etc/fstab file, you must have *root* permission. The new /etc/fstab record will look like this:

   NameOfPhysicalDevice   *NameOfPhysicalDevice*   ignore

2. Make certain that the *sybase* login account owns the raw partition. To accomplish this, enter the following command:

```
chown sybase NameOfPhysicalDevice
```

3. Modify the read, write, and execute permissions for the raw partition such that only the *sybase* login account can read from, or write to, the raw partition. To accomplish this, enter the following command:

```
chmod 600 NameOfPhysicalDevice
```

If you have chosen an operating system file, then be certain that the *sybase* login account owns it, and be certain that the *sybase* login account is the only login account that can read from, or write to, the operating system file.

To initialize a physical device so that the SQL Server can use it, log on to the SQL Server as an account with **sa_role** privileges and enter these commands:

```
1>use master
2>go
1>disk init name = "NameOf DatabaseDevice",
2>physname = "NameOfPhysicalDevice",
3>vdevno = VirtualDeviceNumber,
4>size = NumberOf 2KBlocks
5>[, vstart = StartingVirtualAddress,
6>cntrltype = DiskControllerNumber]
7>go
```

where:

NameOf DatabaseDevice—the name of the database debvice must conform to the rules for Sybase identifiers. It is beneficial to the database Administrator when the elected names reflect the intended use of the device.

NameOfPhysicalDevice—the name assigned by the operating system to the raw disk partition, or the name of an operating system file.

VirtualDeviceNumber—a unique numeric identifier. It is known only to the SQL Server process and has no relevancy to the host computer on the which the SQL Server executes. Legal data values range between 1 and 255. However, the highest virtual device number must be less than the total number of physical devices (and disk partitions) for which your host computer has been configured. Virtual device number 0 represents the **d_master** device (i.e., the **master** device). To determine the highest virtual device number for your host computer, log on to the SQL Server and execute the sp_configure `devices` system procedure. To determine all of the virtual device numbers currently in use on your host computer, run this query:

```
1>use master
2>go
1>select distinct low/16777216
2>from sysdevices
3>order by low
4>go
```

NumberOf2KBlocks—you must specify the size of the new database device in 2K blocks. The smallest a database device can be is 1 MB, or 512 2K blocks. If the intended use of this new database device is to support a new database, then the size of the database device must be greater than either the value of the `database size` configuration variable, or the size of the *model* system database, whichever of the two is larger. In addition, be certain to use all possible space within a given disk partition (but do not use values that are not whole megabytes, e.g., 101.57 MB).

StartingVirtualAddress—the offset, given as a count of 2K blocks, for the SQL Server to begin using the new database device. The default, and preferred, value of this offset is zero.

DiskControllerNumber—the identity of the disk's controller. The default value of the disk controller is zero.

Executing the `disk init` command accomplishes the following:

1. Maps the disk, raw partition, or operating system file to the new database device's name.
2. Records the name of the new database device in the `master..sysdevices` system table.
3. Prepares the device for the storage of databases and their objects.

After a database device has been created, it can be:

1. Allocated to the pool of space available to a specific database, database objects, or transaction log.
2. Designated as a default database device.

This command changes the *master* system database, so to ensure its recovery, be certain to dump the *master* system database. As this command changes the contents of system tables, it cannot be executed within a transaction.

If the `disk init` command fails during its execution, you will have to shut down and restart the SQL. Restarting the SQL Server will free up the virtual device number that you assigned to the new database device. Once it is freed up, you will be able to reuse it.

It is always good practice to store your `disk init` command scripts in a safe place, as you may very well need them at some later point in time (when you least expect to). Storing database administration scripts in a safe place is a general rule that you should apply to all types of the SQL Server administration scripts you create.

If you are administering a SQL Server, and these `disk init` command scripts are no longer available to you, then be certain to reconstruct. You can reconstruct the required `disk init` command script by examining the database device information stored within the `master..sysdevices` table. Here are the column names to look within for the information you need (to record):

1. `name`—the name assigned to the database device.

2. `physname`—the name of the physical device.

3. `low`—the first virtual page numbers assigned to the database device.

4. `high`—the last page numbers assigned to the database device.

To obtain this information, run this query, and record its results set:

```
1>use master
2>go
1>select name, physname, low, high
2>from sysdevices
3>order by name
4>go
```

If you value your merit bonus or paycheck, then do not live on the bleeding edge without these scripts, and without the records of the necessary `master..sysdevices` data, on hand. Be certain to protect the system (and cover yourself) by collecting these scripts and this information.

It is critically important to understand that if the data within `master..sysdevices` becomes corrupted (as is known to happen on occasion), and you do not have access to these `disk init` command scripts and to this uncorrupted `master..sysdevices` information, you'll find yourself "up the stream without a paddle." It's not a pretty sight when a database Administrator cannot reestablish database devices.

Mirroring a Database Device

To protect your data against disk-drive failure, and to give you nonstop recovery in the event of a disk-drive failure, you can have the SQL

Server duplicate data on one database device, called the *primary,* to another database device, called the *mirror.* However, this enhanced recoverability comes at a price: there may be a performance degradation during writes, and you will have to buy more disk drives.

When you elect to mirror a logical device, the two database devices are kept in sync with one another because the SQL Server directs write operations to both the primary and the mirror database devices. You have two options for supporting write operations to mirrored database devices: serial or nonserial. If you use serial writes, then the SQL Server writes to the primary database device first, it waits until that write operation completes, and then it writes to the mirror database device, and waits until the write operation to the mirror completes. With serial writes, you can be assured the write to the primary occurs in the event of a power failure. The total time it takes a serial write operation to complete is the sum total of the time it takes to write to the primary plus the time it takes to write to the mirror. If you use nonserial writes, then the write operations to the primary and to the mirror take place at the same time, and the SQL Server waits for both concurrent writes to complete. The total time it takes a nonserial write operation to complete will be the time it takes to write to the primary or to the mirror, whichever is greatest. With nonserial writes you cannot be assured that either write operation completed in the event of a power failure.

When mirroring is enabled the SQL Server will distribute read operations to both the primary and the mirror database device. The SQL Server will use the results of the first read operation that completes, and will simply discard the one that finishes in second place. This ability of the SQL Server to distribute read operations across both the primary and the mirror database devices can result in enhanced read operation performance.

In the event of a disk-drive failure, the database device that resides on the damaged disk drive is automatically, and transparently, taken off-line by the SQL Server, and an error message is written to the error log to that effect. After the disk-drive failure, the remaining database device will support all read and write operations. After the damaged disk drive is replaced, and reinitialized, it can be brought back into sync with the surviving database device while the SQL Server is on-line, without disruption to active user processes.

Assuming you have the extra disk space, or the capital to buy more disk drives, determining which database devices to mirror can become a bit complicated. At minimum, the *master* and the *systemprocs* system databases should be mirrored because their availability, and recoverability, is critically important to the SQL Server. After these system databases, you will need to consider user databases, and their transaction logs, that are critically important to your business, and which can operate successfully with write operation performance degradation. Refer to the chapter on the *tempdb* system database for a discussion of mirroring the *tempdb* system database using operating system files (this is a must for production environments).

To have the SQL Server create a software mirror, log on to the SQL Server as an account with **sa_role** privileges and enter these commands:

```
1>use master
2>go
1>disk mirror
2>name = " NameOfDatabaseDevice",
3>mirror = " NameOfPhysicalDevice"
4>[,writes = { serial | noserial }]
5>go
```

where:

> *NameOfDatabaseDevice*—the name of the database device that will be mirrored (i.e., it will be the primary database device). This cannot be a dump device.
>
> *NameOfPhysicalDevice*—the name, assigned by the operating system to the raw disk partition, or the name of an operating system file that will be the mirror database device. If the primary database device is a raw disk partition, then the mirror should also be a raw disk partition (if it is not, then you will lose asynchronous I/O capability). Due to the inherent volatility of operating system files, it seldom makes sense to use an operating system file as the primary or as the mirror in a software mirror setup that supports production databases which are to be recovered. This physical device cannot be a dump device.
>
> serial | noserial—serial is the default write operation type, so if you want to override the default, then you must specify writes = noserial.

Executing this command while the primary device is in use will not interfere with SQL Server operations. This command changes the *master* system database, so to ensure its recovery, be certain to dump the *master* system database. As this command changes the contents of system tables, it cannot be executed within a transaction.

Unmirroring a Database Device

If you need to begin the process of replacing the damaged disk drive (or if you are merely changing disk drives) that supported mirroring, then you will have to disable the SQL Server software mirror so that the affected database device is no longer available to the SQL Server.

To unmirror a database device, log on to the SQL Server as an account with **sa_role** privileges and enter these commands:

```
1>use master
2>go
1>disk unmirror
2>name = " NameOfDatabaseDevice",
3>[,side = { "primary" | secondary }]
4>[,mode = { retain | remove }]
5>go
```

where:

> *NameOfDatabaseDevice*—the name of the database device that will be unmirrored. A database device can be unmirrored when it is in use, but there are some exceptions to this policy. You cannot unmirror a database device while a dump database, a load database, a dump transaction, or load transaction command is in progress on the database (but, you can unmirror a database device while a dump transaction with truncate_only, or with no_log, is in progress).

> [,side = { "primary" | secondary }]—if you do not use this optional parameter string, then, by default, the mirror (i.e., secondary) database device is unmirrored. If you want to specify that the primary database device is to be unmirrored, then you must specify side = "primary".

> [,mode = { retain | remove }]—if you do not use this optional parameter string, then, by default, the unmirroring will be temporary (i.e., retain). Be certain to use the default if you plan to remirror the database device later on, using exactly the same configuration as you have right now. If you specify remove, then all references to the current software mirror configuration will be purged from the SQL Server.

When a mirrored database device fails, the SQL Server automatically executes this command (with retain). This command changes the *master* system database, so to ensure its recovery, be certain to dump the *master* system database. As this command changes the contents of system tables, it cannot be executed within a transaction.

Remirroring a Database Device

To remirror a database device, log on to the SQL Server as an account with **sa_role** privileges and enter these commands:

```
1>use master
2>go
1>disk remirror
2>name = " NameOfDatabaseDevice",
3>go
```

where:

NameOfDatabaseDevice—the name of the database device that will be remirrored.

When a database device is remirrored, the SQL Server automatically resyncs (copies the data from the current primary database device to the new secondary database device) without interrupting active user processes. This command changes the *master* system database, so to ensure its recovery, be certain to dump the *master* system database. As this command changes the contents of system tables, it cannot be executed within a transaction.

Dropping a Database Device

Occasionally, you will need to drop a database device. To accomplish this task, log on to the SQL Server as an account with **sa_role** privileges and enter these commands:

```
1>use master
2>go
1>sp_dropdevice NameOfDatabaseDevice
2>go
```

where:

NameOfDatabaseDevice—the name of the database device you want to drop.

Before you can drop a database device, however, it must not be in use by any database. So, if it is in use by a database, then you must drop the database before you drop the database device.

While the `sp_dropdevice system` command removes all references to the database device recorded in the `master..sysdevices` system table, the SQL Server has a process that is still accessing the dropped database device. The only means by which you have to kill this rogue process is to shut down the SQL Server. Once you restart the SQL Server, the virtual device number will also be available for reuse.

Also, the `sp_dropdevice` system command does not delete an underlying operating system file. To delete the underlying operating system file, you will have to execute the appropriate operating system command. This command changes the *master* system database, so to ensure its recovery, be certain to dump the *master* system database. As this command changes the contents of system tables, it cannot be executed within a transaction.

Reporting on Database Device Usage

Contained within `master..sysdevices` are the database devices (i.e., operating system files or raw partitions), as well as *dump devices* (used to back up databases, i.e., tape, operating system file, or raw partition) that the SQL Server uses.

The `master..sysdevices` table contains a row for each database device, and each dump device, in use by the SQL Server. Whenever you execute the `disk init` system command, a new row is added to the `master..sysdevices` table.

To retrieve database device information, stored within the `master..sysdevices` table, the `sp_helpdevice` system procedure can be used. The `sp_helpdevice` system procedure can be used in either of two ways:

1. Pass the name of the database device to the system command when you execute it. When used in this way, only information about that particular database device will be displayed. For example:

```
1>use master
2>go
1>sp_helpdevice NameOfDatabaseDevice
2>go
```

2. Execute the system command without passing the name of a database device to it. When used in this way, information about *all* database devices available to the SQL Server will be displayed. For example:

```
1>use master
2>go
1>sp_helpdevice
2>go
```

By default, anyone with a valid SQL Server login account can execute the `sp_helpdevice` system command.

When used in either of these two ways, the `sp_helpdevice` system command will provide the following information about a database device:

1. The database device name.

2. The physical device name.

3. A brief text description of the device (i.e., device size, type, mirroring).

4. The status field is a bit map used to indicate the type of device (i.e., database device or dump device) and to show whether or not the device is a default storage device or one used to support disk mirroring.

5. The control type (e.g., a database device, or some type of dump device).

6. The device number.

7. The low and high (the first and last) page numbers assigned to the database device.

The d_master Device

The *master* device, named **d_master,** is a special database device that is made during SQL Server installation, via the `buildmaster` utility. The device number of **d_master** is always zero.

At SQL Server installation time, the *master, model,* and *tempdb,* system databases are, by default, stored on the **d_master** database device.

The entire *master* system database, and its transaction log, will forever be contained on the **d_master** device. As the *master* system database cannot be moved, or expanded on, to any other database device, it is extremely important for the database administrator to ensure that no other user-defined databases are created on the **d_master** device, and that no user-defined database objects (e.g., tables, indexes, etc.), are stored on the **d_master** device.

The first four *pages* of the **d_master** device, called the *config* block, are set aside for use by the SQL Server. To collect information about all site databases, the config block is read by the SQL Server at boot time.

Default Database Devices

The SQL Server is capable of making default decisions about the storage location of user-defined databases. These are default decisions in that specific database devices are, or can be, designated as being default database devices. However, an account with **sa_role** privileges has the ability to override the designated default database devices. In addition, an account with **sa_role** privileges also has the ability to specify which database devices are to be the default database devices.

The default database device for *all* user-defined databases is the **d_master** database device. The **d_master** database device is established as the default database device at installation time. However, the database Administrator can change this fact by designating other database devices to be default database devices.

To display the names of the database devices that are default database devices, log on to the SQL Server and enter these commands:

```
1>use master
2>go
1>select name
2>from sysdevices
3>where status & 1 = 1
4>order by name
5>go
```

Alternatively, you can find all database devices that have been designated as default database devices by executing the `sp_helpdevice` system command, without passing it the name of a database device. Within the description field of the `sp_helpdevice` output, the phrase "default device" will be associated with all default database devices.

To designate a particular database device to be a default database device, log on to the SQL Server as an account with **sa_role** privileges and enter these commands:

```
1>use master
2>go
1>sp_diskdefault NameOfDatabaseDevice defaulton
2>go
```

This command changes the *master* system database, so to ensure its recovery, be certain to dump the *master* system database. As this command changes the contents of system tables, it cannot be executed within a transaction.

To stop the **d_master** device from continuing to be a default database device, log on to the SQL Server as an account with **sa_role** privileges, and enter these commands:

```
1>use master
2>go
1>sp_diskdefault d_master defaultoff
2>go
```

This command changes the *master* system database, so to ensure its recovery, be certain to dump the *master* system database. As this command changes the contents of system tables, it cannot be executed within a transaction.

With the SQL Server, one or more database devices can be designated as default database devices. Whenever you create (or alter) a database without specifying its storage location, the default database devices are automatically filled up in alphabetical order by database device name as listed in `master..sysdevices`. As soon as the storage space in the first default database device is used up, then the second default database device is used, until all storage space assigned to default database devices is consumed (at which time you begin the process, once again, of creating new database device).

When choosing which available database devices to designate as default database devices, do not use the following:

1. The **d_master** database device.
2. Any database device that supports a database transaction log.
3. The database device that supports the *model,* the *sybsecurity,* or the *tempdb* system databases.
4. Database devices that support *on-line transaction processing* (OLTP) databases. In that OLTP databases will quickly consume any available storage space, they should be kept separate from the default database devices. Unless OLTP databases are kept off of default database devices, new databases can be carelessly created, populated with data, consume all available storage in the default database devices, and thereby bring the OLTP application to a grinding halt.

Finally, as a general rule, it seldom makes good sense to enable Sybase disk mirroring on default database devices.

Reestablishing a Database Device

Like a stroke of lightning and the rolling thunder that follows, events can arise that corrupt the integrity of the data stored within the `master..sysdevices` table. When these events happen, as they may when you least expect them to, it's time to reestablish the database devices. You reestablish database devices by using the `disk reinit` system command.

To reestablish a database device so that the SQL Server can use it once again, log on to the SQL Server as an account with **sa_role** privileges and enter these commands:

```
1>use master
2>go
1>disk reinit name = "NameOfDatabaseDevice",
2>physname = "NameOfPhysicalDevice",
3>vdevno = VirtualDeviceNumber,
4>size = NumberOf2KBlocks
5>[, vstart = StartingVirtualAddress,
```

```
6>cntrltype = DiskControllerNumber]
7>go
```

where:

NameOfDatabaseDevice—the name of the existing database device.

NameOfPhysicalDevice—the name, assigned by the operating system, to the existing raw disk partition, or the name of the existing operating system file.

VirtualDeviceNumber—a unique numeric identifier. It is known only to the SQL Server process and has no relevancy to the host computer on the which the SQL Server executes. Legal data values range between 1 and 255. However, the highest virtual device number must be less than the total number of physical devices (and disk partitions) for which your host computer has been configured. Virtual device number 0 represents the **d_master** device (i.e., the *master* device). While it is true that the value you use for the vdevno disk reinit command parameter need not be the same as that previously assigned to the database device, you must be certain that you do not reassign a virtual device number that is currently in use. Also, as the master..sysdevices table is now corrupted, it is far too late for you to determine (by examining sysdevices) which virtual device number is already assigned.

NumberOf2KBlocks—you must specify the size of the new database device in 2K blocks. The smallest a database device can be is 1 MB, or 512 2K blocks. If the intended use of this new database device is to support a new database, then the size of the database device must be greater than either the value of the database size configuration variable, or the size of the *model* system database, whichever of the two is larger. In addition, be certain to use all possible space within a given disk partition.

StartingVirtualAddress—the offset, given as a count of 2K blocks, for the SQL Server to begin using the new database device. The default, and preferred, value of this offset is zero.

DiskControllerNumber—the identity of the disk's controller. The default value of the disk controller is zero.

This command changes the *master* system database, so to ensure its recovery, be certain to dump the *master* system database. As this command changes the contents of system tables, it cannot be executed within a transaction.

If you have done the wise thing, and stored the disk init command scripts, as well as the information you recorded from master..sysdevices, in a safe place, then they will now be used to reestablish the database's devices. Simply copy the disk init command scripts to a new file, and change each instance of the work init to reinit. With this done, you will have correctly established the literal data values for the name, physname, size, and vdevno disk reinit parameters (as well as those values for the optional vstart and cntrltype parameters).

To be on the safe side, ensure that the literal data value you are about to assign to a disk reinit command size parameter is correct. Review the results set you produced when you queried the master..sysdevices system table (refer to the end of the preceding "Creating a Database Device" section of this chapter), and perform this calculation: subtract the value of master..sysdevices.high and subtract from it the value of master..sysdevices.low, then add one to the results. Compare the results to the corresponding size parameter. It is extremely critical that you use the correct value for the disk reinit command size parameter. If you do not, then (odds are) you will corrupt your (production) database. Corrupting (production) databases is no way to influence people, and win friends!

Be sure to refer to the System 11 System Administration Guide on recovering the *master* database, as the use of the disk refit system command is applied after the disk reinit system command as part of the procedure for recovering the *master* system database.

Disk Fragments

When space, on a database device, has been allocated to a database, a disk fragment is created. Space for a database is allocated when you execute the create database or the alter database command statements. Each contiguous disk fragment is represented by a data row within the *sysusages* system table. There will be two, or more, data rows within the *sysusages* system table for discontiguous disk fragments. However, there is a hard limit or 128 data rows within the *sysusages* system table for any individual database.

The internal function of the *sysusages* system table is to map the logical page identifiers used within a database to the virtual page identifiers used by the SQL Server. To accomplish this, the *sysusages* system table contains the following information:

1. dbid—the identifier of the database that is using this disk fragment.
2. segmap—the identifier of segments that are mapped to this disk fragment.
3. lstart—the identifier of the first logical page of this disk fragment.
4. vstart—the identifier of the first virtual page of this disk fragment.
5. size—the count of the pages in this disk fragment.

Allocation Units

When you create a database device, the `disk init` command partitions that database device into one or more allocation units. An allocation unit is a grouping of 256 contiguous 2K logical database pages. Each allocation unit contains 32 extents.

Extents

An extent is a contiguous block of eight 2K doubly linked pages. The SQL Server uses the extent construct as the *unit of disk space management* when allocating, or deallocating, disk real estate to a specific principal database object (e.g., table, index, etc).

There are many events that result in an extent being allocated or deallocated:

1. Whenever a table, or index, is created, the SQL Server allocates an extent to that principal database object.

2. Whenever you drop a table, or index, the SQL Server deallocates the extent(s) it consumed.

3. Whenever a table, or index, requires more disk space, the SQL Server allocates another extent to that principal database object.

4. Whenever a table, or index, no longer needs a specific extent, the SQL Server deallocates that specific extent.

Each time an extent is allocated, or deallocated, the SQL Server updates the allocation unit page that manages the extents that support that database object.

SQL Server Kernel Configuration for bcp

To enhance the performance of copying large volumes of bulk data, when using the **bcp** utility, the SQL Server `number of pre-allocated extents` configuration parameter can be configured to specify the number of pre-allocated extents allocated in a single trip to the page manager. This kernel configuration parameter is only used by the **bcp** utility. The default value for the `number of pre-allocated extents` SQL Server configuration parameter is 2. The range of values for the `number of pre-allocated extents` SQL Server configuration parameter is 0 to 31.

Specifying the value of the `number of pre-allocated extents` configuration parameter to a value greater than the default value, will result in the **bcp** utility allocating the specified count of extents each time more space is required to support the data load. For the given specified count of extents, a single extent allocation log record will be written to the transaction log.

To set the value of the number of pre-allocated extents SQL Server configuration parameter to 10, for example, log on to the SQL Server as an account with **sa_role** privileges and enter these commands:

```
1>use master
2>go
1>sp_configure "number of pre-allocated extents", 10
2>go
```

For this change to take effect, you will have to shut down, and then restart the SQL Server. This command changes the *master* system database, so to ensure its recovery, be certain to dump the *master* system database. As this command changes the contents of system tables, it cannot be executed within a transaction.

Pages

The SQL Server uses the page construct as the *unit of disk I/O* for accessing, or modifying, data. Each page is 2K in size. The first 32 bytes of each page are assigned to the page header.

The SQL Server supports eight types of pages:

1. Data page.
2. Index page.
3. Text/image page.
4. *Global allocation map* (GAM) page.
5. Allocation unit page.
6. Generic *object allocation map* (OAM) page.
7. Extent OAM page.
8. Distribution page.

Data page

A data page is composed of three main parts:

1. Page header—a 32-byte field that contains information about:
   - The contents of the data page (e.g., the number of this data page).
   - The numbers of the previous and the next data pages (the first data page in the doubly linked page chain is assigned the literal data value of zero, and the last data page in the doubly linked page chain is also assigned the literal data value of zero).
   - The identity of the table this data page belongs to.

- The next data row number of this data page.
- The minimum length of a data row on this data page.
- The offset to the available space on this data page.

2. Data rows—a formatted structure that contains the following elements:

   - The number of variable-length columns in this data row.
   - The data row number (an index into the offset table that points to where the data row is located on the data page).
   - The data contained in the data row's fixed-length columns.

   Offsets of fixed-length columns in a data row are recorded within the corresponding data row within the *syscolumns* table. For data rows that contain variable-length columns, the following will be recorded:

   - The total length of the data row.
   - The data contained in the data row's variable-length column(s).
   - The offset from the beginning of the data row to the end of the variable-length column data.
   - The sizes of the variable-length columns within the data row.

   Fixed-length columns appear in the data row in the same order in which they appeared in the `create table` command statement. However, while variable-length columns are positioned in the variable-length portion on the data row, they are still positioned as they appear in the `create table` command statement. The maximum number of data rows in a data page is 256. After subtracting the 32-byte page header overhead, you would think that the maximum length of a data row would be 2016 bytes. Right? Unfortunately, you would be mistaken if you reached that conclusion. In SQL Server land, because each data row recorded within a transaction log incurs a 54-byte overhead, the maximum size of a data row is actually 1962 bytes.

3. Row offset table—used to record the location (in bytes) of each data row, relative to the beginning of the data page. The data row offset table is located at the very end of the data page. Each data row on the data page has a SQL Server generated row number. This internal number is used to index into the data row offset table.

To simplify scanning, space on the data page is used contiguously. If a data row is deleted or inserted on a data page, other data rows will be moved to keep the space contiguous. However, the data rows are not positioned on the data pages in any specific physical order (i.e., ascending by data row ID).

Note that individual data rows will never span multiple data pages. For example, in that a data row cannot exceed 1962 bytes, if the size of an individual data row is greater than 981 bytes, then each data page will contain one, and only one, data row. It may be worth pointing out that you can use this feature of the SQL Server to simulate row-level locking (that is, if you are really certain you want to burden the SQL Server with all that locking overhead).

Index page

Before we dive into the subject of index pages, it may be helpful to briefly discuss indexes and how the SQL Server supports them.

Indexes are distinct storage structures that allow rapid access to information stored on data pages. An index can speed up data access because, fundamentally, it is a logical pointer to the exact data page that contains the information you are searching for (this is the case with a clustered index; however, a nonclustered index also includes the data row identifier).

It is on the index pages where index rows are recorded, or entered. Each index row, or entry, contains the literal data values of the key columns that make up the index, the associated data page logical pointer, and, where applicable, the data row identifiers. A *key column* is a column within a table that declares, or participates in the declaration of, a given index. At minimum, the declaration of an index includes one, or more, table column names.

Internally, the SQL Server builds a dedicated B-Tree (binary tree) structure to store, and manage, each user-defined index. The B-Tree structure has been enhanced to support the growth of the index, and is populated with index pages. The SQL Server uses B-Tree search algorithms to scan index pages for matching data page identifiers (and data row identifiers when applicable), based on the literal data values of key columns addressed by a submitted query.

Whenever a B-Tree search is conducted, the SQL Server analyzes the index row located in the middle of the index page. If that row is a match, then the search stops. However, if the row is not a match, then the index page is halved, and the B-Tree search continues in the direction indicated by the key column comparison.

An index B-Tree is a special type of balanced, multileveled, data structure that is comprised of three separate sections:

1. A single index root page that is your entry way into the index. The index root page contains the first and last entry in the index. The page identifier of the index root page is stored within `sysindexes..root`. Each database you create contains its own `sysindexes` system table.

2. The index node pages make up the binary tree itself. The index node pages are sometimes called *intermediate pages* because they exist between the top of the B-Tree, which represents the index root page, and bottom of the B-Tree, which represents the index leaf pages. Every entry in an index node page contains the number of the previous and the next index page in the page chain; these numbers are the index page pointers. Therefore, each index node page participates in a (doubly linked) index page chain. Each given index page chain, within a given index, is called an *index level*. By default, the SQL Server automatically assigns the number 0 to the bottom, or lowest, index level. As the index is traversed from the bottom to the top level, or root, the numbers automatically assigned to the index level increase monotonically (i.e., 0, 1, 2, 3, etc.). The page identifier of the first index node page of the lowest-level index page chain is stored within `sysindexes..first`.

3. The index leaf pages are at the lowest index level. Index leaf pages are always stored in index sequence sort order.

A B-Tree is a balanced data structure because all index leaf pages are the same distance from the index root page. The distance between the index root page and all associated index leaf pages is automatically maintained by the SQL Server whenever a new index row is added to, or whenever an existing index row is deleted from the index.

Without getting into a discussion of the use of indexes, two basic types of indexes are supported by the SQL Server:

1. *Clustered.*   Enforces a user-defined physical-sorted order to the placement of data rows within data pages. As a consequence of the clustered index's ability to impose by force the placement of data rows, there can be one, and only one, clustered index per table. If a table lacks a clustered index, then its data rows are not distributed across a B-Tree structure, but are, instead, stored in a heap structure. Every table that has a clustered index will have a data row in `sysindexes` where the `indid` column's literal data value has been set to one. The intermediate-level index pages, or index leaf pages, contain logical pointers to data pages. Within the intermediate-level index pages of a clustered index, there is one, and only one, entry for each data page in the table. At the leaf level of the clustered index are data pages. In that only the first data row of each data page in the table has a logical pointer in an index page, a clustered index is sometimes referred to as a *sparse index*.

2. *Nonclustered.*   Enforces a user-defined physical-sorted order to the key columns that make up the nonclustered index. However, the placement of data rows within the data pages is *not* physically ordered by a nonclustered index. A given table can have up to 249

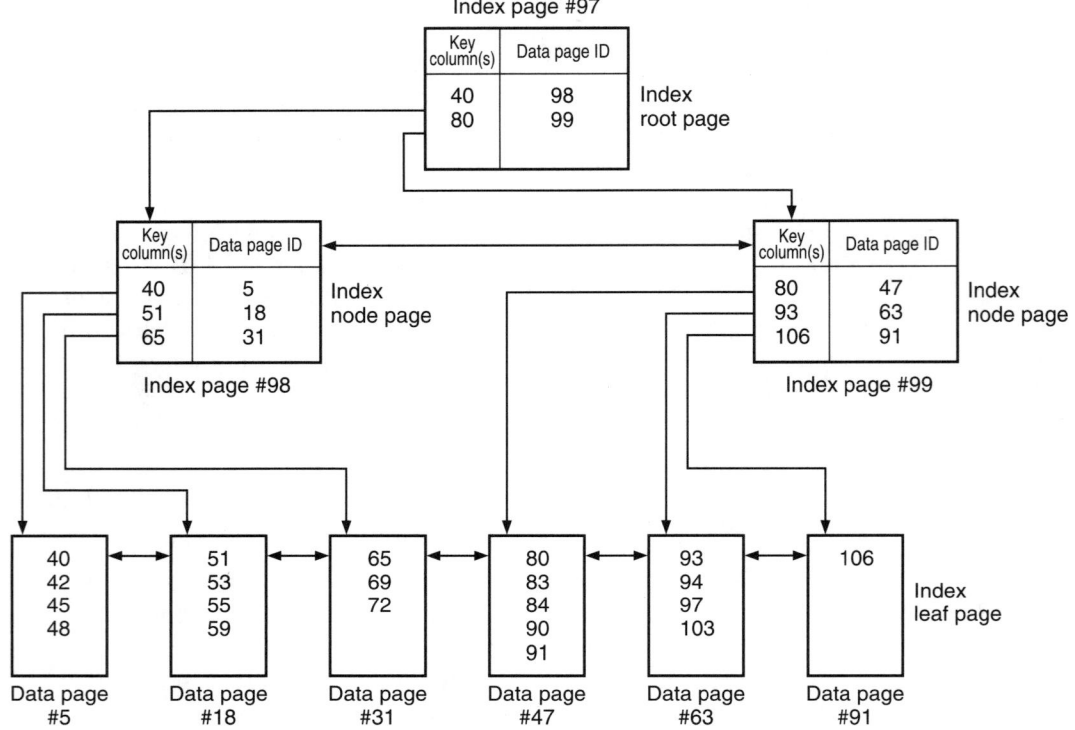

Figure 3.1   Detail of unique clustered index.

nonclustered indexes associated with it. Every table that has a non-clustered index will have a data row in sysindexes where the indid column's literal data value has been set to be greater than one. The lowest-level index pages, or index leaf pages, contain logical pointers to each data row within the table's data pages. In that each data row on each data page in the table has a logical pointer in an index page, a nonclustered index is sometimes referred to as a *dense index*.

In addition to their ability to regulate (in the case of clustered indexes) the distribution of data rows within data pages, indexes can be used to impose data row uniqueness within a table. When you define an index to be unique, the SQL Server ensures that two or more data rows, with identical key columns, will not be placed within a given table. When used in this way, indexes serve as a data-integrity tool.

An index page is composed of two main parts:

1. Page header—a 32-byte field that contains information about:

   ■ The number of this index page.

   ■ The identity of the table this index belongs to.

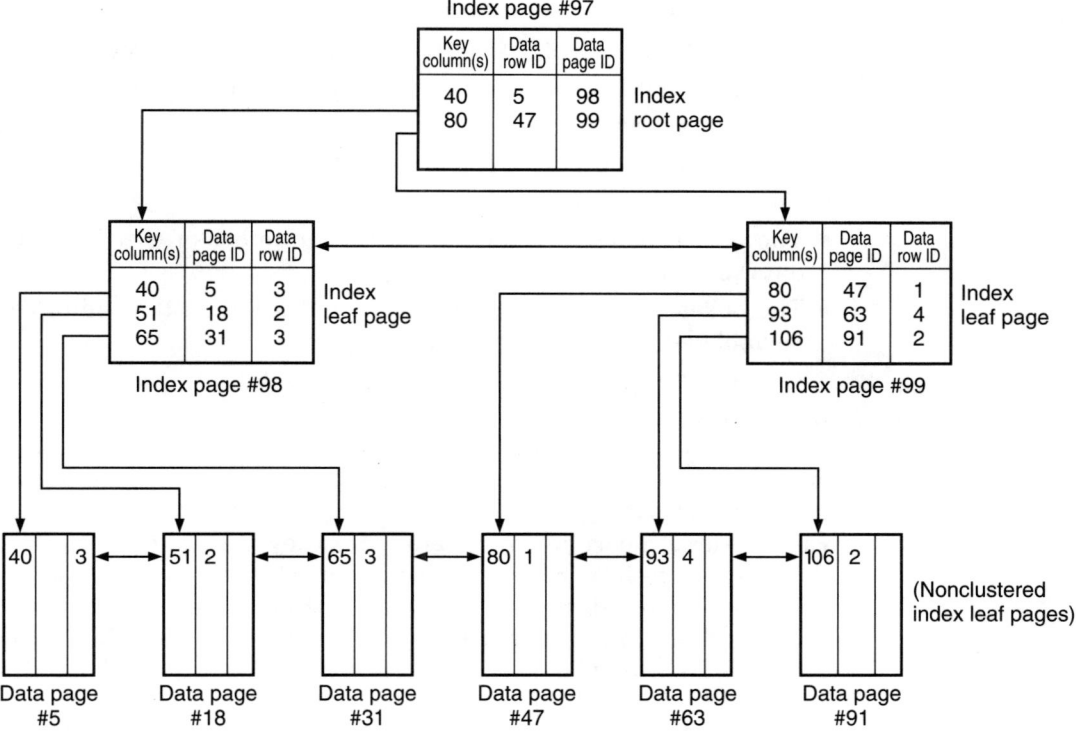

Figure 3.2   Detail of unique nonclustered index.

- The index level.
- The index identifier.
- The number of the previous and next index page in the page chain (these are the index page pointers).
- The offset of the last index row on this index page.
- The offset of the next index row on this index page.
- A time stamp used for managing changes to this index page.
- The minimum length of an index row on this index page.
- Bit flags that are used to hold system-level information.

The SQL Server uniquely identifies an index through the combination of index identifier and the identity of the table that the index belongs to.

The SQL Server uniquely identifies an individual index page chain through the combination of index level, the index identifier, and the identity of the table that the index belongs to.

2. Index rows—a formatted structure that contains different elements, depending upon the type of index you have created.

Clustered index rows contain:

- The number of variable-length columns in this index row.
- The data contained in fixed-length key columns.
- The total length of the index row.
- The data contained in variable key columns.
- The adjust structures.
- The 5-byte pointer to the logical page number of the (index or data) page at the next lower index level.
- The offset from the beginning of the index row to the end of the variable-length key column data.

Offsets of fixed-length columns in an index row are recorded within the corresponding index row within the `syscolumns` system table. Fixed-length columns appear in the index row in the same order in which they appeared in the `create index` command statement. However, while variable-length columns are positioned in the variable-length portion on the index row, they are still positioned as they appear in the `create index` command statement.

Nonclustered index rows contain everything stored in a clustered index row, but differ in that they also contain the identifier of the data row they point to.

The maximum size of an index row, just like a data row, is also 1962 bytes. And, just like a data row, an index row will never span multiple index pages.

To simplify scanning, space on the index page is used contiguously. If an index row is deleted or inserted on an index page, other index rows will be moved to keep the space contiguous.

Like all database servers, your choice of data type has a significant impact on performance. Specifically, the use of variable-length data types, such as varchar, seriously extends index search time for the SQL Server. Index pages, unlike the data page, do not contain an offset table of index row numbers. As a result, whenever an index contains variable-length key columns, the SQL Server must use a sliding binary search. With this variation of a binary search, if there is space available on the index page located in cache, then the bottom of that index page is used to store a binary search table. But, if that index page does not have space available on it, then the SQL Server has to create an internal index row offset table within which it performs a binary search. It is the run-time construction of these offset tables that significantly contributes to query performance degradation.

In that nonclustered indexes contain the data page and data row identifiers, any inserting or deleting of data rows forces the updating of nonclustered index leaf pages. Updating of the nonclustered index must take place, else the nonclustered index would become inconsistent, totally defeating its purpose. Therefore, because of the need to maintain consistency, the use of nonclustered indexes will, whenever row insertion or deletion occurs, introduce (potentially significant) overhead.

Text/image page

Two SQL Server data types, text and image, hold large literal data values. The text data type can hold up to 2,147,483,647 bytes of printable characters. The image data type can hold up to 2,147,483,647 bytes of binary data.

Because of their extremely large size, the SQL Server does not store text and image data values in database tables. The actual text and image data is stored on a separate set of linked data pages. Only a pointer to the location of the text and image data is stored within the database tables.

By default, the actual text and image data is located on the same segment as the table containing the text or image column(s). Also, by default, another data row is added to the sysindexes table. This additional data row records the identity of the linked chain of text or image pages.

Each text or image page holds a maximum of 1800 bytes of data. For database tables with more than one text or image column, all text or image data is held within the same chain of linked data pages.

Page splitting

When a data or index row is created, it is added to an existing data or index page. However, when the space available on a data or index page is not enough to contain the new data or index row, then a page split occurs. When a page split occurs a new data or index page is allocated, and the existing data or index rows are divided between the old and the new pages. This movement of one-half of the rows to one page and the other half of the rows to the other page is referred to as keeping the index pages in balance.

The use of variable-length data types also has a negative impact on the manner in which page-split events are handled by the SQL Server. If, during a page-split event, the new row is too large to fit on either the old or new page, then a second new page is allocated, and the new, large row is stored on it.

Because nonclustered indexes contain the data page and data row identifiers, page splitting forces the updating of nonclustered index leaf pages. Therefore, the use of nonclustered indexes will, whenever page splitting occurs, introduce (potentially significant) SQL Server overhead.

Page shrinking

Whenever the SQL Server encounters an index page with only one index row remaining on it, then that index row is moved to another index page and the blank index page is deallocated. Alternatively, when the last index row on an index page is deleted, then that blank index page is also deallocated. Both of these events are called *page shrinking*.

Because nonclustered indexes contain the data page and data row identifiers, page shrinking forces the updating of nonclustered index leaf pages. Therefore, the use of nonclustered indexes will, whenever page shrinking occurs, introduce (potentially significant) overhead.

Run-time management of indexes

During B-Tree searching, page splitting, and shrinking, indexes must still be managed to support active processes; therefore, the SQL Server strives to achieve these design goals:

1. Maximize the number of processes searching the index. Whenever an index page is searched, the SQL Server takes short-term locks, called resource locks, to ensure that the index remains consistent. When the individual index page B-Tree search is concluded, that index page's resource lock is immediately released.

2. Keep the index pages balanced.

3. Minimize the possibility of deadlocks by splitting and shrinking indexes pages, while the index is subjected to a B-Tree search.

Overflow page

If an index is not unique, then duplicate key columns can be added to the database. If the index row with the duplicate key column is inserted at the end of the index page that lacks enough space to contain the new index row, then an overflow page is allocated by the SQL Server and the new index row is stored there. Therefore, overflow pages contain only index rows, and these index rows ordinarily match the key column of the last row in the previous index page.

Allocation and management of physical data storage

The System 11 SQL Server uses three schemes for allocating and managing physical data storage:

1. Global allocation map (GAM) page.

2. Allocation unit page.

3. Object allocation map (OAM) page.

Global allocation map

Each time the SQL Server creates a database, it allocates and initializes a global allocation map (GAM) for that database. The GAM itself is stored in the database's `sysgams` system table.

The SQL Server uses the GAM pages whenever it determines that a database needs a free extent. By using the GAM page the SQL Server avoids having to scan each allocation page to determine if a free extent exists within a given database.

Access to a GAM requires the use of a spinlock. A *spinlock* is a mechanism used by the SQL Server to synchronize and control access to the GAM by multiple SQL Server threads. If the GAM's spinlock is locked, then other threads attempt to access the GAM "spin," and repeatedly test the lock until it becomes available.

The GAM is a bit map that records the allocation units belonging to a given database. Each bit in the map corresponds to an individual allocation unit. GAM page bit maps have 16,128 bits (from the 2048-byte page subtract 32 bytes for the page header, then, as there are 8 bits in a byte, multiply the result times 8), where each bit represents an individual allocation unit. As such, each individual GAM page can hold allocation unit information for, at maximum, 8 GB of data space allocated to that database.

When the SQL Server first creates a GAM, it marks the entire extent, within which the first GAM page is contained, as reserved. Next, all pages in the extent are then linked together in a page chain. A single GAM page chain is therefore capable of storing information about 64 GB of allocation information for a given database.

There are two features to understand about GAM pages:

1. GAM pages do not have object allocation map pages.

2. GAM pages are not dynamically allocated. They are only allocated when the data or log space of a given database is altered (and only if another GAM page is required to record the database alteration).

A GAM bit is turned off (i.e., is set equal to 0) when:

1. An extent is deallocated.

2. The `dbcc checkalloc` (*NameOfDatabase*, `fix`) Transact-SQL command completes running.

A GAM bit is set on (i.e., is equal to 1) when:

1. The allocation unit represented by this particular bit has run out of free extents.

2. The `dbcc checkalloc` (*NameOfDatabase*, `fix`) Transact-SQL command is run.

Allocation unit page

Within each allocation unit, the very first page of the very first extent is always the allocation unit page. The allocation unit page is used to hold information about the data stored within that allocation unit. The information held on the allocation unit page is an array data structure that records how the remaining 255 2K pages are being used by the occupying database.

An allocation unit page is used to record:

1. Allocated extents—the identity of extents that are being used by each specific principal database object.

2. Free extents—the identity of extents not yet assigned to any specific principal database object.

An allocation unit page is composed of six main parts:

1. Page header—a 32-byte field.

2. An unused reserved space of 16 bytes in length.

3. A 512-byte section to record the 32 extents.

4. A 128-byte section that stores object allocation map page identifiers (the logical page numbers) affiliated with an extent allocated to some principal database object. This number, also called the extent OAM page number, allows direct access to the OAM page. The extent OAM page number is stored on the allocation page that manages the respective extent. The extents that have been allocated to different principal database objects will have different extent OAM page numbers. Each OAM page identifier is 4 bytes long.

5. An unused space of 1328 bytes in length.

6. A 32-byte section used by `dbcc checkalloc` (a database consistency check utility).

Object allocation map

Most tables, and all indexes (the American term for more than one index; however, if English is your cup of tea, then feel free to mentally substitute the word indices in its place), have their own bit map called an object allocation map (OAM).

The function of the OAM is to hold usage information about the pages that have been allocated to a given table, or to a given index. In so doing, the OAM provides a precise representation of the allocation information for a given principal database object and serves as an efficient means by which to both drop or truncate a table, or to drop an index. In addition, the OAM also assists the SQL Server in allocating new pages proximate to other pages that are already allocated to a given principal database object.

The OAM lists all of the allocation unit page numbers on which there are extents that have been assigned to a principal database object. Furthermore, the OAM contains information about the exact count of used and unused pages in extents allocated to the given principal database object on a given allocation page.

Whenever a new page is about to be allocated to or about to be deallocated from a database object, the OAM is analyzed and kept up-to-date. Whenever the count of extents within an OAM reaches zero, then that entry is deleted from the OAM. However, because it may not always be possible to abort a deallocation, for example, the extent has been reallocated, this entry is not deleted during the respective transaction. But, the very next time the OAM is accessed, the deallocation takes place.

The OAM is recorded on pages allocated to the principal database object. The OAM is stored on the first page of the first segment of a given database.

The System 11 SQL Server supports two types of OAM pages:

1. Generic OAM page.
2. Extent OAM page.

Generic object allocation map page

A Generic OAM page is composed of two main parts:

1. Page header—a 32-byte field.
2. Body—each OAM entry is 8 bytes in size. There is one OAM entry for each allocation unit that has extents allocated to the principal database object. If there are pages allocated to a principal database object that span multiple allocation units, then there will be multiple OAM entries in the body of the OAM page.

Note that not all tables have an OAM. Tables that exists solely in memory (`syscurconfigs`, `sysengines`, `syslocks`, `sysmonitors`, `sysprocesses`, and `systestlog`), the `syslogs` and the `sysgams` tables, do not have an OAM. However, all user-created tables and indexes do have an OAM.

Extent object allocation map page

To enhance page allocation performance, the Extent OAM page was added to System 11 SQL Server. The Extent OAM page is used by the

SQL Server to directly access the Generic OAM page containing the OAM entry for the allocation page when allocating and deallocating pages. As a consequence, unlike previous versions of the SQL Server where multiple OAM page scans were required during page allocation and deallocation (a very costly activity for large tables and indexes), page allocation and deallocation proceeds within minimal disk I/O and scanning overhead.

An Extent OAM page is composed of six parts:

1. Page header—a 32-byte field.

2. Object statistics section of 16 bytes.

3. A 1928-byte space containing 241 OAM entries. Each OAM entry is 8 bytes in size. There is one OAM entry for each allocation unit that has extents allocated to the principal database object. If there are pages allocated to a principal database object that span multiple allocation units, then there will be multiple OAM entries in the body of the OAM page.

4. The 4-byte identity of the last scanned (i.e., detected by the SQL Server) OAM page.

5. A 60-byte section containing fifteen 4-byte allocation hints. An allocation hint is information that the SQL Server uses to begin searching for an unused page. When a principal database object is created, space for allocation hints is automatically set aside and stored solely within the first OAM page. Allocation hints are created when pages are allocated, or when pages are deallocated.

6. An 8-byte OAM page identifier (identity column attribute).

Data and index page allocation

Within the SQL Server there are a number of events that cause a page to be allocated:

1. A table is created.

2. An index is created.

3. A data page splits.

4. An index page splits.

5. An overflow page is created.

6. A distribution page is created when the `update statistics` command statement is executed, or when an index is created for a nonempty table.

The SQL Server also allocates pages when:

1. The transaction log grows.
2. A **bcp** is undertaken.
3. The data is being sorted.

To optimize disk access, the SQL Server strives to allocate the new (data or index) page near existing allocated pages (to which the new page will automatically be linked). However, it is not always possible for the SQL Server to accomplish this goal. To allocate a page, in accordance with this goal, the SQL Server proceeds as follows:

1. To ensure that the OAM is not corrupted, the SQL Server takes an exclusive lock on the respective OAM.
2. To allocate the new data or index page (sometimes called the target page) near an existing allocated page, check for an unused page in the extent that includes the target page. If possible, then allocate that page.
3. If it is not possible to allocate an unused page in the extent that includes the target page, then search of an unused page in any of the extents of the table, or index, on this allocation page. If possible, then allocate an unused page in any of the extents of the table, or index, on this allocation page.
4. If it is not possible to allocate an unused page in any of the extents of the table or index on this allocation page, then examine all extents on each allocation page listed within the table's or index's OAM. The implication of this is that the SQL Server is scanning the OAM pages. The SQL Server uses page utilization (=(Number of used pages/(Number of used pages + Number of unused pages) * 100) to decide when to perform an OAM page scan to find unused pages. This parameter (page utilization) is configurable on a serverwide basis. Don't get bent out of shape! Unused pages are not wasted; they can be used at a later time. However, the SQL Server is not wasting time trying to find those unused pages right now. Anytime the SQL Server scans OAM pages, the identifier of the OAM page most recently determined to have an unused page is stored on the Extent OAM page. By storing the last OAM page scanned within the Extent OAM page, the SQL Server can begin its next scan by starting with that OAM page identifier, thereby avoiding rescanning recently searched, but unpromising, OAM pages. If possible, then allocate an unused page in any of the extents of the table or index on this allocation page.

5. Now, if it is not possible to find an unused page, scan all OAM pages and allocate an unused page in any extents of the table or index on any allocation page.

6. If it is not possible to allocate an unused page in any extents on each allocation page listed within the table's or index's OAM, then allocate a new extent, update the GAM, and allocate an unused page from within the new extent.

7. If it is not possible to allocate a new extent, then examine all other allocation pages on all segments to which the table or index is mapped. To ensure that unavailable extents are not searched, only those extents that are available according to the respective GAM are examined. If possible, allocate a page from another allocation page on one of the segments to which the table or index is mapped.

8. If it is not possible to allocate a page from another allocation page on one of the segments to which the table or index is mapped to, then allocate a new extent, update the GAM, and allocate an unused page from within the new extent.

9. If it is possible, by any of the means described above, to allocate a new page, then update the OAM of the respective extent by marking the page as being allocated. At this point in the process, if it is not possible by any of the means described above to allocate a new page, then the SQL Server will raise an 1105 error.

10. Update the used and unused page counts within the respective OAM.

11. Initialize the new page.

12. To ensure page allocation consistency, the SQL Server will obtain an exclusive lock on the neighboring page(s).

13. The SQL Server next records the page allocation event within the database's transaction log.

14. Finally, the new page is linked into the table or index page chain.

SQL server kernel configuration for page utilization

The page utilization percent SQL Server configuration parameter is used internally by the SQL Server to control whether the SQL Server will scan the OAM to find unused data pages before allocating a new extent to a table (or index) or, conversely, the SQL Server will merely allocate a new extent when a new page is needed. Having the SQL Server scan the OAM minimizes the proliferation of unused data and index pages in extents already allocated to a table or index.

The default value of the `page utilization percent` SQL Server configuration parameter is 95. The range of legal values for the `page utilization percent` SQL Server configuration parameter is 1 through 100. If the value of this parameter is set to 100, then the SQL Server will always scan the OAM pages to find unused data (or index) pages before allocating a new extent to the table. When the value of the `page utilization percent` SQL Server configuration parameter is set lower than 100, the SQL Server calculates the ratio of used and unused pages (using this formula: 100 * used pages/(used pages + unused pages)), and compares that ratio to the value of the `page utilization percent` SQL Server configuration parameter. If the value of the `page utilization percent` SQL Server configuration parameter is greater than the ratio of used and unused pages, then the SQL Server will not search the OAM page(s), but will instead simply allocate a new extent. Setting a low value for the `page utilization percent` SQL Server configuration parameter increases the rate of data row inserts, but it definitely increases the percentage of unused pages.

To set the value of the `page utilization percent` SQL Server configuration parameter to 90, for example, log on to the SQL Server as an account with **sa_role** privileges and enter these commands:

```
1>use master
2>go
1>sp_configure "page utilization percent", 90
2>go
```

This command changes the *master* system database, so to ensure its recovery, be certain to dump the *master* system database. As this command changes the contents of system tables, it cannot be executed within a transaction.

This change takes effect immediately. Finally, the behavior of the **bcp** utility is not influenced by the `page utilization percent` SQL Server configuration parameter. The SQL Server allows the **bcp** utility to manage its extent allocation in an entirely different manner from other types of transactions.

Distribution page

The distribution page contains information about index key values that are used by the statistical query optimizer. The subject of distribution pages will be revisited and explored in depth when we study the statistical query optimizer.

Memory Resource Management

Introduction

To respond to an end user's query, the literal data values stored within data (and index) pages must be examined. This examination of data (and index pages) is done by the SQL Server within memory. If the required pages are already in memory, then the SQL Server does not need to perform disk I/O to bring the pages into memory.

The more disk I/O the SQL Server has to perform to satisfy an end user's query, the more disk I/O overhead it must perform, the greater will be the degradation in performance. Therefore, allocating sufficient memory to the SQL Server can significantly improve performance because page access can be performed at memory speeds, not at disk speeds.

Nonetheless, memory management is a double-edged sword. When managed correctly, memory resources can definitely enhance SQL Server performance. However, if memory is managed incorrectly, then the converse is true, that is, performance goes right down the proverbial tubes.

SQL Server Memory Resource Usage

SQL Server 11, like its predecessors, uses memory to support the following components:

1. SQL Server Executable Code.

2. Static Memory allocated to the SQL Server Kernel.

3. Consumer configurable SQL Server memory parameters.

4. Nondata Cache Data Structures used by the SQL Server Kernel.

5. Execution Stack Region—each user connection supported by the SQL Server is allocated its own execution stack. This is a region where these user-connection execution stacks are localized.

6. Audit Queue—audit records generated by user processes are held herein until the audit records can be processed and written to the audit trail by the SQL Server. This queue is optional.

7. Procedure Cache—active query plans, (occasionally) query trees, rules, defaults, views, check constraints, triggers, and stored procedures are located here. In addition, it contains a "scratch" area used when compiling stored procedures and triggers.

8. Data Cache (also referred to as Buffer Cache)—contains GAM pages, OAM pages, data pages, index pages, and transaction log pages. The Data Cache can be partitioned into the Default Data Cache and consumer-created Named Data Caches. Both the Default Data Cache and the individual Named Data Caches can be further partitioned into a maximum of four Memory Pools each. Specific databases, tables, indexes, text, and image data can be explicitly bound to Data and Named Data Caches.

SQL Server Kernel Configuration for Memory

The maximum amount of memory you can configure for a System 11 SQL Server is 2,147,483,647 2K pages, or approximately 4 GB. If the host computer you are going to run the SQL Server on has less than 4 GB of memory, then the maximum amount of memory you can configure for that SQL Server will be limited to the quantity of memory available on that host computer.

To determine the quantity of memory available to the SQL Server on that host computer, you have to calculate the amount of memory that will be taken by the operating system, and all heavyweight threads that will be executing on the host computer, and subtract that amount from the amount of installed memory.

However, life is seldom as simple as the preceding equation. You will most likely have to take into consideration swap space and shared memory settings within the host computer's operating system. Some operating systems, such as UNIX, have a user-configurable limit on the amount of shared memory a given heavyweight thread can obtain from the operating system. For example, you may have a host computer with 1 GB of calculated memory available to the SQL Server, while the operating system has set shared memory to 512K. In this case, even though there is 1 GB of calculated memory available to the SQL Server, the maximum amount of memory the SQL Server can be configured for is only 512K. As regards swap space, you should not configure the amount of memory for the SQL Server beyond the size of the operating system's swap space, or you will run into problems when you try to start the SQL Server or while the SQL Server is running. Fortunately, both swap space and shared memory are configurable parameters, so discuss these issues with the operating system's Administrator before configuring SQL Server memory. Remember, if you increase the SQL Server memory beyond swap space the SQL Server will start to page fault, so be careful.

When you start up the SQL Server, it makes a request from the operating system for a specific quantity of memory resources. To determine what that specific quantity of memory resources is, log on to the SQL Server, as any valid Sybase account, and enter these commands:

```
1>use master
2>go
1>sp_configure
2>go
```

This command will display for you most categories of SQL Server configuration parameters, their current settings, their default settings, the quantity of memory resource that specific configuration parameter setting consumes, and, where applicable, the previous value of the configuration parameter setting. It is the value displayed for the run_value parameter that represents the quantity of memory resource the SQL Server requests from the operating system when it is started (i.e., booted).

At boot time, the SQL Server will, from the quantity of memory resources specified in the run_value configuration parameter, parcel out memory resources to:

1. The SQL Server Executable Code.
2. Static Memory allocated to the SQL Server Kernel.
3. Nondata Cache Data Structures used by the SQL Server Kernel.
4. Some miscellaneous SQL Server overhead (around 5 percent of the value of the run_value configuration parameter).

The remaining memory resources are allocated to Cache (which in turn is broken out into Data Cache and Procedure Cache).

The amount of memory that the SQL Server Executable Code Region consumes is beyond your control. Depending on what platform you are running the SQL Server on, and what the SQL Server's exact release level is, the SQL Server Executable Code Region will take up between 2.5 MB to 3 MB. Fortunately, you do have the ability to configure, and influence, memory resource usage by the other components. To determine the amount of memory the SQL Server Executable Code Region consumes, log on to the SQL Server as an account with **sa_role** privileges and enter these commands:

```
1>use master
2>go
1>dbcc traceon(3604)
2>go
1>dbcc memusage
2>go
1>dbcc traceoff(3604)
2>go
```

The command displays information on the following aspects of the SQL Server memory resource utilization:

Configured Memory—represents the total amount of memory resources allocated to the SQL Server from the operating system.

Code Size—represents the size of the SQL Server Executable Code Region.

Kernel Structures—represents a combination of the static overhead, and overhead directly related to user-configurable SQL Server parameter settings.

Server Structures—represents a combination of the static overhead, and overhead directly related to user-configurable SQL Server parameter settings.

Page Cache—represents the amount of memory configured for Data Cache, including the internal overhead that comes with supporting the Data Cache.

Proc Buffers—represents the total number of 2K pages assigned to procedure buffers. A procedure buffer is a 76-byte data structure that is used by the SQL Server to manage compiled database objects residing within the Procedure Cache. For the SQL Server, compiled database objects are check constraints, defaults, rules, stored procedures, triggers, and views. When the SQL Server brings a compiled object into Procedure Cache, it automatically associates a procedure buffer with each copy of the compiled object. Here's a bit of interesting trivia: unlike most SQL Server data structures, a procedure buffer can span pages. OK, so that fact is not all that interesting.

Proc Headers—represents the total number of 2K pages assigned to procedure headers. Compiled database objects are stored within procedure headers. And, depending on the physical size of the compiled object, it may be stored in more than one procedure header. The total number of compiled database objects that can be stored within the SQL Server Procedure Cache is constrained to the number of procedure headers, or the number of procedure buffers, whichever is less. Keep in mind that compiled database can span more than one procedure header, so, when the size of the compiled database objects is greater than a single procedure header, the total number of compiled database objects in Procedure Cache will be less than the total number of procedure headers.

Now that you've got a handle on determining the actual size of your installed SQL Server Executable Code Region, let's move on to some memory configuration parameters:

1. user connections
2. number of open databases
3. number of extent i/o buffers
4. total memory

Each user process that accesses the SQL Server does so through a user connection. The maximum number of user connections allowed to a given SQL Server is constrained by the operating system that supports that SQL Server. Each process the underlying operating system supports is limited to a finite number of file descriptors its kernel has been configured to support. This limitation applies to the SQL Server process itself, just as to any other process supported by the operating system. However, when configuring multiple SQL Server engines to run on a multiprocessor platform, the limit of file descriptors for the SQL Server increases linearly.

When the SQL Server boots up, it is given, by the operating system, a static number of file descriptors (i.e., the value set for user connections). From the total count of file descriptors, the SQL Server takes a number of file descriptors for its own internal use:

1. One for each logical database device.
2. One for each SQL Server engine for the interfaces file.
3. One for each SQL Server engine for the error log.
4. One for each SQL Server engine for the standard output file.
5. One for each SQL Server engine for the configuration file.
6. One for each SQL Server engine for internal processing.
7. One for the Checkpoint process.
8. One for the HouseKeeper process (if not disabled).

9. One for each threshold (that is currently executing).

10. One for the Audit System (if enabled).

11. One for the Backup Server (if enabled).

12. Two for each SQL Server engine's network affinity migration channel.

13. One for each master network listener on Engine 0 (i.e., one for every *master* entry in the SQL Server's interface file entry).

To determine the current value of the `user connections` SQL Server configuration parameter, log on to the SQL Server as any Sybase account and enter these commands:

```
1>use master
2>go
1>select @@max_connections
2>go
```

Before we explore setting the value of the `user connections` configuration parameter, we need to examine another related SQL Server configuration parameter: `default network packet size`. Every user connection uses three network buffers: one read buffer, one read overflow buffer, and one write buffer. Each network buffer is equal in size, in bytes, to the `default network packet size` SQL Server configuration parameter.

These three network buffers contribute to the overhead of each user connection that, in turn, contributes to the total SQL Server memory overhead. To calculate just how much network buffer memory overhead is actually created, use this formula:

```
default network packet size * 3 * user connections
```

To determine the current value of the `default network packet size` SQL Server configuration parameter, log on to the SQL Server as any Sybase account and enter these commands:

```
1>use master
2>go
1>sp_configure "default network packet size"
2>go
```

The default value for the `default network packet size` SQL Server configuration parameter is 512 bytes. Therefore, if your SQL Server is configured for 64 user connections, then memory overhead is 512 bytes * 3 * 64, or 98,304 bytes. If you were to double the setting for the `default network packet size` SQL Server configuration parameter and increase it to 1024 bytes, then the memory overhead would increase to 196,608 bytes.

Bear with me now, because, when it comes to the `user connection` SQL Server configuration parameter, things get a bit more complicated. The memory overhead associated with the `user connection` SQL Server configuration parameter is also directly related to the `stack size` SQL Server configuration parameter. We will explore the `stack size` SQL Server configuration parameter in detail a little bit later in this chapter. To calculate just how much memory overhead is actually created on a per `user connection` basis, use this formula:

```
(default network packet size * 3)
                    + stack size + stack guard area size
```

To determine the current value of the `stack size` SQL Server configuration parameter, log on to the SQL Server as any Sybase account and enter these commands:

```
1>use master
2>go
1>sp_configure "stack size"
2>go
```

As you know, the default value for the `default network packet size` SQL Server configuration parameter is 512 bytes. While the default setting of the stack size SQL Server configuration parameter is specific to your platform, it is typically 28,672 bytes. And, the `stack guard area size` is 2048 bytes. Therefore, if your SQL Server is using these default settings, the memory overhead for each user connection is (512 * 3) + 28,672 + 2048, or 32,256 bytes. If you have set the `user connection` SQL Server configuration parameter to 64, and kept the other two SQL Server configuration parameters at their default settings, then the total memory overhead for the user connections would be 2,064,384 bytes. If you have doubled the `default network packet size` SQL Server configuration parameter, then the memory overhead for each user connection would be 2,162,688 bytes.

To set the value of the `user connections` SQL Server configuration parameter to 64, log on to the SQL Server as an account with **sa_role** privileges and enter these commands:

```
1>use master
2>go
1>sp_configure "user connections", 64
2>go
```

As the `user connections` SQL Server configuration parameter is a static parameter, the SQL Server must be shut down and restarted for the new setting to take effect. This command changes the *master* system database, so to ensure its recovery, be certain to dump the *master* system database itself. This command changes the contents of system tables, so it cannot be entered in a transaction.

There are two important facts to understand about user-connection memory overhead:

1. It is present within the SQL Server whether or not a user process actually connects to the SQL Server. When the SQL Server boots up, it sets aside memory to account for the user-connection overhead.

2. The user-connection overhead is taken away from memory resources available to both the Procedure Cache and the Data Cache.

Because of these two facts, you need to carefully judge the impact of increasing the settings of the `default network packet size`, the `stack size`, and the `user connections` SQL Server configuration parameters. If you are drowning in memory, this memory overhead may be insignificant. If you are not one of the lucky ones, and memory is tight, then be certain to proceed clearly.

Last, but not least, if you set the value of the `user connections` configuration parameter higher than the operating system limit, you will not overcome the operating system limit, and will only create serious SQL Server run-time problems.

The SQL Server configuration parameter, `number of open databases`, sets the maximum number of databases that can be open concurrently on SQL Server. This number of concurrently opened databases includes all user databases, as well as all SQL Server system databases (*master, model, sybsystemprocs, tempdb* databases), and, if you elected to use the SQL Server auditing utility, the optional *sybsecurity* database. While an account with **sa_role** privileges can set the value of the `number of open databases` SQL Server configuration parameter between 5 and 2,147,483,647, the default setting is 12. In addition, during run time, the maximum number of concurrently opened databases is pragmatically limited to the total number of databases that exist within a given SQL Server (i.e., you can't open more databases than you actually have).

To determine the current value of the `number of open databases` SQL Server configuration parameter, log on to the SQL Server as any Sybase account and enter these commands:

```
1>use master
2>go
```

```
1>sp_configure "number of open databases"
2>go
```

To determine the amount of memory required for the total count of open databases, use the following formula:

$$\text{number of open databases} * 17\text{ KB}$$

As you can see, as long as the number of concurrently opened databases remains relatively small, the overhead is not too excessive. However, it can really add up when you approach, or exceed, 80 open databases (e.g., 80 * 17 KB = 1,360,000 bytes). In addition, each open database itself adds an additional 644 bytes of memory overhead.

To set the value of the number of open databases SQL Server configuration parameter to 80, log on to the SQL Server as an account with **sa_role** privileges and enter these commands:

```
1>use master
2>go
1>sp_configure "number of open databases", 80
2>go
```

As the number of open databases SQL Server configuration parameter is a static parameter, the SQL Server must be shut down and restarted for the new setting to take effect. This command changes the *master* system database, so to ensure its recovery, be certain to dump the *master* system database itself. This command changes the contents of system tables, so it cannot be entered in a transaction.

There are two important facts to understand about open database memory overhead:

1. It is present within the SQL Server whether or not a user process actually opens a SQL Server database. When the SQL Server boots up it sets aside memory to account for the open database overhead.
2. The open database overhead is taken away from memory resources available to both the Procedure Cache and the Data Cache.

The number of extent i/o buffers SQL Server configuration parameter sets the number of work buffers for use by the create index command. Each work buffer is the size of an extent (i.e., 8 data pages * 2048 bytes per data page, or 16,384 bytes in size).

To determine the current value of the number of extent i/o buffers SQL Server configuration parameter, log on to the SQL Server, as any Sybase account and enter these commands:

```
1>use master
2>go
1>sp_configure "number of extent i/o buffers"
2>go
```

The default setting of the `number of extent i/o buffers` SQL Server configuration parameter is zero. The implication of this is that whenever the `create index`, **bcp,** or **dbcc** commands are executed, the SQL Server reads and writes to disk pages one at a time for intermediate sort results and for index pages to disk, one page at a time.

While you can set the `number of extent i/o buffers` SQL Server configuration parameter to a value between 0 and 2,147,483,647, it is recommended that this SQL Server configuration parameter not be set to a value greater than 100 (as the potential benefits by doing so are negligible). If you set the `number of extent i/o buffers` SQL Server configuration parameter to a value of 10, then there will 163,840 bytes set aside for the work buffers.

Once you increase the value of the `number of extent i/o buffers` SQL Server configuration parameter beyond zero, then index creation, **bcp,** and **dbcc** processes, are speeded up because the SQL Server will read and write to disk on an extent, and not on a page, basis. However, there is a catch: only one index creation process, or **bcp** process, can use these work buffers at a time. As a consequence, all but the first active index creation processes, or **bcp** processes, or **dbcc** processes, will read and write to pages to disk, a single page at a time. Nevertheless, if your SQL Server installation supports frequent index creation, or **bcp** processes, and you have sufficient memory resources, then it is worth investigating the benefits you can potentially achieve by creating these work buffers.

To set the value of the `number of extent i/o buffers` SQL Server configuration parameter to 10, log on to the SQL Server as an account with **sa_role** privileges and enter these commands:

```
1>use master
2>go
1>sp_configure "number of extent i/o buffers", 10
2>go
```

As the `number of extent i/o buffers` SQL Server configuration parameter is a static parameter, the SQL Server must be shut down and restarted for the new setting to take effect. This command changes the *master* system database, so to ensure its recovery, be certain to dump the *master* system database itself. This command changes the contents of system tables, so it cannot be entered in a transaction.

There are two important facts to understand about extent i/o buffer memory overhead:

1. It is present within the SQL Server whether or not a **bcp** job is running, a **dbcc** process is running, or an index is being created. When the SQL Server boots up, it sets aside memory to account for the extent i/o buffer memory overhead.

2. The extent i/o buffer memory overhead is taken away from memory resources available to both the Procedure Cache and the Data Cache.

The `total memory` SQL Server configuration parameter establishes the quantity of memory, in 2K units, that the SQL Server obtains from the operating system. To boot successfully, the operating system must allocate this amount of memory resource to the SQL Server. If the SQL Server cannot get this amount of memory resource from the underlying operating system, then it will not boot.

To determine the current value of the `total memory` SQL Server configuration parameter, log on to the SQL Server as any Sybase account and enter these commands:

```
1>use master
2>go
1>sp_configure "total memory"
2>go
```

The displayed value is in 2K page units. While the value of `total memory` can range from 3,850 to 2,147,483,647 2K, its default value is specific to the platform you will be running the SQL Server on. Use the following formula to determine the value you should set the `total memory` SQL Server configuration parameter to:

`total memory` = SQL Server Executable Code Size + (per user connection overhead * number of user connections) + (number of open databases * 644 bytes) + (number of extent i/o buffers * 16K) + (number of locks * 32 bytes) + (number of devices * 45,056 bytes) + size of Procedure Cache + total Data Cache size

To set the value of the `total memory` SQL Server configuration parameter to 256,000 2K units, or 512 MB, log on to the SQL Server as an account with **sa_role** privileges and enter these commands:

```
1>use master
2>go
1>sp_configure "total memory", 256000
2>go
```

As the `total memory` SQL Server configuration parameter is a static parameter, the SQL Server must be shut down and restarted for the new setting to take effect. This command changes the *master* system database, so to ensure its recovery, be certain to dump the *master* system database itself. This command changes the contents of system tables, so it cannot be entered in a transaction.

As you can infer from the preceding formula, you may well have to reset the value of the `total memory` SQL Server configuration parameter whenever you adjust the values of any of the related Server configuration parameters. Remember, before resetting the `total memory` SQL Server configuration parameter proceed clearly.

The Execution Stack Region

At boot time, the SQL Server allocates a fixed amount of memory resource to the Execution Stack Region. The Execution Stack Region is the memory area in which the SQL Server keeps track of the context, as well as the local data, of each user connection supported by an individual stack. The memory address space, the user's query, and the SQL Server data structures corresponding to a user connection, is the context of the user connection.

Each user connection has its own exclusive stack within the Execution Stack Region. This stack is retained by the user connection for the life of the connection. Once the user drops their connection to the SQL Server, that area of the Execution Stack Region becomes available to the next connection that will be established.

The size of each individual stack is the same for all user connections. Given this constraint, all user-connection contexts are, of necessity, the same size. Unfortunately, not all user-connection contexts are created equally. For example, an individual user process may be composed of complex predicate expressions, or may invoke heavily nested, stored procedures, or may contain extremely long select lists.

Given the absence of a suitable SQL Server utility, unless you actually execute a given transaction, there is no way to determine exactly how much stack space a given transaction will require within the SQL Server. As a consequence, individual user connections can, and sometimes do, experience stack overflow events. Whenever a stack overflow event occurs, the SQL Server writes an error message to its error log, and then rolls back the transaction.

Configuring the execution stack region

There are two SQL Server parameters you can use to configure the Execution Stack Region:

1. stack size

2. stack guard size

To determine the current value of the stack size SQL Server configuration parameter, log on to the SQL Server as any Sybase account and enter these commands:

```
1>use master
2>go
1>sp_configure "stack size"
2>go
```

The default, and minimum, setting for the stack size SQL Server configuration parameter is platform specific. The maximum allowable stack size is 2,147,483,647 2K pages. Whatever value you set the stack size SQL Server configuration parameter to, that value must always be an even multiple of the SQL Server's page size, which, on most platforms, is 2048 bytes.

Determining the correct value at which to set the stack size SQL Server configuration parameter equal to is at the best of times an experimental process, but is usually a case of trial and error. It would be easy to state that the stack size SQL Server configuration parameter should be set to hold the largest and most complex query that the SQL Server must support. However, as we discovered earlier in this chapter, the memory overhead associated with user connections is subtracted from Procedure Cache and Data Cache memory resources.

Significant increases in memory overhead, as a result of increasing the value of the stack size SQL Server configuration parameter can seriously degrade SQL Server performance. As a consequence of increasing the value of the stack size SQL Server configuration parameter, there will be less memory in which to store compiled database objects, and data, index, and transaction log pages. Therefore, before you increase the value of the stack size SQL Server configuration parameter, try to decrease the size and complexity of the monster query from hell by rewriting it. Unfortunately, life sometimes demands a nonminimalistic solution, and the beast has to be left on the prowl. The bottom line is that the largest and most complex query that supports the business has to run without experiencing a stack overflow event.

To set the value of the stack size SQL Server configuration parameter to 32,768 bytes, log on to the SQL Server as an account with **sa_role** privileges and enter these commands:

```
1>use master
2>go
```

```
1>sp_configure "stack size", 32768
2>go
```

As the stack size SQL Server configuration parameter is a static parameter, the SQL Server must be shut down and restarted for the new setting to take effect. This command changes the *master* system database, so to ensure its recovery, be certain to dump the *master* system database itself. This command changes the contents of system tables, so it cannot be entered in a transaction.

When you alter the value of the stack size SQL Server configuration parameter, the SQL Server verifies that the new value is an even multiple of the platform page size. If it is not an even multiple of 2048, then the SQL Server rounds it up to the nearest multiple of the platform page size.

More than likely, if you increase the value of the stack size SQL Server configuration parameter, you will also have to increase the value of the total memory SQL Server configuration parameter to preserve the quantity of memory allocated to Procedure Cache and to Data Cache.

To determine the current value of the stack guard size SQL Server configuration parameter, log on to the SQL Server as any Sybase account and enter these commands:

```
1>use master
2>go
1>sp_configure "stack guard size"
2>go
```

The default, and minimum, setting for the stack guard size SQL Server configuration parameter is 4096 bytes. The maximum allowable stack size is 2,147,483,647 2K pages. Whatever value you set the stack guard size SQL Server configuration parameter to, that value must always be an even multiple of the SQL Server's page size, which, on most platforms, is 2048 bytes.

The stack guard area is a configurable overflow stack located at the end of each stack. And, at the end of the stack guard area itself is a proprietary 4-byte structure called the guardword. During run time, the SQL Server checks every user connection to determine if its process has entered the stack's stack guard area. If the process has entered the stack's stack guard area, then the SQL Server will kill the transaction, generate a 3625 error message, and return control to the user connection's application. If a user-connection process succeeds in overflowing the stack boundary, the guardword structure is altered, and the SQL Server will print an error message to that effect in its error log, and will then shut itself down. If the user-connection process grows beyond both the stack and the stack guard area, then the SQL Server will print an error message to that effect in its error log, and will then shut itself down. If you continuously experience these events, then consider increasing the size of the stack guard area (that is, after you already tried to rewrite the process, and have already increased the stack size).

To set the value of the `stack guard size` SQL Server configuration parameter to 8192 bytes, log on to the SQL Server as an account with **sa_role** privileges and enter these commands:

```
1>use master
2>go
1>sp_configure "stack guard size", 8192
2>go
```

As the `stack guard size` SQL Server configuration parameter is static, the SQL Server must be shut down and restarted for the new setting to take effect. This command changes the *master* system database, so to ensure its recovery, be certain to dump the *master* system database itself. This command changes the contents of system tables, so it cannot be entered in a transaction.

When you alter the value of the `stack guard size` SQL Server configuration parameter, the SQL Server verifies that the new value is an even multiple of the platform page size. If it is not an even multiple of 2048, then the SQL Server rounds it up to the nearest multiple of the platform page size.

More than likely, if you increase the value of the `stack guard size` SQL Server configuration parameter, you will also have to increase the value of the `total memory` SQL Server configuration parameter to preserve the quantity of memory allocated to Procedure Cache and to Data Cache.

The Audit Queue

The System 11 SQL Server contains an optional Audit system, consisting of:

1. The *sybsecurity* system database.

2. A collection of system-stored procedures that can be used to configure a variety of supported auditing features.

3. The Audit Queue, into which audit records are written prior to being flushed to the audit trail that is stored on disk.

If you elect to use the Audit System, then you must install it. A step in the Audit System installation process covers the creation of the *sybsecurity* system database. This system database contains all of the system table contained within the *model* system database, as well as these two additional system tables:

1. *sysaudits*—the audit trail records are stored herein.
2. *sysauditoptions*—contains the systemwide values you have set for the Audit System configuration parameters.

When a user-defined audit event occurs, a corresponding 424-byte audit record is written into an in-memory Audit Queue Buffer. The audit record remains in memory until the Audit System writes, that is, flushes, the contents of the *sysaudits* system table onto a data page residing on disk.

On average, the contents of the Audit Queue are written to disk once every 20 seconds, unless, of course, the audit process preempts the write to disk because it is busy writing audit records into the in-memory Audit Queue. However, if the Audit Queue fills up, and runs out of available Buffers, then the audit process will put user connections that produce audit records to sleep, while it flushes the audit records out to disk. Once sufficient space within the Audit Queue becomes available, the audit process once again begins writing audit records into the Audit Queue. As you can well imagine, if this series of events happens frequently, overall SQL Server performance will degrade significantly.

It is important to realize that the audit records are initially stored within volatile storage (i.e., memory). If the SQL Server crashes, then the portion of the audit trail that resides in memory is lost. The black art is to size the Audit Queue such that the thread that writes to the in-memory Buffers does not go to sleep, while at the same time, the risk of exposure to lost audit records due to a SQL Server crash is simultaneously minimized.

For a detailed explanation of the optional Audit System, and how to use and manage it, refer to the System 11 Sybase SQL Server Security Administration Guide and the System 11 Sybase SQL Server Security Features User's Guide.

Cache and Cache Manager Internals

The System 11 SQL Server comes with a single Default Data Cache, a single Procedure Cache, and zero or many consumer-created Named Data Caches. Each SQL Server cache is made up of a number of components that exhibit unique behavior:

Spinlock—each cache has its own spinlock. The function of the spin-lock is to reduce access contention on the cache.

Page—an identical copy of a 2K page of data, index, transaction log, and so on, read from disk and copied into Data Cache in response to a user's query. The pages, under the control of the Cache Manager, are uniquely identified through a combination of their database identifier and their logical page number.

Buffer Header—contains information on a given Buffer, such as the location of the Buffer on the MRU/LRU Chain (queue), the state of the Buffer (e.g., the buffer is dirty), whether the Buffer is, or is not, on the Kept Chain. The Buffer Header itself is relatively small, about 100 bytes in size.

Buffer—an individual Buffer contains a Buffer Header linked to a page. The SQL Server Cache Manager ensures that each data, index, or transaction log page in Data Cache, and each stored procedure, trigger, and so on, in Procedure Cache, is paired off with a Buffer that is dedicated to the referenced principal database object. The Buffer points to a specific page, and serves to regulate its stay within Data Cache, or within the Procedure Cache, as the case may be. When the SQL Server boots, a Buffer Header is linked to a page. While the SQL Server is running, that linkage is maintained. However, it is infor-mation within the page (data and index information) that changes during run time.

Buffer Mass—with System 11 SQL Server, a Buffer is actually a block of individual Buffers equal to the disk I/O size of the Memory Pool in which they reside. The disk I/O size of a Memory Pool can be one page (2K), two pages (4K), four pages (8K), and a single extent consisting of eight pages (16K). A Buffer is managed as a unit of disk I/O called a Buffer Mass, that is, all pages in a Buffer are read from disk, written to disk, or flushed from the cache simultaneously, in mass.

Memory Pool—also referred to as a Buffer Pool, this is a circular linked list of Buffer Masses. Memory Pools come in just four sizes: 2K, 4K, 8K, and 16K. Every Data Cache, whether it is the Default Data Cache or a user-created Named Data Cache, always contains one (default) mandatory 2K Memory Pool. Each Memory Pool has its own MRU/LRU Chain.

Hash Table—a bit map that contains the list of Buffer Masses cur-rently residing within a cache. The Hash Table (sometimes referred to as the hash bucket) enables the SQL Server to rapidly determine whether a given page is within a cache or whether the Cache Man-ager must undertake a disk I/O read to bring a copy of that page into a cache. Each Memory Pool has its own hash table. When an individual page in a Buffer Mass in the Hash Table is referenced by a user transaction, its reference bit is set to "referenced," and when a Buffer in the Hash Table is no longer referenced by a user transaction, its reference bit is set to "unreferenced."

Most Recently Used/Least Recently Used (MRU/LRU) Chain—a circular queue consisting of a doubly linked list of Buffer Masses that are currently available to the Cache Manager so that it can read new pages from disk into cache. Each Memory Pool has its own MRU/LRU Chain.

Buffer Wash Marker—contained within each MRU/LRU chain is a Buffer Wash Marker. The Buffer Wash Marker's purpose in life is to demarcate the position within the MRU/LRU Chain where Buffers, following after the marker toward the LRU side of the chain, are either in the process of being written to disk by the Cache Manager, or are clean.

Memory Pool Wash Area—the portion of the MRU/LRU Chain, between the Buffer Wash Marker and the end of the LRU chain is referred to as the Memory Pool Wash Area.

Kept Chain—a circular queue that contains the list of Buffer Masses that are currently in use by end-user processes. Each Memory Pool has its own Kept Chain. The Buffer Masses in this list are not currently available for replacement by the Cache Manager. After the Buffer Mass is placed on the Kept Chain it is hashed.

Hash Function—the purpose of the Hash Function is to grab a free Buffer Mass (according to the invoked caching strategy and the determined-target Memory Pool), place the Buffer Mass on the Kept Chain, and then hash it. If the target is a 2K Memory Pool, then the Buffer Mass will be hashed on a single page identifier. If the target is a 4K, an 8K, or a 16K Memory Pool, then the Buffer Mass will be hashed on the extent identifier and allocation page identifier. When reading pages into memory, a gain in overall system throughput is achieved because the SQL Server first scans the Hash Table for the referenced page, instead of searching the MRU/LRU Chain or the Kept Chain. If the requested page is found within a Buffer Mass in the Hash Table, then the SQL Server will take, and hold, a resource lock on the page, while rows within the requested page are referenced on behalf of the user's transaction. If the requested page(s) does not exist within the Hash Table, and space is needed, then a Buffer Mass on the Memory Pool's MRU/LRU Chain will be unhashed and the corresponding reference bits will be reset to "unreferenced" on all pages within the Buffer Mass.

The Cache Manager and Reads from Disk

Before a page is brought into cache, the Cache Manager will determine which cache (i.e., the Default Data Cache, one of the consumer-created Named Data Caches, or the Procedure Cache) that the page is to be brought into, and which Memory Pool (the default 2K, or consumer-created 4K, 8K, or 16K) within that cache the page will eventually reside.

If the page belongs to a compiled object, then it will be brought into the Procedure Cache. If the page belongs to a table, index, or transaction log, and if the table, index, or transaction log has not been explicitly bound to a Named Data Cache, then the page will be brought into the Default Data Cache. If the table, index, or transaction log has been explicitly bound to a Named Data Cache, then the page will be brought into that specific Named Data Cache to which it has been bound.

Once the target cache has been determined, then the Cache Manager will make the final determination of which Memory Pool within the target cache the page will take up residency. In the process of deciding which cache Memory Pool the page is to be placed, the Cache Manager will attempt to use hints provided to it by the Query Optimizer. The System 11 SQL Server allows you to suggest a caching strategy (i.e., make a hint, when to create a select, update, or delete query statement. In addition, the Query Optimizer itself can make recommendations to the Cache Manager regarding which caching strategy to use for a particular query.

When you create a select, update, or delete query statement against a table, you can specify a caching strategy by:

1. Indicating which size Memory Pool to use by invoking the `prefetch` command option.

2. Requesting a Buffer Mass replacement strategy, such as, LRU or Fetch-And-Discard, by invoking either the `lru` command option or the `mru` command option.

With System 11, the SQL Server Cache Manager can use either of two caching strategies when reading pages from disk:

1. The LRU Replacement Strategy, where pages are read sequentially into Buffer Masses on the LRU portion of the MRU/LRU Chain within the target Memory Pool.

2. The Fetch-And-Discard Strategy (which is also referred to as the MRU Replacement Strategy), where pages are read into the Buffer Mass(es) that immediately precede the Wash Marker within the target Memory Pool, used, and then rapidly moved to the LRU end of

the MRU/LRU Chain so that the Buffer can be quickly reused by another query. Essentially, this replacement strategy is used when a page is needed only once by a given query and that page is not already in data cache. If another query needs the same page again, then the page will probably have to be read again from disk into data cache.

When a query statement includes a caching strategy hint, the Query Optimizer will produce instructions to the Cache Manager that include the recommended caching strategy. In the absence of caching strategy hints, the Query Optimizer will still suggest to the Cache Manager which caching strategy to use. However, the Query Optimizer makes these suggestions based upon the limited perspective of the single query it is optimizing. The Cache Manager, on the other hand, makes its decisions in light of all active queries. Depending upon the Cache Manager's knowledge of pages currently in cache, the current state of these pages, the availability of Memory Pool Buffer Masses, and other factors, the Cache Manager may act on the caching strategies passed to it through, or by, the Query Optimizer, or the Cache Manager may elect to ignore them in some cases.

If a Memory Pool of the recommended size exists within the target data cache(s), the Cache Manager will examine the Memory Pool for the available Buffer Masses, and will grab the free Buffers if it can. If there are no available Buffer Masses in the recommended Memory Pool, then the Cache Manager follows these rules as it proceeds:

1. If the unavailable recommended Memory Pool size is 16K, then the Cache Manager will examine the 8K Memory Pool for available Buffers, and will grab them if it can. If there are no available Buffers in the 8K Memory Pool, then the Cache Manager will examine the 4K Memory Pool for available Buffers, and will grab them if it can. If there are no available Buffers in the 4K Memory Pool, then the Cache Manager will examine the 2K Memory Pool for available Buffers, and will grab them if it can. If there are no available 2K Memory Pool Buffers, then Cache Manager will wait for available Buffers.

2. If the unavailable recommended Memory Pool size is 8K, then the Cache Manager will examine the 4K Memory Pool for available Buffers, and will grab them if it can. If there are no available Buffers in the 4K Memory Pool, then the Cache Manager will examine the 2K Memory Pool for available Buffers, and will grab them if it can. If there are no available 2K Memory Pool Buffers, then Cache Manager will wait for available Buffers.

3. If the unavailable recommended Memory Pool size is 4K, then the Cache Manager will examine the 2K Memory Pool for available Buffers, and will grab them if it can. If there are no available 2K Memory Pool Buffers, then Cache Manager will wait for available Buffers.

4. If the unavailable recommended Memory Pool size is 2K, then the Cache Manager will not examine any of the larger-sized Memory Pools. Instead, the Cache Manager will wait for 2K Buffers to become available.

If a Memory Pool of the recommended size does not exist within the target data cache(s), the Cache Manager will determine which Memory Pool to use.

If Buffer Masses are available in a large Memory Pool of the recommended size, but one of the requested pages already exists in the 2K Memory Pool, then the remaining requested pages will also be placed in the 2K Memory Pool as well.

Finally, within each allocation unit, the very first page of the very first extent is always the allocation unit page. If the requested page is the allocation unit page, then this page and the other seven data pages on the very first extent will always be placed within the 2K Memory Pool.

The LRU Replacement Strategy

The Cache Manager will elect to use the LRU Replacement Strategy when:

1. Query specifies the LRU Replacement Strategy because the transaction statement declares that this strategy is to be used.

2. Query indicates that the requested page will be used more than once by the transaction.

3. Query will be modifying the contents of the requested page(s).

4. Query tree indicates that root and intermediate-level index pages of a clustered index are requested.

5. The transaction requires an OAM page.

6. Join Query where the Inner table of the Join Query can fit entirely within the data cache.

When the Cache Manage follows the LRU Replacement Strategy, pages are read sequentially, replacing Buffers on the LRU portion of the MRU/LRU Chain within the target Memory Pool. The LRU portion of the queue is that set of Buffers that are actually available to the

Cache Manager so that it can allocate a Buffer to support reading a required page from disk. When a page is first read into cache, it is paired off with a Buffer from the LRU side of the LRU/MRU Chain. Once the Buffer Mass is obtained by the Cache Manager it is placed on the MRU end of the MRU/LRU Chain, and hashed. In this way, the most commonly referenced data pages tend to remain in data cache. As more pages are read into cache, and as the page is aged over time, the Buffer Mass will migrate toward the LRU end of the MRU/LRU Chain.

When a query invokes an index, index and data pages move into data cache in a certain order: first the root page, then intermediate-level page, followed by the index leaf pages, and then the data pages. Index pages are different from data pages in one important aspect: if they are not already in data cache when invoked, they are read into data cache and placed onto the MRU side on the chain and move toward the LRU side of the chain as more index pages are read into data cache. As a consequence, the root page and pages from the higher levels of an index tend to remain within data cache.

Because the behavior of data and index pages is dissimilar, in cache they are aged by the SQL Server in a significantly different manner. Recall that the index leaf pages of a clustered index are data pages, and the index leaf pages of the nonclustered index contain logical pointers to each data rows within the table's data pages. As a consequence of queries, the leaf level of either index will tend to be the last pages read, and would, therefore, tend to reside on the MRU side of the chain. To compensate for this tendency, the SQL Server's Buffer Cache Manager ages data pages from the MRU side of the chain at a faster rate then it ages index pages.

Also, while data pages will make only a single traversal of the MRU/LRU Chain, the System 11 SQL Server allows you to configure the Cache Manager such that index pages, as well as OAM pages, can traverse the MRU/LRU Chain multiple times. This special index page and OAM page caching strategies will be discussed in a later section of this chapter. However, the default Cache Manager configuration allows only a single traversal of the MRU/LRU Chain by index or OAM pages.

The Fetch-And-Discard Replacement Strategy

The Cache Manager will elect to use the Fetch-And-Discard Replacement Strategy when:

1. Query requires a Heap table to be scanned.

2. Join Query involves scanning a Heap table that is not the Inner table of the join.

3. Query does a table scan, even though the table has a clustered index, because the columns in the clustered index do not support columns referenced in the query.

4. Query covers an nonclustered index and a leaf-level index page will be scanned.

5. Optimizer decides not to use an index, but to do a table scan instead, because requested rows will be returned faster by reading the pages directly, rather than by traversing the levels of index pages.

6. Table is a Work table.

7. Range queries (i.e., queries that contain the comparison operators `">"`, `"<"`, `"> x and < y"`, the keyword `"between"`, or match character strings using "like `"string%"`",) that use a clustered index.

8. Inner table in a Join Query where the Inner table is too large to fit entirely within the data cache.

9. Outer table in Join Query, because the Outer table needs only to be read a single time.

10. Query selects text or image column(s).

Whenever possible, a 16K Memory Pool will be used to support the Fetch-And-Discard Replacement Strategy.

The Cache Manager and Data Modifications

How the Cache Manager handles insert, update, and delete statements is relatively more complex than the manner by which it supports select statements. While a single individual query will read pages from disk into data cache, many different queries can potentially modify any page in data cache.

The goal of the Cache Manager is to successfully walk a razor's edge. The Cache Manager likes to hold disk I/O overhead to a minimum by retaining modified pages in cache so that if other user processes also want to modify the same page, that page will already reside in cache. On the other hand, it must also, eventually, write dirty pages to disk, and make the Buffer Masses they reside on available to new read queries.

If the page to be modified is not in cache, then it is read from disk using the LRU Replacement Strategy, the page is modified and begins its movement toward the LRU end of the MRU/LRU Chain as other pages move into the data cache.

If the page to be modified in already in cache, then it is moved to the top of the MRU side of the MRU/LRU Chain, and it begins its movement toward the LRU end of the MRU/LRU Chain as other pages move into the data cache.

The Cache Manager and Writes To Disk

Within the SQL Server there is a process called Checkpoint which is responsible for ensuring that if the SQL Server must be restarted, the recovery of databases can be accomplished in a suitable period of time (this time quantum is user configurable). The Checkpoint process periodically examines the total number of changes to each database and, when it determines that the recovery of an individual database will take longer than the configured time period, it scans the data cache(s) and flushes any dirty pages out to disk.

In addition to Checkpoint, the System 11 SQL Server contains a HouseKeeper process that also flushes any dirty pages out to disk when idle time arises between processing events.

In the MRU/LRU Chain there is a Wash Point on the LRU side of the buffer chain. Over time, dirty pages migrate over to the LRU side of the buffer chain. When these dirty pages pass over the Wash Point, the Cache Manager schedules them to be written to the database. This type of event is called Buffer Washing. The location of the Wash Point within the MRU/LRU Chain is tunable and is established at SQL Server boot time.

In addition to buffer washing, checkpoints, and housekeeping, there are seven other events that cause the contents of the cache to be written to a database:

1. When pages in the transaction log are written to disk at the end of a transaction.

2. When newly allocated pages are written to disk.

3. When all initialized pages are written to disk because the `load database` command is executed.

4. When all initialized pages are written to disk because the `create database` command is executed using the `for load` option.

5. When all initialized pages are written to disk because the `alter database` command is executed using the `for load` option.

6. When dirty pages are written to disk because the `fast bulk copy` command completes successfully.

7. When dirty pages are written to disk because the `select into` command completes successfully.

Reporting on Fetch-And-Discard
Replacement Strategy on an Object Basis

By default, the Fetch-And-Discard Replacement Strategy is enabled on all tables, indexes, text, and image objects. However, if your account has **sa_role** privileges, or if you are the owner of a given table or index, then you can disable and reenable use of the Fetch-And-Discard Replacement Strategy for that object. If you disable the Fetch-And-Discard Replacement Strategy for an object, then all of its pages are read into data cache using the LRU Replacement Strategy.

To view the current status of the Fetch-And-Discard Replacement Strategy for a given table, log on to the SQL Server as any valid account and enter these commands:

```
1>use NameOfDatabase
2>go
1>sp_cachestrategy NameOfDatabase, [NameOfObjectOwner.]
   NameOfTable
2>go
```

where:

NameOfDatabase—the name of the database that contains the table whose caching strategy information you want to view.

NameOfObjectOwner—the name of the Sybase account that owns the table whose caching strategy information you want to view. If you are also the owner of the table, then you do not have to specify a value for this parameter.

NameOfTable—the name of the table whose caching strategy information you want to view.

To view the current status of the Fetch-And-Discard Replacement Strategy for a given index, log on to the SQL Server as any valid account and enter these commands:

```
1>use NameOfDatabase
2>go
1>sp_cachestrategy NameOfDatabase, [NameOfObjectOwner.]Name
   OfTable, NameOfIndex
2>go
```

where:

NameOfDatabase—the name of the database that contains the index whose caching strategy information you want to view.

NameOfObjectOwner—the name of the Sybase account that owns the index whose caching strategy information you want to view. If you are also the owner of the index, then you do not have to specify a value for this parameter.

NameOfTable—the name of the table with the index whose caching strategy information you want to view.

`NameOfIndex`—the name of the index whose caching strategy information you want to view.

Disabling Fetch-And-Discard Replacement Strategy on an Object Basis

If you are the owner of the object, or if your account has **sa_role** privileges, and you want to disable the use of the Fetch-And-Discard Replacement Strategy for a given table, then log on to the SQL Server as that account which owns the object or as an account with **sa_role** privileges and enter these commands:

```
1>use NameOfDatabase
2>go
1>sp_cachestrategy NameOfDatabase, [NameOfObjectOwner.]Name
   OfTable
2>"table only", mru, "off"
3>go
```

where:

NameOfDatabase—the name of the database that contains the table for which you want to disable the Fetch-And-Discard Replacement Strategy.

NameOfObjectOwner—the name of the Sybase account that owns the table for which you want to disable the Fetch-And-Discard Replacement Strategy. If you are also the owner of the table, then you do not have to specify a value for this parameter.

NameOfTable—the name of the table for which you want to disable the Fetch-And-Discard Replacement Strategy.

This change takes effect immediately. This command changes the *master* system database, so to ensure its recovery, be certain to dump the *master* system database. As this command changes the contents of system tables, it cannot be executed within a transaction.

If you are the owner of the object, or if your account has **sa_role** privileges, and you want to disable the use of the Fetch-And-Discard Replacement Strategy for a given index, then log on to the SQL Server as that account which owns the object or as an account with **sa_role** privileges and enter these commands:

```
1>use NameOfDatabase
2>go
1>sp_cachestrategy NameOfDatabase, [NameOfObjectOwner.]Name
    OfTable, NameOfIndex
2>mru, "off"
3>go
```

where:

NameOfDatabase—the name of the database that contains the index for which you want to disable the Fetch-And-Discard Replacement Strategy.

NameOfObjectOwner—the name of the Sybase account that owns the index for which you want to disable the Fetch-And-Discard Replacement Strategy. If you are also the owner of the index, then you do not have to specify a value for this parameter.

NameOfTable—the name of the table with the index for which you want to disable the Fetch-And-Discard Replacement Strategy.

NameOfIndex—the name of the index for which you want to disable the Fetch-And-Discard Replacement Strategy.

This change takes effect immediately. This command changes the *master* system database, so to ensure its recovery, be certain to dump the *master* system database. As this command changes the contents of system tables, it cannot be executed within a transaction.

If you are the owner of the object, or if your account has **sa_role** privileges, and you want to disable the use of the Fetch-And-Discard Replacement Strategy for a given text or image object, then log on to the SQL Server as that account which owns the object or as an account with **sa_role** privileges and enter these commands:

```
1>use NameOfDatabase
2>go
1>sp_cachestrategy NameOfDatabase, [NameOfObjectOwner.]Name
    OfTable
2>"text only", mru, "off"
3>go
```

where:

NameOfDatabase—the name of the database that contains the table that contains the text or image object for which you want to disable the Fetch-And-Discard Replacement Strategy.

NameOfObjectOwner—the name of the Sybase account that owns the table that contains the text or image object for which you want to disable the Fetch-And-Discard Replacement Strategy. If you are also the owner of the table, then you do not have to specify a value for this parameter.

NameOfTable—the name of the table that contains the text or image object for which you want to disable the Fetch-And-Discard Replacement Strategy.

This change takes effect immediately. This command changes the *master* system database, so to ensure its recovery, be certain to dump the *master* system database. As this command changes the contents of system tables, it cannot be executed within a transaction.

If you are the owner of the object, or if your account has **sa_role** privileges, and you want to disable the use of the Fetch-And-Discard Replacement Strategy for a given table, and all indexes, text, and image objects associated with it, then log on to the SQL Server as that account which owns the object or as an account with **sa_role** privileges and enter these commands:

```
1>use NameOfDatabase
2>go
1>sp_cachestrategy NameOfDatabase, [NameOfObjectOwner.]Name
   OfTable
2>mru, "off"
3>go
```

where:

NameOfDatabase—the name of the database that contains the table for which you want to disable the Fetch-And-Discard Replacement Strategy for itself and for all indexes, text, and image objects associated with it.

NameOfObjectOwner—the name of the Sybase account that owns the table for which you want to disable the Fetch-And-Discard Replacement Strategy for itself and for all indexes, text, and image objects associated with it. If you are also the owner of the table, then you do not have to specify a value for this parameter.

NameOfTable—the name of the table for which you want to disable the Fetch-And-Discard Replacement Strategy for itself and for all indexes, text, and image objects associated with it.

This change takes effect immediately. This command changes the *master* system database, so to ensure its recovery, be certain to dump the *master* system database. As this command changes the contents of system tables, it cannot be executed within a transaction.

Enabling Fetch-And-Discard Replacement Strategy on an Object Basis

If you are the owner of the object, or if your account has **sa_role** privileges, and you want to reenable the use of the Fetch-And-Discard Replacement Strategy for a given table, then log on to the SQL Server as that account which owns the object or as an account with **sa_role** privileges and enter these commands:

```
1>use NameOfDatabase
2>go
1>sp_cachestrategy NameOfDatabase, [NameOfObjectOwner.]Name
    OfTable
2>"table only", mru, "on"
3>go
```

where:

NameOfDatabase—the name of the database that contains the table for which you want to reenable the Fetch-And-Discard Replacement Strategy.

NameOfObjectOwner—the name of the Sybase account that owns the table for which you want to reenable the Fetch-And-Discard Replacement Strategy. If you are also the owner of the table, then you do not have to specify a value for this parameter.

NameOfTable—the name of the table for which you want to reenable the Fetch-And-Discard Replacement Strategy.

This change takes effect immediately. This command changes the *master* system database, so to ensure its recovery, be certain to dump the *master* system database. As this command changes the contents of system tables, it cannot be executed within a transaction.

If you are the owner of the object, or if your account has **sa_role** privileges, and you want to reenable the use of the Fetch-And-Discard Replacement Strategy for a given index, then log on to the SQL Server as that account which owns the object or as an account with **sa_role** privileges and enter these commands:

```
1>use NameOfDatabase
2>go
1>sp_cachestrategy NameOfDatabase, [NameOfObjectOwner.]Name
    OfTable, NameOfIndex
```

```
2>mru, "on"
3>go
```

where:

NameOfDatabase—the name of the database that contains the index for which you want to reenable the Fetch-And-Discard Replacement Strategy.

NameOfObjectOwner—the name of the Sybase account that owns the index for which you want to reenable the Fetch-And-Discard Replacement Strategy. If you are also the owner of the index, then you do not have to specify a value for this parameter.

NameOfTable—the name of the table with the index for which you want to reenable the Fetch-And-Discard Replacement Strategy.

NameOfIndex—the name of the index for which you want to reenable the Fetch-And-Discard Replacement Strategy.

This change takes effect immediately. This command changes the *master* system database, so to ensure its recovery, be certain to dump the *master* system database. As this command changes the contents of system tables, it cannot be executed within a transaction.

If you are the owner of the object, or if your account has **sa_role** privileges, and you want to reenable the use of the Fetch-And-Discard Replacement Strategy for a given text or image object, then log on to the SQL Server as that account which owns the object or as an account with **sa_role** privileges and enter these commands:

```
1>use NameOfDatabase
2>go
1>sp_cachestrategy NameOfDatabase, [NameOfObjectOwner.]Name
   OfTable
2>"text only", mru, "on"
3>go
```

where:

NameOfDatabase—the name of the database that contains the table that contains the text or image object for which you want to reenable the Fetch-And-Discard Replacement Strategy.

NameOfObjectOwner—the name of the Sybase account that owns the table that contains the text or image object for which you want to reenable the Fetch-And-Discard Replacement Strategy. If you are also the owner of the table, then you do not have to specify a value for this parameter.

NameOfTable—the name of the table that contains the text or image object for which you want to reenable the Fetch-And-Discard Replacement Strategy.

This change takes effect immediately. This command changes the *master* system database, so to ensure its recovery, be certain to dump the *master* system database. As this command changes the contents of system tables, it cannot be executed within a transaction.

If you are the owner of the object, or if your account has **sa_role** privileges, and you want to reenable the use of the Fetch-And-Discard Replacement Strategy for a given table, and all indexes, text, and image objects associated with it, then log on to the SQL Server as that account which owns the object or as an account with **sa_role** privileges and enter these commands:

```
1>use NameOfDatabase
2>go
1>sp_cachestrategy NameOfDatabase, [NameOfObjectOwner.]Name
  OfTable
2>mru, "on"
3>go
```

where:

NameOfDatabase—the name of the database that contains the table for which you want to reenable the Fetch-And-Discard Replacement Strategy for itself and for all indexes, text, and image objects associated with it.

NameOfObjectOwner—the name of the Sybase account that owns the table for which you want to reenable the Fetch-And-Discard Replacement Strategy for itself and for all indexes, text, and image objects associated with it. If you are also the owner of the table, then you do not have to specify a value for this parameter.

NameOfTable—the name of the table for which you want to reenable the Fetch-And-Discard Replacement Strategy for itself and for all indexes, text, and image objects associated with it.

This change takes effect immediately. This command changes the *master* system database, so to ensure its recovery, be certain to dump the *master* system database. As this command changes the contents of system tables, it cannot be executed within a transaction.

Reporting on Prefetch on an Object Basis

By default, the use of prefetch (i.e., the use of large Memory Pools) is enabled on all tables, indexes, text, and image objects. However, if you are the SQL Server System Administrator, or if you are the owner of a given table or index, then you can disable and reenable use of the prefetch for that object. If you disable the use of prefetch for an object, then all of its pages are read into data cache using the 2K Memory Pool.

To view the current status of the use of prefetch for a given table, log on to the SQL Server as any valid account and enter these commands:

```
1>use NameOfDatabase
2>go
1>sp_cachestrategy NameOfDatabase, [NameOfObjectOwner.]Name
    OfTable
2>go
```

where:

NameOfDatabase—the name of the database that contains the table whose use of prefetch you want to view.

NameOfObjectOwner—the name of the Sybase account that owns the table whose use of prefetch you want to view. If you are also the owner of the table, then you do not have to specify a value for this parameter.

NameOfTable—the name of the table whose use of prefetch you want to view.

To view the current status of the use of prefetch for a given index, log on to the SQL Server as any valid account and enter these commands:

```
1>use NameOfDatabase
2>go
1>sp_cachestrategy NameOfDatabase, [NameOfObjectOwner.]Name
    OfTable, NameOfIndex
2>go
```

where:

NameOfDatabase—the name of the database that contains the index whose use of prefetch you want to view.

NameOfObjectOwner—the name of the Sybase account that owns the index whose use of prefetch you want to view. If you are also the owner of the index, then you do not have to specify a value for this parameter.

NameOfTable—the name of the table with the index whose use of prefetch you want to view.

NameOfIndex—the name of the index whose use of prefetch you want to view.

Disabling Prefetch on an Object Basis

If you are the owner of the object, or if your account has **sa_role** privileges, and you want to disable the use of prefetch for a given table, then log on to the SQL Server as that account which owns the object, or as an account with **sa_role** privileges and enter these commands:

```
1>use NameOfDatabase
2>go
1>sp_cachestrategy NameOfDatabase, [NameOfObjectOwner.]Name
    OfTable
2>"table only", prefetch, "off"
3>go
```

where:

NameOfDatabase—the name of the database that contains the table for which you want to disable the use of prefetch.

NameOfObjectOwner—the name of the Sybase account that owns the table for which you want to disable the use of prefetch. If you are also the owner of the table, then you do not have to specify a value for this parameter.

NameOfTable—the name of the table for which you want to disable the use of prefetch.

This change takes effect immediately. This command changes the *master* system database, so to ensure its recovery, be certain to dump the *master* system database. As this command changes the contents of system tables, it cannot be executed within a transaction.

If you are the owner of the object, or if your account has **sa_role** privileges, and you want to disable the use of prefetch for a given index, then log on to the SQL Server as that account which owns the object or as an account with **sa_role** privileges and enter these commands:

```
1>use NameOfDatabase
2>go
1>sp_cachestrategy NameOfDatabase, [NameOfObjectOwner.]Name
    OfTable, NameOfIndex
```

```
2>prefetch, "off"
3>go
```

where:

NameOfDatabase—the name of the database that contains the index for which you want to disable the use of prefetch.

NameOfObjectOwner—the name of the Sybase account that owns the index for which you want to disable the use of prefetch. If you are also the owner of the index, then you do not have to specify a value for this parameter.

NameOfTable—the name of the table with the index for which you want to disable the use of prefetch.

NameOfIndex—the name of the index for which you want to disable the use of prefetch.

This change takes effect immediately. This command changes the *master* system database, so to ensure its recovery, be certain to dump the *master* system database. As this command changes the contents of system tables, it cannot be executed within a transaction.

If you are the owner of the object, or if your account has **sa_role** privileges, and you want to disable the use of prefetch for a given text, or image object, then log on to the SQL Server as that account which owns the object or as an account with **sa_role** privileges and enter these commands:

```
1>use NameOfDatabase
2>go
1>sp_cachestrategy NameOfDatabase, [NameOfObjectOwner.]Name
   OfTable
2>"text only", prefetch, "off"
3>go
```

where:

NameOfDatabase—the name of the database that contains the table that contains the text or image object for which you want to disable the use of prefetch.

NameOfObjectOwner—the name of the Sybase account that owns the table that contains the text or image object for which you want to disable the use of prefetch. If you are also the owner of the table, then you do not have to specify a value for this parameter.

NameOfTable—the name of the table that contains the text or image object for which you want to disable the use of prefetch.

This change takes effect immediately. This command changes the *master* system database, so to ensure its recovery, be certain to dump the *master* system database. As this command changes the contents of system tables, it cannot be executed within a transaction.

If you are the owner of the object, or if your account has **sa_role** privileges, and you want to disable the use of prefetch for a given table, and all indexes, text, and image objects associated with it, then log on to the SQL Server as that account which owns the object or as an account with **sa_role** privileges and enter these commands:

```
1>use NameOfDatabase
2>go
1>sp_cachestrategy NameOfDatabase, [NameOfObjectOwner.]Name
   OfTable
2>prefetch, "off"
3>go
```

where:

NameOfDatabase—the name of the database that contains the table for which you want to disable the use of prefetch for itself and for all indexes, text, and image objects associated with it.

NameOfObjectOwner—the name of the Sybase account that owns the table for which you want to disable the use of prefetch for itself and for all indexes, text, and image objects associated with it. If you are also the owner of the table, then you do not have to specify a value for this parameter.

NameOfTable—the name of the table for which you want to disable the use of prefetch for itself and for all indexes, text, and image objects associated with it.

This change takes effect immediately. This command changes the *master* system database, so to ensure its recovery, be certain to dump the *master* system database. As this command changes the contents of system tables, it cannot be executed within a transaction.

Enabling Prefetch on an Object Basis

If you are the owner of the object, or if your account has **sa_role** privileges, and you want to reenable the use of prefetch for a given table, then log on to the SQL Server as that account which owns the object or as an account with **sa_role** privileges and enter these commands:

```
1>use NameOfDatabase
2>go
```

```
1>sp_cachestrategy NameOfDatabase, [NameOfObjectOwner.]Name
  OfTable
2>"table only", prefetch, "on"
3>go
```

where:

NameOfDatabase—the name of the database that contains the table for which you want to reenable the use of prefetch.

NameOfObjectOwner—the name of the Sybase account that owns the table for which you want to reenable the use of prefetch. If you are also the owner of the table, then you do not have to specify a value for this parameter.

NameOfTable—the name of the table for which you want to reenable the use of prefetch.

This change takes effect immediately. This command changes the *master* system database, so to ensure its recovery, be certain to dump the *master* system database. As this command changes the contents of system tables, it cannot be executed within a transaction.

If you are the owner of the object, or if your account has **sa_role** privileges, and you want to reenable the use of prefetch for a given index, then log on to the SQL Server as that account which owns the object or as an account with **sa_role** privileges and enter these commands:

```
1>use NameOfDatabase
2>go
1>sp_cachestrategy NameOfDatabase, [NameOfObjectOwner.]Name
  OfTable, NameOfIndex
2>prefetch, "on"
3>go
```

where:

NameOfDatabase—the name of the database that contains the index for which you want to reenable the use of prefetch.

NameOfObjectOwner—the name of the Sybase account that owns the index for which you want to reenable the use of prefetch. If you are also the owner of the index, then you do not have to specify a value for this parameter.

NameOfTable—the name of the table with the index for which you want to reenable the use of prefetch.

NameOfIndex—the name of the index for which you want to reenable the use of prefetch.

This change takes effect immediately. This command changes the *master* system database, so to ensure its recovery, be certain to dump the *master* system database. As this command changes the contents of system tables, it cannot be executed within a transaction.

If you are the owner of the object, or if your account has **sa_role** privileges, and you want to reenable the use of prefetch for a given text or image object, then log on to the SQL Server as that account which owns the object or as an account with **sa_role** privileges and enter these commands:

```
1>use NameOfDatabase
2>go
1>sp_cachestrategy NameOfDatabase, [NameOfObjectOwner.]Name
   OfTable
2>"text only", prefetch, "on"
3>go
```

where:

NameOfDatabase—the name of the database that contains the table that contains the text or image object for which you want to reenable the use of prefetch.

NameOfObjectOwner—the name of the Sybase account that owns the table that contains the text or image object for which you want to reenable the use of prefetch. If you are also the owner of the table, then you do not have to specify a value for this parameter.

NameOfTable—the name of the table that contains the text or image object for which you want to reenable the use of prefetch.

This change takes effect immediately. This command changes the *master* system database, so to ensure its recovery, be certain to dump the *master* system database. As this command changes the contents of system tables, it cannot be executed within a transaction.

If you are the owner of the object, or if your account has **sa_role** privileges, and you want to reenable the use of prefetch for a given table, and all indexes, text, and image objects associated with it, then log on to the SQL Server as that account which owns the object or as an account with **sa_role** privileges and enter these commands:

```
1>use NameOfDatabase
2>go
1>sp_cachestrategy NameOfDatabase, [NameOfObjectOwner.]Name
   OfTable
2>prefetch, "on"
3>go
```

where:

> *NameOfDatabase*—the name of the database that contains the table for which you want to reenable the use of prefetch for itself and for all indexes, text, and image objects associated with it.
>
> *NameOfObjectOwner*—the name of the Sybase account that owns the table for which you want to reenable the use of prefetch for itself and for all indexes, text, and image objects associated with it. If you are also the owner of the table, then you do not have to specify a value for this parameter.
>
> *NameOfTable*—the name of the table for which you want to reenable the use of prefetch for itself and for all indexes, text, and image objects associated with it.

This change takes effect immediately. This command changes the *master* system database, so to ensure its recovery, be certain to dump the *master* system database. As this command changes the contents of system tables, it cannot be executed within a transaction.

If you are the owner of the object, or if your account has **sa_role** privileges, and you want to reenable the use of prefetch for that table, and all indexes, text, and image objects associated with it, then log on to the SQL Server as that account which owns the object or as an account with **sa_role** privileges and enter these commands:

```
1>use NameOfDatabase
2>go
1>sp_cachestrategy NameOfDatabase, [NameOfObjectOwner.]Name
  OfTable
2>prefetch, "on"
3>go
```

where:

> *NameOfDatabase*—the name of the database that contains the table for which you want to reenable the use of prefetch for itself and for all indexes, text, and image objects associated with it.
>
> *NameOfTable*—the name of the table for which you want to reenable the use of prefetch for itself and for all indexes, text, and image objects associated with it.

This change takes effect immediately. This command changes the *master* system database, so to ensure its recovery, be certain to dump the *master* system database. As this command changes the contents of system tables, it cannot be executed within a transaction.

Disabling and Enabling Prefetch
on a Session Basis

With System 11 SQL Server, you can choose to disable the use of large Memory Pools on a per-user-session basis as well as on a per-object basis, even if the Query Optimizer recommends using, or the Cache Manager wants to use, prefetch capabilities.

To disable prefetch on a per-user-session basis, include this command in Transact-SQL statements you submit to the SQL Server:

```
set prefetch off
```

If prefetch has been turned off for a given session, then it cannot be overridden by using the prefetch option in your subsequent select, update, or delete statements. If prefetch is enabled on for a given object, then you can still disable prefetch for a given session.

If you subsequently want to enable prefetch for that same user session, then include this command in a later portion of the Transact-SQL statements you submit to the SQL Server:

```
set prefetch on
```

If prefetch has been disabled for a specific object, then this command line cannot override that setting.

SQL Server Kernel Configuration
for the Cache Manager

The System 11 SQL Server provides for parameters for use in configuring the Cache Manager:

1. memory alignment boundary
2. total data cache size
3. number of index trips
4. number of oam trip

The memory alignment boundary SQL Server configuration parameter establishes the boundary on which Data Caches are aligned. The default value of the memory alignment boundary SQL Server configuration parameter is 2048. The maximum allowable stack size is 16,384. Whatever value you set the memory alignment boundary SQL Server configuration parameter to, that value must always be an even multiple of 2048.

To determine the current value of the memory alignment boundary SQL Server configuration parameter, log on to the SQL Server as any Sybase account and enter these commands:

```
1>use master
2>go
1>sp_configure "memory alignment boundary"
2>go
```

Unlike the other SQL Server memory configuration parameters we will explore, the SQL Server configuration parameter is included solely for the support of specific hardware platforms. As such, it is strongly recommended that it not be modified by the product consumer without assistance from the Sybase Technical Support organization.

The total data cache size SQL Server configuration parameter designates the quantity of memory resource that is available for data, index, and transaction log pages.

To determine the current value of the total data cache size SQL Server configuration parameter, log on to the SQL Server, as any Sybase account, and enter these commands:

```
1>use master
2>go
1>sp_configure "total data cache size"
2>go
```

The value of this SQL Server configuration parameter is internally calculated, and is not, therefore, directly set by the consumer. However, an account with **sa_role** privileges significantly influences the value of the total data cache size SQL Server configuration parameter indirectly. As we were shown previously, at boot time, the SQL Server will parcel out memory resources to:

1. The SQL Server Executable Code.

2. Static Memory allocated to the SQL Server Kernel.

3. Nondata Cache Data Structures used by the SQL Server Kernel.

4. Some miscellaneous SQL Server overhead (around 5 percent of the value of the run_value configuration parameter).

The remaining memory resources are allocated to cache (which in turn is broken out into Data Cache and Procedure Cache). An account with **sa_role** privileges indirectly influences the value of the total data cache size SQL Server configuration parameter through its handling of these system factors:

1. The quantity of memory provided to the SQL Server by the underlying operating system and hardware platform.

2. The values to which an account with **sa_role** privileges sets these SQL Server configuration parameters:

   —total memory

   —number of user connections

   —default network packet size

   —stack size

   —number of open databases

   —number of devices

   —number of open database objects

   —number of extent i/o buffers

   —number of locks

   —procedure cache percent

The number of index trips SQL Server configuration parameter represents the number of times an aged index page moves along the MRU/LRU queue before the Cache Manager designates it as a candidate for swapping out to disk.

To determine the current value of the number of index trips SQL Server configuration parameter, log on to the SQL Server as any Sybase account and enter these commands:

```
1>use master
2>go
1>sp_configure "number of index trips"
2>go
```

The default value of the number of index trips SQL Server configuration parameter is zero. The maximum allowable value of the number of index trips SQL Server configuration parameter is 65,535.

When the value of the number of index trips SQL Server configuration parameter is increased, the longer the period of time the index pages will stay in Data Cache. Conversely, when this configuration parameter is decreased, the shorter the period of time the index pages will stay in Data Cache.

To set the value of the number of index trips SQL Server configuration parameter to 5, log on to the SQL Server, as an account with **sa_role** privileges, and enter these commands:

```
1>use master
2>go
```

```
1>sp_configure "number of index trips", 5
3>go
```

As the number of index trips SQL Server configuration parameter is dynamic, the new value will take effect immediately. This command changes the *master* system database, so to ensure its recovery, be certain to dump the *master* system database itself. This command changes the contents of system tables, so it cannot be entered in a transaction.

For SQL Servers that support high-volume transactions, there is a high probability that index pages will be needed again and again. In these cases, keeping aged index pages in Data Cache for a longer period of time can increase performance. However, a balance must be reached between the size of the index and its duration within Data Cache.

If a small Data Cache is shared by multiple database objects and the transaction volume is high, then problems can arise when the value of the number of index trips SQL Server configuration parameter is set too high. When all of these preceding conditions are present, then the Data Cache will be saturated with aged index pages, and user processes will have to wait extended periods of time for Data Cache space to become available. If the wait period is too long, then the user processes will time-out.

The number of oam trip SQL Server configuration parameter represents the number of times an aged object allocation map (OAM) page moves along the MRU/LRU queue before the Cache Manager designates it as a candidate for swapping out to disk.

To determine the current value of the number of oam trip SQL Server configuration parameter, log on to the SQL Server as any Sybase account and enter these commands:

```
1>use master
2>go
1>sp_configure "number of oam trip"
2>go
```

The default value of the number of oam trip SQL Server configuration parameter is zero. The maximum allowable value of the number of oam trip SQL Server configuration parameter is 65,535.

When the value of the number of oam trip SQL Server configuration parameter is increased, the longer the period of time the OAM pages will stay in Data Cache. Conversely, when this configuration parameter is decreased, the shorter the period of time the OAM pages will stay in Data Cache.

As explained in the previous chapter, every table and index has an OAM page. The OAM page stores the identity of the allocation page of each allocation unit in which the table or the index is assigned space. It is the function of the allocation page to store the information about the table's or the index's extent and page utilization within that allocation unit.

An OAM page is capable of storing information on the mapping for between 2000 to 63,750 pages related to a given table or index. Whenever a new page needs to be created for a table or an index, the SQL Servers manipulate the corresponding OAM page. In processes involving a lot of OAM page manipulation, such as during **bcp** runs or index creation for example, significant performance improvements can be realized by increasing the value of the `number of oam trip` SQL Server configuration parameter.

To set the value of the `number of oam trip` SQL Server configuration parameter to two, log on to the SQL Server as an account with **sa_role** privileges and enter these commands:

```
1>use master
2>go
1>sp_configure "number of oam trip", 2
3>go
```

As the `number of oam trip` SQL Server configuration parameter is dynamic, the new value will take effect immediately. This command changes the *master* system database, so to ensure its recovery, be certain to dump the *master* system database itself. This command changes the contents of system tables, so it cannot be entered in a transaction.

The HouseKeeper

When a data, index, or transaction log page, residing in mixed data cache, is modified, its image is at variance with the image of that page residing on disk. Such a page is called a dirty page, and is, by the SQL Server's Cache Manager, automatically marked as such.

The HouseKeeper is an internal System 11 SQL Server function that washes Buffers contained within data caches (of type "mixed only" as the HouseKeeper does not do any Buffer washing in data caches of type "log only"), that is, it writes dirty pages to disk during idle CPU cycles. Here's how it works:

1. The HouseKeeper thread is set at the lowest process priority, that is, it is one level below a user process. Setting it at this level ensures that it will run if and only if, there are no other tasks for the SQL

Server to undertake. It waits for a SQL Server idle CPU cycle. If there are no idle SQL Server CPU cycles, then the HouseKeeper does not run. However, when an idle SQL Server CPU cycle becomes available, the process priority of the HouseKeeper is raised to that of a user process, and it is then run.

2. Just as soon as it starts to run, it searches the MRU/LRU Chain for dirty buffer pages.

3. It starts from the Wash Marker and advances up the MRU. As it advances up the MRU, is cleans one buffer page at a time, but it flushes batches of buffers to avert flooding the system with disk I/O writes.

4. If the SQL Server has enough idle time for the HouseKeeper thread to search and reach the MRU end of the queue (all active buffer pools in all configured caches) then a free checkpoint is taken in all databases, and all dirty pages are written out to disk.

SQL Server Kernel Configuration for the HouseKeeper

System 11 provides a single SQL Server parameter by which to tune the Housekeeper: `housekeeper free write percent`. The purpose of the `housekeeper free write percent` SQL Server configuration parameter is to constrain the activity of the HouseKeeper so that it does not write dirty pages unnecessarily. This configuration parameter limits the ability of the HouseKeeper process to take advantage of the additional free writes the HouseKeeper process initiates.

Placing constraints on normal HouseKeeper behavior is beneficial in processing situations where pages are repeatedly updated. In such situations, normal HouseKeeper behavior would generate additional disk I/O overhead by moving dirty pages out of Data Cache too soon, only to have them immediately copied back into Data Cache because they need to be updated once again.

To determine the current value of the `housekeeper free write percent` SQL Server configuration parameter, log on to the SQL Server as any Sybase account and enter these commands:

```
1>use master
2>go
1>sp_configure "housekeeper free write percent"
2>go
```

The default value of the `housekeeper free write percent` SQL Server configuration parameter is 20. The value of the `housekeeper` free write percent SQL Server configuration parameter is a number between 0 and 100. The value of the housekeeper free write percent SQL Server configuration parameter allows the HouseKeeper to use a specific number of additional free writes. The formula for determining the value at which to set the housekeeper free write percent SQL Server configuration parameter is as follows:

$$\text{(actual number of writes} - \text{possible number of writes)} / \text{possible number of writes}$$

To limit the HouseKeeper to using only half of the additional free writes, set the value of the housekeeper free write percent SQL Server configuration parameter to 50 by logging on to the SQL Server as an account with **sa_role** privileges and enter these commands:

```
1>use master
2>go
1>sp_configure "housekeeper free write percent", 50
2>go
```

As the housekeeper free write percent SQL Server configuration parameter is dynamic, the new value will take effect in the SQL Server immediately. This command changes the *master* system database, so to ensure its recovery, be certain to dump the *master* system database itself. This command changes the contents of system tables, so it cannot be entered in a transaction.

To disable the HouseKeeper, set the value of the housekeeper free write percent SQL Server configuration parameter to 0 by logging on to the SQL Server as an account with **sa_role** privileges and enter these commands:

```
1>use master
2>go
1>sp_configure "housekeeper free write percent", 0
2>go
```

An unanticipated side effect of setting the value of the housekeeper free write percent SQL Server configuration parameter to zero is the checkpoints will take place less frequently, and as a consequence, the time it takes to recover any database will be increased. This command changes the *master* system database, so to ensure its recovery, be certain to dump the *master* system database itself. This command changes the contents of system tables, so it cannot be entered in a transaction.

The Relationship between Procedure Cache and Data Cache

After the SQL Server Executable takes its share of memory, and after the (optional) Audit Queue is configured, the remaining memory is allocated to the Cache. From this Cache space, Procedure Cache and Data Cache are apportioned according to the value that has been set for the `procedure cache percent` configuration parameter.

Procedure Cache

The Cache Manager uses an MRU/LRU Chain within the Procedure Cache to store active, compiled objects (using at least one buffer per object), for example, rules, defaults, views, check constraints, triggers, stored procedures, active query plans, and query trees:

Rules—constrain the literal data values that can be entered into a particular table's column, or into table columns of a specific user-defined data type.

Defaults—specify the default literal data value of a particular table column.

Check Constraints—limit the literal data values that can be inserted into a table column. They define the search condition which any literal data value must satisfy before it is permitted by the SQL Server to be inserted into a table column.

View—is a "virtual" table whose definition is usually founded upon a subset of columns in one, or more, underlying tables (or other views). The literal definition of a view is stored within the system catalogs of the database in which it is created. However, each time the view is invoked by a user connection it must be "resolved." *View resolution* is the process of validating the existence and accuracy of the definition of the underlying columns and tables (or other views), of converting table names into their object IDs and column names into their column IDs, and then translating the query of the view into a query on the underlying tables. FYI—view resolution is a significant performance overhead.

Stored Procedures—is a compiled assortment of Transact-SQL statements saved within the SQL Server under an identifier, a name. In addition to the collection of SQL Server supplied, stored procedures (called *system procedures*), authorized Sybase accounts can create stored procedures within user databases. When a stored procedure is created, the ASCII text of the procedure is inserted into the database's *syscomments* system table. The stored procedure's Query tree is inserted into the database's *sysprocedures* system table.

Trigger—is a special type of stored procedure, bound to a specific table, that executes when a user process causes a change in the contents of the table, such as when data is inserted, deleted, or updated.

Query Tree—is an internal "normalized" representation of a Transact-SQL statement, stored procedure, view, trigger, rule, or default. Query trees are stored within the database's *sysprocedures* system table. When a compiled object (stored procedure, view, trigger, rule, or default) is executed, its Query tree is read from disk and brought into Procedure Cache. Query trees are constructed through a process called *resolution*. Query resolution is the process of validating the existence and accuracy of the definition of the related columns and tables (or views), converting table names and column names into their column IDs, and then transforming the query into an internal representation. A Query tree is built whenever a Transact-SQL statement executes (keep this fact in mind if your application uses ad hoc queries or submits Transact-SQL statements), or whenever a compiled object is first created (keep this fact in mind if your application periodically recreates stored procedures).

Query Plan—is an optimized series of steps requisite to executing a query, including the specific methods chosen by the SQL Server for access to each table within the query tree. The process of constructing a query plan is called *compilation*. A query plan is built when a Transact-SQL statement executes, or whenever a stored procedure (or trigger) is first executed. When a stored procedure executes, the SQL Server reads its query tree from the *sysprocedures* system table and places it within Procedure Cache. Next, the SQL Server creates a query plan and places it in Procedure Cache as well. The SQL Server uses the following information to construct the query plan: the query tree, the statistics corresponding to each table and index referenced within the procedure, and the literal data values of the parameters passed to the procedure when it is first executed. It is important to realize that query plans are held only in the Procedure Cache during run time and are not written out to permanent storage. As a consequence, a stored procedure's query plan must be rebuilt if the SQL Server has been rebooted since the procedure was last executed.

When a user process invokes a stored procedure, or trigger, the SQL Server scans the Procedure Cache MRU/LRU Chain for its corresponding query plan. If the query plan is located, it is automatically placed on the MRU end of the chain, and the execution of the stored procedure, or trigger, is initiated.

If, after scanning the Procedure Cache's MRU/LRU Chain, the SQL Server determines that the invoked stored procedure's query plan is not in memory, then its corresponding query tree is read from the *sysprocedures* system table, and brought into the Procedure Cache. After the supporting query tree reaches Procedure Cache, the SQL Server, using the literal data values passed in the procedure's parameters, compiles the required query plan. The query plan is then placed on the MRU end of the chain, and execution of the procedure starts.

If more than one active user process invokes the same stored procedure, or trigger, then multiple copies of the stored procedure, or trigger, will be brought into the Procedure Cache.

While procedures are reusable, only one user can run a single copy of procedure's query plan at a time (i.e., they are not reentrant). When more than one user connection tries to run the same procedure at the same point in time, the SQL Server will create supplementary query plans (based upon the literal data values of the parameters provided by each user connection). However, once a user connection is finished using a given query plan, that query plan becomes available for reuse by any other user connection.

Plans and compiled objects that migrate to the LRU end of the MRU/LRU Chain, that are not in use, are aged out of the Procedure Cache.

SQL Server Kernel Configuration for Procedure Cache

The SQL Server provides a single parameter by which to configure the Procedure Cache: `procedure cache percent`. The purpose of the `procedure cache percent` SQL Server configuration parameter is to establish the percentage of available cache that will be allocated to the Procedure Cache (with the remainder going to the Data Cache).

To determine the current value of the `procedure cache percent` SQL Server configuration parameter, log on to the SQL Server as any Sybase account and enter these commands:

```
1>use master
2>go
1>sp_configure "procedure cache percent"
2>go
```

The default value of the `procedure cache percent` SQL Server configuration parameter is 20. The value of the `procedure cache percent` SQL Server configuration parameter is a number between 1 and 99.

Establishing the proper value for the `procedure cache percent` SQL Server configuration parameter is, under the best of situations, an empirical process. However, more often then not, the process is one of trial and error. A good place to start is to get an idea of the minimum Procedure Cache size. The minimum Procedure Cache size would allow at least one copy of each frequently used compiled object to reside simultaneously in the Procedure Cache. To establish the minimum value of the `procedure cache percent` SQL Server configuration parameter, follow these steps:

1. Determine the total count of all compiled objects supported by the SQL Server. Count just the stored procedures, views, and triggers.

2. Determine the size of each compiled object. To obtain that information, log on to the SQL Server as any Sybase account and enter this command:

```
select(count(*)/8) +1 from sysprocedures where id =
    object_id("NameOfObject")
```

the displayed results indicate the size of the object as its total count of 2K pages.

4. Determine the average size of the objects.

5. Increase the minimum size by another 10 percent to play it safe, since the minimum size of the Procedure Cache will equal the total count of compiled objects times the average compiled object size.

Alternatively, you could determine the proper value for the `procedure cache percent` SQL Server configuration parameter by using this formula:

$$\text{Procedure Cache size} = (\text{maximum number of concurrent users}) * (\text{size of largest compiled object}) * 1.25$$

Using either of the preceding formulas, the value of the `procedure cache percent` SQL Server configuration parameter would then be:

`procedure cache percent` = Procedure Cache size / available cache

Data Cache

The SQL Server uses the Data Cache to store data, index, and transaction log pages in memory. Perhaps the most significant improvement of the SQL Server by System 11 has been in the area of the Data Cache and its management. Unlike its predecessors, with System 11 you have support for the following facilities and capabilities:

1. Default Data Cache.

2. Named Data Cache(s).

3. Mixed Cache(s).

4. Memory Pools.

5. Configuration of disk I/O (2K, 4K, 8K, or 16K) on a per Memory Pool basis.

6. The ability to bind databases, and principal data objects to specific Data Caches.

7. A variety of powerful caching strategies.

With these new capabilities, you can realize significant performance improvements by binding to Data Caches such things as:

Constantly used tables, and their indexes.

The *tempdb* system database.

Highly active database transaction logs.

Text or image page chains.

The `master..sysindexes` system table and its own index.

The database system tables *sysobjects, syscolumns,* and *sysprotects.*

At boot time, as we have seen, after all mandatory memory resource requirements are satisfied, all remaining memory resources are assigned to Data Cache. When the SQL Server is installed it contains only the Default Data Cache. All Data Cache needs are supported by this sole Default Data Cache. It is up to the consumer to create any additional Named Data Caches, and to bind any database objects specifically to them.

Memory Pools

A Memory Pool (also referred to as a Buffer Pool) is a circular-linked list of Buffers. Memory Pools come in just four sizes: 2K, 4K, 8K, and 16K. Every Data Cache, whether it is the Default Data Cache or a user-created Named Data Cache, always contains one (default) mandatory 2K Memory Pool.

The creation of 4K, 8K, and 16K Memory Pools is done at the consumer's discretion. But, there is a maximum of only four Memory Pools per Data Cache that can be created by the consumer. Furthermore, in a given Data Cache, you cannot create two Memory Pools of the same size. That is, a Data Cache can contain one and only one 2K Memory Pool, can contain one and only one 4K Memory Pool, and so on.

The Data Cache's mandatory 2K Memory Pool is used to support internal SQL Server utilities and specific Transact-SQL commands that perform their own extent disk I/O and Buffer management, outside of the Cache Manager. These are the SQL Server and Transact-SQL commands that require a 2K Memory Pool to accomplish their tasks:

1. `create database`
2. `alter database`
3. `create index`
4. `drop table`
5. `disk init`
6. **dbcc** commands (all of which perform large quantities of disk I/O)

When it comes to the execution of **dbcc** commands and memory resources usage, there are a number of important factors to understand:

1. If you have set the value of the `number of extent i/o buffers` SQL Server configuration parameter to zero, and if you have not configured any Named Data Caches, then all **dbcc** commands will use 2K Memory Pool within the Default Data Cache.

2. If you have set the value of the `number of extent i/o buffers` SQL Server configuration parameter to one or greater, and if the extent I/O 8K Work Buffers are not already supporting another command, then the executing **dbcc** `checkalloc` and **dbcc** `tablealloc` commands will use those 8K Work Buffers.

3. If you have configured a Named Data Cache with a 16K Memory Pool, and you have bound one or more tables to that Named Data Cache, then when you execute a **dbcc** `checkdb` or **dbcc** `checktable` command, it will use the 16K Memory Pool.

4. If you have configured a Named Data Cache with a 16K Memory Pool, and you have bound one or more tables to that Named Data Cache, then when you execute a **dbcc** `checktable` command, it will use only the Named Data Cache's 2K Memory Pool when examining indexes.

As regards internal SQL Server utilities' usage of 2K Memory Pools, it is important to understand the following facts:

1. Unless the Default Data Cache is configured with a 4K Memory Pool, the SQL Server will use the Default Data Cache's 2K Memory Pool to support unbound transaction logs.

2. Unless a Named Data Cache to which a transaction log is bound is configured with a 4K Memory Pool, the SQL Server will use the

Named Data Cache's 2K Memory Pool to support the bound transaction log.

3. When a database is being recovered, the SQL Server uses a 2K Memory Pool. As a consequence, during database recovery all transaction log pages are read into, and transactions are rolled backward and forward within, the 2K Memory Pool. If the database has been bound to a Named Data Cache, then the 2K Memory Pool within the Named Data Cache is used to support the recovery of the database. If, alternatively, the database has not been bound to a Named Data Cache, then the 2K Memory Pool within the Default Data Cache is used to support the recovery of the unbound databases.

4. When the SQL Server starts up, the 2K Memory Pool within the Default Data Cache is used to recover all databases, regardless of whether a given database has been bound to a Named Data Cache or not.

At present, the largest Memory Pool you can create is just 16K in size (i.e., a single extent). This limitation exists because the SQL Server Page Manager (that brings pages off of disk and returns them to the Cache Manager) is not capable of guaranteeing that extents adjacent to one another on disk are actually being used by the same database object (i.e., table, index, etc.). However, when the SQL Server uses a 16K Memory Pool, an extent (containing eight pages) is read into Data Cache in a single disk read, thereby eliminating the majority of the disk I/O time related to disk-head positioning and individual-page seeking. The eight pages in the extent are managed as a single disk I/O unit within the Cache Manager. As such, the Cache Manager will age all pages in the extent in the same manner, and will write all eight pages to disk at the same point in time.

For queries and Transact-SQL commands that access pages sequentially, 16K Memory Pools can provide significant performance gains when the pages themselves have been physically stored in a sequential order. If you are using these Transact-SQL commands heavily:

dbcc checkdb

dbcc checktable

update statistics

bcp in, and out, on heap structures

or, if the SQL Server is supporting queries that:

1. Allocate several pages, such as select into

2. Traverse the leaf levels of nonclustered indexes

3. Involve table scans of either single tables, or join queries (particularly in those cases where the join query repeatedly rereads the inner table)

4. Manipulate text or image data types

the deployment 16K Memory Pools is highly recommended.

For a given Data Cache, you can view the Memory Pools it contains by logging on to the SQL Server as any valid Sybase account and entering the command:

```
1>use master
2>go
1>sp_poolconfig NameOfDataCache
2>go
```

where:

NameOfDataCache—the name of the existing Data Cache whose Memory Pools you want to examine.

Memory Pool Wash Area

Every Memory Pool contains a Wash Area. The portion of the MRU/LRU Chain, between the Buffer Wash Marker and the end of the LRU Chain is referred to as the Wash Area. The default size of the Wash Area is 256 Buffers, unless, that is, the Memory Pool itself has fewer than 512 Buffers. When the Memory Pool has fewer that 512 Buffers, the default size of the Wash Area is 20 percent of the Buffers contained in the Memory Pool. As will be demonstrated later in this chapter, an account with **sa_role** privileges can set the size of the Wash Area. The minimum setting of the Wash Area is ten Buffers, and the maximum setting of the Wash Area is 80 percent of the size of the Memory Pool.

Pages within the Wash Area are either clean or are in the process of being asynchronously written to disk by the Cache Manager. Once written to disk, the Buffer is designated as being clean. In that the Cache Manager places new pages at the end of the LRU Chain, the Wash Area must be sized such that pages are written to disk before they reach the end of the LRU Chain. If the Wash Area is too small, then the SQL Server will have to wait for clean buffers, and as a consequence, performance will noticeably degrade.

Creating a Memory Pool

As has been stated, the Default Data Cache and all Named Data Caches will always contain a mandatory, and default, 2K Memory Pool.

With System 11, the potential now exists for an account with **sa_role** privileges to create a 4K, an 8K, and a 16K Memory Pool within every existing Data Cache.

If the only Memory Pool that exists in a Data Cache is the mandatory and default 2K, then the SQL Server will perform disk I/O in 2K units, a single page at a time, for all database objects bound to the Data Cache. By creating 4K, 8K, or 16K Memory Pools, you can significantly enhance SQL Server performance by taking advantage of the relatively larger 4K, 8K, and 16K disk I/O units.

Your decision to apportion a Data Cache into multiple Memory Pools must be based upon a solid understanding of the queries the Data Cache will support, and upon the behavior of the application that it supports. With that knowledge in hand, create a 4K, 8K, or 16K Memory Pool in an existing Data Cache by logging on to the SQL Server as an account with **sa_role** privileges, and enter these commands:

```
1>use master
2>go
1>sp_poolconfig NameOfDataCache, "MemoryPoolSize [P|K|M|G]",
2>"ConfiguredMemoryPoolK",
3>["AffectedMemoryPoolK"]
4>go
```

where:

NameOfDataCache—the name of the existing Data Cache in which you want to create the new Memory Pool.

MemoryPoolSize—this parameter specifies the size of new Memory Pool you are creating. The size of the new Memory Pool can be specified in four units of measurement: P for pages; K for kilobytes; M for megabytes, and G for gigabytes. The default unit of measurement is kilobytes. The default size of a Memory Pool is 512K. The minimum size of a Memory Pool is 512K.

ConfiguredMemoryPoolK—this parameter is used to specify the Buffer disk I/O unit. When creating a Memory Pool, the legal values are 4K, 8K, and 16K. When creating a new Memory Pool, there is no default Buffer disk I/O unit. You must select an appropriate Buffer disk I/O unit. In that all Data Caches automatically contain a mandatory 2K Memory Pool, 2K is not a legal value to be used for this parameter when creating a Memory Pool. The combination of *NameOfDataCache* and *ConfiguredMemoryPoolK*—uniquely identifies this Memory Pool. Remember, for a given Data Cache, there can be only one mandatory 2K Memory Pool, only one optional 4K Memory Pool, only one optional 8K Memory Pool, and only one optional 16K Memory Pool.

AffectedMemoryPoolK—this optional parameter specifies the existing Memory Pool from which memory resources will be deallocated. This deallocated memory resource will be reallocated to the new Memory Pool you are creating. If you do not pass this optional parameter to this command, then, by default, memory resources will be deallocated from the Data Cache's 2K Memory Pool. If, however, within the referenced Data Cache, a 4K, an 8K, or a 16K Memory Pool already exists, then you can deallocate memory resources from one of them if you so choose. Remember, you cannot decrease the mandatory 2K Memory Pool Size below 512K.

This command changes the *master* system database, so to ensure its recovery, be certain to dump the *master* system database itself. This command changes the contents of system tables, so it cannot be entered in a transaction.

Here are a number of important facts to consider prior to executing the sp_poolconfig command:

1. You create new Memory Pools while the SQL Server is running, the new Memory Pools take effect immediately. You do not have to restart the SQL Server after the successful completion of the sp_poolconfig command to ensure that the new Memory Pool is in place.

2. The SQL Server can support only one active sp_poolconfig command on a given Data Cache at a time. As a consequence, if you issue a second sp_poolconfig command before the first command completes executing, then the SQL Server will put the second instance of the sp_poolconfig command to sleep until such point in time as the first instance of the sp_poolconfig command completes executing.

3. In that the creation of a Memory Pool involves the deallocation and reallocation of memory resources, the act of creating Memory Pools can definitely have adverse effects on the run time performance of a SQL Server that supports a production system. Therefore, it is advisable to create Memory Pools during off-peak production hours.

4. When you create a Memory Pool, the SQL Server will attempt to allocate all requested memory resources for the new Memory Pool. If this is not possible, then it will allocate as much memory resource as it can. As a consequence, you must not assume that the planned deallocation and reallocation of memory resources actually proceeded in the manner you expected. Therefore, be certain to read the informational message the SQL Server displays after the

`sp_poolconfig` command completes executing. That message will tell you the requested Memory Pool size as well as the actual size of the newly created Memory Pool. Be clear about this: you do not want to be robbing Peter to pay Paul.

5. When the SQL Server is restarted after the successful completion of an `sp_poolconfig` command, all newly created Memory Pools are materialized in accordance with their configured size.

6. In the process of deallocating and reallocating memory resources to support the execution of the `sp_poolconfig` command, the SQL Server can only allocate free Buffers. The SQL Server must wait until sufficient quantities of Buffers are not in use or not dirty (i.e., that contain changes that have not yet been written to disk) to complete the memory resource allocation process.

7. The process of allocating free Buffers from an existing Memory Pool to the new Memory Pool does involve some overhead. As such, SQL Server performance can degrade during the free Buffer allocation phase.

8. When a Memory Pool is created within a Data Cache to which compiled objects have been bound, the compiled objects will be recompiled the next time they are executed.

9. When a Memory Pool is created within a Data Cache to which a database has been bound, all compiled objects contained within that bound database will be recompiled the next time they are executed.

10. You should consider creating a 4K Memory Pool within the Default Data Cache. This Memory Pool will be used by all transaction logs whose databases have not been bound to a mixed-type Named Data Cache, and will be used by transaction logs that have not individually been bound to a logonly-type Named Data Cache.

11. Be certain to monitor and study the behavior of the newly created Memory Pool to confirm that its utilization and its Buffers' disk I/O units are appropriate for the application it is supporting.

Also, when deallocating memory resources from any 2K Memory Pool, keep in mind that the affected 2K Memory Pool must remain large enough to support:

1. Database recovery.

2. Any transaction log that may use it.

3. The execution of `alter database`, `create database`, `create index`, dbcc's `disk init`, and `drop table` commands.

Modifying the Size of a Memory Pool

The amount of memory resources allocated to a given Memory Pool can be altered after its creation. To modify the memory resources allocated to a 2K, a 4K, an 8K, or a 16K Memory Pool, log on to the SQL Server as an account with **sa_role** privileges and enter these commands:

```
1>use master
2>go
1>sp_poolconfig NameOfDataCache, "MemoryPoolSize [P|K|M|G]",
2>"ConfiguredMemoryPoolK",
3>["AffectedMemoryPoolK"]
4>go
```

where:

NameOfDataCache—the name of the existing Data Cache that contains the Memory Pool you want to modify.

MemoryPoolSize—this parameter specifies the new size of the Memory Pool you are modifying. The size of the new Memory Pool can be specified in four units of measurement: P for pages, K for kilobytes, M for megabytes, and G for gigabytes. The default unit of measurement is kilobytes. The minimum size of a Memory Pool is 512K (unless, that is, you plan to drop a 4K, an 8K, or a 16K Memory Pool).

ConfiguredMemoryPoolK—this parameter is used to specify the Buffer disk I/O unit of the Memory Pool you are modifying. The legal values are 4K, 8K, and 16K. You do not configure the 2K Memory Pool, as its size is the balance of memory resources not already allocated to any 4K, 8K, or 16K Memory Pool contained within the referenced Data Cache. The combination of *NameOfDataCache* and *ConfiguredMemoryPoolK* uniquely identifies this Memory Pool.

[*AffectedMemoryPoolK*]—this optional parameter specifies the existing Memory Pool from which memory resources will be deallocated. This deallocated memory resource will be reallocated to the new Memory Pool you are creating. If you do not pass this optional parameter to this command, then, by default, memory resources will be deallocated from the Data Cache's 2K Memory Pool. If, however, within the referenced Data Cache, a 4K, an 8K, or a 16K Memory Pool already exists, then you can deallocate memory resources from one of them if you so choose. Remember, you cannot decrease the mandatory 2K Memory Pool Size below 512K.

This command changes the *master* system database, so to ensure its recovery, be certain to dump the *master* system database itself. This command changes the contents of system tables, so it cannot be entered in a transaction.

Here are a number of important facts to consider prior to modifying a Memory Pool:

1. You modify Memory Pools while the SQL Server is running. The changes to the referenced Memory Pools take effect immediately. You do not have to restart the SQL Server after the successful completion of the `sp_poolconfig` command to ensure that the modified Memory Pools are in place.

2. The SQL Server can support only one active `sp_poolconfig` command at a time on a given Data Cache. As a consequence, if you issue a second `sp_poolconfig` command before the first command completes executing, then the SQL Server will put the second instance of the `sp_poolconfig` command to sleep until such point in time as the first instance of the `sp_poolconfig` command completes executing.

3. In that the modification of Memory Pools involves the deallocation and reallocation of memory resources, the act of modifying Memory Pools can definitely have adverse effects on the run-time performance of a SQL Server that supports a production system. Therefore, it is advisable to modify Memory Pools during off-peak production hours.

4. When you modify a Memory Pool, the SQL Server will attempt to allocate all requested memory resources for the Memory Pool. If this is not possible, then it will allocate as much memory resource as it can. As a consequence, you must not assume that the planned deallocation and reallocation of memory resources actually proceeded in the manner you expected. Therefore, be certain to read the informational message the SQL Server displays after the `sp_poolconfig` command completes executing. That message will tell you the requested Memory Pool size as well as the actual size of the modified Memory Pools. Be clear about this: you do not want to be robbing Peter to pay Paul.

5. When the SQL Server is restarted after the successful completion of an `sp_poolconfig` command, all modified Memory Pools are materialized in accordance with their configured sizes.

6. In the process of deallocating and reallocating memory resources to support the execution of the `sp_poolconfig` command, the SQL Server can only allocate free Buffers. The SQL Server must wait until sufficient quantities of Buffers are not in use or not dirty (i.e., that contain changes that have not yet been written to disk) to complete the memory resource allocation process.

7. The process of allocating free Buffers from an existing Memory Pool to and from the modified Memory Pools does involve some overhead. As such, SQL Server performance can degrade during the free Buffer allocation phase.

8. When a Memory Pool is modified within a Data Cache to which compiled objects have been bound, the compiled objects will be recompiled the next time they are executed.

9. When a Memory Pool is modified within a Data Cache to which a database has been bound, all compiled objects contained within that bound database will be recompiled the next time they are executed.

10. Be certain to monitor and study the behavior of the modified Memory Pool to confirm that their utilization and their Buffers' disk I/O units are appropriate for the application it is supporting.

11. When configuring a Memory Pool for use by a transaction log, you should size the Memory Pool to increase the number of times that active processes reread log pages from memory versus from disk. Also, the Buffer Mass of the Memory Pool should be configured to match the Buffer Mass of the transaction log. By default, the Buffer Mass size of a transaction log is 4K, so the Buffer Mass of the Memory Pool should also be 4K. However, is there is no 4K Memory Pool in the data cache, then the SQL Server will use the 2K Memory Pool to support the transaction log.

Also, when deallocating memory resources from any 2K Memory Pool, keep in mind that the affected 2K Memory Pool must remain large enough to support:

1. Database recovery.

2. Any transaction log that may use it.

3. The execution of `alter database`, `create database`, `create index`, dbcc's, `disk init` and `drop table` commands.

Modifying a Memory Pool Wash Area

The Wash Area of every Memory Pool is configurable. Normally, the default size of the Wash Area is appropriate. However, you may need to adjust a Memory Pool Wash Area in large Data Caches that support very high rates of data modification, such as is typically the case with *on-line transaction processing* (OLTP) applications. In these types of situations, it is worth investigating whether a Memory Pool Wash Area that is 1 to 2 percent of the Memory Pool size is beneficial to SQL Server performance or not.

To modify the size of a Memory Pool Wash Area, log on to the SQL Server as an account with **sa_role** privileges and enter these commands:

```
1>use master
2>go
1>sp_poolconfig NameOfDataCache, "BufferDiskI/OUnit",
2>"wash=size[P|K|M|G]"
3>go
```

where:

NameOfDataCache—the name of the existing Data Cache in which you want to create the new Memory Pool.

BufferDiskI/OUnit—this parameter is used to specify the Memory Pool whose Wash Area is to be modified. The Memory Pool is identified according to the Buffer disk I/O unit it supports. The legal values to be used for this parameter are `"2K,"` `"4K,"` `"8K,"` and `"16K."`

`wash=`*size*`[P|K|M|G]`—this parameter specifies the new size of the Memory Pool Wash Area in units of pages, kilobytes, megabytes, or gigabytes. For example, when this parameter is defined in this manner, `wash=1024K`, a Memory Pool Wash Area will be set to 1024K. The minimum number of Buffers in the Wash Area is 10 Buffer disk I/O units, for example, if the Memory Pool supports 4K disk I/O units, then the minimum size its Memory Pool Wash Area can be is 20 pages. The maximum size a Memory Pool Wash Area can be is 80 percent of the Memory Pool size.

This command changes the *master* system database, so to ensure its recovery, be certain to dump the *master* system database itself. This command changes the contents of system tables, so it cannot be entered in a transaction.

Here are a number of important facts to consider prior to modifying a Memory Pool Wash Area:

1. You modify a Memory Pool Wash Area while the SQL Server is running. The changes to the referenced Memory Pools Wash Area take effect immediately. You do not have to restart the SQL Server after the successful completion of the `sp_poolconfig` command to ensure that the modified Memory Pool Wash Area is in place.

2. The SQL Server can support only one active `sp_poolconfig` command on a given Data Cache at a time. As a consequence, if you issue a second `sp_poolconfig` command before the first command completes executing, then the SQL Server will put the second

instance of the `sp_poolconfig` command to sleep until such point in time as the first instance of the `sp_poolconfig` command completes executing.

3. The act of modifying a Memory Pool Wash Area can definitely have adverse effects on the run-time performance of a SQL Server that supports a production system. Therefore, it is advisable to modify Memory Pool Wash Areas during off-peak production hours.

4. When you modify a Memory Pool Wash Area, the SQL Server will attempt to resize it using the values you provided. Be certain to read the informational message the SQL Server displays after the `sp_poolconfig` command completes executing. That message will tell you the requested Memory Pool Wash Size as well as the actual size of the modified Memory Pool Size.

5. When the SQL Server is restarted after the successful completion of an `sp_poolconfig` command, all modified Memory Pools are materialized in accordance with their configured sizes.

6. If you set the Memory Pool Wash Area such that is becomes too large, the SQL Server will move Buffers past the Buffer Wash Marker too quickly. When a Buffer moves past the Buffer Wash Marker, the Cache Manager writes the Buffer to disk and marks the Buffer as being clean. The clean Buffer will remain in the Wash Area until it reaches the end of the LRU. If the SQL Server executes another query that would modify the page contained within the clean Buffer, the SQL Server must perform the disk I/O required to bring a fresh copy of the page back into Data Cache. As a consequence, the SQL Server will have performed an unnecessary write on that page. Keep in mind that Buffers are written in disk I/O units, so, in the case of 4K, 8K, and 16K Memory Pools, the unnecessary writes will involve two, four, or eight pages respectively.

7. If you set the Memory Pool Wash Area such that is becomes too small, SQL Server may not be able to find a clean Buffer at the end of the LRU Chain. Once again, in the case of 2K, 4K, 8K, and 16K Memory Pools, the SQL Server will have to locate one clean page, two clean pages, four clean pages and eight clean pages, respectively. If a clean Buffer is not available, then the SQL Server will be forced to wait for clean Buffers to become available before it reads in the new page images from disk proceed. Forcing the SQL Server to wait for available Buffers will seriously degrade SQL Server performance.

8. When a Memory Pool is modified within a Data Cache to which compiled objects have been bound, the compiled objects will be recompiled the next time they are executed.

9. When a Memory Pool is modified within a Data Cache to which a database has been bound, all compiled objects contained within that bound database will be recompiled the next time they are executed.

10. Be certain to monitor and study the behavior of the modified Memory Pool Wash Area to confirm that its new size is appropriate for the application it is supporting.

Dropping a Memory Pool

You can drop any 4K, 8K, or 16K Memory Pool that you have created. However, it is not possible to drop a Data Cache's 2K Memory Pool. To drop a 4K, an 8K, or a 16K Memory Pool, log on to the SQL Server as an account with **sa_role** privileges and enter these commands:

```
1>use master
2>go
1>sp_poolconfig NameOfDataCache, "OK", "BufferDiskI/OUnit",
2>"wash=size[P|K|M|G]"
3>go
```

where:

NameOfDataCache—the name of the existing Data Cache in which you want to create the new Memory Pool.

OK—this parameter resets the size of the Memory Pool to 0 kilobytes. This completely removes the memory resources allocated to the Memory Pool being dropped.

BufferDiskI/OUnit—this parameter is used to specify the Memory Pool that is to be dropped. The Memory Pool is identified according to the Buffer disk I/O unit it support (e.g., 4K, 8K, or 16K). The legal values to be used for this parameter are "4K," "8K," and "16K."

These changes take effect immediately. This command changes the *master* system database, so to ensure its recovery, be certain to dump the *master* system database itself. This command changes the contents of system tables, so it cannot be entered in a transaction.

Here are a number of important facts to consider prior to modifying a Memory Pool:

1. Be certain that none of the Buffers contained within the Memory Pool you want to drop are being used by any active transactions.

2. When you drop a Memory Pool, the SQL Server will attempt to deallocate all requested memory resources for that Memory Pool. If

the Memory Pool you are trying to drop contains Buffers that are in use by an active transaction or are dirty and not yet written to disk, SQL Server will move as many Buffers as possible to the 2K Memory Pool and then print an informational message. Be certain to read the informational message the SQL Server displays after the `sp_poolconfig` command completes executing. That message will tell you the requested Memory Pool size as well as the actual size of the dropped Memory Pool. If the Memory Pool you attempted to drop contained any Buffers that were linked to an active transaction, those Buffers will still be present within the Memory Pool you tried to drop. The SQL Server could not move those Buffers because they were being used by an active transaction(s). Once the active transaction completes and the dirty Buffers are flushed to disk, you will have to reissue the command statements to complete the process of dropping the Memory Pool.

3. When a Memory Pool is dropped, the memory resources previously allocated to it are reallocated to the 2K Memory Pool.

4. You drop Memory Pools while the SQL Server is running. The changes to the referenced Memory Pools take effect immediately. You do not have to restart the SQL Server after the successful completion of the `sp_poolconfig` command to ensure that the drop Memory Pools is gone, and that its previously allocated memory resources have been reallocated to the Data Cache's 2K Memory Pool.

5. The SQL Server can support only one active `sp_poolconfig` command at a time on a given Data Cache. As a consequence, if you issue a second `sp_poolconfig` command before the first command completes executing, then the SQL Server will put the second instance of the `sp_poolconfig` command to sleep until such point in time as the first instance of the `sp_poolconfig` command completes executing.

6. In that dropping a Memory Pool involves the deallocation and reallocation of memory resources, the act of dropping a Memory Pool can definitely have adverse effect the run-time performance of a SQL Server that supports a production system. Therefore, it is advisable to drop Memory Pools during off-peak production hours.

7. When the SQL Server is restarted after the successful completion of an `sp_poolconfig` command, all dropped Memory Pools will not materialize and the Data Cache's 2K Memory Pool will come back on-line in accordance with its new size.

8. In the process of deallocating and reallocating memory resources to support the execution of the `sp_poolconfig` command, the SQL

Server can only allocate free Buffers. The SQL Server must wait until sufficient quantities of Buffers are not in use or are not dirty (i.e., that contain changes that have not yet been written to disk) to complete the memory resource allocation process.

9. The process of allocating free Buffers from a dropped Memory Pool to the 2K Memory Pool does involve some overhead. As such, SQL Server performance can degrade during the free Buffer allocation phase.

10. When a Memory Pool is dropped, the 2K Memory Pool has been modified. If this happens within a Data Cache to which compiled objects have been bound, the compiled objects will be recompiled the next time they are executed.

11. When a Memory Pool is dropped, the 2K Memory Pool has been modified. If this happens within a Data Cache to which a database has been bound, all compiled objects contained within that bound database will be recompiled the next time they are executed.

Default Data Cache

When you install the System 11 SQL Server "right out of the box" it comes with a single, mandatory Default Data Cache that contains a 2K Memory Pool. When the SQL Server is booted, after all mandatory memory resource requirements are satisfied, the remaining memory resources are assigned to Data Cache, and then, a specific percentage of the Data Cache is allocated to Procedure Cache. By default, the remaining memory resources are the reserve of the mandatory Default Data Cache. The minimum size of the Default Data Cache is 512K.

Basically, the Default Data Cache mimics the pre-System 11 Data Cache. And, like its ancestors, it always has a 2K Memory Pool and is always a "mixed" data cache. With System 11, two types of data caches are possible:

1. *Mixed.*   The data cache is capable of supporting all types of pages, for example, data pages, index pages, and transaction log pages.

2. *Logonly.*   The data cache is capable of supporting just transaction log pages.

Regarding data cache type: the Default Data Cache (while it is a mixed data cache) is always of type "default"; while Named Data Caches can be of either "mixed" or "logonly," they can never be of type "default." As its mandatory "mixed" data cache, the SQL Server uses the Default Data Cache to:

1. Manage all data, index, and transaction log pages brought into memory (unless, that is, you purposefully subdivide the Default Data Cache by creating Named Data Caches, and then take the necessary steps of explicitly binding databases and database objects to these Named Data Caches). Typically, frequently accessed data pages, higher- and lower-level index pages, system tables (such as *sysobjects* and *sysindexes*), and active transaction log pages for each database will reside within the Default Data Cache

2. Support database recovery

3. Support the `load database` and the `load transaction`, commands

At first glance it might not make sense why, even after Named Data Caches have been created, the SQL Server would still continue to use the Default Data Cache to support database recovery, as well as the `load database` and the `load transaction`, commands. Actually, it makes very good sense for the SQL Server to exhibit this type of behavior. As you will see, not only can the configuration of data caches drastically change over time (such as dropping a Named Memory Cache, or changing its type to "logonly,"), but the configuration of which databases and which databases objects are or are not bound to the data caches can change drastically over time as well. These types of configuration changes to Named Data Caches can make database recovery impossible in some contexts. By supporting these utilities within the mandatory Default Data Cache, the consumer can safely proceed after such configuration changes.

Reporting on Default Data Cache

To view the configuration of the Default Data Cache, log on to the SQL Server, as any valid Sybase account, and enter these commands:

```
1>use master
2>go
1>sp_cacheconfig "default data cache"
2>go
```

In response to this command sequence, the SQL Server will display a report on the Default Data Cache that is composed of two blocks of information. In the first block, at the top of the report, will be displayed:

Cache Name—this is the name of the configured data cache.

Status—indicates the current status of the data cache. The legal values for this column are:

Pend/Act—this value means that the data cache was created, but the SQL Server has not been started since it was created; however, its status will transition to "active" after the SQL Server has been restarted.

Active—the data cache is currently active within the SQL Server.

Pend/Del—the cache is active, but will be dropped just as soon as the SQL Server has been restarted. The value displayed within the "Config Value" column of this report should be zero.

Type—denotes the data cache type (i.e., whether the data cache is "mixed" or "logonly"). However, when the literal value of the data cache name is "default data cache", then the displayed type will be "Default." Note that only the Default Data Cache is of type "Default."

Config Value—represents the size of the data cache (when the SQL Server will be restarted).

Run Value—represents the size of the data cache that SQL Server is currently using. The size of the Default Data Cache is the size of data cache memory resources not explicitly configured for other Named Data Caches.

In the second block, at the bottom of the report, will be displayed information about each Memory Pool configured in the data cache:

IO Size—denotes the size of the Buffer disk I/O units in a given Memory Pool.

Wash Size—denotes the size of the Wash Area of a given Memory Pool.

Config Size—indicates the configured size of the Memory Pool.

Run Size—indicates the current run size of the Memory Pool.

Configuring the Default Data Cache

It is possible to reconfigure the Default Data Cache (e.g., create a 4K, an 8K, or a 16K Memory Pool within the Default Data Cache, modify a Memory Pool Wash Size, or resize the Default Data Cache such that it grabs its own piece of the data cache pie).

The techniques for creating a 4K, an 8K, or a 16K Memory Pool within the Default Data Cache are the same as those you use for configuring memory pools in Named Data Caches, and have already been addressed.

To ensure that the Default Data Cache will retain a fixed amount of the available data cache, log on to the SQL Server as an account with **sa_role** privileges and enter these commands:

```
1>use master
2>go
1>sp_cacheconfig "default data cache", "CacheSize [P|K|M|G]"
2>go
```

where:

CacheSize—this parameter specifies the size of the Default Data Cache you want to set. Size can be specified in units of pages (P), kilobytes (K), megabytes (M), and gigabytes (G). When specifying unit size in megabytes or in gigabytes, the size can be indicated in floating-point values. Specifying the unit of measurement is optional, so if you do not specify a unit of measurement, the default size will be in kilobytes. The minimum size of the Default Data Cache is 512K. Essentially, as the intention is to have the Default Data Cache support databases and database objects that are not explicitly bound to Named Data Caches, you want to be certain that its size is suitable for its intended purpose.

This command changes the *master* system database, so to ensure its recovery, be certain to dump the *master* system database itself. This command changes the contents of system tables, so it cannot be entered in a transaction.

Here are two important facts to keep in mind when configuring the size of the Default Data Cache:

1. After the `sp_cacheconfig` command completes successfully, you must restart the SQL Server before the new Default Data Cache size can take effect.

2. When you change the configuration of the Default Data Cache, the spinlock on the Default Data Cache prohibits all other processes from accessing the Default Data Cache. Even though the spinlock is held by the `sp_cacheconfig` process for a brief amount of time, invoking the `sp_cacheconfig` process does degrade SQL Server performance while it is running.

Named Data Caches

With the System 11 SQL Server, the consumer has the ability to improve performance by dividing the Default Data Cache into one or more separate Named Data Caches, and by then binding databases and database objects to these Named Data Caches. By default, all database and database objects reside within the Default Data Cache. So, it is important to realize that the SQL Server will use these Named Data

Caches only after you have expressly bound databases or database objects to them.

Like the Default Data Cache, each Named Data Cache contains a default 2K Memory Pool, and can be configured to contain a 4K, an 8K, and a 16K Memory Pool that will support larger disk I/O units.

Reporting on All Named Data Caches

To view all configured data caches within your SQL Server, log on to the SQL Server as any valid Sybase account and enter these commands:

```
1>use master
2>go
1>sp_cacheconfig
2>go
```

In response to this command sequence, the SQL Server will display a report on all data caches, which is composed of two or more blocks of information. In the first block, at the top of the report, will be displayed:

Cache Name—this is the name of each data cache.

Status—indicates the current status of each data cache. The legal values for this column are:

Pend/Act—this value means that the data cache was created, but the SQL Server has not been started since it was created; however, its status will transition to "active" after the SQL Server has been restarted.

Active—the data cache is currently active within the SQL Server.

Pend/Del—the cache is active, but will be dropped just as soon as the SQL Server has been restarted. The value displayed within the "Config Value" column of this report should be zero.

Type—denotes the type of each data cache (i.e., whether the data cache is "mixed" or "logonly"). However, when the literal value of the data cache name is "default data cache", then the displayed type will be "Default." Note that only the Default Data Cache is of type "Default."

Config Value—represents the size of each data cache (when the SQL Server will be restarted).

Run Value—represents the size of the each cache that SQL Server is currently using. The size of the Default Data Cache is the size of data cache memory resources not explicitly configured for other Named Data Caches.

Following the first report block, will be one block for each configured data cache. Each successive individual data cache block will display information about each Memory Pool configured in each data cache:

IO Size—denotes the size of the Buffer disk I/O units in a given Memory Pool.

Wash Size—denotes the size of the Wash Area of a given Memory Pool.

Config Size—indicates the configured size of the Memory Pool.

Run Size—indicates the current run size of the Memory Pool.

Access to the Default Data Cache, as well as to all Named Data Caches, takes place via a spinlock. When the sole data cache is the Default Data Cache, then all SQL Server processes that need dynamic access to memory resources must contend for that single spinlock. By creating multiple data caches, with their own spinlocks, the contention on the Default Data Cache's spinlock is significantly diminished. In those cases where the SQL Server is running on *symmetrical multi-processor* (SMP) platforms, this single spinlock contention scenario can be further diminished by running multiple SQL Server engines in combination with Named Data Caches.

Now, it is tempting to think of Named Data Caches as a cure-all for your performance problems. After all, you can readily bind databases, the *tempdb* system database, transaction logs, and heavily active database objects to data cache. But, like so many other easy things in life that are viewed superficially, you may soon discover that you have taken a good thing too far, and crossed the line into carelessly micromanaging the data cache. The studied analysis of application queries, database object usage patterns, and skillful indexing must not be abandoned for data cache quick fixes. Subsequent sections of this chapter explain how to configure data cache to improve SQL Server performance in meaningful ways.

Creating a Named Data Cache

The System 11 SQL Server enables you to partition the Default Data Cache into a maximum of 65,536 separate Named Data Caches. By default, each Named Data Cache has a:

1. Minimum size of 512K.

2. Data Cache type of "mixed."

3. 2K Memory Pool to which all allocated memory resources are assigned.

Every Named Data Cache consumes a relatively small amount of memory resources from the Default Data Cache to support structures that manage the Named Data Cache. In that the memory resources for the new Named Data Cache, and its associated management overhead, are taken from the Default Data Cache, it is prudent to determine just how much memory resources will be taken to support management overhead. To obtain an estimate to the overhead, log on to the SQL Server, as any Sybase account, and enter these commands:

```
1>use master
2>go
1>sp_helpcache "SizeOfCache[P,K,M,G]"
2>go
```

where *SizeOfCache*, given in units of pages, kilobytes, megabytes, or gigabytes, indicates the actual size of the new Named Data Cache you want to create. You may be amazed at just how much management overhead there is for the planned Named Data Cache. For example, a 200M data cache has slightly more than 10M of management overhead.

When running the sp_helpcache command to determine data cache overhead, here are two important facts to keep in mind:

1. This command will correctly calculate the data cache overhead only in those cases where the does not exceed 74 GB.

2. In that this command creates a temporary table, you cannot invoke it from within a transaction.

To create a Named Data Cache, log on to the SQL Server as an account with **sa_role** privileges and enter these commands:

```
1>use master
2>go
1>sp_cacheconfig [NameOfDataCache [,"CacheSize[P|K|M|G]"]
  [, logonly | mixed ]]
2>go
```

where:

NameOfDataCache—this is the name of the data cache you want to create. The name must be unique, and cannot be longer than 30 bytes in length. Unlike most other Sybase identifiers, the data cache name can contain special characters and spaces.

CacheSize—this optional parameter specifies the size of the Named Data Cache you want to create. Size can be specified in units of pages (P), kilobytes (K), megabytes (M), and gigabytes (G). When specifying unit size in megabytes or in gigabytes, the size can be indicated in floating-point values. Specifying the unit of measurement is optional, so if you do not specify a unit of measurement, the default size will be in kilobytes. The minimum size of a Named Data Cache is 512K. If you choose not to use this optional parameter, then the Named Data Cache will be created at the default size, 512K. Essentially, as the intention is to have the new Named Data Cache support databases and database objects that are explicitly bound to it, you want to be certain that its size is suitable for its intended purpose.

`logonly | mixed`—this optional parameter specifies the Named Data Cache type (i.e., logonly or mixed). If you elect not to use this optional parameter, then the Named Data Cache type will be mixed.

This command changes the *master* system database, so to ensure its recovery, be certain to dump the *master* system database itself. This command changes the contents of system tables, so it cannot be entered in a transaction.

Here are a few important facts to keep in mind when creating a Named Data Cache:

1. Unless you explicitly bind a database, or bind database objects to the Named Data Cache you created, the new Named Data Cache will not be used by the SQL Server.

2. After the `sp_cacheconfig` command completes successfully, you must restart the SQL Server before the new Named Data Cache can take effect.

3. Before you can bind databases, or bind database objects to, or configure 4K, 8K, or 16 Memory Pools for the new Named Data Cache, the SQL Server must have been restarted since the point in time when the new Named Data Cache was created.

4. The memory resources assigned to the new Named Data Cache are deallocated from the Default Data Cache.

5. When you create the new Named Data Cache, the SQL Server will attempt to deallocate memory resources from the Default Data Cache. And, the SQL Server will not allow the size of the Default Data Cache to be less than 512K. So, be certain to read the informational message the SQL Server displays after the `sp_cacheconfig` command completes executing. That message will tell you the requested Named Data Cache size as well as the actual size of the Named Data Cache.

6. Keep in mind that the HouseKeeper does not run against any data cache of type logonly.

Next, we will take up the topic of data cache configuration. By understanding the various aspects of caching, and the alternative caching strategies, one gains the understanding of why data cache needs to be configured in certain ways. With that understanding in hand, data caches can be correctly configured to meet your processing requirements.

Configuring a Named Data Cache

There are a number of goals you want to attain when configuring Named Data Caches:

1. Reduce the number of disk reads by taking advantage of (relatively) larger disk I/O units.
2. Reduce the number of disk writes that results from data, index, and log pages being flushed from data cache by competing processes.
3. Reduce the length of time that competing processes hold locks by managing the locked resources in data cache, as opposed to performing disk I/O.
4. Reduce data cache spinlock contention on SMP platforms.

When you accomplish any of the above goals, in an informed manner, you will observe significant SQL Server performance improvements.
Named Data Caches can be configured by:

1. Dividing the Named Data Cache into a 2K, a 4K, an 8K, and a 16K Memory Pools.
2. Resizing a Named Data Cache Memory Pool.
3. Altering the Wash Area Size of a Named Data Cache Memory Pool.
4. Dropping a 4K, an 8K, or a 16K Named Data Cache Memory Pool.
5. Binding databases or database objects to Named Data Caches.
6. Dropping database or database object bindings from Named Data Caches.
7. Changing the type of a Named Data Cache.
8. Resizing the Named Data Cache.

In this chapter we have already covered items one through four. Because of their complexity, items five and six are covered in the chapters dealing with databases, with tables and indexes, and with transaction log management. And, item seven, also a very complex topic, is covered in the chapter on transaction log management.

To resize a Named Data Cache, log on to the SQL Server as an account with **sa_role** privileges and enter these commands:

```
1>use master
2>go
1>sp_cacheconfig NameOfDataCache, "CacheSize[P|K|M|G]"
2>go
```

where:

NameOfDataCache—this is the name of the data cache whose size you want to change.

CacheSize—this parameter specifies the size of the Named Data Cache you want to set. Size can be specified in units of pages (P), kilobytes (K), megabytes (M), and gigabytes (G). When specifying unit size in megabytes or in gigabytes, the size can be indicated in floating-point values. Specifying the unit of measurement is optional, so if you do not specify a unit of measurement, the default size will be in kilobytes. Essentially, as the intention is to have the new Named Data Cache support databases and database objects that are explicitly bound to it, you want to be certain that its size is suitable for its intended purpose.

This command changes the *master* system database, so to ensure its recovery, be certain to dump the *master* system database itself. This command changes the contents of system tables, so it cannot be entered in a transaction.

Here are a few important facts to keep in mind when resizing a Named Data Cache:

1. After the `sp_cacheconfig` command completes successfully, you must restart the SQL Server before the new Named Data Cache size can take effect.

2. Before you can bind databases, or bind database objects to, or configure 4K, 8K, or 16 Memory Pools for the new Named Data Cache, the SQL Server must have been restarted since the point in time when the Named Data Cache was resized.

3. If you increase the size of the Named Data Cache, then memory resources are deallocated from the Default Data Cache.

4. When you increase the size of the Named Data Cache, the SQL Server will attempt to deallocate memory resources from the Default Data Cache. And, the SQL Server will not allow the size of the Default Data Cache to be less than 512K. So, be certain to read

the informational message the SQL Server displays after the `sp_cacheconfig` command completes executing. That message will tell you the requested Named Data Cache size as well as the actual size of the Named Data Cache.

5. When you increase the size of a Named Data Cache, all new memory resources are assigned to its 2K Memory Pool.

6. If you decrease the size of the Named Data Cache, then memory resources are reallocated to the Default Data Cache.

7. When you decrease the size of a Named Data Cache, all the memory resources to be deallocated must be available within its 2K Memory Pool. That is, the size of the Named Data Cache can never be smaller than its 2K Memory Pool. So, keeping this constraint in mind, you may need to move memory resources into the 2K Memory Pool from the other memory pools before you decrease the size of the Named Data Cache.

8. When configuring a Named Data Cache for use by a transaction log, you should size the Named Data Cache to increase the number of times that active processes reread log pages from memory, versus from disk. Also, most of the space in the Named Data Cache should be configured to match the Buffer Mass of the transaction log.

Dropping a Named Data Cache

If you want to drop a Named Data Cache, you merely set its size to zero. To drop a Named Data Cache, log on to the SQL Server as an account with **sa_role** privileges and enter these commands:

```
1>use master
2>go
1>sp_cacheconfig NameOfDataCache, "0"
2>go
```

where:

NameOfDataCache—this is the name of the data cache whose size you want to change.

This command changes the *master* system database, so to ensure its recovery, be certain to dump the *master* system database itself. This command changes the contents of system tables, so it cannot be entered in a transaction.

Here are a few important facts to keep in mind when dropping a Named Data Cache:

1. After the `sp_cacheconfig` command completes successfully, the status of the Named Data Cache is set to `Pend/Del`. You must restart the SQL Server before the change can take effect. Until you restart the SQL Server, the data cache will remain active. The status of all bound databases and database objects will be marked invalid, but they will continue to use the dropped Named Data Cache until such point in time as the SQL Server has been restarted.

2. Before dropping the Named Data Cache, it is recommended that you drop all database and database objects bindings to the Named Data Cache.

3. You cannot drop the Default Data Cache.

5

Databases

Introduction

The SQL Server is technically advanced software used to store, manage, and manipulate information, and executable processes, of value to its intended user. A database is an organized collection of data structures and executable processes that share a causal relationship. Whenever you create, modify, destroy, or read information being managed by a SQL Server, you are doing so within the context of a database. A given SQL Server is capable of supporting up to 32,727 databases.

As everything within a SQL Server revolves around databases, it is not possible to explore databases without touching upon many related, and complex, topics, for example, transaction logs, system commands, and so on. When these related topics are encountered in this chapter, they are dealt with at a high level. If the readers wish to explore such topics at a greater depth, then it is advised that they review the Table of Contents, Glossary, and Index in their search for more information on their topic of interest.

Principal SQL Server Database Objects

Another way of defining a database is to state that it is an explicit collection of principal database objects. The term *object* is used here to simply indicate something in the real world that can be formally represented within the SQL Server. The SQL Server supports a limited number of object categories, collectively referred to as principal database objects:

- Tables
- Stored procedures

- Indexes
- Views
- Triggers (a type of stored procedure)
- Defaults
- Rule constraints.

Within each object category, there can be, within a given database, multiple instances of a given category of principal database objects, or none for that matter (e.g., a database can contain a hundred or more tables, and no triggers). In other chapters of this book we explore these object categories in depth, so they will merely be listed here. If you are curious about them, then jump ahead to their respective chapters.

System Databases and User Databases

The SQL Server supports two types of databases:

1. *User databases.* A database that you create yourself, and into which are placed principal database objects that you own, design, and implement.
2. *System databases.* These are special databases that support the SQL Server itself. The System 11 SQL Server contains five system databases:
   a. The *master* system database.
   b. The *model* system database.
   c. The *tempdb* system database.
   d. The *sybsystemprocs* system database.
   e. The *sybsecurity* system database.

We will first examine the system databases and then move on to an investigation of user databases.

Updating System Tables

By default, the SQL Server automatically prohibits any modification of the system tables. This constraint is in place to ensure the integrity of the system tables. However, on occasion, it become necessary to modify system tables (e.g., to change a login account's `suid`) and to disable this constraint so that stored procedures and triggers which modify system tables can be created. To disable this constraint on modifying system tables, the SQL Server has the `allow updates to system tables` configuration parameter.

To allow system tables to be modified, log on to the SQL Server as an account with **sso_role** privileges, and enter these commands:

```
1>use master
2>go
1>sp_configure "allow updates to system tables", on
2>go
```

Here are some important facts to understand about setting the `allow updates to system tables` **SQL Server configuration parameter on:**

1. Changes to the `allow updates to system tables` **SQL Server configuration parameter take effect immediately.**

2. Corrupting a system table can create serious problems within the SQL Server. To protect against such corruption, always use the `begin transaction` statement when changing a system table. Just as soon as the modifying command completes, read the changed value(s) to confirm that the desired goal was achieved. Then, and only then, commit the transaction.

3. While the constraint against modifying system tables is disabled, any login account with **sa_role** privileges can create triggers or stored procedures that modify system tables, and these types of login accounts can directly modify system tables.

4. While the constraint against modifying system tables is disabled, any login account can create triggers or stored procedures that modify system tables.

5. If you want to ensure that no other login account will create stored procedures or triggers that can modify system tables, then be certain to place the SQL Server in single-user mode before you disable the constraint against modifying system tables.

6. Immediately after completing your tasks, run the `sp_configure "allow updates to system tables", off` command to enable the constraint against modifying system tables.

7. The stored procedures and triggers created to modify system tables will continue to modify them even after the constraints against modifying has been reenabled.

The *master* System Database

The *master* system database contains system tables that keep track of information about:

1. The SQL Server as a whole.

2. The *master* system database itself.

The *master* system database, the *master* system database's transaction log, and its system tables are created when you install the SQL Server. The *master* system database and the *master* system database's transaction log always reside on the **d_master** database device. The *master* system database is contained entirely on the **d_master** database device and cannot be expanded onto any other.

Please note that it is not possible to move the *master* system database or the *master* system database's transaction log off of the **d_master** database device. Also, it is important to realize that if it becomes necessary, the **d_master** database device will be reinitialized. When the **d_master** device is reinitialized, any database or transaction log located on the **d_master** database device (other than the *master* system database itself) may well be clobbered.

Since the *master* system database's transaction log is located on the same device as the database itself, you must always use the `dump database` command to back up the *master* system database. Use the `dump transaction` with the `truncate_only` option periodically to purge the transaction log of the *master* system database.

Back up the *master* system database with the `dump database` command each time you create, alter, or drop any device, database, or database object, and each time you execute a stored procedure that changes it.

System Tables and the *master* System Database

All Sybase-supplied tables in the *master* system database are considered system tables. It is within these system tables that the *master* system database keeps track of:

1. Character sets and their sort order (in *syscharsets*).
2. User-configurable SQL Server environment variables with their default values (in *sysconfigures*).
3. User-configurable SQL Server environment variables with their current values (in *syscurconfigures*—this table is built dynamically during run time).
4. The databases on the SQL Server (in *sysdatabases*).
5. The tape and disk database devices in the system (in *sysdevices*).
6. SQL Server engines currently running (in *sysengines*).
7. The languages known to the SQL Server (in *syslanguages*).
8. Every network protocol available for connecting to the SQL Server (in *syslisteners*).

9. The active locks (in *syslocks*—this table is built dynamically during run time).

10. Users who hold serverwide roles (in *sysloginroles*).

11. Login accounts (in *syslogins*).

12. System error, or warning, messages returned by the SQL Server (in *sysmessages*).

13. Ongoing processes (in *sysprocesses*).

14. Remote login accounts (in *sysremotelogins*).

15. Remote servers that this SQL Server can interact with, that is, remote SQL Servers, Open Servers, or Backup Servers (in *sysservers*).

16. Server roles (in *syssrvroles*).

17. The storage space allocated to each database (in *sysusages*).

The *model* System Database

The *model* system database (as well as the *master* and the *tempdb* system databases) is placed, at installation time, on the **d_master** database device. Within the *model* system database are the system tables, principal database objects, and user-defined data types required for each SQL Server user database.

The *model* system database is used as a template for constructing user databases. Each time the `create database` command is executed, the SQL Server makes a copy of the *model* system database and then extends the size of the new database as specified within the `create database` command. As regards the size of a new user database, it is important to know that its size cannot be smaller than the size of the *model* system database.

Modifying the *model* system database

These are some of the typical changes that are made to the *model* system database:

1. Changing its size.

2. Creating rules, user-defined data types, defaults, tables, views, or stored procedures within it so that user databases, and the *tempdb* system database automatically have these objects.

3. Locating *model* system database's principal database objects and user-defined data types on specific segments.

4. Adding login accounts that are to have access to all new databases and the *tempdb* system database.

5. Setting database permissions, particularly for the **guest** login account, so that it has access to all new databases, and the *tempdb* system database.

6. Setting database configuration options for all new databases and for the *tempdb* system database. By default, the database configuration options are set to off within the *model* system database.

When you install SQL Server, the *model* system database is only 2 MB, or 1024 2K blocks, in size. To determine the current size of the *model* system database log on to the SQL Server as any Sybase account and, enter these commands:

```
1>use model
2>go
1>sp_helpsegment
2>go
```

Information on all segments within the *model* system database will then be displayed.

You can use the `alter database` command to change the size of the *model* system database. However, if you intend on increasing the size of the *model* system database, then you must keep in mind the hard-and-fast rule that the size of the *model* system database can never be larger than the size of the *tempdb* system database. We will explore the `alter database` command syntax when we discuss altering the size of user databases later in this chapter.

While the *master* system database and all of its principal database objects must remain on the **d_master** database device, the *model* system database and its principal database objects can be created, or located, on database devices other than **d_master.**

Always keep in mind that every modification you make to the *model* system database (without exception) is reflected in each new database you create, and in the *tempdb* (each time the SQL Server boots) system database. Therefore, when you modify the *model* system database, you must be extremely careful not to corrupt the *model* system database. As the *model* system database is used as the template for the *tempdb* system database, as well as for all new user databases, their quality cannot be any better than the *model* system database; specifically, if the *model* system database is corrupted then all new user databases, and the *tempdb* system database, will be corrupted as well. To avoid damaging the *model* system database, obey the following rules:

1. Be certain to make a backup copy of the *model* system database with the `dump database` system command each time you modify the *model* system database. In case of media failure, or *model* system database corruption, you can restore the *model* system database as you would a user database.

2. Be sure to keep a script of these changes to the *model* system database so that you can reapply them in the event of a catastrophic failure.

3. Always run the `sp_checkreswords` system command on the *model* system database after you make any modifications to it. This system command will check the *model* system database to determine if it contains identifiers (such as user names, login names, remote login names, user-defined data types names, principal database object names, column names, database device names, and segment names) that are reserved keywords (i.e., a collection of words that you must not use for identifiers).

4. Consider the possible negative impact of the modification(s) to the *tempdb* system database and to all future user databases.

5. Just like all other databases, the *model* system database has its own transaction log. However, the *model* system database does not have a separate log segment. Always use the `dump transaction` with the `truncate_only` option to purge the *model* system database's transaction log after each database dump.

The model system database and booting the SQL Server

When a SQL Server is booted, it performs database recovery in this order:

1. Recover *master* system database.

2. Recover *sybsecurity* system database.

3. Recover *model* system database.

4. Create *tempdb* (using *model* as its template) system database.

5. Recover *sybsystemprocs* system database. (Client processes can connect to the SQL Server at this point in time, but they cannot access user databases.)

6. Recover user databases, in ascending order by `master..sysdatabase.dbid`.

If, at step four, there are problems with the *model* system database, then the *tempdb* system database cannot be created and so the SQL

Server may not boot. Therefore, take all necessary precautions to ensure that the *model* system database is not corrupted.

The *tempdb* System Database

Each time the SQL Server boots, it creates the *tempdb* system database, using the *model* system database as its template. The *tempdb* system database is shared by all login accounts to create temporary tables, and the SQL Server uses the *tempdb* system database to store, manage, and modify internal work tables. If there are problems with the *model* system database, then these problems will exist within the *tempdb* system database as well.

By default, when the SQL Server is installed:

1. The *tempdb* system database and its transaction log are installed on the **d_master** device.
2. It is 2 MB in size.
3. The `select into/bulkcopy` option is enabled. Be sure to keep this database option enabled on the *tempdb* system database.

While an account with **sa_role** privileges can change the size of the *tempdb* system database, its size:

1. Cannot be less than the size of the *model* system database.
2. Must be at least the size of the largest work table (including its clustered index).

And, as regards the *tempdb* system database:

1. Its database space can be monitored by the use of segment thresholds.
2. Always use the database option `ddl in tran` set to `false` in *tempdb* system database (and in *model* system database) lest the system grind to a halt because data definition language commands hold locks on its system tables, such as *sysobjects,* which is used to store representations of work and temporary tables.

Temporary Tables

At boot time, SQL Server explicitly grants `create table` permission in the *tempdb* system database to all login accounts. When you create a temporary table, you can create user-defined data types, rules, defaults, and indexes for use with the temporary table. However, you cannot create views or triggers on temporary tables. If you want the user-defined data types, rules, or defaults to persist beyond the current boot session, then you will have to add them to the *model* system database.

Client process can explicitly create temporary tables within the *tempdb* system database in two different ways:

1. Prefix the temporary table identifier with the "#" symbol. This type of temporary table can be accessed only by the session that created it (i.e., other SQL Server sessions cannot read or write to such a table). The first 13 bytes of this type of temporary table's name, including the # symbol, must be unique for the session. If the user-assigned name of this type of temporary table is longer than 13 bytes, the SQL Server automatically truncates the name to 13 bytes in length. If the user-assigned name of this type of temporary table is shorter than 13 bytes, the SQL Server automatically pads the end of the name with the "_" symbol to make it 13 bytes in length. Next, the SQL Server assigns a 17-byte number suffix to the temporary table name. Using this suffix, the SQL Server is able to restrict access to the temporary table from all but the session which created it. Unlike a user table, a temporary table name cannot be changed. Such temporary tables, created by a stored procedure, are dropped when the stored procedure stops executing or when the table is explicitly dropped using the drop-table command. Temporary tables created outside of stored procedures are dropped when the client session logs out of the SQL Server (that is, when their current session ends), or when the table is explicitly dropped using the drop-table command.

2. Prefix the temporary-table identifier with the "`tempdb..`" character string. This type of temporary table exists either until its owner explicitly drops it or until the SQL Server is rebooted. The same user can access the temporary table across successive sessions. A suffix is not added to the temporary-table identifier. Even though permissions on this type of temporary table default to the public login account, no other login account can access or manipulate this type of temporary table.

Temporary tables are not recoverable, nor does the SQL Server take locks on temporary tables because they are always used by a single process.

Work Tables

The query optimizer creates its own temporary tables called work tables. The work table holds all the intermediate results of queries that are ordered and/or grouped, and then the final select is done. When all results are returned, the table is dropped automatically.

A work table is a system-generated temporary table, generated for intermediate results for certain types of queries or for certain processing strategies. These queries that may implicitly create work tables in the *tempdb* system database are:

1. `select distinct`—a work table is created to sort the results of the query so that no duplicates are returned.

2. `select ... order by`—a work table is created for queries using `order by` only when the table(s) involved in the query does not have a clustered index on the column(s) listed in the `order by` clause. The query optimizer will weigh the cost of sorting by the nonclustered index on the columns listed in the `order by` clause against the cost of creating a work table for the columns in the `order by` clause and sorting the work table. If the query optimizer decides that the estimated cost of using the nonclustered index is cheaper (in terms of disk I/O), a work table will not be created to support the query.

3. `select ... group by`—always forces creation of a work table for intermediate query results. This type of statement will cause a temporary clustered index to be created on the work table for internal join processing. This temporary clustered index exists only until the query is completed. The creation of these temporary clustered indexes on the work tables requires that there be sufficient space in the *tempdb* system database to hold 120 to 150 percent of the size of the work table.

4. `select ... where not exists`—queries that use both the `where not exists` clause and a join will have a work table created to hold the intermediate query results. The intermediate query results are processed through an internal call to the `group by` function. A temporary clustered index will be created on the work table that supports the internal join processing.

5. `select ... where ... or ...`—this statement will cause a temporary clustered index to be created on the work table to be created that supports the internal join processing.

6. `select into ...`—a work table will be created to store the selected data before it is inserted into the target table.

7. Scalar aggregation—when a transaction uses an aggregate function (`avg`, `count`, `max`, `min`, or `sum`) a single value is produced by the SQL Server. Internally, the SQL Server creates a work table, and its clustered index, to assist the process of scalar aggregation.

8. Reformatting—when the SQL Server query optimizer determines that a table which participates in a join query is large and does not have an index which can be used to support the join query, the query optimizer may invoke a processes called *reformatting*. There are a

series of steps that are followed during the reformatting process. First, from the smaller of the two tables in the join query, all required join columns from the qualifying rows will be taken and inserted into a work table. Next, a clustered index is created on the join columns contained within the work table. The newly created clustered index is composed of the columns that support the join from the work table to the larger join table. Last, the SQL Server will use this clustered index to obtain the qualifying rows from each table that participates in the join query. As you can see, there is really quite a bit of disk I/O going on to build the work table and its clustered index. So, if the optimizer determines that the join query can be accomplished more efficiently by repeatedly performing table scans on the large table, versus the reformatting process, then the reformatting process will not be invoked.

9. When system procedures execute, they select data into work tables.

And like temporary tables, the SQL Server does not take locks on work tables because they are always used by a single process.

The *tempdb* Transaction Log

As a consequence of supporting these types of tasks, the *tempdb* system database and its transaction log can be subjected to heavy disk I/O loads. Every time a work table is created within the *tempdb* system database, allocation page log records are written to disk. In addition, as memory resources are limited, the *tempdb* system database data, index, and log pages may displace other data, index, and log pages from the Default Data Cache.

The *tempdb* system database transaction log behaves like a user database transaction log with the option `trunc log on chkpt` enabled. But data management is more difficult with the *tempdb* system database because it is more difficult to get information about space use: work tables cannot be referenced by the user, and the log is truncated during every cycle of the checkpoint process, about every 60 seconds. This occurs whether the `trunc log on chkpt` option is set on the *tempdb* system database or not.

To better manage this work load, the System 11 SQL Server allows you to place the *tempdb* system database on a raw device, or in an operating system file, and then to bind the *tempdb* system database to its own mixed Named Data Cache. If your goal is to make the *tempdb* system database perform at its fastest possible rate, then you will want to place it in an operating system file and then bind it to its own mixed Named Data Cache. In production environments, the *tempdb* system database should be mirrored on operating system files as well.

Locating the *tempdb* System Database

It is on the **d_master** database device that Sybase, by default, always locates the *tempdb* system database and the *tempdb* system database's transaction log. Under normal conditions, disk I/O for a *master* database is high. However, disk I/O activity is extremely high when the **d_master** database device is mirrored.

Therefore, in all cases where the *tempdb* system database resides on the **d_master** database device, the performance of database operations that are dependent upon access to the *tempdb* system database will be significantly constrained by the disk I/O activities that support the **d_master** database device. Recall that these operations place a load on the *tempdb* system database's transaction log as well as on the *tempdb* system database. It is highly recommended that you move the *tempdb* system database and transaction log from the **d_master** database device to some other device. This relocation of the *tempdb* system database is critically important for those sites where the **d_master** database device is mirrored. When you mirror the **d_master** database device, be certain to unmap all *tempdb* system database segments (except for the system segment) from the **d_master** database device and map them to another device.

Since the SQL Server does not provide up-to-date recovery of *tempdb* system database, in case of media failure, there is no need to move the *tempdb* system database's transaction log on to a separate device unless the load on its transaction log is so high that contention arises.

Given the fact that the *tempdb* system database is not recovered, it may seem that it does not make sense to mirror the *tempdb* system database. However, to run, the SQL Server needs the *tempdb* system database. If the disk on which the *tempdb* system database resides fails, then the SQL Server will crash. In production environments, to protect the SQL Server, the *tempdb* system database should be mirrored to protect against media failures that would crash the SQL Server.

Also, just like any other database, you can increase *tempdb* system database performance by spreading it across multiple devices. When you spread a database across multiple disk drives, the increased number of I/O channels improves overall I/O rates.

Binding the *tempdb* System Database to Named Data Cache

Having made the case for binding the *tempdb* system database to its own mixed Named Data Cache, be certain to look at these things before you take the plunge:

1. Determine which queries in your application(s) are using *tempdb* system database resources.

2. For those queries which use the *tempdb* system database, you must produce show plans that include statistic I/Os. These show plans will indicate, among other things, the counts and sizes of the work tables that are automatically being generated to support these queries.

3. Determine when those queries that use the *tempdb* system database are being executed.

4. Do your best to determine the length of time the temporary and work tables that these queries generate are residing within the *tempdb* system database.

With these metrics in hand you will be able to estimate the amount and frequency of disk I/O activity associated with the *tempdb* system database. Use this estimate to establish the size of the *tempdb* system database and the amount of data cache resources it will require.

It is being assumed that you will already have, as good practice, moved the *tempdb* system databases on to an operating system file. Also, it is being assumed that you have previously created a mixed Named Data Cache intended for the exclusive use of the *tempdb* system database, and have subsequently restarted the SQL Server so that the status of the newly created Named Data Cache is "Active."

Because the SQL Server takes exclusive locks on all data, index, and log pages when binding a database to a data cache, when you explicitly bind the *tempdb* system database to a Named Data Cache, it must be in "single-user mode." So, to bind the *tempdb* system database to a mixed Named Data Cache, log on to the SQL Server as an account with **sa_role** privileges and enter these commands:

```
1>use master
2>go
1>sp_dboption tempdb, single, true
2>go
1>use tempdb
2>go
1>checkpoint
2>go
1>sp_bindcache NameOfDataCache, tempdb
2>go
1>use master
2>go
1>sp_dboption tempdb, single, false
2>go
```

where

NameOfDataCache—is the name of the mixed Named Data Cache to which you want to exclusively bind the *tempdb* system database. This Named Data Cache must exist before you execute the `sp_bindcache` command. Be certain that the data cache is of type "mixed," since you cannot bind the *tempdb* system database to a data cache of type "logonly." Also, the status of this data cache must be "Active," that is, the SQL Server must have been restarted since the point in time when this data cache was created, else the *tempdb* system database cannot be bound to it.

This change will take effect immediately. This command changes the *master* system database, so to ensure its recovery, be certain to dump the *master* system database. As this command changes the contents of system tables, it cannot be used within a transaction.

Here are a few important facts to keep in mind when binding the *tempdb* system database to its exclusive mixed Named Data Caches:

1. The *tempdb* system database must be in single-user mode before it can be bound to its exclusive mixed Named Data Cache.

2. When you bind the *tempdb* system database to its mixed Named Data Cache you must be in (i.e., using) the *master* system database.

3. If the *tempdb* system database is already bound to another Named Data Cache, the old binding is dropped and the new one is created (i.e., you do not have to unbind the database before you create its new binding).

4. When you bind the *tempdb* system database to a Named Data Cache, any of its pages in memory are flushed to disk. They will be located in the Named Data Cache to which they are bound once a user process needs to access them.

5. You cannot bind the *tempdb* system database to a Named Data Cache if the user process that is doing the database binding also has a cursor open on any temporary table contained within the *tempdb* system database.

6. The Named Data Cache to which the *tempdb* system database is being bound must be of type "mixed."

7. Configure the mixed Named Data Cache to which the *tempdb* system database is bound to contain a 16K Memory Pool. All queries that use the `select ... into` construct will then take advantage of the 16K Memory Pool.

8. Unlike tables in other user databases, the individual temporary and work tables contained within the *tempdb* system databases cannot

be bound to another Named Data Cache. The tables contained within the *tempdb* system database are dropped every time the SQL Server is restarted. Therefore, it makes it a practical impossibility to support binding of specific temporary tables. Binding the *tempdb* system database to a mixed Named Data Cache is an all-or-nothing proposition (i.e., all tables within the *tempdb* system database are bound to exactly the same mixed Named Data Cache, or none of them are bound to any mixed Named Data Cache).

The *sybsystemprocs* System Database

Within the SQL Server all system commands are implemented as stored procedures whose identifiers are prefixed with "sp_" character string. Prior to System 10, all SQL Server system commands resided within the *master* system database. Starting with System 10, all SQL Server system commands now reside within the *sybsystemprocs* system database. As the *master* system database must reside solely on the **d_master** database device, the prior placement of system commands within the *master* system database placed a strain of the storage capacity of the **d_master** database device. The introduction, in System 10, of the *sybsystemprocs* system database is aimed at alleviating this storage capacity problem. In addition the *sybsystemprocs* system database provides these added benefits:

1. If the *master* system database is unfortunately corrupted, then the system procedures are still safe.

2. Unlike its predecessors, the *master* system database can be recovered without having to concern yourself with the need to rebuild or restore the system procedures. As a consequence, the recovery of the *master* system database can proceed, relative to its predecessors, at a faster pace.

3. The *sybsystemprocs* system database can be restored without having to concern yourself with the need to rebuild or restore the *master* system database.

4. Users of the System 11 SQL Server are able to store their own user-defined stored procedures without worrying about consuming the limited storage capacity of the **d_master** database device.

5. You can, if you so choose, place the *sybsystemprocs* system database on a mirrored operating system file-based database device.

When a system command is entered, the SQL Server searches for that system command within the database the process is running against. If the system command is not found within that database, then the *sybsystemprocs* system database is searched. If the SQL Server fails to find it there, then the *master* system database is searched.

Like any other database, you can change the *sybsystemprocs* system database. These are some of the typical changes that can be made to the *sybsystemprocs* system database:

1. Change its size.

2. Modify the definitions of the stored procedures it contains.

3. Add new principal database objects to it, specifically user-defined system commands created by an account with **sa_role** privileges.

4. Locate *sybsystemprocs* principal database objects on specific segments.

5. Add Sybase accounts to it.

To avoid damaging the *sybsystemprocs* system database, obey the following rules:

1. Be certain to make a backup copy of the *sybsystemprocs* system database with the `dump database` command each time you modify the *sybsystemprocs* system database. In case of media failure, or *sybsystemprocs* system database corruption, you can restore the *sybsystemprocs* system database as you would a user database.

2. Be sure to keep a script of these changes to the *sybsystemprocs* system database so that you can reapply them in the event of a catastrophic failure.

3. Always run the `sp_checkreswords` system command on the *sybsystemprocs* system database after you make any modifications to it.

4. Just like all other databases, the *sybsystemprocs* system database has its own transaction log. However, the *sybsystemprocs* system database does not have a separate log segment. Always use the `dump transaction` with the `truncate_only` option to purge the *sybsystemprocs* system database's transaction log after each database dump.

The *sybsecurity* System Database

The SQL Server offers an audit trail for such events as:

1. Logging on and off the SQL Server.

2. The destruction of principal database objects.

3. The execution of stored procedures and triggers.

4. Actions caused by a particular Sybase account.

5. Transact-SQL, and system, commands that reference a particular principal database object.

6. Transact-SQL, and system, commands that reference a particular database.

7. Any system command that requires a special role in order to execute.

The SQL Server uses the *sybsecurity* system database to store its audit-trail information.

SQL Server Kernel Configuration for Databases

To configure the kernel for databases, the SQL Server provides you with a couple of parameters:

1. `default database size`
2. `number of open databases`
3. `number of open objects`

The `default database size` SQL Server configuration parameter establishes the default count of megabytes allocated to a new user database if you do not specify a size of the new database when you issue the `create database` command. If, when you issue the `create database` command, you specify a size of the new database, then that size will take precedence over the default database size. The default value of the `default database size` SQL Server configuration parameter is 2 MB. The range of values for this configuration parameter is 2 to 10,000 MB. In that new databases start with a copy of the *model* system database, you must be certain that the `default database size` SQL Server configuration parameter is always at least as large as the *model* system database.

To specify that the default size of new user databases will be 10 MB, log on to the SQL Server as an account with **sa_role** privileges and enter these commands:

```
1>use master
2>go
1>sp_configure "default database size", 10
2>go
```

For this change to take effect, you will have to shut down and then restart the SQL Server. This command changes the *master* system database, so to ensure its recovery, be certain to dump the *master* system database. As this command changes the contents of system tables, it cannot be used within a transaction.

The `number of open databases` SQL Server configuration parameter constrains the maximum number of system and user databases that can be open concurrently on the SQL Server. The default value of the `number of open databases` SQL Server configuration parameter is 12. The legal values for this configuration parameter range from 5 to 2,147,483,647 databases. As each open database consumes 17 KB of memory, you should not increase the value of the `number of open databases` SQL Server configuration parameter beyond the total number of databases on your SQL Server or beyond the practical limits of your system's support threshold.

To specify that the maximum number of databases simultaneously open on the SQL Server (e.g., 100 databases), log on to the SQL Server as an account with **sa_role** privileges and enter these commands:

```
1>use master
2>go
1>sp_configure "number of open databases", 100
2>go
```

For this change to take effect, you will have to shut down and then restart the SQL Server. This command changes the *master* system database, so to ensure its recovery, be certain to dump the *master* system database. As this command changes the contents of system tables, it cannot be used within a transaction.

The `number of open objects` SQL Server configuration parameter specifies the maximum number of principal database objects that can be open concurrently within the SQL Server. The default value of this configuration parameter is 500. The legal values for the `number of open objects` SQL Server configuration parameter range from 100 to 2,147,483,647 database objects. If the `number of open objects` SQL Server configuration parameter is set too low on your SQL Server, then an error message to that effect will be written into the SQL Server's error log each time an attempt is made to exceed the value. When this event occurs, just set the value a bit higher. Even though the overhead associated with the `number of open objects` SQL Server configuration parameter is minimal, do not go overboard when setting its value.

To specify that the maximum number of database objects simultaneously open on the SQL Server (e.g., 1000 database objects), log on to the SQL Server as an account with **sa_role** privileges and enter these commands:

```
1>use master
2>go
```

```
1>sp_configure "number of open objects", 1000
2>go
```

For this change to take effect, you will have to shut down, and then restart the SQL Server. This command changes the *master* system database, so to ensure its recovery, be certain to dump the *master* system database. As this command changes the contents of system tables, it cannot be used within a transaction.

Creating a User Database

Any Sybase account that is a legal user of the *master* system database, and to whom permission to create a database has been granted, can create a new user database. However, by default, this permission is limited to accounts with **sa_role** privileges.

To create a new user database, log on to the SQL Server as an authorized Sybase account and enter these commands:

```
1>use master
2>go
1>create database NameOfDatabase
2>[ on { default | NameOfDatabaseDevice } [ = size ]
3>[,NameOfDatabaseDevice [ = size ] ...]
4>[ log on NameOfDatabaseDevice [ = size ]
5>[,NameOfDatabaseDevice [ = size ]] ...]
6>[ with override ]
7>[ for load ]
8>go
```

where:

NameOfDatabase—the name of the new user database must conform to the rules for Sybase identifiers, and each database name must be unique within the SQL Server. It is beneficial to everyone (who will need to access this database) that you choose a name that reflects the intended use of the database.

[on { default—the purpose of the optional on clause is to enable you to specify the name(s) of one or more database devices upon which the database will reside. If you elect not to use the optional on clause, or if you use it in combination with the default reserved word, then the new user database will be placed on any of the default database devices listed within master..sysdevices, or on any default database device associated with that particular valid Sybase account. By default, that database device, as previously explained, would be the **d_master** database device. An additional consequence of not electing to use the optional on clause is that the size of your new user database will be the value of the database size SQL Server configuration parameter, or the size of the *model* system database, whichever of the two is larger.

NameOfDatabaseDevice—the name of the database device on which the database will reside. It is not possible when using the create database command to reference a database device that does not already exist within the master..sysdevices system table. If you do not comply with this requirement, then this command will fail.

[= size]—specifying the size of your new user database is optional. By default, the smallest a new user database can be is the value of the database size SQL Server configuration parameter, or the size of the *model* system database, whichever of the two is larger. If you skip the on clause, or if you do not specify the size of the database, then the size will be the SQL Server default database size. Unless you have modified the database size SQL Server configuration parameter, or the size of the *model* system database, then the smallest database size is 2 MB. However, if you elect to specify the size of the new user database, then you must do so by specifying its size in megabyte counts (e.g., = 2) for a database size that equals 2 MB. The largest value you can assign to size, on a per-database-device basis, is 2048 (i.e., 2048 MB). If you assign a value to size that is smaller than the SQL Server default database size, the create database command will fail (and you will receive an error message stating this fact). Also, if you assign more space to the new user database than is actually available on that referenced database device (or on the default database device), and if that available space is not less than the SQL Server default database size, then the create database command will still complete successfully, and you will receive a message that indicates the actual size of the new user database.

[,*NameOfDatabaseDevice* [= size] ...]—it is possible for a user database to reside on multiple database devices, and to consume varying amounts of space on those respective database devices. Therefore, when creating a new user database, you can, right from the start, assign space to that new user database from multiple database devices. However, an individual database cannot use more than 128 disk fragments, nor can it use more than 32 segments.

[log on *NameOfDatabaseDevice* [= size]—The purpose of the optional log on clause is to enable you to specify the name(s) of one or more database devices upon which the database's transaction log will reside. If you elect not to use the optional log on clause, then the transaction log will reside on the same database device as the database's data and index pages (this is generally not a good thing to have occur). There are a number of very good reasons why a transaction log should not reside on the same database device as the database's data and index pages:

1. To guarantee that the new user database is fully recoverable, the transaction log should not reside on a database device that will contain the data and index pages of this new user database. In the unfortunate event that the disk drive on which you have placed either the database or the transaction log crashes, then you can recover either the database or the transaction log from its respective dump.

2. It can significantly improve SQL Server performance. When the data and index pages are on a separate database device from that of the transaction log, and when these database devices are located on different disk drives, reads and writes to the database devices can take place concurrently, instead of linearly as is the case when both the pages and the log reside on the same database device.

3. It allows you to constructively use the `dump transaction log` command, not just the `dump database` command. This backup flexibility can reduce the amount of time it takes to do a backup, and it can contribute to reducing the amount of tape or disk space you need to set aside for doing backups.

4. The pages and the log are not forced to compete against each other for the same area of disk space. Instead, you can assign a fixed amount of disk space that is individually dedicated to each.

5. The SQL Server automatically creates a default `free-space threshold` to monitor the transaction log, and, additionally, allows you to create other free-space thresholds on both the data and log sections of the user database.

As regards the optional `size` parameter to the optional `log on` clause, the general rule is to assign a value to the `size` parameter that equals 10 to 25 percent of the size of the new user database. However, the actual size of a database's transaction log is really dependent upon the type, length, volume, and frequency of the (open) write transactions submitted to the database and the frequency at which you take transaction log dumps. For example, because deferred updates take up twice as much log space as direct updates, you need to know when deferred versus direct updates are taking place. Note that if you choose not to use the optional `size` parameter to this optional clause, then the transaction log will be given 2 MB of disk space.

`[ ,`*NameOfDatabaseDevice* `[ =` `size` `]] ...]`—it is possible for a transaction log to reside on multiple database devices, and to consume varying amounts of space on those respective database devices. Therefore, when creating a new user database, you can, right from the start, assign space to that new transaction log from multiple database devices.

[with override]—the purpose of this optional clause is to allow you to place both the data and the log on the same nondefault database device. On those SQL Servers where disk space is at a premium, having this option can make the difference in creating or not creating a new user database, or recovering or not recovering a database from a dump. Note that when you use this option, you are entirely dependent upon the dump database command.

[for load]—this option is used to load the new database from an existing database dump. You will need to invoke this capability of the create database command whenever you undertake to move an existing database from its current host computer to another host computer, or whenever you are forced to recover a database after a disk crash. Creating a new database with this option places constraints on how you can initially use this database. Before you actually load the database you can use only these commands: load database, drop database, and alter database ... for load; the SQL Server restricts you from using any other commands against the database. Fortunately, after you successfully run the load database command, the command restriction is permanently lifted. There are also constraints related to database device usage by the dump database and those database devices earmarked for use by the new database.

This change takes effect immediately. This command changes the *master* system database, so to ensure its recovery, be certain to dump the *master* system database. As this command changes the contents of system tables, it cannot be used within a transaction.

When the create database command executes successfully, the following course of action will be undertaken by the SQL Server:

1. Checks the name you have chosen for the database to ensure that it does not violate Sybase rules for an identifier, and ensures that the name of the new database is unique within the SQL Server.

2. Checks that the names of the database device are correct, and confirms that they in fact have space available to support this new user database.

3. Assigns a unique numeric identifier to the new user database.

4. Assigns space to the new user database from each of the specified database devices, and these disk fragment assignments are recorded within the master..sysusages system table.

5. Inserts a row, representing this new user database, into the master..sysdatabases system table.

6. Places a copy of the *model* system database inside the new user database space. As a consequence, the new user database inherits the following items:

- The system tables that are common to all databases.
- Database configuration options as set within the *model* system database.
- Rules, user-defined data types, defaults, tables, views, or stored procedures that exist within the *model* system database.
- Sybase accounts that exist within the *model* system database.
- Database permissions, particularly for the **guest** account, that exist within the *model* system database.

7. Initializes all required pages in all referenced database devices that were not initialized as a result of copying the *model* system database into the new user database space if the `for load` option has not been invoked. If the `for load` option has been invoked, then the SQL Server does not do that task. As you might imagine, the time it takes the SQL Server to complete this step can be a considerable; just how much time depends on the speed of your host computer and on the amount of space you have assigned to this new user database. To get a good feeling for how long this may take, on average, you can record the elapsed time it takes to create each new user database and use these measurements as a basis for guesstimating in the future.

As indicated in the preceding outline, the SQL Server always modifies the *master* system database whenever you successfully create a new user database. This command changes the *master* system database, so to ensure its recovery, be certain to dump the *master* system database. As this command changes the contents of system tables, it cannot be used within a transaction.

Because a copy of the *model* system database is used to create each new user database, the SQL Server is restricted to making one, and only one, new user database at a time. If you attempt to create two or more new user databases simultaneously, the SQL Server will allow the first one to proceed, but will abort the other `create database` commands.

User Database System Tables

A collection of 20 system tables are automatically defined whenever you create a new user database. These system tables are:

1. *sysalternates*. Contains Sybase accounts that are aliases to Sybase accounts in this database.

2. *sysattributes.*   For each object in the database, this table records object-attribute definitions that have been configured via system procedures.

3. *syscolumns.*   Contains the names of all columns in all tables and views, as well as the names of all parameters associated with all stored procedures that exist in this database.

4. *syscomments.*   Contains the definitions of defaults, rules, table constraints, stored procedures, triggers, and views that exist in this database.

5. *sysconstraints.*   Holds the check and referential constraints associated with a table or column in this database.

6. *sysdepends.*   Records the stored procedures, tables, and views that are referenced by stored procedures, triggers, or views or in this database.

7. *sysindexes.*   Records each clustered index, each nonclustered index, each table that does not have a clustered index, and each table that has a column of text or image data type in this database.

8. *syskeys.*   Holds the definition of each primary, foreign, and common key in this database.

9. *syslogs.*   This is the database's transaction log.

10. *sysobjects.*   Holds the identity of every check constraint, default, log, referential constraint, rule, stored procedure, table (temporary and work tables within the *tempdb* system database), trigger, and view in this database.

11. *syspartitions.*   Contains one row for each page chain (partition) of a partitioned table.

12. *sysprocedures.*   Holds the identity of every check constraint, declarative default, default, rule, stored procedure, trigger, and view in this database.

13. *sysprotects.*   Contains user-permission information on every `grant` and `revoke` permission command executed within this database.

14. *sysreferences.*   Contains the referential-integrity constraints declared on a column or on a table in this database.

15. *sysroles.*   Maps Server role identifiers to Local role identifiers in this database.

16. *sysegments.*   Records the identity of every segment used by this database.

17. *systhresholds.*   Records each threshold in this database.

18. *systypes.*   Contains all the definitions of all SQL Server defined data types, as well as all user-defined data types.

19. *sysusermessages.* Holds the user-defined messages that can be returned by the SQL Server.

20. *sysusers.* Records the groups, roles, and users allowed in this database.

Each new user database picks up all of these system tables when the copy of the *model* system database is placed within its space during the process that creates the new user database.

Database Options

Database-wide settings that an account with **sa_role** privileges, or an account with **dbo** privileges, can elect to change are called *database options*. These SQL Server database options, and their default values, are as follows:

1. abort tran on log full—this option's default value is false. This option determines what happens to a running transaction when it crosses the database transaction log's last-chance threshold. When set to the default value, the SQL Server will merely suspend the running transaction and then automatically restart it as soon as free space exists once again within the database's transaction log. When the value of this option is set to true, then all active user transactions that need to write to the filled database transaction log are automatically killed by the SQL Server until free space exists once again within the database's transaction log.

2. allow nulls by default—this option's default value is false. When the value of this option is set to false, the default value of a column is not null, which prohibits null from being assigned to a column, unless you specifically state in the column's definition that nulls are allowed. When the value of this option is set to true, the default value of a column is changed from not null to null, thereby putting your SQL Server in compliance with ANSI '89 SQL standard.

3. auto identify—this option's default value is false. When the value of this option is set to true, every time a table is created in this database, without specifying either an IDENTITY column, a primary key constraint, or a unique constraint, an IDENTITY column is automatically defined in each new table created within this database.

4. dbo use only—this option's default value is false. When the value of this option is set to true, only an account with **dbo** privileges may use the database.

5. ddl in tran—this option's default value is false. When the value of this option is set to true, a limited suite of data definition language

Transact-SQL commands can be executed from within a user transactions in the database. The suite of permitted data-definition language Transact-SQL commands is limited to: `alter table`, `create default`, `create index`, `create procedure`, `create rule`, `create schema`, `create table`, `create trigger`, `create view`, `drop default`, `drop index`, `drop procedure`, `drop rule`, `drop table`, `drop trigger`, `drop view`, `grant`, and `revoke`.

6. `identity in nonunique index`—this option's default value is false. If you set this option to true, and if the table already has an IDENTITY column, then that IDENTITY column will automatically be included by the SQL Server in all indexes you create on that table. As a consequence, all indexes on that table will be unique indexes, and so these unique indexes will then be used to support updatable cursors (this will ensure that the cursor will always be positioned at the correct row the next time `fetch` command is performed on the cursor) and isolation level 0 reads.

7. `no chkpt on recovery`—this option's default value is false. When the value of this option is set to false, a checkpoint record is attached to the database after it is recovered when the SQL Server is restarted, and, as an additional precaution, the database's sequence number is automatically changed by the SQL Server Checkpoint process. The checkpoint record ensures that the restarted SQL Server will not attempt to needlessly recover the database, when doing so would be inappropriate, and causes any following load of the database's transaction log to fail. When the value of this option is set to true, a database does not get a checkpoint record from the recovery process, and the database's sequence number is not changed by the automatic SQL Server Checkpoint process.

8. `no free space acctg`—this option's default value is true. When the value of this option is set to true, free-space accounting, and the execution of threshold actions for nonlog segments, are disabled. As a consequence, the rows-per-page value for each table is not automatically kept up to date by the SQL Server. As a result, system procedures that estimate nonlog segment usage by the database will likely produce incorrect information. When the value of this option is set to false, database recovery is significantly increased because, during the recovery process, free-space counts are recalculated for every nonlog segment associated with the database. Finally, you cannot disable free-space accounting on log segments.

9. `read only`—this option's default value is false. When the value of this option is set to true, user transactions that would modify data

within the database are prohibited, but user transactions that only read data are permitted.

10. `select into/bulk copy`—this option's default value is false. When the value of this option is set to true, the use of `writetext, select into` a permanent table, or `fast bulk copy` into a table that does not have an index or trigger associated with it, is allowed. As a consequence of setting the value of this option to true, two factors must be considered. First, when `writetext, select into,` and `fast bulk copy` commands are used, except for corresponding page allocations and page deallocations, a record of their use is not recorded within the database's transaction log. Second, because these commands are not recorded within the database's transaction log, it is not possible to use the `dump transaction` system command. It is strongly advised that, once these unlogged commands complete executing, the value of this option be set to false, and then the `dump database` system command be executed on this database. In this way, you will be in a position to fully recover the database, if need be.

11. `single user`—this option's default value is false. When the value of this option is set to true, only one Sybase account at a time may be connected to this database.

12. `trunc log on chkpt`—this option's default value is false. When the value of this option is set to false, the database's transaction log will fill up until an account with **dbo** or **sa_role** privileges successfully issues the `dump transaction` system command. When the value of this option is set to true, committed, and rolled back, transactions are removed from the database's transaction log each time the database's checkpoint process is run automatically by the SQL Server. The purpose of this option of automatic committed and rolled back transaction removal is to decrease the chance that the database transaction log's last-chance threshold will be crossed, and to ensure that the database transaction log does not fill up. As a consequence of setting the value of this option to true, it is not possible to use the plain vanilla `dump transaction` system command. Therefore, in most cases, it is inappropriate to set the value of this option to true for production databases because a copy of the database's transaction log is not made prior to truncating the transaction log. However, it is appropriate to set the value of this option to true when the database and its transaction log are not located on separate segments, or when the ability to recover a database is not necessary, as is the case in some development or testing environments. When the value of this option is set to true, to be able to recover the database you must use the `dump database`

system command. Finally, it is important to realize that the database's transaction log is not truncated when the `checkpoint` system command is executed when the value of this option is set to true. However, you can still use the `truncate only` command option.

13. `trunc. log on chkpt.`—refer to the `trunc log on chkpt` option.

Setting Database Options

To set a database option, log on to the SQL Server as an account with **dbo** or with **sa_role** privileges, and enter these commands:

```
1>use master
2>go
1>sp_dboption NameOfDatabase, "database option", { true | false }
2>go
1>checkpoint
2>go
```

where:

NameOfDatabase—the name of the user database whose database options you want to change.

"database option"—the specific Boolean database option you want to set. Be certain to enclose the given database option within quotation marks.

`{ true | false }`—the literal value of a database option can be set to either true or false.

`checkpoint`—the new database option setting will not take effect until this command is issued (or, until the SQL Server is restarted).

This command changes the *master* system database, so to ensure its recovery, be certain to dump the *master* system database. As this command changes the contents of system tables, it cannot be used within a transaction.

To set database options for all new user databases that you will create, set a given database option within the *model* system database. However, this approach has its drawbacks:

1. The setting of a given database option may not be appropriate for all new user databases.

2. As the *model* system database is used to define the *tempdb* system database at SQL Server start-up, certain problems can arise within the *tempdb* system database. For example, it is not advisable to set

the value of the `ddl in tran` database option to true within the *model* system database, because the execution of data-definition language Transact-SQL commands necessitates the holding of locks within the system tables, such as *sysobjects*. Because the *tempdb* system database is shared by all databases, if the value of the `ddl in tran` database option is set to true, then the performance of the SQL Server can degrade rapidly.

3. As the *model* system database is used to define all new user databases, setting the value of the `trunc log on chkpt` database option to true, can be problematic. You will not be able to load the new user database with data and log dumps from a source database. Therefore, if within the *model* system database the value of the `trunc log on chkpt` database option has been set to equal true, then first set the `trunc log on chkpt` database option to false within the new user database and then load new user database by using the data and log dumps from the source database. If you prefer, then reset the `trunc log on chkpt` database option to true after the data and log dumps have completed successfully.

There are some constraints associated with the `sp_dboption` system procedure:

1. As the *master* system database's database options cannot be changed, it cannot be used on the *master* system database.

2. No one can be using the database when you set one of its database options.

3. During SQL Server run time, the change in a database option takes place only after running the `checkpoint` command.

Granting Create-Database Permission to a Login Account

Any Sybase account that is a legal user of the *master* system database, and to whom permission to create a database has been granted, can create a new user database. It is strongly advised, to protect the SQL Server installation, and to carefully manage the use of database device resources, that the privilege of creating new user databases be highly restricted. However, if you have a trusted and skilled login account, and you want to permit that login account to create databases within the SQL Server, then log on to the SQL Server as an account with **sa_role** privileges and enter these commands:

```
1>use master
2>go
```

```
1>grant create database to loginame
2>go
```

where:

loginame—the name of the login account to which you want to grant permission to create user databases. Every database this login account creates will own and assume the role of **dbo** (i.e., database owner).

Determining Database Ownership

To determine the Sybase account that owns a given database, log on to the SQL Server as any valid Sybase account and enter these commands:

```
1>use master
2>go
1>sp_helpdb NameOfDatabase
2>go
```

where:

NameOfDatabase—the name of the user database for which you want to determine ownership.

The sp_helpdb system command provides a collection of information about the database, one piece of information of which is the login account that owns the database.

Changing Database Ownership

The login account that creates a user database owns that database. However, only an account with **sa_role** privileges can change ownership of a given user database.

To change ownership of a given user database, log on to the SQL Server as an account with **sa_role** privileges and enter these commands:

```
1>use NameOfDatabase
2>go
1>sp_changedbowner loginame
2>go
1>checkpoint
2>go
```

where:

NameOfDatabase—the name of the user database for which you want to change ownership.

`loginame`—the name of the Sybase account that will now be the owner of the database.

This command changes the *master* system database, so to ensure its recovery, be certain to dump the *master* system database. As this command changes the contents of system tables, it cannot be used within a transaction.

After the `sp_changedbowner` system command completes successfully, an account with **sa_role** privileges must grant the appropriate permissions within the user database to the new database owner.

Use of the `sp_changedbowner` system command has these additional constraints:

1. You must be using the database whose ownership you want to change.

2. You cannot change the ownership of the *master* system database. The *master* system database is always owned by the Sybase **sa** account.

3. The Sybase account must exist before you can assign ownership of a user database to it.

4. The Sybase account cannot be a user of the database to which you are assigning ownership. If the Sybase account is currently a user of the database to which you want to assign ownership, then log on to the SQL Server as an account with **sa_role** privileges and enter these commands:

```
1>use NameOfDatabase
2>go
1>sp_dropuser loginame
2>go
1>checkpoint
2>go
```

5. The Sybase account cannot have an alias in the database to which you are assigning ownership. An alias is a Sybase account that can act as the **dbo** of a user database. If the Sybase account currently has an alias **dbo** in the database to which you want to assign ownership, then log on to the SQL Server as an account with **sa_role** privileges and enter these commands:

```
1>use NameOfDatabase
2>go
```

```
1>sp_dropalias loginame
2>go
1>checkpoint
2>go
```

6. If you want to transfer aliases, and their permissions, to the new database owner, then log on to the SQL Server as an account with **sa_role** privileges and enter these commands:

```
1>use NameOfDatabase
2>go
1>sp_changedbowner loginame, true
2>go
1>checkpoint
2>go
```

7. If you execute the `sp_changedbowner` system command without using the optional true parameter, then all aliases that currently exist within the user database, and their respective permissions within the given user database, will automatically be dropped by the SQL Server.

8. You should not use the `sp_changedbowner` system command to change ownership of the *sybsystemprocs* system database.

Functions of the dbo

Login accounts that own a database assume the privileges and responsibilities of the **dbo.** The **dbo** has the ability to accomplish any task within, as well as grant permissions to other login accounts that use the database it owns.

Any accounts with **dbo** privileges in a given database can execute these commands (which cannot be transferred to any other user of their database except where noted) in that database:

1. `checkpoint` (shared with accounts that have **sa_role** privileges).

2. `dbcc` (shared with accounts that have **sa_role** privileges).

3. `drop database` (shared with accounts that have **sa_role** privileges).

4. `dump database` (shared with accounts that have **oper_role** privileges).

5. `dump transaction` (shared with accounts that have **oper_role** privileges).

6. `grant` object-creation permission to other login accounts that use their database (shared with accounts that have **sa_role** privileges).

7. `load database` (shared with accounts that have **oper_role** privileges).

8. `load transaction` (shared with accounts that have **oper_role** privileges).

9. `revoke` object-creation permission to other login accounts that use their database (shared with accounts that have **sa_role** privileges).

10. `setuser` (shared with accounts that have **sa_role** privileges).

11. `sp_addalias` (shared with accounts that have **sa_role** privileges).

12. `sp_adduser` (shared with accounts that have **sa_role** privileges).

13. `sp_addgroup` (shared with accounts that have **sa_role** privileges).

14. `sp_changegroup` (shared with accounts that have **sa_role** privileges).

15. `sp_dropalias` (shared with accounts that have **sa_role** privileges).

16. `sp_dropuser` (shared with accounts that have **sa_role** privileges).

17. `sp_dropgroup` (shared with accounts that have **sa_role** privileges).

Any accounts with **dbo** privileges can also grant and revoke these permissions to any user of the database they own:

1. `create default` (shared with accounts that have **sa_role** privileges).

2. `create index` (shared with accounts that have **sa_role** privileges).

3. `create procedure` (shared with accounts that have **sa_role** privileges).

4. `create rule` (shared with accounts that have **sa_role** privileges).

5. `create table` (shared with accounts that have **sa_role** privileges).

6. `create view` (shared with accounts that have **sa_role** privileges).

7. `grant` permissions on system tables and principal database objects within the database (shared with accounts that have **sa_role** privileges).

8. `revoke` permissions on system tables and principal database objects within the database (shared with accounts that have **sa_role** privileges).

Creating a Database Group

Groups are mechanisms which allow a database owner to create a name for a collection of users of the database. Creating groups in a database is an advantageous way to grant and revoke permissions for principal database objects to a single entity, instead of to individual users of a database.

Each database contains a group called *public*. Every login account that is added to a given database is a member of the public group. A login account can be a member of one other group, but it will always be a member of the public group regardless of which other one it may belong to.

To create a new group within a database, log on to the SQL Server as an account with **dbo** privileges, or as an account with **sa_role** privileges, and enter these commands:

```
1>use NameOfDatabase
2>go
1>sp_addgroup NameOfGroup
2>go
```

where:

NameOfDatabase—the name of the database in which you want to create the new group.

NameOfGroup—the name of the group you want to create within the specified database. The name of the group cannot match the name of a login account that has been added to the specified database. The name must be unique across groups within the database and must comply with all rules for identifiers.

Once a group has been created, permissions within the database can be granted to it and users of the database can become members of the group. Once this command completes successfully, the group is immediately valid within the database and can be used immediately. This command changes the database's system tables, so to ensure its recovery, be certain to dump its transaction log and then dump the database itself. Also, because this command changes the contents of the system tables it cannot be executed within a transaction.

Reporting on Users of a Database

Before you add a login account, a user, to a database, you should produce a report of all users within a given database. To determine which login accounts are users of a database, log on to the SQL Server as any user of the target database and enter these commands:

```
1>use NameOfDatabase
2>go
```

```
1>sp_helpuser [loginame]
2>go
```

where:

NameOfDatabase—the name of the database for which you want to produce a report of all users, or a single user, within that database.

[loginame]—the login name of the user within the database for which you want to produce a report. If this optional parameter is not provided, then a report on all users in the database will be produced.

The report this command produces will contain user name(s), user ID within the database (uid), the group name, the user's login name (this will be **dbo** for the login account that owns the database or that has been aliased to the **dbo**), and the user's default database.

Adding a User to a Database

Before a login account can use a given database, the login account must be added to that database. To add a login account to a given database, log on to the SQL Server as an account with **dbo** privileges, or as an account with **sa_role** privileges, and enter these commands:

```
1>use NameOfDatabase
2>go
1>sp_adduser loginame[, UserNameInDatabase [, NameOfGroup ]]
2>go
```

where:

NameOfDatabase—the name of the database to which you want to add the login account.

loginame—the login name of the user that you want to add to a database.

UserNameInDatabase—this optional parameter is the name you want to give to the login account in this database. If you do not use this optional parameter, then the name of the user will be the same as the name of their login account. If you do not want to create a user name for this login account, but you do want to have this login account to be a member of a group (in addition to the public group), then you must provide the character string null for this parameter. You must not enclose the character string null in quotes (" ").

NameOfGroup—this optional parameter is the name of the group to which you want this login account to be a member. If you do not use this optional parameter, then the login account will only be a member of the public group in this database. Even if you specify another group, the user will still belong to the public group. A user and a group it belongs to cannot share the same name.

Once this command completes successfully, the login account is immediately valid within the database and can be used immediately. Once a login account has been added to a database, permissions within the database can be granted to it and it can execute the `use` database command. It will use the database as its default database if another database has not already been assigned to it, and can use the `sp_modifylogin` system procedure to make this database its default database. This command changes the database's system tables, so to ensure its recovery be certain to dump its transaction log and then dump the database itself. Also, because this command changes the contents of the system tables, it cannot be executed within a transaction.

Adding the "guest" User to a Database

The SQL Server allows you to create a user named "guest" in any database, which enables every login account to use that database (just so long as the guest login has not been dropped from the *master* or *tempdb* system databases) with the permissions granted to the guest user, as well as those granted to the public group. This is, in most production environments, a serious breach of security.

To add the guest user to a given database, log on to the SQL Server as an account with **dbo** privileges, or as an account with **sa_role** privileges, and enter these commands:

```
1>use NameOfDatabase
2>go
1>sp_adduser guest
2>go
```

where:

NameOfDatabase—the name of the database to which you want to add the guest login account.

Once this command completes successfully, the guest user is immediately valid within the database and can be used immediately. Once a login account has been added to a database, permissions within the database can be granted to it and it can execute the `use` database command. This command changes the database's system tables, so to ensure its recovery be certain to dump its transaction log and then dump the database itself. Also, because this command changes the contents of the system tables, it cannot be executed within a transaction.

Aliasing a User in a Database

The SQL Server allows two or more login accounts to act as if they were the same user in a database. The act of setting up such a collective identity is called *aliasing*. More often than not, aliasing is used to allow multiple login accounts to be a **dbo** of the same database.

To alias a login account in a given database, log on to the SQL Server as an account with **dbo** privileges, or as an account with **sa_role** privileges, and enter these commands:

```
1>use NameOfDatabase
2>go
1>sp_addalias loginame, UserNameInDatabase
2>go
```

where:

NameOfDatabase—the name of the database in which you want to create an alias.

loginame—the login name of the user that you want to have aliased. A login account can be aliased to only one other login account at a time.

UserNameInDatabase—the name of the login account in this database which you want to alias. If the database owner will be aliased, then parameter will be the character string dbo. To determine which login accounts are aliased to **dbo,** pass the character string dbo to the **sp_helpuser** system procedure.

Once this command completes successfully, the alias is immediately valid within the database and can be used immediately. This command changes the database's system tables, so to ensure its recovery, be certain to dump its transaction log and then dump the database itself. Also, because this command changes the contents of the system tables, it cannot be executed within a transaction.

Removing an Alias from a User in a Database

To alias a login account in a given database, log on to the SQL Server as an account with **dbo** privileges, or as an account with **sa_role** privileges, and enter these commands:

```
1>use NameOfDatabase
2>go
```

```
1>sp_dropalias loginame
2>go
```

where:

NameOfDatabase—the name of the database in which you want to drop an alias.

loginame—the login name of the user who's alias you want to remove.

Once this command completes successfully, the alias is immediately invalid within the database. This command changes the database's system tables, so to ensure its recovery, be certain to dump its transaction log and then dump the database itself. Also, because this command changes the contents of the system tables, it cannot be executed within a transaction.

Changing a Database User's Group Membership

At any given time, a login account can be a member of another group in addition to the public group. Membership in a database group can be changed at any point in time by an account with **dbo** privileges, or by an account with **sa_role** privileges.

To change the group a login account is a member of, log on to the SQL Server as an account with **dbo** privileges, or as an account with **sa_role** privileges, and enter these commands:

```
1>use NameOfDatabase
2>go
1>sp_changegroup NameOfGroup, UserNameInDatabase
2>go
```

where:

NameOfDatabase—the name of the database in which you want to change group membership.

NameOfGroup—the name of the group to which you want this login account to be a member. If the login account is to be a member of the public group, then the character string public must be enclosed in quotes (""). A user and a group it belongs to cannot share the same name.

UserNameInDatabase—the name of the user in this database that you want to change group membership for. If the login account has not been given a user name in the database, then this parameter will be set to the name of the login account.

Once this command completes successfully, the login account's group membership takes effect immediately within the database. This command changes the database's system tables, so to ensure its recovery, be certain to dump its transaction log and then dump the database itself. Also, because this command changes the contents of the system tables, it cannot be executed within a transaction.

Reporting on User Permissions in a Database

Database users, groups, and roles can be granted permission to create defaults, procedures, rules, tables, and views. In the chapters that follow, we will explore granting and revoking these permissions for database users, groups, and roles. In this chapter, however, we will explain the way to determine which object-creation permissions have been granted to a database user, a group, and a role.

To produce a report of user, group, and role permission within a database, log on to the SQL Server as any valid login account and enter these commands:

```
1>use NameOfDatabase
2>go
1>sp_helprotect [Name]
2>go
```

where:

NameOfDatabase—the name of the database in which you want to report on user, group, and role permissions.

[Name]—this optional parameter is the name of the user, group, or role for which you want a report of their permissions within the database. If you do not provide this optional parameter, then permissions for all users, groups, and roles within the database will be reported.

When the command completes executing, the SQL Server will produce a report showing the create-object permissions that exist for the database user, group, or role.

Dropping a User from a Database

You can drop users from a database only if they:

1. Do not own a principal database object, as well as a threshold, in the database. You will have to drop these principal database objects and thresholds from the database before you can drop the user from the database.

2. Have not granted permissions to any other user of the database. You will have to revoke these permissions within the database before you can drop the user from the database.

To drop a (qualified) user from a database, log on to the SQL Server as an account with **dbo** privileges, or as an account with **sa_role** privileges, and enter these commands:

```
1>use NameOfDatabase
2>go
1>sp_dropuser UserNameInDatabase
2>go
```

where:

NameOfDatabase—the name of the database from which you want to drop the user.

UserNameInDatabase—the name of the user in this database that you want to drop. If the login account has not been given a user name in the database, then this parameter will be set to the name of the login account. If other users are aliased to this user, then their alias is dropped as well. This name cannot be the **dbo.**

Once this command completes successfully, dropping the user will take effect immediately within the database. This command changes the database's system tables, so to ensure its recovery, be certain to dump its transaction log and then dump the database itself. Also, because this command changes the contents of the system tables, it cannot be executed within a transaction.

Dropping the "guest" User from a Database

If you want to shore up the security hole provided by the **guest** login account then it will have to be dropped from the *master* system database, the *tempdb* system database, and from every user database it has been added to. When you drop the **guest** login account from the *master* and the *tempdb* system databases, the "guest" mechanism will not function within user databases. You must still ensure that the **guest** login account does not own any principal database object or threshold in the database, and that it has not granted any permissions to any other login account in the database.

To drop the **guest** login account, log on to the SQL Server as an account with **dbo** privileges, or as an account with **sa_role** privileges, and enter these commands:

```
1>use NameOfDatabase
2>go
1>sp_dropuser "guest"
2>go
```

where:

NameOfDatabase—the name of the database in which you want to drop the **guest** login account.

Once this command completes successfully within both the *master* and the *tempdb* system databases, the "guest" mechanism in all user databases will be disabled. This command changes the database's system tables, so to ensure its recovery, be certain to dump its transaction log and then dump the database itself. Also, because this command changes the contents of the system tables, it cannot be executed within a transaction.

Dropping a Group from a Database

To drop a group, you must be certain that no users are members of that group. If there is a user member in the group you wish to drop then the SQL Server will display an error message to that effect. In that all database users are members of the public group, you cannot drop the public group.

To drop a group from a database, log on to the SQL Server as an account with **dbo** privileges, or as an account with **sa_role** privileges, and enter these commands:

```
1>use NameOfDatabase
2>go
1>sp_dropgroup NameOfGroup
2>go
```

where:

NameOfDatabase—the name of the database from which you want to drop the group.

NameOfGroup—the name of the group you want to drop from the database.

Once this command completes successfully, the group is immediately invalid within the database and is purged from the database. This command changes the database's system tables, so to ensure its recovery, be certain to dump its transaction log and then dump the database itself. Also, because this command changes the contents of the system tables, it cannot be executed within a transaction.

Placing a Database in dbo use only Mode

By default, all authorized users of a database can access that database concurrently. However, situations arise, like running database consistency checks or making repairs to indexes and tables, where you would prefer that only the database owner can access a given database. To set a database into `"dbo use only"` mode, log on to the SQL Server as an account with **dbo** privileges, or as an account with **sa_role** privileges, and enter these commands:

```
1>use master
2>go
1>sp_dboption NameOfDatabase, "dbo use only", true
2>go
1>checkpoint
2>go
```

where:

NameOfDatabase—the name of the database that you want to limit access to only the database owner.

As soon as this command completes successfully, no other account other than the **dbo** can begin to access the database. Any current users of the database will remain within that database until they log off, or until their process is killed by an account with **sa_role** privileges.

To enable other users to access the database once again, merely run the above commands, but replace the character string `true` with the character string `false`.

Checking Database Consistency

Despite the best efforts put forward by the developers of the System 11 SQL Server, database consistency can be lost as a result of product bugs or the SQL Server crashing. The goal of Sybase is to make the need to check database consistency a thing of the past. But, while significant improvements have been made with System 11, that goal has not yet been reached. Therefore, you may need to schedule times when you check the consistency of each and every system and user database that is managed by the SQL Server.

The SQL Server has a utility called the *database consistency checker* (**dbcc**) that database owners can use to check the logical and physical consistency within the databases they own. It is important to understand that in order for the **dbcc** utility to do its work, it takes and holds locks on the database object it is checking. As a consequence of taking these locks, serious contention problems can arise within the database, and performance can grind to a halt. So, be certain to execute the **dbcc** utility when doing so avoids contention within the database.

The **dbcc** utility can detect, and (sometimes) correct logical and physical inconsistencies within databases before (and after) these inconsistencies result in a database outage. Your goal should be to discover the database inconsistency as soon as possible and then take the necessary steps to repair whatever damage occurred (if possible).

The **dbcc** utility has three facilities that accounts with **dbo** or **sa_role** privileges can use to check the overall consistency of the database they own (plus facilities for checking and repairing tables and indexes as well):

1. dbcc checkdb
2. dbcc checkcatalog
3. dbcc checkalloc

The dbcc checkdb utility runs these checks on all tables in the database to ensure that they are consistent as regards:

1. Data page linkages.
2. Index page linkages.
3. Sort order of the index.
4. All pointers (e.g., allocation page pointers, OAM page pointers).
5. Data rows on every data page have an entry in the first OAM page to maps to their respective locations on the data page. If a data row is not accounted for on the OAM page, then the OAM page will be updated.
6. Index rows on every index page have an entry in the first OAM page to maps to their respective locations on the index page. If an index row is not accounted for on the OAM page, then the OAM page will be updated.

To run the dbcc checkdb utility, log on to the SQL Server as the **dbo** and execute this command:

```
1>dbcc checkdb [(NameOfDatabase [, skip_ncindex]) ]
2>go
```

where:

> *NameOfDatabase*—this optional parameter is the name of the database that you own and want to run this **dbcc** utility against. If you do not provide this optional parameter, then the current database will be checked.

> `skip_ncindex`—this optional parameter allows the `dbcc checkdb` utility to skip the checking of nonclustered indexes on user tables in the current database. As it is possible to simply rebuild corrupted nonclustered indexes without fear of loss of data, using this option can decrease the time it takes to check the database. The default is to check all indexes.

The SQL Server will produce a report of this consistency check and error messages of any inconsistency it encounters. If errors are reported, then read the Trouble Shooting Guide and contact Sybase Technical Support, if need be, for assistance in recovering consistency.

If you have bound the tables the `dbcc checkdb` utility is checking to a Named Data Cache with a 16K Memory Pool, then the `dbcc checkdb` utility will use that 16K Memory Pool when checking their consistency. However, the `dbcc checkdb` utility will always use a 2K Memory Pool when checking the consistency of the table indexes.

The `dbcc checkcatalog` utility checks consistency within and between the database's system tables, and verifies that:

1. Every data type recorded in the *syscolumns* system table has a corresponding entry in the *systypes* system table.

2. Every table and view within the *sysobjects* system table has at least one corresponding entry in the *syscolumns* system table.

3. The last checkpoint recorded within the *syslogs* system table is OK.

To run the `dbcc checkcatalog` utility, log on to the SQL Server as the **dbo,** and execute this command:

```
1>dbcc checkcatalog[NameOfDatabase]
2>go
```

where:

> *NameOfDatabase*—this optional parameter is the name of the database that you own and want to run this **dbcc** utility against. If you do not provide this optional parameter, then the current database will be checked.

The SQL Server will produce a report of this consistency check, display the segments used by this database, and produce error messages of any inconsistency it encounters. If errors are reported, then read the Trouble Shooting Guide and contact Sybase Technical Support, if need be, for assistance in recovering consistency.

The dbcc checkalloc utility is used to verify that:

1. All pages, of all types, are accurately allocated.
2. No page is allocated that is not being used.
3. No page that is being used is not allocated.

To run the dbcc checkalloc utility, log on to the SQL Server as the **dbo** and execute this command:

```
1>dbcc checkalloc[NameOfDatabase] [, nofix]
2>go
```

where:

> *NameOfDatabase*—this optional parameter is the name of the database that you own and want to run this **dbcc** utility against. If you do not provide this optional parameter, then the current database will be checked.

> nofix—this optional parameter is the default for this command. You need not specify it.

The SQL Server will produce a report of this consistency check, and will produce error messages of any inconsistency it encounters. If the SQL Server's memory has been configured to support extent I/O work buffers, then the dbcc checkalloc facility will use them to do its work and will complete at significantly faster rates.

If errors are reported, then read the Trouble Shooting Guide and contact Sybase Technical Support, if need be, for assistance in recovering consistency. You can elect to attempt to fix the reported problems, but doing so can result in lost data (and may not succeed). To run the dbcc checkalloc utility to fix reported problems, log on to the SQL Server as the **dbo** and place the database into "dbo use only" mode, have all active processes against the database terminated, and then execute this command:

```
1>dbcc checkalloc[NameOfDatabase] fix
2>go
```

where:

> *NameOfDatabase*—this optional parameter is the name of the database that you own and want to run this **dbcc** utility against. If you

do not provide this optional parameter, then the current database will be checked.

fix—if you specify this optional parameter, then the utility will attempt to fix the corruption problem(s). However, loss of data may occur.

Changing the Name of a Database

In addition to changing the owner of a user database, you can also change the name. However, only an account with **sa_role** privileges can change the name of a database.

Before an account with **sa_role** privileges can rename a user database, these preliminaries must be satisfied:

1. You cannot rename a database if it contains a table that references or that is referenced by a table in another database. It is possible, within a SQL Server, for external database tables to place foreign key constraints on a primary key of a table in the database about to be renamed. To determine if this case is applicable, then, as a valid Sybase account (that has permissions to use the database that is to be renamed), log on to the SQL Server and enter these commands:

```
1>use NameOfDatabase
2>go
1>select object_name(tableid), db_name(frgndbname)
2>from sysreferences
3>where frgndbname is not NULL
4>go
```

In addition, it is possible for external database tables to place primary key constraints on a foreign key of a table in the database about to be renamed. To determine if this case is applicable:

```
1>use NameOfDatabase
2>go
1>select object_name(reftabid), db_name(pmrydbname)
2>from sysreferences
3>where pmrydbname is not NULL
4>go
```

If, after running either of these queries, you discover that foreign key constraints or primary key constraints exist within the database about to be renamed, then, as the table owner, or an account with **dbo** or **sa_role** privileges that is impersonating the table owner, enter these commands:

```
1>use NameOfDatabase
2>go
```

```
1>alter table NameOfTable
2>drop constraint NameOfConstraint
3>go
```

After the database has been renamed, be certain to re-create all of the constraints that you dropped. This command changes the database, so be sure to dump the database's transaction log and then dump the database.

2. As is demonstrated in later chapters, it is possible within a System SQL Server for views, stored database procedures, and triggers to explicitly reference a database by its name. Once you change a name of a database, the views, stored database procedures, and triggers will continue to work properly until the point in time when they are recompiled. To correct this problem, you will have to update the definitions of all affected views, stored database procedures, and triggers that will be affected by the new database name. To determine which views, stored database procedures, and triggers are potentially impacted by this change in database names, you will use the sp_depends system command (this command is covered in depth in a later chapter). Once you identify the impacted views, stored database procedures, and triggers, then, after the database is renamed, you will have to modify their respective definitions so that they reference the database by its new name, drop their current incarnations from the database, and then re-create them.

3. An account with **sa_role** privileges must place the user database into single-user mode. To accomplish this you must make certain that no one is currently using the database you intend to rename. To determine if anyone is using the database, then as a valid Sybase account (that has permission to use the database that is to be renamed), log on to the SQL Server and execute the sp_who command. If there are no other users currently in the database, then within the output of this command you will see "sa_role" as the login name for processes that support the sp_who system command, and you will see "NULL" as the login name for all SQL Server system processes. If any other processes or login names are displayed, then you will not be able to bring the database into single-user mode. Take the time to contact everyone who is running a process within the database and ask them to exit from the database. If you are unable to reach them and it is crucial that you immediately proceed with the renaming of the database, then you can terminate their processes. The spid column in the output from the sp_who command contains the Sybase process identifier of each process that is present within the current database. To terminate an offending process, log on to the SQL Server as an account with **sa_role** privileges and enter these commands:

```
1>use NameOfDatabase
2>go
1>kill spid
2>go
```

Repeat the `kill` command for each offending process, as necessitated. When it is possible to bring the database into single-user mode, then, as an account with **dbo,** or **sa_role** privileges, enter these commands:

```
1>use master
2>go
1>sp_dboption NameOfDatabase, "single user", true
2>go
1>checkpoint
2>go
```

This ensures that no one else can gain access to the database from this point forward through the renaming process.

To change the name of a given user database, log on to the SQL Server as an account with **sa_role** privileges and enter these commands:

```
1>use master
2>go
1>sp_renamedb OldNameOfDatabase, NewNameOfDatabase
2>go
```

where:

OldNameOfDatabase—the current name of the database whose name you want to change. This cannot be a system database.

NewNameOfDatabase—the new name of the user database must conform to the rules for Sybase identifiers, and each database name must be unique within the SQL Server. It is beneficial to everyone (who will need to access this database) that you choose names that reflect the intended use of the database.

This command changes the *master* system database, so to ensure its recovery, be certain to dump the *master* system database. As this command changes the contents of system tables, it cannot be used within a transaction.

A final word of warning about using the `sp_renamedb` system command: if the database you want to rename is under the control of a Sybase Replication Server, then you must not rename that database, because, if you rename a database that has been assimilated into a replication system, then you will significantly corrupt that replication system.

Displaying Information about Principal Database Objects within a Database

To obtain information about the principal database objects within a current database, log on to the SQL Server as any valid Sybase account (that has permission to use the database you want to examine) and enter these commands:

```
1>use NameOfDatabase
2>go
1>sp_help
2>go
```

When completed executing, this command will display information about user tables and views, system tables, indexes, triggers, stored procedures, the database's transaction log, user-defined data types (their base Sybase data types, length, and any rule or default bound to it, and nullability), rules, defaults, checks, and referential constraints, as well as the Sybase account that owns each principal database object.

Determining the Size of a Database

The size of a database includes both the data space and the log space assigned to it. To determine the size of a database, log on to the SQL Server as any valid Sybase account (that has permission to use the database you want to examine) and enter these commands:

```
1>use NameOfDatabase
2>go
1>sp_helpdb NameOfDatabase
2>go
```

When the sp_helpdb system command is executed as shown above, the following three sets of data will be displayed:

Group 1

name—the name of the database.

db size—the total size of the database, including data- and log-space assignments.

owner—the name of the Sybase account that is the owner of the database.

dbid—the database's numeric identifier.

created—the month, day, and year in which the database was created.

status—displays the current status of the database. There are two categories of database status: one that represents the status of settable database options, and one that represents the status automatically set by the SQL Server itself. Examples of status messages: crashed while loading database, database suspect, or database name has changed.

Group 2

device_fragments—the name of the database device on which the database has been placed.

size—the size, in megabytes, of the device fragment.

usage—indicates if the device fragment is being used to hold log records, data pages, or both log records and data pages.

free kbytes—the space, in kilobytes, within the device fragment that has not been allocated to store data pages or log records.

Group 3

device—the name of the database device on which this database has been placed.

segment—indicates if the device is being used as a log segment, a master segment, or a default data segment.

Determining the Database Devices Used by a Database

To determine the database devices being used by a given database, log on to the SQL Server as any valid Sybase account and enter these commands:

```
1>use master
2>go
1>sp_helpdb NameOfDatabase
2>go
```

Determining the Amount of Space a Database Is Using

Determining the amount of space a database is currently consuming can only be known for the tables, clustered indexes, and nonclustered indexes the database includes.

To determine the amount of space a database is currently consuming, log on to the SQL Server as any valid Sybase account (that has permission to use the database you want to examine) and enter these commands:

```
1>use NameOfDatabase
2>go
1>sp_spaceused
2>go
```

When the `sp_spaceused` system command is executed as shown above, the following two sets of data will be displayed:

Group 1

> `database_name`—the name of the database.
>
> `database_size`—the total amount of data space, in megabytes, allocated to this database (via the `create database` and `alter database` commands).

Group 2

> `reserved`—the total amount of space that has been reserved for use by tables and indexes included within this database. Space is reserved for a database whenever the SQL Server automatically assigns a new extent to this database.
>
> `data`—displays how much space is actually being used, as opposed to being reserved for use, by tables within this database.
>
> `index_size`—reveals how much space is actually being used, as opposed to being reserved for use, by clustered and nonclustered indexes within this database.
>
> `unused`—indicates the amount of space that has been reserved for use by this database, but which is not yet being used by any table or index within this database.

If you add together the `data`, `index_size` and `unused` displayed values, then they should equal the amount of reserved space.

To determine how much of the allocated space still remains to be reserved by this database, then subtract the amount of reserved space from the size of the database.

Changing the Size of a Database

Just about every database you create will require more disk space over time. This need for space can be accommodated prior to the point in time when it is needed, or during run time when client processes have been suspended by the SQL Server because the log segment has run out of space.

To alter the size of a database, log on to the SQL Server as an account with **dbo** or **sa_role** privileges and enter these commands:

```
1>use master
2>go
1>alter database NameOfDatabase
2>[ on { default | NameOfDatabaseDevice } [ = size ]
3>[, NameOfDatabaseDevice [ = size ]] ...]
4>[ log on { default | NameOfDatabaseDevice } [ = size ]
5>[, NameOfDatabaseDevice [ = size ]] ...]
6>[ with override ]
7>[ for load ]
8>go
```

where:

NameOfDatabase—the name of the existing database whose size you want to increase.

[on { default—the purpose of the optional on clause is to enable you to specify the name(s) of one or more database devices upon which the database will be extended. If you elect not to use the optional on clause, or if you use it in combination with the default reserved word, then the database will be extended onto any of the default database devices listed within master..sysdevices, or on any default database device associated with that particular Sybase account. By default, that database device would, as previously explained, be extended onto the **d_master** database device. An additional consequence of not electing to use the optional on clause, is that the size of your database will be increased by only 1 MB.

NameOfDatabaseDevice—the name of the database device must conform to the rules for Sybase identifiers. It is not possible when using the alter database command to reference a database device that does not already exist within the master..sysdevices system table. If you do not comply with this requirement, then this command will fail.

[= size]—specifies the size by which your database is to be increased. The smallest default amount by which a database can be increased is 1 MB. The largest value you can assign to size, on a per-database-device basis, is 2048 (i.e., 2048 MB). If you assign more space to the database than is actually available on that referenced database device (or on the default database device), then the alter database command will still complete successfully by assigning as much space as possible, and you will receive a message that indicates the actual size by which the database was increased.

[, *NameOfDatabaseDevice* [= size] ...]—it is possible for a database to reside on multiple database devices and to consume varying amounts of space on those respective database devices. Therefore, when altering the size of a database, you can simultaneously assign space to that database from multiple database devices. However, an individual database cannot use more than 128 disk fragments, nor can it use more than 32 segments.

[log on *NameOfDatabaseDevice* [= size]—the purpose of the optional log on clause is to enable you to specify the name(s) of one or more database devices upon which the database's transaction log will reside. When you use this optional clause, all disk fragments (on the database device referenced on the on clause) become log segments. If you elect not to use the optional log on clause, then the transaction log will reside on the same database device as the database's data and index pages (this is generally not a good thing to have occur). There are a number of very good reasons why a transaction log should not reside on the same database device as the database's data and index pages:

1. To guarantee that the database is fully recoverable, the transaction log should not reside on a database device that will contain the data and index pages of this database. In the unfortunate event that the disk drive on which you have placed either the database or the transaction log crashes, then you can recover either the database or the transaction log from their respective dump.

2. It can significantly improve SQL Server performance. When the data and index pages are on a separate database device from that of the transaction log, and when these database devices are located on different disk drives, reads and writes to the database devices can take place concurrently, instead of linearly as is the case when both the pages and the log reside on the same database device.

3. It allows you to use the dump transaction log command, not just the dump database command. This backup flexibility can reduce the amount of time it takes to do a backup, and it can contribute to reducing the amount of tape or disk space you need to set aside for doing backups.

4. The pages and the log are not forced to compete against each other for the same area of disk space. Instead, you can assign a fixed amount of disk space that is individually dedicated to each.

5. The SQL Server automatically creates a default free-space threshold monitoring on the transaction log, and, additionally,

enables you to create other free-space thresholds on both the data and log sections of the database.

As regards the optional `size` parameter to the optional `log on` clause, the general rule is to assign a value to the `size` parameter that equals 10 to 25 percent of the size of the new user database. However, the actual size of a database's transaction log is really dependent upon the type, length, volume, and frequency of the (open) write transactions submitted to the database, and the frequency at which you take transaction log dumps. For example, because deferred updates take up twice as much log space as direct updates, you need to know when deferred versus direct updates are taking place. Note that, if you choose not to use the optional `size` parameter to this optional clause, then the transaction log will be given 1 MB of disk space.

`[ ,` *NameOfDatabaseDevice* `[ = size ]] ... ]`—it is possible for a transaction log to reside on multiple database devices and to consume varying amounts of space on those respective database devices. Therefore, when altering the size of a database, you can simultaneously assign space to that transaction log from multiple database devices.

`[ with override ]`—the purpose of this optional clause is to allow you to place both the data and the log on the same nondefault database device. When you do use this optional clause, all disk fragments (on the database device referenced on the `on` clause) become system and default segments. On SQL Servers where disk space is at a premium, having this option can make the difference in altering or not altering a database, or recovering or not recovering a database from a dump. Note that when you use this option, you are entirely dependent upon the `dump database` command.

`[ for load ]`—this option is used only immediately after you have used the `create database ... for load` command. This option to `alter database` command enables you to recreate the database device allocations and segment usage of the database being loaded from the dump image. There are also constraints related to database device usage by the `dump database` and those database devices earmarked for use by the new database.

This command changes the *master* system database, so to ensure its recovery, be certain to dump the *master* system database. As this command changes the contents of system tables, it cannot be used within a transaction.

If the SQL Server suspended a client process because the log ran out of space, then they will automatically be reawakened once the `alter` database command completes successfully. When you use the alter database command to extend a database onto a database device that is currently being used by that database, the SQL Server automatically maps the standard system and default segments to that database device.

Use of the alter database command has these additional constraints:

1. You must be using the *master* system database when using this Transact-SQL command.

2. If you are increasing the space for the *master* system database, then you are limited to extending its space within the **d_master** database device.

3. If the database whose space you are extending is being dumped while you are trying to extend is space allotment, then the alter database command will stall and will not continue processing until after the dump is completed.

Whenever you execute the alter database command, be absolutely certain to back up *master* system database. If you fail to back up the *master* system database after you have altered a database, and the *master* system database becomes corrupted, then your ability to recover the altered database is up for grabs. However, you may be lucky enough to recover the altered database through the use of the disk refit command; but don't bank on it.

SQL Server Kernel Configuration for Database Recovery

The SQL Server provides two configuration parameters for database recovery:

1. print recovery information
2. recovery interval in minutes

The print recovery information SQL Server configuration parameter is a toggle switch that establishes what type of information the SQL Server displays on the console during database recovery. The default setting for the print recovery information SQL Server configuration parameter is 0 (off). When in the off setting, the SQL Server displays on the console only the name of the database and a brief informational message stating that the database's recovery is in progress. When the setting of the print recovery information SQL Server configuration parameter is 1 (on), then the SQL Server displays on the console informational messages on each and every individual transaction that is processed during recovery, stating that it has been committed or aborted.

To specify that the `print recovery information` SQL Server configuration parameter is to be toggled on, log on to the SQL Server as an account with **sa_role** privileges and enter these commands:

```
1>use master
2>go
1>sp_configure "print recovery information", on
2>go
```

For this change to take effect, you will have to shut down, and then restart the SQL Server. This command changes the *master* system database, so to ensure its recovery, be certain to dump the *master* system database. As this command changes the contents of system tables, it cannot be used within a transaction.

The `recovery interval in minutes` SQL Server configuration parameter is covered in Chap. 6.

Dumping a Database

To recover a database after a media failure, you will need a good dump image of the database. You can dump a database while there are active processes running against it, or when it is not in use. When you create a dump image of a database, you write a copy of all allocated pages (both pages allocated to the database, as well as those allocated to that database's transaction log) to a Sybase dump device. To ensure that you are creating a good dump image of a database, you should run the **dbcc** utility on the database (and make any repairs as needed) prior to creating a database dump image.

Other than making dump images of your database at regularly scheduled intervals, you should dump the database after changing the contents of its system tables, after creating indexes, after any unlogged transactions occur (e.g., fast **bcp,** `select into ...`, or non-logged `writetext` commands), and after taking a dump of the database's transaction log using either the `"with no_log"` or `"with truncate_only"` options.

To create a dump image of an entire database, including its transaction log, log on to the SQL Server as an account with **dbo, sa_role,** or **oper_role** privileges and enter these commands:

```
1>use NameOfDatabase
2>go
1>dump database NameOfDatabase
2>to NameOfDumpDevice
3>go
```

where:

NameOfDatabase—the name of the database for which you want to create a dump image of the entire database.

NameOfDumpDevice—the name of the SQL Server dump device to which you want to write the database's dump image.

For a detailed coverage of the `dump database` command syntax for use with the SQL Server Backup Server, refer to the System 11 System Administration Guide from Sybase.

Loading a Database

Recovering a system or user database after a media-failure event requires loading each impacted database with its latest dump image, and, where applicable, transaction log dumps. The processes for recovering a system or user database are very detailed and exacting and have significant variations for system versus user databases.

To determine the correct method to use when recovering a system or user database after a media failure, refer to the System 11 System Administration Guide from Sybase and follow each and every step of the recovery process exactly as specified in the guide. If you have been making dump images at regularly scheduled intervals, and after each time you changed the contents of its system tables or created indexes, and after any unlogged transactions occur (e.g., fast **bcp,** `select into` ..., or nonlogged `writetext` commands), you should be able to recover the database(s) just fine. Good luck, and remember to follow the recovery instructions exactly as they are documented.

Binding a Database to a Named Data Cache

Well, once you've built a Named Data Cache and created a user database, the next step is to bind the database (and/or, its database objects) to a Named Data Cache.

As has been previously explained, if neither a given database nor the objects it contains, have been explicitly bound to a specific Named Data Cache, then they will reside within the Default Data Cache. However, things sometimes get crowded in Default Data Cache and access to heavily used databases can benefit from a little more elbowroom.

Before you explicitly bind a specific database object to a specific Named Data Cache, you need to know the present size of the database in question. This information is critically important because you do not want to bind the database to a Named Data Cache that is too small to handle the binding. To determine the present size of the database that you want to explicitly bind to a Named Data Cache, log on to the SQL Server as any valid Sybase account and enter these commands:

```
1>use NameOfDatabase
2>go
1>sp_spaceused
2>go
```

where:

NameOfDatabase—the name of the database whose present size you need to know.

Once the command completes executing, all related-size information about the database will be displayed. With these measurements in hand, you can make an informed decision as to which Named Data Cache you should correctly bind the database.

Once you have convinced yourself that SQL Server performance will improve by binding a given database to a Named Data Cache, you will bind that database to one and only one Named Data Cache. However, this restriction does not prohibit you from binding objects contained in that database, such as indexes, transaction logs, or tables, to other Named Data Caches. The database binding basically provides a mandatory data cache binding for all objects in the bound database that have not been explicitly bound to some other Named Data Cache.

Because the SQL Server takes exclusive locks on all data, index, and log pages when binding a database to a data cache, when you explicitly bind the database to a Named Data Cache, it must be in `single` user mode. So, to bind database to a Named Data Cache, log on to the SQL Server as an account with **sa_role** privileges and enter these commands:

```
1>use master
2>go
1>sp_dboption NameOfDatabase, single, true
2>go
1>use NameOfDatabase
2>go
1>checkpoint
2>go
1>use master
2>go
1>sp_bindcache NameOfDataCache, NameOfDatabase
2>go
1>sp_dboption NameOfDatabase, single, false
2>go
```

where

NameOfDataCache—the name of the Named Data Cache to which you want to bind the database. This Named Data Cache must exist before you execute the `sp_bindcache` command. Since you cannot bind a database to a data cache of type "logonly," be certain that the data cache is of type "mixed." Also, the status of this data cache must be "Active," that is, the SQL Server must have been restarted since the point in time when this data cache was created, else nothing can be bound to it.

NameOfDatabase—the name of the database that you want to bind to a given Named Data Cache. By default, all database objects contained within this database will now be bound to a specific Named Data Cache (keep in mind that you can still bind this database's database objects elsewhere, if you so choose). This database must exist before you execute the `sp_bindcache` command. Also, you cannot bind the *master* system database to any data cache.

This change takes effect immediately. This command changes the *master* system database, so to ensure its recovery, be certain to dump the *master* system database. As this command changes the contents of system tables, it cannot be used within a transaction.

Here are a few important facts to keep in mind when binding databases to Named Data Caches:

1. The database that is to be bound to the Named Data Cache must be in single-user mode.

2. When you bind a database to a Named Data Cache you must be in (i.e., using) the *master* system database.

3. If the database you are binding to a given Named Data Cache is already bound to another Named Data Cache, the old binding is dropped and the new one is created (i.e., you do not have to unbind the database before you create its new binding).

4. When a database is bound to a Named Data Cache, all compiled objects that reference database objects contained within the newly bound database are recompiled the next time they are executed by a user process.

5. If you drop a database that is bound to a Named Data Cache, then all of its related bindings are automatically dropped by the SQL Server.

6. When you bind a database to a mixed Named Data Cache, the SQL Server must acquire exclusive locks on all table, index, and log pages residing in data cache. The SQL Server will cause the

`sp_bindcache` command to sleep until these exclusive locks can be acquired. In addition, these exclusive locks will degrade the performance of any transaction that requires locks on the affected table, index, or log pages. Once these exclusive locks are acquired, the SQL Server will flush all related dirty pages to disk and drop all related clean pages from the data cache. When these pages are needed once again to support a query, they are read into the mixed Named Data Cache to which they have been bound. As a consequence, the performance of the queries that first read the pages back into data cache will degrade.

7. You cannot bind a database to a Named Data Cache if either of these two conditions are present:

   ■ There is an isolation level zero read taking place on any table in the databases.

   ■ The user process that is doing the database binding also has a cursor open on any table contained within the databases being bound.

8. The Named Data Cache to which the database is being bound must be of type "mixed."

9. The *master* system database cannot be bound to a data cache.

10. If a Named Data Cache to which a database is currently bound is dropped, the data cache binding records remain within the system catalogs, but are marked as invalid. As a consequence, warning messages about the database binding will be written to the SQL Server error log each time the SQL Server boots (i.e., it is restarted). If you subsequently re-created the Named Data Cache (using exactly the same name), the bindings will automatically take effect and will be marked as valid once the status of the Name Data Cache becomes "Active." So, unless you intend to re-create a dropped Named Data Cache to which a database is bound, you should unbind the database from the Named Data Cache before you drop the Named Data Cache.

Binding System Tables to Named Data Cache

Each database contains a system table called *sysindexes*. This system table contains a record of each table and index and the identity of the segments where each table, index, and chain of text/image pages is stored. Given the types of records the *sysindexes* system table contains, it is subjected to constantly high data-access rates. As such, you will, in general, realize performance improvements by binding the user database's *sysindexes* system table and its index (also named *sysindexes*) to a mixed Named Data Cache.

If your SQL Server has a database that supports a good deal of ad-hoc queries, then you will realize an overall performance improvement by binding these system tables it contains as well:

1. The *sysobjects* system table—contains records of all database objects contained within the database.

2. The *syscolumns* system table—contains records of all columns contained within the database.

3. The *sysprotects* system table—contains records of all user permissions within the database.

Every time an ad hoc query executes, these three tables are accessed to help the SQL Server parse and compile ad hoc queries.

Because the SQL Server takes exclusive locks on all related data pages when binding a system table to a data cache, when you explicitly bind a system table to a Named Data Cache, the database it is contained within must be in `single` user mode. So, to bind a system table to a mixed Named Data Cache, log on to the SQL Server as an account with **sa_role** privileges and enter these commands:

```
1>use master
2>go
1>sp_dboption NameOfDatabase, single, true
2>go
1>use NameOfDatabase
2>go
1>checkpoint
2>go
1>use master
2>go
1>sp_bindcache NameOfDataCache, NameOfDatabase,
  NameOfSystemTable
2>go
1>sp_dboption NameOfDatabase, single, false
2>go
```

where

NameOfDataCache—the name of the mixed Named Data Cache to which you want to exclusively bind the system table. This Named Data Cache must exist before you execute the `sp_bindcache` command. Be certain that the data cache is of type "mixed," since you cannot bind a system table to a data cache of type "logonly." Also, the status of this data cache must be "Active," that is, the SQL Server must have been restarted since the point in time when this data cache was created, else the system table cannot be bound to it.

NameOfDatabase—the name of the database that contains the system table you want to bind to a mixed data cache. This database must exist before you can bind any of its system tables to a Named Data Cache.

NameOfSystemTable—the name of the system table that you want to bind to the Named Data Cache. The *sysattributes* and the *sysallocdb* system tables cannot be bound to data cache.

This command changes the database, so to ensure its recovery, be certain to dump its transaction log and then dump the database itself. Here are a few important facts to keep in mind when binding a system table to a mixed Named Data Cache:

1. The database that contains the system table must be in single-user mode before the system table can be bound to a mixed Named Data Cache.

2. When you bind a system table to a mixed Named Data Cache you must be in (i.e., using) the database that contains the system table.

3. Binding the system table to Named Data Cache takes effect immediately (i.e., you do not have to restart the SQL Server).

4. If the system table is already bound to another Named Data Cache, the old binding is dropped and the new one is created (i.e., you do not have to unbind the system table before you create its new binding).

5. When you bind the system table to a Named Data Cache, any of its pages in memory are flushed to disk. They will be located in the Named Data Cache to which they are bound once a user process needs to access them.

6. You cannot bind the system table to a Named Data Cache if either of these two conditions are present:

   ■ There is an isolation level zero read taking place on the system table.

   ■ The user process that is doing the database binding also has a cursor open on the system table.

7. The Named Data Cache to which the system table is being bound must be of type "mixed."

8. When you bind the system table to a mixed Named Data Cache, the SQL Server must acquire exclusive locks on all related table, index, and log pages residing in data cache. The SQL Server will cause the binding process to sleep until these exclusive locks can be acquired. In addition, these exclusive locks will degrade the performance of any transaction that requires locks on the affected

table, index, or log pages. Once these exclusive locks are acquired, the SQL Server will flush all related dirty pages to disk and drop all related clean pages from the data cache. When these pages are needed once again to support a query, they are read into the mixed Named Data Cache to which they have been bound. As a consequence, the performance of the queries that first read the pages back into data cache will degrade.

9. If a Named Data Cache to which the system table is currently bound is dropped, the data cache binding records remain within the system catalogs, but are marked as invalid. As a consequence, warning messages about the system table binding will be written to the SQL Server error log each time the SQL Server **boots** (i.e., it is restarted). If you subsequently re-created the Named Data Cache (using exactly the same name), the bindings will automatically take effect and will be marked as valid, once the status of the Name Data Cache becomes "Active." So, unless you intend to re-create a dropped Named Data Cache to which a database object is bound, you should unbind the system table from the Named Data Cache before you drop the Named Data Cache.

10. It is not necessary to specify the system table owner name because it is owned by **dbo.**

Binding System Table Indexes to Named Data Cache

You can bind the index of a system table (or the index of any table for that matter) to a different data cache then the one the system table uses or is explicitly bound to. In fact, it is permissible to bind only a table's index(es) to a Named Data Cache, and not bind the table itself. Now, if you bind a clustered index to a Named Data Cache, the explicit binding only affects the root index page and the intermediate index pages. The leaf pages of the index, which in fact are the table's data pages, are not affected whatsoever by the explicit index binding.

Because the SQL Server takes exclusive locks on all related index pages when binding a system table's index to a data cache, when you explicitly bind a system table index to a Named Data Cache, the database it is contained within must be in `single` user mode. So, to bind a system table's index to a mixed Named Data Cache, log on to the SQL Server as an account with **sa_role** privileges and enter these commands:

```
1>use master
2>go
1>sp_dboption NameOfDatabase, single, true
```

```
2>go
1>use NameOfDatabase
2>go
1>checkpoint
2>go
1>use master
2>go
1>sp_bindcache NameOfDataCache, NameOfDatabase,
  NameOfSystemTable,
2>NameOfSystemTableIndex
3>go
1>sp_dboption NameOfDatabase, single, false
2>go
```

where

NameOfDataCache—the name of the mixed Named Data Cache to which you want to exclusively bind the system table. This Named Data Cache must exist before you execute the sp_bindcache command. Be certain that the data cache is of type "mixed," since you cannot bind the system table to a data cache of type "logonly." Also, the status of this data cache must be "Active," that is, the SQL Server must have been restarted since the point in time when this data cache was created, else the system table cannot be bound to it.

NameOfDatabase—the name of the database that contains the system table whose index you want to bind to a mixed data cache. This database must exist before you can bind any of its system tables to a Named Data Cache.

NameOfSystemTable—the name of the system table whose index you want to bind to the Named Data Cache.

NameOfSystemTableIndex—the name of the system table index that you want to bind to the Named Data Cache.

When binding a system table's index to a Named Data Cache, be certain to keep in mind the same set of important facts related to binding a system table to a mixed Named Data Caches.

This command changes the database, so to ensure its recovery, be certain to dump its transaction log and then dump the database itself.

Unbinding a System Table from Named Data Cache

The SQL Server takes exclusive locks on all related data pages when a system table is unbound from a data cache. Therefore, when you unbind a system table from a Named Data Cache, the database it is contained within must be in `single` user mode. So, to unbind a system table from a mixed Named Data Cache, log on to the SQL Server as an account with **sa_role** privileges and enter these commands:

```
1>use master
2>go
1>sp_dboption NameOfDatabase, single, true
2>go
1>use NameOfDatabase
2>go
1>checkpoint
2>go
1>use master
2>go
1>sp_unbindcache NameOfDatabase, NameOfSystemTable
2>go
1>sp_dboption NameOfDatabase, single, false
2>go
```

where

NameOfDatabase—the name of the database that contains the system table you want to unbind from a mixed data cache.

NameOfSystemTable—is the name of the system table that you want to unbind from the Named Data Cache.

Here are a few important facts to keep in mind when unbinding a system table from a mixed Named Data Caches:

1. The database that contains the system table must be in single-user mode before the system table can be unbound from a mixed Named Data Cache.

2. When you unbind a system table from a mixed Named Data Cache you must be in (i.e., using) the database that contains the system table.

3. Unbinding the system table from Named Data Cache takes effect immediately (i.e., you do not have to restart the SQL Server).

4. When you unbind the system table from a Named Data Cache, any of its pages in memory are flushed to disk. They will be relocated in the Default Data Cache once a user process needs to access them.

5. You cannot unbind the system table from a Named Data Cache if either of these two conditions are present:

   - There is an isolation level zero read taking place on the system table.

- The user process that is doing the database unbinding also has a cursor open on the system table.

6. When you unbind the system table from a mixed Named Data Cache, the SQL Server must acquire exclusive locks on all related table, index, and log pages residing in data cache. The SQL Server will cause the `sp_unbindcache` process to sleep until these exclusive locks can be acquired. In addition, these exclusive locks will degrade the performance of any transaction that requires locks on the affected table, index, or log pages. Once these exclusive locks are acquired, the SQL Server will flush all related dirty pages to disk and drop all related clean pages from the data cache. When these pages are needed once again, to support a query, they are read into the Default Data Cache. As a consequence, the performance of the queries that first read the pages back into data cache will degrade.

7. It is not necessary to specify the system table owner name because it is owned by **dbo.**

8. In that the `sp_unbindcache` command modifies system tables, you cannot execute this command from within a transaction.

Unbinding a System Table Index from Named Data Cache

The SQL Server takes exclusive locks on all related index pages when unbinding a system table's index from a data cache. Therefore, when you unbind a system table index from a Named Data Cache, the database it is contained within must be in `single` user mode. So, to unbind a system table's index from a mixed Named Data Cache, log on to the SQL Server as an account with **sa_role** privileges and enter these commands:

```
1>use master
2>go
1>sp_dboption NameOfDatabase, single, true
2>go
1>use NameOfDatabase
2>go
1>checkpoint
2>go
1>use master
2>go
1>sp_unbindcache NameOfDatabase, NameOfSystemTable,
2>NameOfSystemTableIndex
3>go
1>sp_dboption NameOfDatabase, single, false
2>go
```

where

>*NameOfDatabase*—the name of the database that contains the system table you want to unbind from a mixed data cache.
>
>*NameOfSystemTable*—the name of the system table whose index you want to unbind from the Named Data Cache.
>
>*NameOfSystemTableIndex*—the name of the system table index that you want to unbind from the Named Data Cache.

When unbinding a system table's index from a Named Data Cache, be certain to keep in mind the same set of important facts related to unbinding a system table from a mixed Named Data Cache.

Unbinding a Database from a Named Data Cache

At times, it becomes necessary to tear down what you have built, or what you have inherited. The SQL Server takes exclusive locks on all data, index, and log pages when unbinding a database from a data cache. Therefore, when you unbind the database from a Named Data Cache, the database must be in `single` user mode. So, to unbind a database from a Named Data Cache, log on to the SQL Server as an account with **sa_role** privileges and enter these commands:

```
1>use master
2>go
1>sp_dboption NameOfDatabase, single, true
2>go
1>use NameOfDatabase
2>go
1>checkpoint
2>go
1>use master
2>go
1>sp_unbindcache NameOfDatabase
2>go
1>sp_dboption NameOfDatabase, single, false
2>go
```

where

>*NameOfDatabase*—the name of the database that you want to unbind from a given Named Data Cache. By default, all database objects contained within this database will now reside within the Default

Data Cache (keep in mind that you can still bind this database's database objects elsewhere, if you so choose). This database must exist before you execute the `sp_unbindcache` command.

This change takes effect immediately. This command changes the *master* system database, so to ensure its recovery, be certain to dump the *master* system database. As this command changes the contents of system tables, it cannot be used within a transaction.

Here are a few important facts to keep in mind when unbinding databases to Named Data Caches:

1. The database that is to be unbound to the Named Data Cache must be in single-user mode.

2. When you unbind a database to a Named Data Cache you must be in (i.e., using) the *master* system database.

3. When a database is unbound from a Named Data Cache, all compiled objects that reference database objects contained within the newly unbound database are recompiled the next time they are executed by a user process.

4. If you drop a database that is bound to a Named Data Cache, then all of its related bindings are automatically dropped by the SQL Server.

5. When you unbind a database to a mixed Named Data Cache, the SQL Server must acquire exclusive locks on all table, index, and log pages residing in data cache. The SQL Server will cause the `sp_unbindcache` command to sleep until these exclusive locks can be acquired. In addition, these exclusive locks will degrade the performance of any transaction that requires locks on the affected table, index, or log pages. Once these exclusive locks are acquired, the SQL Server will flush all related dirty pages to disk and drop all related clean pages from the data cache. When these pages are needed once again, to support a query, they are read into the Default Data Cache. As a consequence, the performance of the queries that first read the pages back into data cache will degrade.

6. You cannot unbind a database from a Named Data Cache if either of these two conditions are present:

   - There is an isolation level zero read taking place on any table in the databases.

   - The user process that is doing the database unbinding also has a cursor open on any table contained within the databases being bound.

Unbinding All Databases from a Named Data Cache

When it comes to unbinding databases or database objects from Named Data Cache, you have two options:

1. Unbind individual databases and individual database objects from a specific Named Data Cache (as has been demonstrated).

2. Unbind all databases and all database objects from a specific Named Data Cache.

To unbind all database objects from a specific Named Data Cache, the SQL Server provides you with the `sp_unbindcache_all` system procedure. However, the `sp_unbindcache_all` system procedure is only capable of opening eight databases simultaneously. If there are more than eight databases, or if there are database objects from more than eight separate databases, simultaneously bound to this Named Data Cache, the `sp_unbindcache_all` system procedure will not work. If this is the case, your only recourse is to use the `sp_unbindcache` system procedure to reduce the number of bound databases/objects to a level manageable by the `sp_unbindcache_all` system procedure.

To unbind all databases and database objects from Named Data Cache, log on to the SQL Server as an account with **sa_role** privileges and enter these commands:

```
1>use master
2>go
1>sp_unbindcache_all NameOfDataCache
2>go
```

where

NameOfDataCache—the name of the Named Data Cache from which you want to unbind all databases and database objects.

This change takes effect immediately. This command changes the *master* system database, so to ensure its recovery, be certain to dump the *master* system database. As this command changes the contents of system tables, it cannot be used within a transaction.

Here are a few important facts to keep in mind when executing the `sp_unbindcache_all` system command:

1. All databases that are presently bound to the Named Data Cache must be placed in single-user mode before you execute the `sp_unbindcache_all` system command.

2. When you unbind a database from a Named Data Cache you must be in (i.e., using) the *master* system database.

3. When a database or a database object is unbound from a Named Data Cache, all compiled objects that reference database objects contained within the bound database are recompiled the next time they are executed by a user process.

4. If you drop a database that is bound to a Named Data Cache, then all of its related bindings are automatically dropped by the SQL Server.

5. When you unbind a database from a mixed Named Data Cache, the SQL Server must acquire exclusive locks on all table, index, and log pages residing in data cache. The SQL Server will cause the `sp_unbindcache_all` command to sleep until these exclusive locks can be acquired. In addition, these exclusive locks will degrade the performance of any transaction that require locks on the affected table, index, or log pages. Once these exclusive locks are acquired, the SQL Server will flush all related dirty pages to disk and drop all related clean pages from the data cache. When these pages are needed once again, to support a query, they are read into the Default Data Cache. As a consequence, the performance of the queries that first read the pages back into data cache will degrade.

6. You cannot unbind a database from a Named Data Cache if either of these two conditions are present:

   - There is an isolation level zero read taking place on any table in the databases.
   - The user process that is doing the database unbinding also has a cursor open on any table contained within the databases being bound.

Dropping an Undamaged Database

As nothing is permanent, eventually you will come to a point in time when you have to destroy (i.e., drop) a database. When you drop a database you purge the SQL Server of all principal database objects contained within that database, you free all data and log space that had been allocated to that database, removing all traces of the database from the master..sysdatabases and the master..sysusages system tables.

Before an account with **sa_role** privileges can drop a user database, these preliminaries must be satisfied:

1. You cannot drop a database that is in use. You must make certain that no one is currently using the database you intend to drop. To deter-

mine if anyone is using the database, as a valid Sybase account (that has permission to use the database that is to be renamed), log on to the SQL Server, execute the `sp_who` command. If there are no other users currently in the database, then within the output of this command, you will see `"sa_role"` as the login name for the process that supports the `sp_who` system command, and you will see "NULL" as the login name for all SQL Server system processes. If any other processes or login names are displayed, then you will not be able to drop the database. Take the time to contact everyone who is running a process within the database and ask them to exit from it. If you are unable to reach them, and it is crucial that you immediately proceed with the dropping of the database, then you can terminate their processes. The spid column in the output from the `sp_who` command contains the Sybase process identifier of each process that is present within the current database. To terminate an offending process, then, log on to the SQL Server as an account with **sa_role** privileges and enter these commands:

```
1>use NameOfDatabase
2>go
1>kill spid
2>go
```

Repeat the `kill` command for each offending process, as necessitated. Also, ensure that no one else, other than an account with **sa_role** privileges, tries to access to the database, from this point forward through the drop process.

2. You cannot drop a database if it contains a table that references, or that is referenced by, a table in another database. As is demonstrated in later chapters, it is possible for external database tables to place foreign key constraints on a primary key of a table in the database about to be dropped. To determine if this case is applicable, then, as a valid Sybase account (that has permission to use the database that is to be renamed), log on to the SQL Server and enter these commands:

```
1>use NameOfDatabase
2>go
1>select object_name(tableid), db_name(frgndbname)
2>from sysreferences
3>where frgndbname is not NULL
4>go
```

In addition, it is possible for external database tables to place primary key constraints on a foreign key of a table in the database about to be dropped. To determine if this case is applicable,

```
1>use NameOfDatabase
2>go
1>select object_name(reftabid), db_name(pmrydbname)
2>from sysreferences
3>where pmrydbname is not NULL
4>go
```

If, after running either of these queries, you discover that foreign key constraints or primary key constraints exist within the database about to be dropped, then, as the table owner, or as an account with **dbo** or with **sa_role** privileges, enter these commands:

```
1>use NameOfDatabase
2>go
1>alter table NameOfTable
2>drop constraint NameOfConstraint
3>go
```

3. As is demonstrated in later chapters, it is possible within a SQL Server for views, stored database procedures, and triggers to explicitly reference a database by its name. Once you drop a database, the views, stored database procedures, and triggers will continue to execute until the point in time when they are recompiled. To correct this problem, you will have to update the definitions of all views, stored database procedures, and triggers that will be affected by the dropped database. To determine which views, stored database procedures, and triggers are potentially impacted by this dropped database, you will use the sp_depends system command (this command is covered in depth in a later chapter). Once you identify the impacted views, stored database procedures, and triggers, then, after the database is dropped you will have to modify their respective definitions so that they no longer reference the dropped database, drop their current incarnations from the database, and re-create them if need be.

To drop a database, log on to the SQL Server as the Sybase account that owns the database and enter these commands:

```
1>use master
2>go
1>drop database NameOfDatabase
2>go
```

where:

NameOfDatabase—the name of the database you want to destroy.

This command changes the *master* system database, so to ensure its recovery, be certain to dump the *master* system database. As this command changes the contents of system tables, it cannot be used within a transaction.

Use of the `drop database` command has these additional constraints:

1. The `drop database` command does not work on a database that cannot be recovered or used. To drop such a database, an account with **sa_role** privileges must use the `dbcc repair dropdb` utility.
2. If auditing is enabled within the SQL Server, then the *sybsecurity* system database cannot be dropped. Furthermore, only the Sybase System Security Officer can drop the *sybsecurity* system database.

Dropping a Damaged Database

If a database is damaged and cannot be recovered or used, and you wish to drop it, the `drop database` command will not work. To drop a damaged database, log on to the SQL Server as the **sa_role** and enter these commands:

```
1>use master
2>go
1>dbcc dbrepair NameOfDatabase
2>go
```

where:

NameOfDatabase—the name of the damaged database you want to destroy.

This command changes the *master* system database, so to ensure its recovery, be certain to dump the *master* system database. As this command changes the contents of system tables, it cannot be used within a transaction.

6

Transaction Log Subsystem

Introduction

With the release of System 11, Sybase has made significant enhancements to the Transaction Log Subsystem (also known as the Xact Logging Subsystem (XLS)). To address the potential bottlenecks arising on transaction logs, and their management, the System 11 SQL Server offers these improvements over previous product releases:

1. User Transaction Log Caches (also called Private Log Caches).
2. Configuration of Transaction Log disk I/O sizes.
3. Binding a Transaction Log to a Named Data Cache of type "logonly."
4. Convenient way to get information on long-running processes.

Write-Ahead Transaction Log

To facilitate database recovery, every database has its own individual write-ahead transaction log. When you create a user database, the transaction log, the spinlock for the transaction log, the segment on which the transaction log will reside, as well as the **last-chance** threshold for that log segment, are automatically created by the SQL Server for that database.

The write-ahead transaction log is implemented as a heap table, called *syslogs* (in that it is a heap structure, it does not have any indexes). Every time you insert, update, or delete data, you are (eventually) writing log records into *syslogs.* When writing to *syslogs,* you are promoting disk I/O activity. The amount of disk I/O activity due to the logging of transactions can be significant. Any significant increase in disk I/O activity may degrade overall system performance.

There are some SQL Server commands that do not change the state of the database and so are not written to the transaction log by the SQL Server:

1. Truncating a table.

2. Bulk coping data, via the **bcp** utility, into a table that does not have indexes.

3. The `select...into` command.

4. The `writetext` command.

5. The `dump transaction with no_log` command.

SQL Server Failure Events

The purpose of the transaction log is to assist the SQL Server in the recovery of a database under normal conditions (i.e., at SQL Server boot time, and after a failure event).

The SQL Server is designed to handle three types of failure events:

1. *Media.* The physical media that holds the database data is unavailable. Typically, this is due to a hardware failure, such as a disk crash or the failure of a disk controller.

2. *SQL Server.* The SQL Server process terminates, or aborts, in an uncontrolled manner. This may be due to a hardware failure, such as the failure of RAM chips, or bus errors, or the failure of the motherboard. Or it may be due to a SQL Server software bug. When this type of failure event occurs, the SQL Server cannot recover any transaction information that resided solely in memory. You must provide a programmatic, or manual, solution to recover from the loss of memory resident transaction information.

3. *Transaction.* A *logical unit of work* (LUW) does not complete (a completed transaction is a transaction that has either been committed or rolled back). Transaction-failure events occur for any number of reasons. The client process that submitted the transaction might not have the required SQL Server permissions or the required database object permissions. The transaction may have been involved in a deadlocking incident, and ended up on the losing side. The transaction may have exceeded current resource capacities (e.g., the SQL Server ran out of disk space). The transaction may have invoked an explicit rollback.

For all three categories of failure events, the goal of the SQL Server recovery process is to restore the database to a consistent state.

Nonetheless, it is not possible, in all cases, to attain this goal. That is, it is not safe to assume that you can completely recover from any and all types of failure events. Every piece of technology has its limitations, and the SQL Server is no exception to that rule.

In addition, it is not safe to naively assume that a recovered database is, by definition, a consistent database. There are ways to recover a database that do not guarantee its consistency. Sometimes, consistency has to be forsaken in order to simply regain access to the database so that you can assess the damages.

Transaction Log Records

A transaction is both a logical unit of work and a logical unit of recovery. A transaction is capable of being both things because when a transaction is logged it takes the form of a log record. Each log record is a transaction log page. A log record is composed of two main parts:

1. *Log header.* A proprietary fixed-length structure, that, among many other things, indicates the log record type, the *syslogs* row number, the length of the log data, and the transaction identifier.

2. *Log data.* A proprietary variable-length structure whose information content is governed by the log record type. These are the basic types of log records, and their generic descriptions:

   - *Begin transaction record.* Contains such information as the identity (SQL Server site ID; database ID; Sybase user ID; process ID; user log cache ID) of the process that started the transaction, the identity of the database that is controlling the transaction, the entity of the controlling transaction, a time stamp indicating when the transaction was initiated, and a transaction mnemonic (i.e., the name of the transaction).

   - *End transaction log record.* Contains such information as the status of the transaction (e.g., abort, commit, or preparing to commit—if this is a Two-Phase Commit protocol) and a time stamp indicating when the transaction finished.

   - *Direct data row insert log record.* Contains such information as the identity of the table (i.e., the object ID) in which the row was inserted, the identity of the data page in which the row will reside, the offset on the data page where the row will be placed, the "before insert" page time stamp, the "after insert" page time stamp, and the image of the data row that was inserted.

   - *Direct data row delete log record.* Contains such information as the identity of the table (i.e., the object ID) in which the row was removed, the identity of the data page in which the row resides, the offset on the data page from where the row was removed, the "before delete" page time stamp, the "after delete" page time stamp, and the image of the data row that was deleted.

- *Direct index row insert log record.* Contains the same information as the direct data row insert log record.

- *Direct index row delete log record.* Contains the same information as the direct data row delete log record.

- *Deferred data row insert log records.* When a data row `insert` is deferred, the physical location of the row (i.e., the number of the data page in which the row will reside, and the offset on that data page where the row will be placed) is not yet determined. Hence, the use of the term *deferred*. The physical location of the row will be determined at the point in time when the transaction is actually processed internally within the SQL Server. When an `insert` is deferred, two log records are stored within *syslogs*. The first log record contains such information as its row number, the description of the operation being performed, the identity of the controlling transaction, the data being logged, and the status of the transaction. The second log record contains a pointer to the first log record as well as such information as the identity of the table (i.e., the object ID) in which the row was inserted, the identity of the data page in which the row will reside, the offset on the data page where the row will be placed, the "before insert" page time stamp, the "after insert" page time stamp, and the image of the data row that was inserted

- *Deferred data row delete log records.* When a data row `delete` is deferred, two log records are stored within *syslogs*. The first and second log records are the same as those for the deferred data row insert log records.

- *Deferred index row insert log records.* When an index row `insert` is deferred, two log records are stored within *syslogs*. The first and second log records are the same as those for the deferred data row insert log records.

- *Deferred index row delete log records.* When an index row `delete` is deferred, two log records are stored within *syslogs*. The first and second log records are the same as those for the deferred data row delete log records.

- *Split page allocation for a data page.* A new data page is allocated whenever a data page split event occurs. When a data page splits, two log records are produced. The first log record represents the new data page that is being created, and contains such information as: the number of the allocated data page, the status of the new data page, the ID of the object allocation map affected by the page split event, the new data page time stamp, the pointer to the previous data page to which this new data page is linked, the previous data page old time stamp, the previous data page new time stamp, the pointer to the next data page to which this new data page is being linked, the next data page old time stamp, and the next data page new time stamp. The second log record represents the movement of data rows from the old to the new data page, and contains such information as the number of the old data page from which the data rows are being removed, the offset to the point at which the old data page was split, the "before split" time stamp of the old data page, and the "after split" time stamp of the old data page.

- *Split page allocation for an index page.*   A new index page is allocated whenever an index page split event occurs. When an index page splits, two log records are produced with the same format as those that record a data page split.

- *Generic page allocation.*   A page allocation is logged when an overflow data or an index page is created, when the first page of a table or an index is created, when a distribution page is created, or when an OAM page is created. When these page allocation events occur, the format of the log record is the same as the first split log record.

- *Page deallocation.*   For all types of pages, the format of the log record is the same as the first page split log record.

- *Extent allocation.*   Contains such information as: the extent ID, the object ID, the index ID, the object allocation map page number, the status, and the allocation mask (bit map).

- *Extent deallocation.*   Extents can be deallocated due to a database object (such as a table or index) being dropped, or because all pages within the extent itself have been deallocated. In the former case, an extent deallocation log record is created. In the latter case, an extent drop log record is created. The extent deallocation log record contains such information as: the extent ID, the object ID, the index ID, the object allocation map page number, the status, and the deallocation mask (bit map). The extent drop log record contains such information as: the extent ID, the object ID, the index ID, the saved object allocation map page number, status, the allocation page number, and the saved page number

- *Checkpoint.*   Log records indicate that a checkpoint has occurred at this position in the transaction log.

There are two important facts to keep in mind about the SQL Server:

1. When you issue a direct, or deferred, `update` command, the SQL Server records that event as two related events: a delete event followed by an insert event.

2. The unit of disk I/O for a transaction log is now configurable, so log record pages are written to disk as a Buffer Mass.

It is quite possible for a single LUW to produce large volumes of log records (of the most basic types). This is particularly true when records in the LUW are handled by the process on a record basis and not handled, whenever possible, on a batch basis.

For a given period of time or for a given transaction the volume of log records inserted into *syslogs* is directly dependent upon the number of:

1. Data rows being inserted and deleted (remember an update is implemented as a combination of insert and delete log records).

2. Indexes being affected.

3. Data and index pages being allocated or deallocated by the outstanding, and completed, transactions.

Because the purpose of the write-ahead transaction log is to support database recovery, it is not possible to turn off transaction logging. Nonetheless, you can limit the amount of logging associated with certain database operations (e.g., bulk copy loads) but be forewarned: doing so effectively makes the transaction log useless for database recovery. In addition, you can reduce the amount of logging by avoiding deferred updates, inserts and deletes wherever possible, and taking advantage of batching transactions wherever possible (with this technique the creation of begin-and-end transaction log records is kept to an absolute minimum).

Direct Updates

The SQL Server supports two basic types of updates: deferred and direct. Wherever possible, the SQL Server prefers to do direct updates. When a direct update takes place, the following events occur:

1. The affected index and/or data row is located on specified pages.

2. The corresponding log records are written to the transaction log.

3. The changes are made directly to the affected data page and any affected index page (the old index row is deleted and the new index row is inserted).

The SQL Server uses three techniques for supporting direct updates:

1. *In-place updates.*   Used when affected rows on a page are not moved (i.e., the Row ID remains the same and the row pointers in the page's offset table are not modified). An in-place update cannot take place if the total length of a row is changed, the column being updated is part of the clustered index (if such a change were to take place then the index and data rows would have to be resorted), the update statement involves a table join, the column being updated supports a referential-integrity constraint, the column being updated is referenced in a trigger, and the affected table has been marked for replication by a replication system.

2. *Cheap direct updates.*   If an in-place update cannot occur, then the SQL Server tries to change the affected row and then rewrite it at the same offset location on the page. Rows will be moved around the page, but their Row IDs will remain constant, however, their pointers in the row offset table will be modified to reflect their new placements. A cheap update cannot take place if the total length of a row is changed such that it could not remain on the same page, the column being updated is part of the clustered index (if such a change were to take place then the index and data rows would have to be resorted), the update statement involves a table join, the column being updated supports a referential-integrity constraint, the column being updated is referenced in a trigger, and the affected table has been marked for replication by a replication system.

3. *Expensive direct updates.*   If cheap update cannot take place because the total length of a row is changed such that the row cannot remain on the same page or if the affected column is part of the table's clustered index, then the SQL Server will perform an expensive direct update if possible. When an expensive update is performed, the SQL Server conducts a table or index scan to locate the affected row, deletes the affected data row from its current page, deletes the clustered and all nonclustered index entries and then inserts the changed data row on a new data page, and updates all index entries. If the affected table is a heap structure, then the changed data row will be inserted at the end of the heap structure. The SQL Server will use an expensive direct update if the index used to locate the affected row is not being changed by the update statement, the update statement does not involve a table join, the column being updated does not support a referential-integrity constraint, the column being updated is not referenced in a trigger, and the affected table has not been marked for replication by a replication system.

Deferred Updates

When the SQL Server determines that none of the three direct update techniques are feasible, then it resorts to deferred updates. When the SQL Server uses the deferred update method, these events occur:

1. The affected data row is located.
2. Deferred delete and deferred insert log records for the affected current, and new data pages are written to the database's transaction log.
3. The database's transaction log is scanned and the corresponding log records are read.
4. A delete on the affected data page takes place.
5. Deletes on the affected index pages take place.
6. The database's transaction log is rescanned and the corresponding log records are reread.
7. An insert on the affected data page takes place.
8. Inserts on the affected index pages take place.

The deferred update method, relative to the direct update method, produces far more log records and involves repeated scans of the transaction log. It is, therefore, a significant source of performance degradation. Nevertheless, the central aim of the deferred update method is to support transactions that (may) generate revisions all through a table.

Instead of making the changes directly to the data row on a given page, within cache, the SQL Server reads log records in the transaction log. Once the transaction is committed, the transaction log is read, the changes are applied to the relevant pages, and the Cache Manager takes over the task of flushing the dirty pages to disk. The log records are used to support these changes because the cache might lack the memory resources needed to manage all potentially modified pages.

Your transaction will result in a deferred update if any one of the following conditions are present:

1. The update statement includes a join.
2. The affected column supports a referential integrity constraint.
3. The update results in a row being moved to another page while that table is being accessed by a table scan or a clustered index.
4. Revised columns are variable-length data types.
5. Revised columns are NULLABLE.

6. Within a `delete` command, the affected table does not have a unique index. In the absence of a unique index, the query optimizer is incapable of deciding that zero, or only one, data row fits the `delete` statement's **where** clause.

7. Within a single command, the target table into which rows are being inserted cannot be the same as the source table from which the rows are being selected. For example, `insert` *tableA* `select` * from *tableA*.

8. Data rows are being inserted into the target table, and at least one column in the target table is used within the query statement's **where** clause. For example, `insert` *tableA* `select` "*columnAData-Value*", *columnB, columnC* from *tableA* where *columnA* = "`ExtantData-Value`".

9. The affected column is referenced by a trigger.

10. The referenced table has been marked for replication within a replication system.

When executing the deferred update method, revisions are brought to bear on all relevant data rows through the creation of log records that echo the:

1. Old and new literal data values of the column(s) being changed (as when an `update` occurs).

2. New literal data values of a data row (as when an `insert` occurs).

3. Old literal data values of a data row (as when a `delete` occurs)

For the direct update method, the SQL Server applies the changes right into the data page. Unlike a deferred update, the direct update method is not *syslogs* intensive (i.e., there is no need to read log records from the transaction log, the traversal of index B-Trees is reduced, locking contention is minimized, and physical disk I/O is reduced because the SQL Server does not have to retrieve pages from the disk to make the changes), therefore, direct updates are used wherever possible.

The way in which you write your Transact-SQL statements and implement a physical database can produce unwanted deferred updates. One of the tried-and-true techniques for making quick improvements in database performance is to eliminate deferred updates wherever possible (and practical). In general, the performance problems stemming from deferred updates are a very good reason for prohibiting the use of variable-length data types, restricting the use of NULL, and requiring a unique index for each table within a physical database.

Deferred Index Inserts

When an update statement changes the data value of an index column used to find a data row, or when the update statement changes the data value of a column in a unique index, the SQL Server performs a deferred index insert. To ensure data consistency, a query should change a single qualifying data row once and only once. The SQL Server uses the deferred index insert method to ensure that a data row is located only once during an index scan and that a transaction does not violate a uniqueness constraint on the table. These are the events that take place when a deferred index insert occurs:

1. The affected index entries are deleted using the direct update method.
2. The affected data page is updated using the direct update method.
3. The deferred index insert log records are written to the database's transaction log.
4. The database's transaction log is scanned and the corresponding log records are read.
5. The new index entries are inserted using the deferred update method.

User Transaction Log Caches

In previous releases of the Sybase SQL Server, processes, before they wrote to a database, had to acquire the transaction log spinlock. Since they competed for a single spinlock, significant contention could arise as they single-threaded their writes to the transaction log. With the System 11 SQL Server, each user connection is allocated its own region in memory, called User Transaction Log (UTL) Cache (also called Private Log Cache), in which the user connection consolidates and buffers the transaction log records its transactions create. No longer are each user connection's individual log records immediately written to the database's transaction log.

Internally, the Transaction Management subsystem provides an open-session connection to the database's transaction log. Periodically, each open session grabs the transaction log spinlock, and, using a single-threaded technique, flushes its UTL Cache, copying the user-connection process's transaction log records to the database's transaction log in a single-log session. To keep disk-write overhead to a minimum, the SQL Server will store partially filled transaction log Buffer Masses from several processes in the transaction log, and then write them to disk simultaneously (using a technique called *group commit*).

In that a System 11 database's transaction log spinlock need only be obtained when the UTL Caches are periodically flushed to the *syslogs,* contention for the transaction log spinlock prior to writing transaction log records has been significantly reduced. For a System 11 SQL Server running just one engine, transaction logs are written as fast as in System 10 SQL Servers. But, for SQL Servers running multiple engines on symmetrical multiprocessor platforms, transaction log writing is incredibly faster than in previous versions.

Each user connection's UTL Cache is flushed whenever one of these events occur:

1. A user-connection process causes a trigger to be fired.

2. The SQL Server executes a system transaction, such as an OAM page allocation, that, internally, is treated as part of the user-connection process.

3. The next transaction log record Buffer Mass the user connection needs to write cannot fit inside the UTL Cache (i.e., the ULT Cache fills up).

4. The process is completed (i.e., it is committed or aborted). Even if the process is rolled back, all of its related log records in the UTL Cache are still copied to *syslogs.*

5. When a user-connection process modifies a database object (i.e., table, index, etc.), in a database that is not the same one that contained the last database object that the process modified.

6. When, to preserve the write-ahead transaction log, a modified page must be written to disk. Another way of describing this condition is to state that a pinned page is *unpinned.* Pinning a modified page is implemented in two phases: in the first phase the modified page is pinned to the UTL Cache and then flushed from the UTL Cache to the *syslogs* table. Once *syslogs* is flushed to disk, the pin on the page is released. Unpinning always requires the contents of the ULT Cache to be copied to *syslogs* and then written out to disk. As multiple processes can modify a page in a data cache, this is one context in which the exclusivity of a user connection's ULT Cache is compromised.

Unpinning pages in a UTL Cache happens whenever:

1. A checkpoint is taken in the database the user-connection process is associated with.

2. A write operation occurs such that database recoverability must be ensured (e.g., an index page splits, an overflow page is created, etc.).

3. A Buffer Mass, related to the user process, is to be aged out of a data cache. Before the Buffer Mass can be aged out of a data cache, the image of that Buffer Mass in a UTL Cache must be flushed to *syslogs,* and then *syslogs* must be flushed out to disk prior to writing that data cache Buffer Mass image to disk.

The introduction of UTL Caches in System 11 also affects another aspect of SQL Server transaction management. If your process is using the Chained Transaction Mode, the Begin Transaction Log Record is initially written into the process's UTL Cache, and not into the transaction log. In fact, no transaction log records will, in general, be written to the transaction log until at least one log record reflects a change in the state of the database.

Configuring User Transaction Log Caches

There are two parameters that can be configured to tune UTL Caches, on a systemwide basis:

1. `user log cache size`
2. `user log cache spinlock ratio`

The `user log cache size` SQL Server configuration parameter affects, as implied, the size of all ULT Caches. The default, and minimum, size of a UTL Cache is 2048 bytes. The maximum size of a UTL Cache is 2,147,483,647 bytes. Also, the size of a UTL Cache does not have to be specified in multiples of 2K.

When determining the size at which to configure UTL Caches (which is more a black art than a science), keep these ideas in mind:

1. The ideal is to size the UTL Cache such that it is flushed once per transaction.

2. Do not make the UTL Caches bigger than the largest transaction supported by the SQL Server. In that the UTL Cache is flushed when the transaction it contains is completed, allocating more memory than required to store the log records of the largest transaction will just waste memory resources.

3. Do not make the UTL Caches too large, as this will likely increase contention on UTL spinlocks and probably cause them to be flushed too frequently.

4. Do not configure the UTL Cache to support long-running transactions, as this will increase the probability of pages being pinned to a UTL Cache and increase contention. As the probability of pinning

pages to the UTL Caches increases, unpinning will occur more frequently, and the likelihood of the utilizing their full size will diminish with the same frequency.

5. Do not configure the UTL Caches too small as this will make them fill up too quickly and cause them to be flushed to *syslogs* more than once per transaction. When the UTL Caches are flushed too frequently, contention arises on the UTL Caches.

To set the `user log cache size` SQL Server configuration parameter to 6000, for example, log on to the SQL Server as an account with **sa_role** privileges and enter these commands:

```
1>use master
2>go
1>sp_configure "user log cache size", 6000
2>go
1>checkpoint
2>go
```

The `user log cache size` SQL Server configuration parameter is static. As such, the new value you set it to will not take effect until you reboot the SQL Server. This command changes the *master* system database, so to ensure its recovery, be certain to dump the *master* system database. As this command changes the contents of system tables, it cannot be executed within a transaction.

The second UTL Cache SQL Server configuration parameter, `user log cache spinlock ratio`, controls the number of UTL Caches per spinlock. The default value of the `user log cache spinlock ratio` SQL Server configuration parameter is 20. The minimum value of the `user log cache spinlock ratio` SQL Server configuration parameter is 1, and its maximum value is 2,147,483,647. As the total number of UTL Caches is dependent on the configured count of user connections, the number of spinlocks that the SQL Server allocates is directly dependent upon the total number of configured user connections. The default setting of this SQL Server configuration parameter allocates one spinlock per twenty user connections.

When determining the value at which to set the `user log cache spinlock ratio` SQL Server configuration parameter, keep these ideas in mind:

1. The lower you set the value of this SQL Server configuration parameter, the more spinlocks you will have.

2. The more spinlocks you have, the more memory resources are taken from both the Procedure Cache and from all of the data caches. Each spinlock consumes 256 bytes of memory, so tread carefully.

3. If your SQL Server has been configured to support only one engine, then there will be one UTL spinlock for all user connections. As long as the SQL Server supports only one engine, you cannot modify the `user log cache spinlock ratio` SQL Server configuration parameter.

To set the `user log cache spinlock ratio` SQL Server configuration parameter to 12, for example, log on to the SQL Server as an account with **sa_role** privileges and enter these commands:

```
1>use master
2>go
1>sp_configure "user log cache spinlock ratio", 12
2>go
1>checkpoint
2>go
```

The `user log cache spinlock ratio` SQL Server configuration parameter is static. As such, the new value you set it to will not take effect until you reboot the SQL Server. This command changes the *master* system database, so to ensure its recovery, be certain to dump the *master* system database. As this command changes the contents of system tables, it cannot be executed within a transaction.

The Checkpoint Process

Within the SQL Server there is a process, called the Checkpoint, that is responsible for ensuring that if the SQL Server must be restarted, the recovery of databases can be accomplished in a suitable period of time (this time quantum is user configurable).

Once per minute, the sleeping Checkpoint process wakes up and examines the total number of changes to each database and, when it determines that the recovery of an individual database will take longer than the configured time period, it scans the data cache(s) and flushes any dirty pages out of data cache(s), out of UTL Caches, and out of *syslogs,* to disk. If a given database has set the `trunc log on chkpt` option on, then the Checkpoint process will truncate the database's transaction log. After working its way through the databases, it then goes back to sleep.

Configuring the Recovery Interval

You can adjust the frequency at which the Checkpoint process does its thing by changing the value of the `recovery interval in minutes` SQL

Server configuration parameter. The default value of the recovery interval in minutes SQL Server configuration parameter is 5. The minimum value of the recovery interval in minutes SQL Server configuration parameter is 1, and its maximum value is 32,767.

The recovery interval in minutes SQL Server configuration parameter establishes the maximum number of minutes, on a per-database basis, that the SQL Server should take to recover any database after a SQL Server failure event occurs. It is the function of the recovery process to roll forward, or roll back, transactions starting from the oldest active transaction (which is indicated by the last Checkpoint Log Record in the transaction log). On average, Sybase estimates that it will take a System 11 SQL Server one minute to recover a database whose transaction log contains 6000 log records. However, your recovery period will vary depending on the types of log records contained within the transaction log, on how powerful your machine is, and how you have your SQL Server configured and tuned.

To set the recovery interval in minutes SQL Server configuration parameter to 10 minutes, for example, log on to the SQL Server as an account with **sa_role** privileges and enter these commands:

```
1>use master
2>go
1>sp_configure "recovery interval in minutes", 10
2>go
1>checkpoint
2>go
```

In that the recovery interval in minutes SQL Server configuration parameter is dynamic, the consequences of changing its value will take effect immediately. This command changes the *master* system database, so to ensure its recovery, be certain to dump the *master* system database. As this command changes the contents of system tables, it cannot be executed within a transaction.

When setting the value of the recovery interval in minutes SQL Server configuration parameter, keep these facts in mind:

1. If you decrease the value of the recovery interval in minutes SQL Server configuration parameter, the Checkpoint process will run more frequently and slow down the SQL Server ever so slightly.

2. If you increase the value of the recovery interval in minutes SQL Server configuration parameter, the time it takes you to recover the database may be unacceptable to the business process(es) you are supporting.

The SQL Server Transaction Log and Text or Image Data Types

When you first assign a literal data value to a text or image column (i.e., you initialize it), the SQL Server allocates at least one data page, creates a pointer to the allocation page for the chain of linked data pages, and then stores that pointer in the table.

Whenever a text or image column is deleted, the SQL Server replaces the existing pointer with NULL and deallocates all of the data pages in the chain. These data pages are then available for allocation.

Whenever a text or image column is updated, the SQL Server first deletes the text or image data (however, the first page in the chain of linked data pages is not deallocated, instead it remains available for future use) and then reinitializes the text or image column.

Normally, text or image data is not logged by the SQL Server. Because of the size of these data types, the logging of text and image data can radically increase the rate at which transaction log resources are consumed.

To avoid the logging of text or image data, you must set the `select into/bulkcopy` database option on, and use the `writetext` command. With the `select into/bulkcopy` option set on, transactions involving text or image data are not, by default, logged. To use the `writetext` command against a temporary table, an account with **sa_role** privileges must enable the `select into/bulkcopy` option on the *tempdb* database.

However, client processes do have the option of logging text or image data on a transaction by transaction basis when using the `writetext` command. You may decide that it is important to be able to recover from failure events that could occur while modifying text or image data. If that is the case, then you will have to log the text or image transaction(s).

Whether your use of `writetext` is logged or not, this command is not capable of causing a trigger to fire. Also, whether the SQL Server does or does not log the actual text or image data, it will always log the data page allocations and deallocations associated with the transaction(s).

The `insert` and `update` commands can also be used on text and image data. Whenever you use these commands on text or image data, the transaction will be logged.

If you are going to log text or image data, then you must be certain to locate the database's *syslogs* on a separate database device and be certain that its size is capable of storing the potentially huge volumes of log records produced by transactions involving text and image data. Else you may end up taking the proverbial long walk off a short pier.

Because the default use of the `writetext` command does not result in the creation of transaction log records, you cannot recover any modifications to the database after you use this command. In addition, you cannot readily recover the database from a transaction log dump after the use of the `writetext` command (unless you purposefully intervene by taking a dump of the database *immediately* after executing the `writetext` command.

If after using `writetext` you issue a `dump transaction` command, the SQL Server will not try to stop `dump transaction` from running. You will not be given any indication by the SQL Server about the uselessness of taking a transaction dump in this context.

Transaction Log Options

The SQL Server database options and their default values that affect transaction logs are as follows:

1. `abort tran on log full`—this option's default value is `false`. This option determines what happens to a running transaction when it crosses the database transaction log's last-chance threshold. When set to the default value, the SQL Server will merely suspend the running transaction and then automatically restart it as soon as free space exists once again within the database's transaction log. When the value of this option is set to `true`, then all active user transactions that need to write to the database transaction log are automatically killed by the SQL Server until free space exists once again within the database's transaction log.

2. `no chkpt on recovery`—this option's default value is `false`. When the value of this option is set to `false`, a checkpoint record is attached to the database after it is recovered when the SQL Server is restarted, and as an additional precaution, the database's sequence number is automatically changed by the SQL Server Checkpoint process. The checkpoint record ensures that the restarted SQL Server will not attempt to needlessly recover the database, when doing so would be inappropriate, and causes any following load of the database's transaction log to fail. When the value of this option is set to `true`, a database does not get a checkpoint record from the recovery process, and the database's sequence number is not changed by the automatic SQL Server Checkpoint process. Instead, both a primary and secondary copy of the database are managed by the SQL Server. For this to work, the value of the `no chkpt on recovery` option must be set to `true` within both the primary and secondary databases. To start things off, a dump of the primary database is taken and loaded into the secondary database. Next, at predetermined intervals, dumps of the primary database's transaction log are taken and then loaded

into the secondary database. By disabling the automatic changing of the respective database sequence number, the primary and secondary database's sequence numbers are kept in sync, thereby ensuring that subsequent transaction log dumps from the primary database can be applied to the secondary database.

3. `select into/bulk copy`—this option's default value is `false`. When the value of this option is set to `true`, the use of `writetext`, `select into` a permanent table, or fast bulk copy into a table that does not have an index or trigger associated with it, is allowed. As a consequence of setting the value of this option to `true`, two factors must be considered. First, when `writetext`, `select into`, and `fast bulk copy` commands are used, except for corresponding page allocations and deallocations, a record of their use is not recorded within the database's transaction log. Second, because these commands are not recorded within the database's transaction log, it is not possible to use the `dump transaction` system command. It is strongly advised that, once these unlogged commands complete executing, the value of this option be set to `false`, and then the `dump database` system command be executed on this database. In this way, you will be in a position to fully recover the database, if need be.

4. `trunc log on chkpt`—this option's default value is `false`. When the value of this option is set to `false`, the database's transaction log will fill up until an account with **dbo** or **sa_role** privileges successfully issues the dump transaction system command. When the value of this option is set to `true`, committed and rolled back transactions are removed from the database's transaction log each time the database's Checkpoint process is run automatically by the SQL Server. The purpose of this option of automatically committed and rolled back transaction removal is to decrease the chance that the database transaction log's **last-chance** threshold will be crossed, and to ensure that the database transaction log does not fill up. As a consequence of setting the value of this option to `true`, it is not possible to use the default `dump transaction` system command. Therefore, in most cases, it is inappropriate to set the value of this option to `true` for production databases because a copy of the database's transaction log is not made prior to truncating the transaction log. However, it is appropriate to set the value of this option to `true` when the database and its transaction log are not located on separate segments, or when the ability to recover a database is not necessary, as is the case in some development, or testing environments. When the value of this option is set to `true`, to be able to recover the database, you must use the `dump database` system command. Finally, it is important to realize that the database's transaction log is truncated

when the `checkpoint` system command is executed when the value of this option to `true`. Also, if the last page of the transaction log is being used by an open transaction and a checkpoint occurs, the transaction log cannot be truncated. When this happens you must use the `dump transaction` *NameOfDatabase* `with no_log` command.

5. `trunc.log on chkpt.`—refers to the `trunc log on chkpt` option.

Setting Transaction Log Options

To set a database option, log on to the SQL Server as an account with **sa_role** privileges and enter these commands:

```
1>use master
2>go
1>sp_dboption NameOfDatabase, "database option", {true|false}
2>go
1>checkpoint
2>go
```

where:

NameOfDatabase—the name of the user database whose options you want to change.

"*database option*"—the specific Boolean database option you want to set. Be certain to enclose the given database option within quotation marks.

`{true|false}`—the literal value of a database option can be set to either `true` or `false`.

`checkpoint`—the new database option setting will not take effect until this command is issued (or, until the SQL Server is restarted).

This command changes the *master* system database, so to ensure its recovery, be certain to dump the *master* system database. As this command changes the contents of system tables, it cannot be executed within a transaction.

There are some constraints associated with the **sp_dboption** system procedure:

1. As the *master* system database's options cannot be changed, it cannot be used on the *master* system database.

2. No one can be using the database when you set one of its options.

3. During SQL Server run time, the change in a database option only takes place after running the `checkpoint` command.

Sizing a Transaction Log

There are two factors to consider when you determine the size of a database's transaction log:

1. Quantity of log records being written to the transaction log.
2. Frequency in which you dump the transaction log.

In general, it is advised that you make the transaction log 10 to 15 percent of the size of the database's data space. Sizing a database's transaction log in this manner is a good start, but you have to be careful. The bottom line is that a database's transaction log must be large enough to handle the largest transaction that will complete within the transaction log. If the general approach is sufficient, then all is well and good. However, it is best for the database Administrator to work closely with the application developers and determine largest transaction(s), and the frequency at which they are executed.

Dumping the transaction log purges the *syslogs* table of Buffer Masses that are no longer needed to roll back transaction or to recover the database. If the `trunc log on chkpt` database option has been enabled in a database, then the SQL Server will automatically purge the transaction log of committed transaction log records.

By matching the frequency of transaction log dumping with the rate and quantity of log writing, you will establish a suitable size for the transaction log.

Placement of a Database's Transaction Log

If you want to be able to recover a database, the first rule to remember is never place a database and its *syslogs* table on the same segment, or on the same database device. And, if you want to be able to recover from a media-failure event in particular, never place a database and its *syslogs* table on the same disk drive.

If you place the database and its *syslogs* table on the same segment, then you will not be able to back up the database's transaction log. You can still use the `dump transaction` command, but in this context the command will only truncate the transaction log; it will not back up the transaction log.

Unfortunately, when responding to a `create database` command, the SQL Server, by default, locates both the database and its *syslogs* table on the next available default database device. Storage space for the database and the *syslogs* table is allocated from the default database devices in alphabetical order by device name (as recorded within the `master..sysdevices` table). If there is enough space on the next available default database device (to hold both the database and *syslogs*), then they will both reside there by default.

Unless you explicitly use the `log on` clause of the `create database` command, the log segment will be located on a default database device. Also, unless you explicitly use the `on` clause of the `create database` command, the database will be located on a default database device. Therefore, by default, both the transaction log and the database may well end up on the same physical disk. Generally, this is not a good thing to have occur.

To make matters worse, SQL Server has established the **d_master** device as the first default database device. As the **d_master** device is the first default database device, it is the exception to the "in alphabetical order by device name" rule. Fortunately, it is possible (and advisable) to change the **d_master** device's status as a default device so that it cannot be used for storage if the user fails to specify a device with the `create database`, or with the `alter database`, commands.

Every time you cause a write to *syslogs*, you promote disk I/O activity. The amount of data activity with logging transactions can be significant. As the volume of rows being inserted into *syslogs* increases, the amount of disk I/O activity rises significantly. Any significant increase in disk I/O activity will degrade overall system performance.

Overall system performance will further degrade when multiple processes (such as accessing the *master* system database, accessing the *tempdb* system database, writing to *syslogs*, or accessing a database) compete for the same disk drive, or for the same disk controller. The higher the degree of competition between processes for limited disk I/O bandwidth, the greater the probability of disk I/O bottlenecks occurring.

Therefore, to avoid disk I/O bottlenecks, you should locate a database and its *syslogs* table on different disks (and off of different disk controllers when possible).

Also, by placing the transaction log on a physical device that is separate from the one that holds the other objects in the database, you have the ability to monitor disk I/O events specific to the transaction log. This capability is extremely important when analyzing SQL Server performance problems, or when determining a suitable size for the transaction log.

However, as always, there is an exception to the above recommendations. If you have a small, noncritical database (i.e., one which you do not need to be recovered if it were to go south), then it is OK to place the transaction log on the same logical device as the rest of the database.

Determining the Location of a Database's Transaction Log

To determine which logical database device(s) a database's transaction log is located on, log on to the SQL Server as any Sybase account and enter these commands:

```
1>use master
2>go
1>sp_helpdb NameOfDatabase
2>go
```

where:

NameOfDatabase—the name of the database whose transaction log you want to determine on which logical device(s) it resides.

Moving the Transaction Log to another Logical Database Device

If you have determined that a database's transaction log has been incorrectly placed, you will have to move the transaction log to another, more suitable, logical database device. The SQL Server provides you with the procedures and a process for moving a transaction log that was initially placed on the same logical device as the rest of the database (i.e., the log on clause was not used when the database was initially created).

To move such a transaction log, log on to the SQL Server as an account with **dbo** or **sa_role** privileges and follow this series of steps.

Step 1.   Place the database into single-user mode by entering these commands:

```
1>use master
2>go
1>sp_dboption NameOfDatabase, single, true
2>go
```

where

NameOfDatabase—the name of the database that contains the transaction log you want to move to another logical device. This database must exist and it must have been created without using the log on clause.

You have now ensured that no new transactions, other than your own, will attempt to write to the transaction log you want to move.

Step 2.   Enter these commands:

```
1>use NameOfDatabase
2>go
1>sp_logdevice NameOfDatabase, NameOfLogicalDevice
2>go
```

where

> *NameOfDatabase*—the name of the database that contains the transaction log you want to move to another logical device. This database must exist and it must have been created without using the `log on` clause.
>
> *NameOfLogicalDevice*—the new logical database device to which you want to move the transaction log. This logical database device must already have been initialized with the `disk init` command, and it must already have been allocated to the database with either the `create database` or the `alter database` command.

Bear in mind that the **sp_logdevice** system procedure does not move the currently allocated transaction log page from its original logical database device. The **sp_logdevice** system procedure will, however, move all transaction log pages to be allocated in the future onto the new logical database device. The currently allocated page will remain on the original logical database device until either of two things happens: the currently allocated transaction log page is filled with new transaction records or the transaction log is dumped.

Step 3.   To get the currently allocated transaction log page over to the new transaction log logical database device, you may have to submit some dummy `insert` or `update` transaction against the database. The object is to fill up the currently allocated transaction log page, which is 2048 bytes in size. However, before you start submitting the dummy transaction, you will need to determine what page is being used right now, by entering these commands:

```
1>dbcc checktable (syslogs)
2>go
```

After this command completes, estimate how many log records you will need to fill the currently allocated transaction log page and then submit the corresponding dummy transaction. When they complete running, then rerun the `dbcc checktable (syslogs)` command to make sure that the page has been filled, and that a new one has been allocated.

Step 4. Determine if there are any active transactions in the database and wait for them to complete. To determine if there are any active transactions, enter these commands:

```
1>sp_who
2>go
```

The display will indicate which processes are running in which databases. As soon as you see that your process is the only one running against the database, then you can proceed to the next step.

Step 5. At this point, you have to remove all log pages from the transaction log. To do this, enter these commands:

```
1>dump transaction NameOfDatabase
2>to NameOfDumpDevice
3>go
```

Step 6. Now, all portions of the transaction log should be on the new logical database device you moved it to. To verify this, enter these commands:

```
1>sp_helplog
2>go
1>dump database NameOfDatabase
2>to NameOfDumpDevice
3>go
```

The name of the logical database device on which the first page of the transaction log is located should be the name of the logical database device to which you moved the transaction log. As you have altered the system catalogs for this database, it is now necessary to dump the database so that it can be recovered if need be.

Step 7. Be certain to place the database back into multiuser mode. To accomplish that, enter these commands:

```
1>use master
2>go
1>sp_dboption NameOfDatabase, single, false
2>go
```

When you move a transaction log using this process, keep these things in mind:

1. After the transaction log has been moved, the space it was located on is now available for use by the rest of the database.

2. A new **last-chance** threshold will be created for the database. Make any changes to this threshold as may be required to restore the behavior of the database's previous last-chance threshold.

If you want to move a transaction log that is not located on the same device as the rest of the database, then you will have to re-create that database on another set of devices (this time correctly placing the transaction log) and then use the Sybase bulk copy (**bcp**) utility to copy the data out of the current database and into the newly created database.

Increasing the Size of a Transaction Log

To increase the size of a transaction log, log on to the SQL Server as an account with **dbo** or **sa_role** privileges and enter these commands:

```
1>use master
2>go
1>sp_dboption NameOfDatabase, single, true
2>go
1>alter database NameOfDatabase
2>log on { default|NameOfDatabaseDevice} [=size]
3>[,NameOfDatabaseDevice [=size]]...]
4>go
1>sp_dboption NameOfDatabase, single, false
2>go
```

where:

NameOfDatabase—the name of the database whose transaction log you want to enlarge.

`log on`—indicates that the command will affect the placement of the database's transaction log.

`[ default`—if you elect not to use the default reserved word, then the new space allocated to the transaction log will be placed on any of the default database devices listed within `master..sysdevices` or on any default database device associated with that particular valid Sybase account. By default, that database device would be the **d_master** database device.

NameOfDatabaseDevice—the name of the database device must conform to the rules for Sybase identifiers. This logical database device must already have been initialized with the `disk init` command. If you do not comply with this requirement, then this command will fail. There are a number of very good reasons why a transaction log should not reside on the same database device as the database's data and index pages:

1. To guarantee that the user database is fully recoverable, the transaction log should not reside on a database device that will contain the data and index pages of this user database. In the unfortunate event that the disk drive on which you have placed either the database or the transaction log crashes, then you can recover either the database or the transaction log from their respective dumps.

2. It can significantly improve SQL Server performance. When the data and index pages are on a separate database device from that of the transaction log, and when these database devices are located on different disk drives, reads and writes to the database devices can take place concurrently instead of linearly, as is the case when both the pages and the log reside on the same database device.

3. It allows you to use the `dump transaction log` command, not just the `dump database`. This backup flexibility can reduce the amount of time it takes to do a backup and can contribute to reducing the amount of tape or disk space you need to set aside for doing backups.

4. The pages and the log are not forced to compete against each other for the same area of disk space. Instead, you can assign a fixed amount of disk space that is individually dedicated to each.

5. The SQL Server automatically creates a default, last-chance threshold monitoring on the transaction log, and, additionally, enables you to create other free-space thresholds on both the data and log sections of the user database.

`[=size]`—specifying the size of your new user database is optional. By default, the smallest value of the `size` configuration variable is 1 (i.e., 1 MB, or 512K pages). The largest value you can assign to `size`, on a per-database-device basis, is 2048 (i.e., 2048 MB). As regards the optional `size` parameter to this optional clause, the general rule is to assign a value to the `size` parameter that equals 10 to 25 percent of the size of the user database. However, the actual size of a database's transaction log is really dependent upon the type, length, volume, and frequency, of the (open) write transactions submitted to the database, and the frequency at which you take transaction log dumps. For example, because the deferred updates take up twice as much log space as the direct, you need to know when deferred, versus direct, updates are taking place. Note that, if you choose not to use the optional `size` parameter to this optional clause, then the transaction log will be given 2 MB of disk space.

`[ ,NameOfDatabaseDevice [=size]]...`—it is possible for a transaction log to reside on multiple database devices and to consume varying amounts of space on those respective database devices. Therefore, when altering user databases, you can assign space to that transaction log from multiple database devices.

This change will take effect at once. This command changes the *master* system database, so to ensure its recovery, be certain to dump the *master* system database. As this command changes the contents of system tables, it cannot be executed within a transaction.

Dumping a Transaction Log

To ensure database recovery and availability of transaction log space, you will need to periodically dump the database's transaction log. You can dump a transaction log while there are active processes within a database, or when the database is not in use. When you create a dump image of a transaction log you write copies of pages within the transaction log to a SQL Server dump device, record the dump event within the transaction log, and then purge the transaction log of inactive log records. Under normal operating conditions, if the `trunc log on chkpt` database option is set on for your database, then you will not need to dump the transaction log.

The SQL Server supports three techniques for dumping transaction logs (in the absence of a media-failure event):

1. Plain vanilla
2. With `truncate_log`
3. With `no_log`

The plain vanilla technique is for use on databases when the `trunc log on chkpt` database option is set off, the database's transaction log is on a segment that does not support tables or indexes, and when operating under normal conditions (i.e., your transaction log has not been filled with log records). To take a plain vanilla dump of a transaction log, log on to the SQL Server as an account with **dbo, sa_role,** or **oper_role** privileges and enter these commands:

```
1>use NameOfDatabase
2>go
1>dump tran[saction] NameOfDatabase
2>to NameOfDumpDevice
3>go
```

where:

NameOfDatabase—the name of the database whose transaction log you want to make a dump image of.

`tran[saction]`—you can enter the full character string or its abbreviation.

NameOfDumpDevice—the name of the SQL Server dump device to which you want to write a copy of the transaction log.

This command will write copies of the transaction log pages to the dump device, writes a dump transaction record into the transaction log, and then purges the transaction log of inactive records.

The `"with truncate_only"` technique is for use on databases where the transaction log is on the same segment that supports tables or indexes (e.g., the *master,* the *model,* and the *sybsystemprocs* system databases) and user databases that do not have the logs on separate segments. To take a `"with truncate_only"` dump of a transaction log, log on to the SQL Server as an account with **dbo, sa_role,** or **oper_role** privileges and enter these commands:

```
1>use NameOfDatabase
2>go
1>dump tran[saction] NameOfDatabase with truncate_only
2>go
```

where:

NameOfDatabase—the name of the database whose transaction log you want to make a dump image of.

`tran[saction]`—you can enter the full character string or its abbreviation.

The `"with truncate_only"` technique does not write copies of the transaction log pages to the dump device, but it does write a dump transaction record into the transaction log, and then purges the transaction log of inactive records. As this technique provides you with no means to recover the database, you must take a dump of the database after using it.

Under abnormal operating conditions, a database transaction log may become full of log records. In such cases, the plain vanilla technique will not work. You will have to, first, try the `"with truncate_only"` technique to free space within the transaction log. However, the `"with truncate _only"` technique may not do the trick in all cases. If after trying the `"with truncate_only"` technique, there is not sufficient free space in the transaction log, then you must use the `"with no_log"` technique to free space within the transaction log. To take a `"with no_log"` dump of a transaction log, log on to the SQL Server as an account with **dbo, sa_role,** or **oper_role** privileges and enter these commands:

```
1>use NameOfDatabase
2>go
1>dump tran[saction] NameOfDatabase with no_log
2>go
```

where:

NameOfDatabase—the name of the database whose transaction log you want to make a dump image of.

`tran[saction]`—you can enter the full character string or its abbreviation.

The `"with no_log"` technique does not write copies of the transaction log pages to the dump device, nor does it write a dump transaction record into the transaction log, but it does purge the transaction log of inactive records. As this technique provides you with no means to recover the database, you must take a dump of the database after using this technique.

Loading a Transaction Log

To recover a system or user database after a media-failure event, requires loading each impacted database with its latest dump image, and, where applicable, transaction log dumps. The processes for recovering a system or user database are very detailed and exacting. They have significant variations for system databases versus user databases.

To determine the correct method to use when recovering a system or user database after a media failure, refer to the System 11 System Administration Guide from Sybase and follow each and every step of the recovery process exactly as specified in the guide. If you have been making dump images at regularly scheduled intervals, and after each time, you changed the contents of its system tables or created indexes, and after any unlogged transaction occurs (e.g., fast `bcp`, `select into...`, or nonlogged `writetext` commands, etc.), you should be able to recover the database(s) just fine. Good luck, and remember to follow the recovery instructions exactly as they are documented.

Configuring "logonly" Type Named Data Cache

On SMP platforms, with the SQL Server running multiple engines, binding a transaction log to a "logonly" type Named Data Cache significantly reduces contention on the database's transaction log spinlock. Also, when that Named Data Cache and its Memory Pool have been sized correctly, you will increase the number of times that processes can reread log pages in cache versus rereading them from disk.

There are a number of contexts in which the transaction log is read:

1. During database recovery, transaction log pages are read from disk into the 2K Memory Pool in the Default Data Cache, and all related transactions that must be rolled back or forward, read their data and index pages into the Default Data Cache.

2. Transactions that are performed in deferred, as opposed to direct, mode require rereading the transaction log to apply changes to affected tables or indexes. Most often, these log pages are still in data cache.

3. When a trigger has referenced inserted and deleted tables the transaction log is read. These tables are constructed during run time by reading records from the transaction log when the trigger queries the affected tables. Most often, these log pages are still in data cache.

4. When a transaction is rolled back, log records from the transaction log are read. Most often, these log pages are still in data cache.

By default, all newly created Named Data Caches are of type "mixed." However, before you can bind a transaction log to a Named Data Cache, you must change its type to "logonly." To change a Named Data Cache's type, log on to the SQL Server as an account with **sa_role** privileges and enter these commands:

```
1>use master
2>go
3>sp_cacheconfig NameOfDataCache, logonly
4>go
```

where:

NameOfDataCache—the name of the data cache whose type you want to change to "logonly."

logonly—this parameter specifies the Named Data Cache type as being "logonly."

This change takes effect immediately. This command changes the *master* system database, so to ensure its recovery, be certain to dump the *master* system database. As this command changes the contents of system tables, it cannot be executed within a transaction.

Here are a few important facts to keep in mind when changing the type of a Named Data Cache:

1. The HouseKeeper does not run against any data cache of type "logonly."

2. You can change the type of the Named Data Cache to "logonly" if, and only if, there are no databases, or any database objects currently bound to the Named Data Cache. So, be sure to unbind all relevant databases and database objects from the Named Data Cache before you attempt to set its type to "logonly."

3. Studies have shown that transaction logs typically perform best when they use a 4K Memory Pool. So, be certain to configure a 4K Memory Pool within all Named Data Caches that are of type "logonly."

Binding a Transaction Log to Named Data Cache

Because the SQL Server takes exclusive locks on log pages when binding a *syslogs* table to a "logonly" type Named Data Cache, the database it is contained within must be in a single-user mode. So, to bind a *syslogs* table to a "logonly" type Named Data Cache, log on to the SQL Server as an account with **sa_role** privileges and enter these commands:

```
1>use master
2>go
1>sp_dboption NameOfDatabase, single, true
2>go
1>use NameOfDatabase
2>go
1>checkpoint
2>go
1>use master
2>go
1>sp_bindcache NameOfDataCache, NameOfDatabase, syslogs
2>go
1>sp_dboption NameOfDatabase, single, false
2>go
```

where

NameOfDataCache—the name of the mixed Named Data Cache to which you want to exclusively bind the transaction log. This Named Data Cache must exist before you execute the sp_bindcache command. Be certain that the data cache is of type "logonly," since you cannot bind the *syslogs* table to a data cache of type "mixed." Also, the status of this data cache must be "Active," that is, the SQL Server must have been restarted since the point in time when this data cache was created, else the *syslogs* table cannot be bound to it. Analysis has shown that most SQL Servers transaction logs perform best with 4K Memory Pools. By default, the SQL Server will use the 2K Memory Pool of data cache the *syslogs* table is bound to, unless that data cache is configured with a 4K Memory Pool. In order to ensure that the transaction log will use the 4K Memory Pool, you must change the transaction log's Buffer Mass (by using the `sp_logiosize` system procedure).

NameOfDatabase—the name of the database that contains the transaction log you want to bind to a "logonly" data cache. This database must exist before you can bind its transaction log to a "logonly" type Named Data Cache.

This change takes effect immediately. This command changes the *master* system database, so to ensure its recovery, be certain to dump the *master* system database. As this command changes the contents of system tables, it cannot be executed within a transaction.

Here are a few important facts to keep in mind when binding a transaction log to a "logonly" type Named Data Cache:

1. When you bind the *syslogs* table to a "logonly" type Named Data Cache you must be in (i.e., using) the database that contains the transaction log.

2. If the *syslogs* table is already bound to another Named Data Cache, the old binding is dropped and the new one is created (i.e., you do not have to unbind the *syslogs* table before you create its new binding).

3. When you bind the *syslogs* table to a Named Data Cache, any of its pages in memory are flushed to disk. They will be located in the Named Data Cache to which they are bound once a user process needs to access them.

4. The Named Data Cache, to which the *syslogs* table is being bound, must be of type "logonly."

5. When you bind the *syslogs* table to a Named Data Cache, the SQL Server must acquire an exclusive lock on the table. The SQL Server will cause the binding process to sleep until this exclusive lock can be acquired. In addition, this exclusive lock will degrade the performance of any transaction that requires locks on the *syslogs* table. Once these exclusive locks are acquired, the SQL Server will flush all related dirty log pages to disk, and drop all related clean log pages from the data cache. When these log pages are needed once

again to support a query, they are read into the mixed Named Data Cache to which they have been bound.

6. If a Named Data Cache to which the *syslogs* table is currently bound is dropped, the data cache binding records remain within the system catalogs, but are marked as invalid. As a consequence, warning messages about the *syslogs* table binding will be written to the SQL Server error log each time the SQL Server boots (i.e., it is restarted). If you subsequently re-created the Named Data Cache (using exactly the same name), the bindings will automatically take effect and will be marked as valid, once the status of the Name Data Cache becomes "Active." So, unless you intend to re-create a dropped Named Data Cache to which a *syslogs* table is bound, you should unbind the *syslogs* table from the Named Data Cache before you drop the Named Data Cache.

7. It is not necessary to specify the table owner name because it is owned by **dbo.**

Determining Transaction Log Buffer Mass Size

With System 11 there are two techniques you can use to determine the transaction log Buffer Mass size for all databases. First, you can find out this information for all databases by reading the SQL Server's error log. When the SQL Server is started, the size of each transaction log's Buffer Mass is written to the error log. Alternatively, you can log on to the SQL Server as any valid Sybase account and enter these commands:

```
1>use master
2>go
1>sp_logiosize "all"
2>go
```

This command sequence will cause the SQL Server to display the transaction log Buffer Mass sizes for all databases, grouped by the name of the data cache.

If you want to know the Buffer Mass size of a given database's transaction log, log on to the SQL Server as any valid Sybase account that is authorized to use that particular database and enter these commands:

```
1>use NameOfDatabase
2>go
1>sp_logiosize
2>go
```

where:

NameOfDatabase—the name of the database that contains the transaction log whose Buffer Mass size you want to know.

This command sequence will cause the SQL Server to display the transaction log Buffer Mass size for just the specified database.

Configuring Transaction Log Buffer Mass Size

For the SQL Server to use the Memory Pool you have previously configured specifically for a transaction log, you must match the Buffer Mass that the transaction log will use to that of the appropriate Memory Pool in the data cache that will support the transaction log (this can be the Default Data Cache, or it can be a "mixed" type Named Data Cache which the transaction log is using because its database has been explicitly bound to it, or it can be a "logonly" type Named Data Cache to which the transaction log itself has been explicitly bound). If the supporting data cache does not contain a Memory Pool whose Buffer Mass size matches that of the transaction log that is bound to it, then the SQL Server will automatically use the data cache's 2K Memory Pool to support the transaction log.

It is being assumed that you have completed all necessary preliminary memory resource management tasks prior to configuring transaction log disk I/O. Sybase has determined that, in general, there is a higher probability of transaction log group commits occurring, versus flushing the transaction log simply because it is full of log pages, when the transaction log uses a 4K Buffer Mass. However, the general case may not apply to your particular application.

To set the Buffer Mass size of a given transaction log to the default size of 4K, log on to the SQL Server as an account with **sa_role** privileges and enter these commands:

```
1>use NameOfDatabase
2>go
1>sp_logiosize "default"
2>go
```

where:

NameOfDatabase—the name of the database that contains the transaction log whose Buffer Mass size you want to set to 4K.

`"default"`—sets the size of the transaction log's Buffer Mass to 4K. Alternatively, you could pass the number 4 to this system procedure to accomplish the same results.

This change takes effect immediately. This command changes the contents the database's system tables, so to ensure its recovery, be certain to dump the database's transaction log, and then dump the database itself. As this command changes the contents of system tables, it cannot be executed within a transaction.

Here are a few important facts to keep in mind when setting a transaction log's Buffer Mass to the default size:

1. If the supporting data cache does not contain a 4K Memory Pool, then the data cache's 2K Memory Pool will be used by the transaction log. Also, if there are 8K or 16K Memory Pools in that data cache, they will not be used by the transaction log.

2. During database recovery, the 2K Memory Pool in the Default Data Cache will be used to support transaction log management, regardless of the Buffer Mass size of the transaction log.

You can also set the Buffer Mass size of a given transaction log to the size of 2K, 8K, or 16K. To set a transaction log's Buffer Mass to 16K, for example, log on to the SQL Server as an account with **sa_role** privileges and enter these commands:

```
1>use NameOfDatabase
2>go
1>sp_logiosize "16"
2>go
```

where:

NameOfDatabase—is the name of the database that contains the transaction log whose Buffer Mass size you want to set to 4K.

16—sets the size of the transaction log's Buffer Mass to 16K.

This change takes effect immediately. This command changes the contents the database's system tables, so to ensure its recovery, be certain to dump the database's transaction log, and then dump the database itself. As this command changes the contents of system tables, it cannot be executed within a transaction.

Here are a few important facts to keep in mind when setting a transaction log's Buffer Mass to a 2K, 8K, or 16K size:

1. If you set the transaction log's Buffer Mass to 8K or to 16K, and the supporting data cache does not contain a Memory Pool whose size matches the size of the transaction log's new Buffer Mass, then the command will fail, and the transaction log's Buffer Mass size will not be changed.

2. If the transaction log is bound to a logonly type Named Data Cache, then any Memory Pool with a larger Buffer Mass than the size of the transaction log's Buffer Mass will not be used to support the transaction log.

3. During database recovery, the 2K Memory Pool in the Default Data Cache will be used to support transaction log management, regardless of the Buffer Mass size of the transaction log.

4. The only legal sizes of transaction log Buffer Masses are 2K, 4K, 8K, and 16K.

Unbinding a Transaction Log from Named Data Cache

In that even the best made plans sometimes go astray, you may need to reverse a decision to bind a transaction log from a "logonly" type Named Data Cache.

Because the SQL Server takes exclusive locks on log pages when binding a *syslogs* table from a "logonly" type Named Data Cache, the database it is contained within must be in "single-user mode." So, to unbind a *syslogs* table from a "logonly" type Named Data Cache, log on to the SQL Server as an account with **sa_role** privileges and enter these commands:

```
1>use master
2>go
1>sp_dboption NameOfDatabase, single, true
2>go
1>use NameOfDatabase
2>go
1>checkpoint
2>go
1>use master
2>go
1>sp_unbindcache NameOfDataCache, NameOfDatabase, syslogs
2>go
1>sp_dboption NameOfDatabase, single, false
2>go
```

where

NameOfDataCache—the name of the mixed Named Data Cache from which you want to unbind the transaction log. This Named Data Cache must exist before you execute the sp_unbindcache command. The status of this data cache must be "Active," that is, the SQL Server must have been restarted since the point in time when this data cache was created, else the system table cannot be unbound from it.

NameOfDatabase—the name of the database that contains the transaction log you want to unbind from a "logonly" data cache. This database must exist before you can unbind its transaction log from a "logonly" type Named Data Cache.

This change takes effect immediately. This command changes the *master* system database, so to ensure its recovery, be certain to dump the *master* system database. As this command changes the contents of system tables, it cannot be executed within a transaction.

Here are a few important facts to keep in mind when unbinding a transaction log from a "logonly" type Named Data Caches:

1. When you unbind the *syslogs* table to a "logonly" type Named Data Cache you must be in (i.e., using) the database that contains the transaction log.

2. When you unbind the *syslogs* table to a Named Data Cache, any of its pages in memory are flushed to disk. They will be located in the Default Data Cache once a user process needs to access them.

3. When you unbind the *syslogs* table to a Named Data Cache, the SQL Server must acquire exclusive locks on the table. The SQL Server will cause the `sp_unbindcache` process to sleep until exclusive locks can be acquired. In addition, this exclusive lock will degrade the performance of any transaction that require locks on the *syslogs* table. Once these exclusive locks are acquired, the SQL Server will flush all related dirty log pages to disk, and drop all related clean log pages from the data cache. They will be located in the Default Data Cache once a user process needs to access them.

4. It is not necessary to specify the table owner name because it is owned by **dbo.**

Determining the Use of Transaction Log Resources

If you are concerned about the use of space available to *syslogs,* then you can log on to the SQL Server as an account with **sa_role** privileges and enter these commands:

```
1>use NameOfDatabase
2>go
1>dbcc checktable (syslogs)
2>go
```

The output produced by the **dbcc** Checkpoint utility will indicate how much space is available to *syslogs*. Unfortunately, if both your database and transaction log are on the same segment, then the **dbcc** Checktable utility will not be able to indicate how much space is available to the *syslogs* table. This is another of many reasons why you should not put *syslogs* on the same segment (or database device) that holds your database.

Also, you can log on to the SQL Server as any valid Sybase account and enter these commands:

```
1>use NameOfDatabase
2>go
1>select count(*) from syslogs
2>go
```

Last, you can log on to the SQL Server as any valid Sybase account and enter these commands:

```
1>use NameOfDatabase
2>go
1>sp_spaceused syslogs
2>go
```

Now, if you intend to use any of the preceding techniques, be forewarned: you will be taking locks on the *syslogs* table, and may be increasing contention into a point where contention may already exist. Avoid using these techniques when doing so will impede active transactions, or will increase the occurrence of deadlock events. To use these techniques wisely, you must be intimately familiar with the behavior of the SQL Server at the point in time when any of these techniques are to be used. At times, they can be used in a prudent and safe manner. At other times, their use can be a serious impediment to the other processes active within the database, and may cause another user process to be rolled back in order to resolve a deadlock event their use introduced into the database. By all means, keep on rockin' in the free world, but keep those little concrete hands off the transaction log.

The *syslogs* Taboo

Ensuring the integrity of *syslogs* is critically important. Be absolutely certain that insert, update, or delete commands are never applied to the contents of any *syslogs* table.

Recall that every insert, update, and delete command is logged (i.e., written) into *syslogs*. If you submit an insert, update, or delete command against *syslogs,* you are attempting to change the database. This change, like all other database changes, will be recorded by appending a log record to *syslogs*. This act of appending a log record must itself be recorded in *syslogs;* ad nauseam. Before you know it, you have created a programmatic loop that executes until the entire log segment is consumed. Unfortunately, the SQL Server will permit an authorized client process to submit changes to *syslogs*. Caveat emptor!

Just how the SQL Server will proceed after the transaction log is full is influenced by the database option `abort tran on log full`. By default, the option is set to false, so the offending transaction will be suspended, only to reawaken when log space has been freed, or increased. Upon being reawakened, the transaction will proceed to consume all newly available log space until it is once again suspended. If the option is set to `true`, then the offending transaction is automatically killed by the SQL Server.

Misuse of the dbcc log Utility

Still, you can read the *syslogs* table in order to manually recover a database. Because log records are not composed of column formatted data, you cannot directly select useful data from *syslogs*. Fortunately, Sybase has provided the **dbcc log** utility. The function of the **dbcc log** utility is to read the *syslogs* data pages into a buffer, and to print out the log records in a human-consumable format. However, you can comprehend the meaning of the **dbcc log** utility output statements if, and only if, you know how to decode them.

The use of the **dbcc log** utility is not entirely risk free. You must not use the **dbcc log** utility against a database that has the `trunc log on chkpt` option enabled. Anytime the transaction log is truncated, log records of completed transactions (i.e., `committed` or `rolled back` transactions, are deleted from *syslogs*. As the log records are deleted, the data pages they resided upon are subject to being deallocated from *syslogs,* and then possibly subsequently reallocated to *syslogs*.

When you enable the database's `trunc log on chkpt` option, the automatic internal Checkpoint process, as one of its tasks, truncates the transaction log. Typically, this automatic internal Checkpoint process fires off once every minute. Given its frequency, it is quite possible for one of the data pages read by the **dbcc log** utility, and hence loaded into a data page cache buffer, to be deallocated and then reallocated. This creates very serious problems for the Cache Manager, and corrupts the OAM. Once the OAM is corrupted, recovery of the database might be possible only through the use of database backups.

As regards the `trunc log on chkpt` option itself, when it is enabled, the Checkpoint process does not make a copy of the transaction log prior to deleting the inactive log records. Because a copy of the log is not made prior to truncating the log, the `trunc log on chkpt` option should not be used on databases that must be recoverable. Therefore, this option should not be enabled on production databases.

There is one exception to this production database rule. It may be appropriate to enable the `trunc log on chkpt` option for a production database during the time period in which you are using the **bcp** utility to upload larger batch files. When this option is enabled, the transaction log will not fill up during the upload process. However, once the upload process completes, be certain to disable the `trunc log on chkpt` option, take a checkpoint of the database, and then take a dump of the database.

If you do enable the `trunc log on chkpt` option, the only way to ensure recoverability of the database is to dump the database. After a media-failure event, you will not be able to take a dump of the transaction log because changes to your database are not recoverable from the transaction log dump (i.e., the transaction log dump is missing the truncated log records).

The master..syslogshold Table

In addition to implementing UTL Caches in the Transaction Log Subsystem, it has been enhanced, as well, in System 11, to manage the `master..syslogshold` system table (which is a heap structure). The SQL Server dynamically populated the *syslogshold* table when queried to store a snapshot of:

1. Representations of the oldest active, uncompleted, transaction in each database it manages (the process must have written at least one log record to a transaction log from a UTL Cache).

2. Representations of each Sybase Replication Server Log Transfer Manager's (also referred to as a Replication Agent) connection that manages the secondary truncation point it has placed within a given transaction log.

For a given database, there will be zero, one, at most, two rows: one for the oldest active transaction, if present, and one for the Log Transfer Manager's connection, if present. Also, keep in mind that, since the *syslogshold* table is populated by a snapshot query, it is only representing the activity in the SQL Server at the specific point in time when the *syslogshold* table was queried. As such, the oldest active transaction may actually have completed before the contents of the *syslogshold* table are returned to you.

The physical definition of the `master..syslogshold` table is:

Column Name	Data Type	Description
dbid	smallint	The ID of the Database that contains the oldest active transaction.
reserved	int	This column is not presently being used by the SQL Server.
spid	smallint	The SQL Server ID of the user process that owns the oldest active transaction in the database. When the process is the Log Transfer Manager's secondary truncation point, the value of this column will always be zero.
Page	int	This is either the number of the first transaction log page associated with the oldest active user process transaction, or it is the number of the secondary truncation page for the Log Transfer Manager.
xactid	char(6)	The SQL Server ID of the oldest active transaction. If this is a Log Transfer Manager's connection that supports its secondary truncation point, then the value stored in this column will always be 0x000000.
masterxactid	char(6)	This column is used to handle multidatabase transaction. If the oldest active transaction is a multidatabase transaction, then this column will store the SQL Server ID of the transaction's master transaction. If the oldest active transaction is not a multidatabase transaction then this column will contain the value 0x000000. Also, if this is a Log Transfer Manager's connection that supports its secondary truncation point, then the value stored in this column will always be 0x000000.
starttime	datetime	This is the date and time when the oldest active transaction was started. Or, in the case of a Log Transfer Manager, the point in time when the secondary truncation point was set within the transaction log.
name	char(67)	This is the name of the oldest active transaction in the database. When a transaction is created, you can provide, as an option to the `begin transaction` command, a name for that transaction. If, when the transaction was created, it was given a name, then that name will be stored in this column. However, if no name was provided when the transaction was created, then the string "`$user_transaction`" will be stored in this column. Additionally, if the nonnamed transaction was started in the ANSI chained mode, then the string "`$chained_ transaction`" will be stored in this column. Transactions started internally by the SQL Server are assigned names, and these names are prefixed with the dollar sign ($) and indicate their purpose in life. In the case of a Log Transfer Manager, the string "`$replication_truncation_point`" will be stored in this column.

Through the introduction of the `master..syslogsholds` table, the System 11 SQL Server provides an easy way to identify the oldest active transaction in a given database and to obtain the information necessary to take appropriate action. This is significant in that log-running transaction can prevent a `dump transaction` from truncating the transaction log.

To determine the specific host computer, the identity of the SQL Server process, and the name of the application associated with the oldest active transactions (and their names and the times they started), log on to the SQL Server as any valid Sybase account and enter these commands:

```
1>use master
2>go
1>select P.hostname, P.hostprocess, P.program_name, H.name,
   H.starttime
2>from sysprocesses P, syslogshold H
3>where P.spid = H.spid
4>and H.spid != 0
5>go
```

In the above query, the purpose in evaluating the literal data value stored in `syslogshold..spid` is being ensured that information about a user process's oldest active transaction, and not a Log Transfer Manager's secondary truncation point, will be selected.

To determine the identity of the SQL Server process and the name of the oldest active transaction that is blocking a transaction log's primary truncation point, and therefore preventing a `dump transaction` from truncating a database's transaction log, log on to the SQL Server as any valid Sybase account and enter these commands:

```
1>use master
2>go
1>select H.spid, H.name
2>from NameOfDatabase..sysindexes I, syslogshold H
3>where I.id = 8
4>and H.page = I.first
5>and H.dbid = db_id("NameOfDatabase")
5>go
```

In this query, `I.id` is being tested for equality to the literal data value 8, because the object identifier for a *syslogs* table is 8. And, the literal data value stored within the `sysindexes..first` column is the page identifier of the first page in the `master..syslogshold` table. Last, the system function `db_id()` returns the identifier of the database in question.

OK, so now that you have this type of information, what are you going to do with it? Well, first, you have to make a call as to whether this transaction is causing a real problem or not. If it is causing a real problem, then you have three options:

1. Go ahead and kill the transaction (using the `kill` command), and then execute the `dump transaction` command as soon as possible. This might not be such a smart thing to do if you are not the owner of the process that created the transaction.

2. Contact the user who owns the offending transaction, persuade them to kill their process, and then execute the `dump transaction` command as soon as possible.

3. Do nothing (i.e., sit on your thumbs) and wait till the stuff hits the fan. Yeah, right. Eventually the transaction log will fill up to such a degree that the `dump transaction` command cannot run successfully, thereby truncating the transaction log. At that point, your only recourse will be to execute the `dump transaction with no_log` command, which will truncate the log without recording the truncation event. After running this command, you should immediately execute the `dump database` command to at least save an image of the database.

When we examine segments and thresholds we will investigate how transaction log's last-chance threshold can automatically alert you to this type of problem.

User-Defined Data Types, Defaults, and Rules

Data Types

A column's data type specifies what kind of information that column will hold, and controls how that data will be physically stored. The SQL Server provides a number of system-supplied data types.

Exact numeric integers. They preserve their accuracy during arithmetic operations.

`tinyint`—1 byte of storage; whole numbers that range from 0 to 255.

`smallint`—2 bytes of storage; whole numbers that range from –32,768 to 32,767.

`int`—4 bytes of storage; whole numbers that range from –2,147,483,648 to 2,147,483,647.

Exact numeric decimals. They preserve their accuracy during arithmetic operations (to the least significant digit), as well as those arithmetic operations that include decimal points. Data stored in numeric and decimal columns is packed to conserve disk space. The exact numeric types accept two optional parameters: precision (specifies the maximum number of decimal digits that can be stored in the column [includes all digits, to the right and left of the decimal point]) and scale (specifies the maximum number of digits that can be stored to the right of the decimal point), enclosed within parentheses and separated by a comma. The combination of precision and scale determines the range of values that can be stored in a decimal or numeric data type column. For the precision parameter, you can specify 1 to 38 digits or use the default of 18 digits. For the scale parameter, you can specify a scale of 0 to 38 digits or use the default scale of 0 digits. Note that the value of the scale parameter must be less than or equal to the value of the precision parameter. Also, the numeric and decimal data types are identical; however, only numeric data types with a scale of 0 can be used for the IDENTITY column.

`numeric(p,s)`—2 to 17 bytes of storage (note that the storage size increases by 1 byte for each additional 2 digits of precision); range -10^{38} to 10^{38}.

`decimal(p,s)`—2 to 17 bytes of storage (note that the storage size increases by 1 byte for each additional 2 digits of precision); range -10^{38} to 10^{38}.

Approximate numeric. They allow rounding during arithmetic operations, and they support all aggregate functions and all arithmetic operations except *modulo.* Approximate numeric data are entered as a mantissa (a signed or unsigned number, with or without a decimal point, in addition, the column's binary precision determines the maximum number of binary digits allowed in the mantissa). followed by an optional exponent (begins with the character "e" or "E," and must be an integer). The literal data value of an approximate numeric column is equal to mantissa $* 10^{\text{exponent}}$.

`float (default precision)`—4 (when the default precision is single precision, i.e., < 16) or 8 bytes (when default precision is double precision, i.e., >= 16) of storage; range (and storage precision) is machine dependent; accepts an optional binary precision parameter.

`double precision`—8 bytes of storage; range (and storage precision) is machine dependent.

`real`—4 bytes of storage; range (and storage precision) is machine dependent.

Character. Used to store strings consisting of letters, numbers, and symbols. Fixed-length character columns that are defined as nullable are automatically transformed into variable-length character data types. Data in variable-length columns is stripped of trailing blanks; storage size is the actual length of the data entered. While fixed-length columns do require more physical storage space than variable-length columns, they are accessed somewhat faster than variable-length columns. Character strings must be enclosed in either single-quote characters (`' '`), or in double-quote characters (`""`). Character strings that include the double-quote character must be surrounded by single-quote characters (`'"'`). Character strings that include the single-quote character should be surrounded by double-quote characters (" ' "). Alternatively, for each quotation mark you want to include in the string, you can enclose a quotation mark in two quotation marks (" " ", or ' ' '). To continue a character string onto the next line, enter a backslash (\) before going to the next line.

char(n)—*n* bytes of storage; 255 bytes or less.

varchar(n)—actual length of data value entered; 255 bytes or less.

nchar(n)—*n* bytes of storage; 255 bytes or less.

nvarchar(n)—*n* bytes of storage; 255 bytes or less.

text—0 or multiple of 2K data pages; range of 2,147,483,647 bytes or less.

Binary-like.   The SQL Server stores bit patterns, such as images, in a hexadecimal-like notation. Binary-like data types begins with the characters "0x", and can include any combination of digits and the uppercase and the lowercase letters "A" through "F." The SQL Server manipulates the binary-like data types in a platform-specific manner.

binary(n)—*n* bytes of storage; 255 bytes or less; literal data values entered into the column are padded with zeros to the full length of the column.

varbinary(n)—actual length of data value entered; 255 bytes or less.

image—0 or multiple of 2K data pages; range of 2,147,483,647 bytes or less.

Monetary.   This data type is used to store monetary data, such as U.S. dollars and other decimal currencies. You can use all aggregate functions and all arithmetic operations, except modulo, with monetary data types.

smallmoney—4 bytes of storage; range –214,738.3648 to 214,738.3647; accurate to one ten-thousandth of a monetary unit; round values up to two decimal places for display purposes.

money—8 bytes of storage; range –922,337,203,685,477.5808 to 922,337,203,685,477.5807; accurate to one ten-thousandth of a monetary unit; round values up to two decimal places for display purposes.

Date/time.   Used to store date and time information.

smalldatetime—4 bytes of storage; range is January 1, 1900 to June 6, 2079; with up-to-the-minute accuracy.

datetime—8 bytes of storage; range is January 1, 1753, to December 31, 9999, with accuracy of up to one three-hundredth of a second.

Bit.   Used for Boolean data (e.g., yes/no, true/false, etc.). *Columns* of this data type cannot be nullable and cannot participate in an *index.*

bit—1 byte of storage holds up to 8 bit columns; assigned data value 0 or 1.

It is important to realize that, when you elect to use variable-length data types in table columns, you significantly increase the likelihood of deferred updates occurring. As is shown in Chap. 6, Transaction Log Subsystem, twice as many log records need to be written for a deferred update versus a direct update. And, as will be made clear in Chap. 11, The Parallel Lock Manager, the consumption of locks is higher for a deferred update versus a direct update. For these two basic reasons, deferred updates are known to seriously degrade SQL Server performance. Due to the overhead incurred during read and write operations involving variable-length data types, it is recommended that you avoid using variable-length data types, unless absolutely necessary, or unless you do not care about SQL Server performance. During a read operation, when the SQL Server reads a row containing variable-length data types, it must calculate the actual physical length of each variable-length field (for every variable-length field) for every row that is scanned.

The NULL Value

NULL is a distinct value that is used to denote that the data value of the column is unknown. When you declare a column's data type, you can specify whether the SQL Server should assign a NULL value to that column if a user transaction does not provide an explicit data value for that column during insertion, and when non-NULL default has not been explicitly bound to the column.

When you declare a column as being nullable, you are in effect doing three things:

1. Declaring that a data value does not need to be entered into this column.

2. Allowing the SQL Server to enter the NULL value as the column's default data value.

3. If the column is a fixed-length data type, then you are automatically converting that column's fixed-length data type into a corresponding variable-length data type. In the SQL Server, only variable-length data types can be nullable. In addition, the SQL Server will not notify you of this data-type conversion. The automatic conversions are shown below:

Data Type	Data Type Converted To
float	floatn
int	intn
smallint	intn
tinyint	intn
decimal	decimaln
numeric	numericn
char	varchar
nchar	nvarchar
binary	varbinary
money	moneyn
smallmoney	moneyn
datetime	datetimn

As the use of NULL values results in the automatic conversion of fixed-length to variable-length data types, their use significantly increases the likelihood of deferred updates occurring and, in turn, degrading SQL Server performance. Therefore, it is recommended that you avoid using the NULL value unless it is absolutely necessary, or unless you do not care about SQL Server performance.

By default, if you do not specify that a column is to accept the NULL value, the SQL Server does not provide the NULL value as the column's default value. However, you can change this on a SQL Server-wide basis by logging on to the SQL Server as an account with **sa_role** privileges and entering these commands:

```
1>use master
2>go
1>sp_dboption "allow nulls by default", true
2>go
```

During SQL Server run time, the change in a database option takes place only after running the checkpoint command. This command changes the *master* system database, so to ensure its recovery, be certain to dump the *master* system database. As this command changes the contents of system tables, it cannot be executed within a transaction.

Data-Type Hierarchy

SQL Server data types are hierarchically ordered. This hierarchical ordering of data types regulates the outcome of computations involving multiple data types, as well as values produced when converting data of one data type to another. The higher the data type is on the food chain, the more dominant it is. Following is the hierarchical ordering to SQL Server data type:

Data Type	Hierarchy Level
floatn	1
float	2
datetimn	3
datetime	4
real	5
numericn	6
numeric	7
decimaln	8
decimal	9
moneyn	10
money	11
smallmoney	12
smalldatetime	13
intn	14
int	15
smallint	16
tinyint	17
bit	18
varchar	19
sysname	19
nvarchar	19
char	20
nchar	20
varbinary	21
timestamp	21
binary	22
text	23
image	24

where 1 is the highest level, and 24 is the lowest, in the hierarchy. It is worth noting that user-defined data types inherit the hierarchical level of the system type on which they are based.

User-Defined Data Types

Within the SQL Server, Sybase accounts can construct their own data types that are based upon the provided SQL Server system data types. In a sense, all you are allowed to accomplish is:

1. Giving the new data type a unique, case-sensitive name (i.e., identifier).
2. Specifying whether or not the new data type allows nulls.

Once a user-defined data type is created, it can be used within `create table` and the `alter table` commands, and defaults and rules can be bound to it, as well, to support the idea of domain. A domain is a finite set of atomic data values, all of the same data type.

User-defined data types have the same data-type hierarchy as the SQL Server-supplied data types on which they are based.

Sybase System 11 SQL Server-Provided User-Defined Data Types

In addition to the base data types, the SQL Server also provides two user-defined data types:

`timestamp`—every time a row containing a column of type time stamp is inserted or updated, the literal data value of the time-stamp column is automatically incremented by the SQL Server. In this sense, time stamp is really a means to accomplish row-level versioning within a table. It is defined as varbinary(8) with NULL allowed. Finally, time stamp cannot be used as the base data type of another user-defined data type.

`sysname`—used within system tables to hold the names or identifiers of principal database objects. It is defined as varchar(30) with NULL not allowed.

The IDENTITY Property

User-defined data types and table columns have a property called IDENTITY, that, if you so choose, can be enabled. A table can have one and only one IDENTITY column. When the IDENTITY property is enabled, the SQL Server will automatically insert a unique, linearly sequential number into the column each time a new row is inserted into the table. In this way, the literal data value of the IDENTITY column uniquely identifies each row in a table.

During run time, as determined by the precision of the column, the SQL Server partitions the domain of possible IDENTITY column values into blocks of linearly sequential numbers, and, for each active table that contains an IDENTITY column, brings a block of these numbers into cache. From these memory-resident blocks, the SQL Server automatically assigns the next sequential number to the IDENTITY column of each new row inserted into the corresponding table. The SQL Server will work its way through this block, assigning all values contained therein, consume them all, then create a new block of values. When creating the new block of values, the SQL Server has to be absolutely certain that the new block will contain the next sequential values. Even though it is unlikely that the SQL Server would crash at this point, or that an account with **sa_role** privileges would enter the `shutdown with no_wait` command into the SQL Server, either of these events could possibly happen. To accommodate these phenomena, the SQL Server references the table and determines the current maximum value of the IDENTITY column. If, at this point, the referenced table page is not in data cache, then the SQL Server must read it from disk (keep in mind that you will be reading more than a single page if the table has been bound to a Memory Pool that is larger than 2K). After successfully referencing the target page, another block of IDENTITY values is created and placed in cache.

Because the blocks of IDENTITY values reside in cache, there is no way to absolutely ensure that the linearly sequential data values derived from a block will end up being stored in a target IDENTITY column. If the SQL Server were to crash, or if an account with **sa_role** privileges were to enter the `shutdown with no_wait` command into the SQL Server, the data values contained within the blocks in memory will be lost forever. When this occurs, gaps will be present in the data-value sequences of IDENTITY columns. Gaps will also be present in the data-value sequences of IDENTITY column when rows are deleted from a table containing an IDENTITY column, when transactions that used a data value from the block are rolled back, or when the literal data value of an IDENTITY column has been established by a manual process.

Here are some other important facts to understand about IDENTITY columns:

1. Normally, the literal data value of IDENTITY columns cannot be modified by user processes; however, there is a way to get around this rule if necessary.

2. NULL values cannot be entered into columns which have their IDENTITY property enabled.

3. The literal data value of the IDENTITY property takes precedence over any default that you might (foolishly) bind to the user-defined data type or the table column.

4. The range of legal values of IDENTITY columns can be 1 through 10 precision −1. You can tune the precision of all IDENTITY columns, on a SQL Server-wide basis, by configuring the `size of auto identity column` SQL Server configuration parameter. However, the maximum legal value of the column's IDENTITY property is always constrained by the individual column's precision.

5. Once the IDENTITY column reaches the constraint of the maximum legal value of the column's precision, then all successive `insert` statements into that table will fail, raising an error message to that effect. If you hit this wall, then there is a way out. You must create a new table that has an identical structure, but the precision of the IDENTITY column must be suitably increased, and you need to give this new table a different name. After the modified table has been created, you can move the data from the old table into the new table by using the `insert` statement, or by using the **bcp** utility. When the data has been moved, you can drop the old table and rename the new table to that of the old table. Be certain to correctly set permissions on the new version of the table, and to re-create whatever triggers are required.

Database Configuration for the IDENTITY Property

The SQL Server provides two IDENTITY-related database configuration parameters that you can toggle on or off for a given database:

1. `auto identity`
2. `identity in nonunique index`

The `auto identity` database option can be used to have the SQL Server automatically include a 10-digit IDENTITY column, called SYB_IDENTITY_COL (scale is always 0), when user tables are created in a given database and the `primary key`, the `unique` constraint, or an IDENTITY column, where not specified in the `create table` statement. To reference this column, you must use either of these two approaches: you can explicitly declare this column's identifier, or you can use the reserved keyword `syb_identity`. To set this database option on log on to the SQL Server as an account with **dbo** or **sa_role** privileges and enter these commands:

```
1>use NameOfDatabase
2>go
1>sp_dboption "auto identity", on
2>go
```

where:

NameOfDatabase—the name of the database in which you want to set this database option.

During SQL Server run time, the change in a database option takes place only after running the `checkpoint` command. To disable this database option, simply toggle the database option to off. This command changes the database, so to ensure its recovery, be certain to dump its transaction log and then dump the database itself. As this command changes the contents of system tables, it cannot be executed within a transaction.

With the `identity in nonunique index` database option set on, the SQL Server will ensure that nonunique indexes automatically contain an IDENTITY column, if and only if the table the index is based on has a column with the IDENTITY property already enabled (regardless of whether the IDENTITY property was enabled explicitly by you or automatically by the SQL Server). The IDENTITY column will be the very last field in the nonclustered index. There are pros and cons about setting this option on, and they all pretty much center around the impacts to the query optimizer. To set this database option on, log on to the SQL Server as an account with **dbo** or **sa_role** privileges and enter these commands:

```
1>use NameOfDatabase
2>go
1>sp_dboption "identity in nonunique index", on
2>go
```

where:

NameOfDatabase—the name of the database in which you want to set this database option.

During SQL Server run time, the change in a database option only takes place after running the `checkpoint` command. To disable this database option, simply toggle the database option to off. This command changes the database, so to ensure its recovery, be certain to dump its transaction log and then dump the database itself. As this command changes the contents of system tables, it cannot be executed within a transaction.

SQL Server Kernel Configuration
for the IDENTITY Property

The SQL Server provides three IDENTITY-related SQL Server systemwide configuration parameters that you can tune:

1. `size of auto identity column`
2. `identity burning set factor`
3. `identity grab size`

The SQL Server `size of auto identity column` configuration parameter complements the `auto identity` database option, by establishing the precision of SYB_IDENTITY_COL columns on a SQL Server-wide basis. Once set, the precision of any existing SYB_IDENTITY_COL column is not affected; only future SYB_IDENTITY_COL columns are affected. The default value is 10. The range of legal values is 1 through 38. To specify a value for this SQL Server configuration parameter to 15, for example, log on to the SQL Server as an account with **sa_role** privileges and enter these commands:

```
1>use master
2>go
1>sp_configure "size of auto identity column", 15
2>go
```

For this change in the `size of auto identity column` SQL Server configuration parameter to take effect, the SQL Server must be shut down and restarted. This command changes the *master* database, so to ensure its recovery, be certain to dump the *master* database. As this command changes the contents of system tables, it cannot be executed within a transaction.

The `identity burning set factor` is used to set the percentage of potential IDENTITY column values that are released into each block. The art of tuning the `identity burning set factor` SQL Server configuration parameter is to balance performance while minimizing the gaps in IDENTITY columns. As has been explained, when the SQL Server crashes, or is `shutdown with nowait`, and when transactions roll back, gaps in IDENTITY column values will arise. The maximum size of IDENTITY column value gap is directly dependent on the `identity burning set factor` SQL Server configuration parameter. The default value of the `identity burning set factor` SQL Server configuration parameter is 5000, and range of values for this configuration parameter is 1 through 9,999,999. To determine the correct value of this parameter for use with the `sp_configure` system command, use this formula: (percentage expressed in decimal form) × 10,000,000. For example, if you want to set the identity burning set factor to 10 percent, then the value of the identity burning set factor SQL Server configuration parameter would be: (.10) × 10,000,000 = 1,000,000.

To specify a value for this SQL Server configuration parameter to 10 percent, for example, log on to the SQL Server as an account with **sa_role** privileges and enter these commands:

```
1>use master
2>go
1>sp_configure "identity burning set factor", 1000000
2>go
```

For this change in the identity burning set factor SQL Server configuration parameter to take effect, the SQL Server must be shut down and restarted. This command changes the *master* database, so to ensure its recovery, be certain to dump the *master* system database. As this command changes the contents of system tables, it cannot be executed within a transaction.

The identity grab size SQL Server configuration parameter works in conjunction with the identity burning set factor SQL Server configuration parameter. The identity grab size SQL Server configuration parameter allows every user process to prefetch or grab into memory a count of preburned IDENTITY column values to use for inserts into IDENTITY columns. The art of tuning the identity grab size SQL Server configuration parameter is to balance performance while minimizing the gaps in IDENTITY columns. Each time a process grabs an IDENTITY column value from the block, a spinlock is taken, released, and not taken again until the prefetched, preburned IDENTITY column values are used up doing inserts into IDENTITY columns. When a process needs to grab a count of additional values that exceeds the remaining preburned values, then a new block of IDENTITY column values is preburned, and the process grabs values from the new preburned block. By increasing the value of the identity grab size SQL Server configuration parameter, contention on the block's spinlock is reduced. This reduction in block spinlock contention can result in slight performance improvements on SMP platforms (and provides no performance benefit on uniprocessor platforms). To ensure the linear sequence of IDENTITY column values, the default value of the identity grab size SQL Server configuration parameter is one. However, if an application process needs to insert contiguous IDENTITY column values and you are comfortable with increasing the likelihood of gaps in IDENTITY column values and willing to forsake linear sequences of IDENTITY column values, then you can tune the identity grab size SQL Server configuration parameter. The range of values for the identity grab size SQL Server configuration parameter is 1 through 2,147,483,647.

To specify a value for this SQL Server configuration parameter to five, for example, log on to the SQL Server as an account with **sa_role** privileges and enter these commands:

```
1>use master
2>go
1>sp_configure "identity grab size", 5
2>go
```

For this change in the identity grab size SQL Server configuration parameter to take effect, the SQL Server must be shut down and restarted. This command changes the *master* database, so to ensure its recovery, be certain to dump the *master* database. As this command changes the contents of system tables, it cannot be executed within a transaction.

Creating a User-Defined Data Type

There are benefits to obtain from creating user-defined data types. You can assign a unique, highly meaningful name to represent a base data type that reflects its intended use. For example, you can create a data type, based on the int data type, named "code" in which you plan to store codes for use in an application. Also, unlike the system data types, you can directly bind defaults and rules to a user-defined data type. When you bind a default, or a rule, directly to a user-defined data type, every table column that is based on the user-defined data type will inherit the default or rule bound to the user-defined data type. The defaults and rules you bind to the user-defined data type will enforce data integrity on every table column that is based on the user-defined data type.

However, before you go ahead and create a user-defined data type in a given database, you should look in that database to determine which user-defined data types already exist therein.

To determine which, if any, user-defined data types exist in a given database, log on to the SQL Server as any Sybase account that is authorized to use that database and enter these commands:

```
1>use NameOfDatabase
2>go
1>sp_help
2>go
```

where:

NameOfDatabase—the name of the database from which you want a listing of principal database objects.

The command will display a listing of all principal database objects contained within the current database, their type, and their owner. At the bottom of the report will be the listing of user-defined data types. For each user-defined data type contained within the database, the report will indicate the name of the user-defined data type, the system data type it is based on, its length, whether or not it allows NULL, the name of the default that is bound to it (if applicable), and the name of the rule that is bound to it (if applicable).

To examine the definition of a given user-defined data type in a given database, log on to the SQL Server as any Sybase account that is authorized to use that database and enter these commands:

```
1>use NameOfDatabase
2>go
1>sp_helptext NameOfUserDefinedDataType
2>go
```

where:

NameOfDatabase—the name of the database that contains the user-defined data type whose definition you want to inspect.

NameOfUserDefinedDataType—the name of the user-defined data type whose definition you want to inspect.

To examine the definition of a default that is bound to a given user-defined data type in a given database, log on to the SQL Server as any Sybase account that is authorized to use that database, and enter these commands:

```
1>use NameOfDatabase
2>go
1>sp_helptext [loginame.]NameOfDefault
2>go
```

where:

NameOfDatabase—the name of the database that contains the user-defined data type whose definition you want to inspect.

[loginame.]—the name of the Sybase account that owns the default. If you are the owner of the default, then you do not have to provide this parameter.

NameOfDefault—the name of the default that is bound to the user-defined data type whose definition you want to inspect.

To examine the definition of a rule that is bound to a given user-defined data type in a given database, log on to the SQL Server as any Sybase account that is authorized to use that database and enter these commands:

```
1>use NameOfDatabase
2>go
1>sp_helptext [loginame.]NameOfRule
2>go
```

where:

NameOfDatabase—the name of the database that contains the user-defined data type whose definition you want to inspect.

[loginame.]—the name of the Sybase account that owns the rule. If you are the owner of the rule, then you do not have to provide this parameter.

NameOfRule—the name of the rule that is bound to the user-defined data type whose definition you want to inspect.

To create a user-defined data type, log on to the SQL Server as the owner or user of the current database and issue the following commands:

```
1>use NameOfDatabase
2>go
1>sp_addtype NameOfUserDefinedDataType, NameOfSystemDataType
2>[ (length) | (precision [, scale)]],
3>"identity" | Nullability
4>go
```

where:

NameOfDatabase—the name of the database in which you want to create the new user-defined data type.

NameOfUserDefinedDataType—the name of the new user-defined data type must comply with the rules for identifiers and must be unique to the owner of the new user-defined data type within the current database. When you create this user-defined data type, you will be its owner.

NameOfSystemDataType—the name of one of the SQL Server-provided base data types. You cannot use time stamp. In those cases where the name of the base data type includes parentheses or commas, be certain to enclose it within single or double quotes.

`(length)`—the char, varchar, nchar, nvarchar, binary, and varbinary base data types should have an indicated length (enclosed within parentheses). If you do not supply a length, then the SQL Server uses the default length of one character.

`(precision [, scale)]`—the float-base data type expects a binary precision (enclosed within parentheses). If you do not supply a binary precision, then the SQL Server uses the machine-dependent default precision. The numeric and decimal data types expect a decimal precision and scale (enclosed within parentheses, separated by a comma). If you do not supply the decimal precision and scale, then the SQL Server uses a default precision of 18 and a default scale of 0.

`"identity"`—indicates that the new user-defined data type has the IDENTITY property. You can specify the IDENTITY property only for numeric data types that have a scale of 0. Because the word identity is a reserved keyword, you must enclose it within single or double quotation marks.

Nullability—indicates how the user-defined data type handles the null value. Acceptable values for this parameter are "null", "NULL", "nonull", "NONULL", "not null", and "NOT NULL".

This change will take effect immediately. This command changes the database, so to ensure its recovery, be certain to dump the database's transaction log, and then dump the database itself. As this command changes the contents of system tables, it cannot be executed within a transaction.

Changing the Name of a User-Defined Data Type

The SQL Server provides you with a system procedure to change the name of a user-defined data type. If you are the owner of the user-defined data type, and you want to change its name, log on to the SQL Server and enter these commands:

```
1>use NameOfDatabase
2>go
1>sp_rename NameOfUserDefinedDatatype, NewNameOfUserDefined-
   Datatype
2>go
```

where:

NameOf Database—the name of the database that contains the user-defined data type that you own, whose name you want to change.

NameOf UserDefinedDatatype—the current name of the user-defined data type that you own, whose name you want to change.

NewNameOf UserDefinedDatatype—the new name you want to assign to the user-defined data type that you own.

This change will take effect immediately. This command changes the database, so to ensure its recovery, be certain to dump the database's transaction log, and then dump the database itself. As this command changes the contents of system tables, it cannot be executed within a transaction.

An account with **dbo** or **sa_role** privileges can change the name of user-defined data types that you own as well as user-defined data types that are owned by any other Sybase account that is authorized to use your database.

Dropping User-Defined Data Types

As long as a user-defined data type is not in use by any table in a given database, then it can be dropped. To drop a user-defined data type that you own, log on to the SQL Server as the account that owns the user-defined data type and execute the following commands:

```
1>use NameOf Database
2>go
1>sp_droptype NameOf UserDefinedDataType
2>go
```

where:

NameOf Database—the name of the database in which you want to drop the user-defined data type.

NameOf UserDefinedDataType—the name of the user-defined data type you want to drop.

This change will take effect immediately. This command changes the database, so to ensure its recovery, be certain to dump the database's transaction log, and then dump the database itself. As this command changes the contents of system tables, it cannot be executed within a transaction.

An account with **dbo** or **sa_role** privileges can drop any user-defined data type in the current database that is owned by another Sybase account.

Defaults

Every table column must store some literal data value. If the table column has not been allowed to store the NULL value, then some other data value must be stored therein. A *default* is a literal data value that has been created and then bound to a table column, or to a user-defined data type on which a table column is based.

When a default is bound to a table column or to a user-defined data type on which a table column is based, the SQL Server will automatically store the default in the table column, if you do not explicitly provide a data value for that column when you insert a row into the table.

Granting Permission to Create Defaults

By default, users of a database do not have permission to create defaults within that database. To grant permission to a user, to a list of users, to the groups (including the `public` group), or to a role, log on to the SQL Server as an account with **dbo** or **sa_role** privileges and enter these commands:

```
1>use NameOfDatabase
2>go
1>grant create default
2>to {public | name_list | role_name}
3>go
```

where:

NameOfDatabase—the name of the database in which you want to grant permission to create defaults to a user, to a list of users, to the groups (including the `public` group), or to a role.

`{public | name_list | role_name}`—the user, list of users, group, or role to which you want to grant create-default permission.

This change will take effect immediately. This command changes the database, so to ensure its recovery, be certain to dump the database's transaction log, and then dump the database itself. As this command changes the contents of system tables, it cannot be executed within a transaction.

Creating a Default

The right to create defaults in a given database rests with the owner of the database. However, any Sybase account that is authorized to use a given database can be granted permission to create defaults by the owner of that database. However, before you go ahead and create a default in a given database, you should look in that database to determine which defaults already exist therein. To determine which, if any, defaults exist in a given database log on to the SQL Server as any Sybase account that is authorized to use that database and enter these commands:

```
1>use NameOfDatabase
2>go
1>sp_help
2>go
```

where:

NameOfDatabase—the name of the database from which you want a listing of principal database objects.

The command will display, for your inspection, a listing of all principal database objects contained within the current database, their type, and their owner. On the left-hand side of the report above the listing of user-defined data types and immediately following the listing of rules, the defaults will be listed, if there are any present within the database. For each default contained within the database, the report will indicate the name of the default and the name of the owner of the default.

To examine the definition of a default in a given database, log on to the SQL Server as any Sybase account that is authorized to use that database and enter these commands:

```
1>use NameOfDatabase
2>go
1>sp_helptext [loginame.]NameOfDefault
2>go
```

where:

NameOfDatabase—the name of the database that contains the default whose definition you want to inspect.

[loginame.]—the name of the Sybase account that owns the default. If you are the owner of the default, then you do not have to provide this parameter.

NameOfDefault—the name of the default whose definition you want to inspect.

To create a default, log on to the SQL Server as a Sybase account authorized in the current database and issue the following commands:

```
1>use NameOfDatabase
2>go
1>create default NameOfDefault
2>as ConstantExpression
3>go
```

where:

NameOfDatabase—the name of the database in which you want to create the new default.

NameOfDefault—the name of the default you want to create. The name of the default must comply with the rules for identifiers, and it must be unique to the owner of the new default within the current database. You will be the owner of this default.

`as` *ConstantExpression*—after the `as`, you enter the constant expression. There are a number of rules for default constant expressions:

1. Enclose character and date constants in quotation marks.
2. You do not need to enclose floating point, integer, or money constants in quotation marks.
3. Binary data constants must have the "0x" prefix.
4. Money data constants must have the "$" prefix.
5. A default constant expression can include SQL Server functions that do not reference another database object, for example, `getdate()`.

This change will take effect immediately. This command changes the database, so to ensure its recovery, be certain to dump the database's transaction log, and then dump the database itself. As this command changes the contents of system tables, it cannot be executed within a transaction.

If you are an account with **dbo** or **sa_role** privileges, you can create defaults that will be owned by another Sybase account that is authorized to use a given database. To create a default that will be owned by another Sybase account, log on to the SQL Server as an account with **dbo** or **sa_role** privileges and enter these commands:

```
1>use NameOfDatabase
2>go
```

```
1>create default loginame.NameOfDefault
2>as ConstantExpression
3>go
```

where:

NameOfDatabase—the name of the database in which you want to create the new default.

`loginame.`—the name of the Sybase account that will own default you have created in the current database.

NameOfDefault—the name of the default you want to create. The name of the default must comply with the rules for identifiers, and it must be unique to the owner of the new default within the current database. You will be the owner of this default.

`as` *ConstantExpression*—after the `as`, you enter the constant expression. There are a number of rules for default constant expressions:

- Enclose character and date constants in quotation marks.
- You do not need to enclose floating point, integer, or money constants in quotation marks.
- Binary data constants must have the "0x" prefix.
- Money data constants must have the "$" prefix.
- A default constant expression can include SQL Server functions that do not reference another database object, for example, `get-date()`.

This change will take effect immediately. This command changes the database, so to ensure its recovery, be certain to dump the database's transaction log, and then dump the database itself. As this command changes the contents of system tables, it cannot be executed within a transaction.

Now that the default has been created, you will need to bind it to a user-defined data type or to a table column. When you do so, be certain the default's data value or built-in function is compatible with the data type of the table column or user-defined data type.

The SQL Server also allows you to create defaults for table columns by using the `default clause` of the `create table` statement, or by using the `default clause` of the `alter table` statement. However, unlike the defaults you create with the preceding technique, these column defaults are limited to the specific table column they were created for. That is, you cannot bind these defaults to any other table column, and you cannot bind them to user-defined data types.

Changing the Name of a Default

The SQL Server provides you with a system procedure to change the name of a default. If you are the owner of the default and you want to change its name log on to the SQL Server and enter these commands:

```
1>use NameOfDatabase
2>go
1>sp_rename NameOfDefault, NewNameOfDefault
2>go
```

where:

NameOfDatabase—the name of the database that contains the default that you own whose name you want to change.

NameOfDefault—the current name of the default that you own whose name you want to change.

NewNameOfDefault—the new name you want to assign to the default that you own.

This change will take effect immediately. This command changes the database, so to ensure its recovery, be certain to dump the database's transaction log, and then dump the database itself. As this command changes the contents of system tables, it cannot be executed within a transaction.

An account with **dbo** or **sa_role** privileges can change the name of a default that you own as well as defaults that are owned by any other Sybase account that is authorized to use your database.

Binding Defaults to User-Defined Data Types

A default you own can be bound to one or more user-defined data types that you also own, just as long as the data value of the default constant does not conflict with the base data type of your user-defined data type. But, it is not possible for you to bind a default you own either to a user-defined data type that you do not own, or to a SQL Server-supplied system data type. Also, if you bind a default to a user-defined data type with the IDENTITY property enabled, the default will have no effect whatsoever on the user-defined data type. The SQL Server will not give you an error message when you bind the default to that user-defined data type, but it will ignore the default and automatically proceed to assign the next sequential number to the table column based on that user-defined data type.

When you bind a default to a user-defined data type, you have two options:

1. Have the default take immediate effect on all existing table columns that are based on the user-defined data type within the current database.

2. Prevent the default from taking effect on all existing table columns based on the user-defined data type, and instead, have the default binding take effect only on future table columns that will be based on the user-defined data type within the current database.

The options are available to you except for the case where existing table columns based on the user-defined data type, within the current database, have previously had their default changed.

Here are two important facts to understand about binding defaults to user-defined data types:

1. If the user-defined data type already has a default bound to it, that default will be unbound, and the new default will replace it.

2. If the default value is a character string, and the user-defined data type is too short to hold the default's data constant, then the SQL Server will, when a row is inserted into the table that contains the user-defined data type, either truncate the default's data constant and store the balance in the column, or it will generate an SQL-STATE exception. The default setting of the SQL Server will merely truncate the default's data constant. However, if for a given session you have previously entered the `set string_rtruncation on` command, then the SQLSTATE exception will be generated upon insert.

To bind a default you own to a user-defined data type that you own, and have that default take immediate effect on all existing table columns that are based on that user-defined data type, log on to the SQL Server as a Sybase account that owns both the default and the user-defined data type and enter these commands:

```
1>use NameOfDatabase
2>go
1>sp_bindefault NameOfDefault, NameOfUserDefinedDataType
2>[futureonly]
3>go
```

where:

NameOfDatabase—the name of the database that contains the default and user-defined data type that you want to bind to one another.

NameOfDefault—the default that you want to bind to the user-defined data type.

NameOf UserDefinedDataType—the name of the user-defined data type that you want to bind the default.

[futureonly]—this optional parameter prevents existing table columns based on the user-defined data type from immediately inheriting the default.

This change will take effect immediately. This command changes the database, so to ensure its recovery, be certain to dump the database's transaction log, and then dump the database itself. As this command changes the contents of system tables, it cannot be executed within a transaction.

An account with **dbo** or **sa_role** privileges can bind the default to the user-defined data type, just as long as both the default and the user-defined data type are both owned by the same Sybase account.

Binding Defaults to Table Columns

A default can be bound to one or more columns, in one or more tables, just so long as the:

1. Value of default constant does not conflict with the table column's data type

2. Table column's data type is not timestamp.

3. IDENTITY

If and only if you own a table, then you can bind defaults that you also own to columns in that table.

Here are some important facts to understand about binding defaults to table columns:

1. If you bind a default to a table column that has the IDENTITY property enabled, the default will have no effect whatsoever on the table column. The SQL Server will not give you an error message when you bind the default to that table column, but it will ignore the default and automatically proceed to assign the next sequential number.

2. If the default value is a character string, and the table column is too short to hold the default's data constant, then the SQL Server will, when a row is inserted into the table, either truncate the default's data constant and store the balance in the column or it will generate an SQLSTATE exception. The default setting of the SQL Server will merely truncate the default's data constant. However, if for a given session you have previously entered the set string_rtruncation on command, then the SQLSTATE exception will be generated upon insert.

3. A table column whose data type is a user-defined data type that has a default bound to it can have a new default bound to it. The column's default will override and replace the default bound to the user-defined data type.

4. If a default has already been bound to a table column, and you want to bind a new default to that same table column, then the current default must be unbound from the table column using the sp_unbindefault command before the new default is bound to the table column.

5. You can bind a default to a table column where the table already contains data. The default will be applied only to new rows that are inserted into the table. Binding the default will not impact the data already stored in the table column (i.e., they retain their current literal data values, even if they contain the NULL value).

To bind a default you own to a column in a table that you own log on to the SQL Server as a Sybase account that owns both the default and the user-defined data type and enter these commands:

```
1>use NameOfDatabase
2>go
1>sp_bindefault NameOfDefault, "NameOfTable.NameOfColumn"
2>go
```

where:

NameOfDatabase—the name of the database that contains the default and table column that you own, and which you want to bind to one another.

NameOfDefault—this is the default that you own and want to bind to the table column that you own.

NameOfTable.NameOfColumn—the name of the table column that you own to which you want to bind a default which you also own. Both the table and the column name are enclosed in quotes, because they contained an embedded punctuation, the period (.) symbol. When you pass a parameter, that contains an embedded punctuation, to a SQL Server system procedure, it must be enclosed in quotation marks.

This change will take effect immediately. This command changes the database, so to ensure its recovery, be certain to dump the database's transaction log, and then dump the database itself. As this command changes the contents of system tables, it cannot be executed within a transaction.

An account with **dbo** or **sa_role** privileges can bind the default to a column in that table, just as long as both the default and the table are both owned by the same Sybase account.

Unbinding a Default from a User-Defined Data Type

A default you own can be unbound from a user-defined data type that you also own. When a default is unbound, the link between it and the user-defined data type is merely broken (i.e., the default is not destroyed, and it remains within the current database and can be used again in the future).

When you unbind a default from a user-defined data type, you have two options:

1. Have the default unbinding take immediate effect on all existing table columns that are based on the user-defined data type within the current database.

2. Prevent the default unbinding from taking effect on all existing table columns based on the user-defined data type.

The options are available to you except for the case where existing table columns based on the user-defined data type within the current database have previously had their default changed.

To unbind a default you own from a user-defined data type that you own, and have that default unbinding take immediate effect on all existing table columns that are based on that user-defined data type, log on to the SQL Server as a Sybase account that owns both the default and the user-defined data type and enter these commands:

```
1>use NameOfDatabase
2>go
1>sp_unbindefault NameOfDefault, NameOfUserDefinedDataType
2>[futureonly]
3>go
```

where:

NameOfDatabase—the name of the database that contains the default and user-defined data type that you own and which you want to unbind from one another.

NameOfDefault—the default that you own and that you want to unbind from your user-defined data type.

NameOfUserDefinedDataType—the name of the user-defined data type that you own, from which you want to unbind the default that you own.

[futureonly]—this optional parameter prevents existing table columns based on the user-defined data type from having their default unbound.

This change will take effect immediately. This command changes the database, so to ensure its recovery, be certain to dump the database's transaction log, and then dump the database itself. As this command changes the contents of system tables, it cannot be executed within a transaction.

An account with **dbo** or **sa_role** privileges can unbind the default from the user-defined data type, just as long as both the default and the user-defined data type are both owned by the same Sybase account.

Unbinding a Default from a Table Column

If and only if you own a table, then you can unbind defaults that you also own from columns in that table. To unbind a default you own from a column in a table that you own, log on to the SQL Server as a Sybase account that owns both the default and the table and enter these commands:

```
1>use NameOfDatabase
2>go
1>sp_unbindefault NameOfDefault, "NameOfTable.NameOfColumn"
2>go
```

where:

NameOfDatabase—the name of the database that contains the default and table column that you own, and which you want to unbind from one another.

NameOfDefault—the default that you own and that you want to unbind from the table column that you own.

NameOfTable.NameOfColumn—the name of the table column that you own from which you want to unbind a default which you also own. Both the table and column name are enclosed in quotes, because they contain an embedded punctuation, the period (.) symbol. When you pass a parameter that contains an embedded punctuation to a SQL Server system procedure, it must be enclosed in quotation marks.

This change will take effect immediately. This command changes the database, so to ensure its recovery, be certain to dump the database's transaction log, and then dump the database itself. As this command changes the contents of system tables, it cannot be executed within a transaction.

An account with **dbo** or **sa_role** privileges can unbind the default from a column in that table.

You will have to use the `alter table` statement to unbind defaults bound, using either the `create table` statement or the `alter table` statement.

Dropping a Default

You can drop a default that you own just as long as that default is not already bound to a user-defined data type or to table column in the current database. If you attempt to drop a default that is being used, then the SQL Server will abort your instruction and display an error message indicating the context(s) in which the default is presently being used in the current database. If you really want to drop the default, then you must first unbind it from all user-defined data types and table columns that are presently using it.

When you drop a default from a nullable column, then the NULL value will become the table column's default data value. And, when you drop a default from a nonnullable column, then the SQL Server will display an error message if the process does not provide a data value for the column when attempting to insert a new row into the table (also, the transaction will fail if a data value is not provided for the column).

To drop an unused default that you own, log on to the SQL Server as a Sybase account authorized in the current database and issue the following commands:

```
1>use NameOfDatabase
2>go
1>drop default NameOfDefault
2>[,NameOfDefault] . . .
3>go
```

where:

NameOfDatabase—the name of the database from which you want to drop the default.

NameOfDefault—the name of the unused default you own that you want to drop.

[,*NameOfDefault*] . . .—the list of names of other unused defaults that you also own and want to drop as well.

This change will take effect immediately. This command changes the database, so to ensure its recovery, be certain to dump the database's transaction log, and then dump the database itself. As this command changes the contents of system tables, it cannot be executed within a transaction.

An account with **dbo** or **sa_role** privileges can drop defaults that are owned by another Sybase account that is authorized to use a given database. To drop a default that is owned by another Sybase account, log on to the SQL Server as an account with **dbo** or **sa_role** privileges and enter these commands:

```
1>use NameOfDatabase
2>go
1>drop default loginame.NameOfDefault
2>[,loginame.NameOfDefault] ...
3>go
```

where:

NameOfDatabase—the name of the database from which you want to drop the default.

`loginame.`—the name of the Sybase account that owns the unused default you want to drop from the current database.

NameOfDefault—the name of the unused default you want to drop.

`[,loginame.`*NameOfDefault*`]` ...—the list of names of other unused defaults you want to drop.

This change will take effect immediately. This command changes the database, so to ensure its recovery, be certain to dump the database's transaction log, and then dump the database itself. As this command changes the contents of system tables, it cannot be executed within a transaction.

Revoking Permission to Create Defaults

To revoke permission to a user, a list of users, the groups (including the `public` group), or to a role, to create defaults, log on to the SQL Server as an account with **dbo** or **sa_role** privileges and enter these commands:

```
1>use NameOfDatabase
2>go
1>revoke create default
2>from {public | name_list | role_name}
3>go
```

where:

NameOfDatabase—the name of the database in which you want to revoke permission to create default from a user, from a list of users, from the groups (including the `public` group), or from a role.

{`public` | `name_list` | `role_name`}—the user, list of users, group, or role for which you want to revoke create-default permission.

Once this command completes successfully, the login account is immediately incapable of creating defaults within the database. This command changes the database's system tables, so to ensure its recovery, be certain to dump its transaction log and then dump the database itself. Also, because this command changes the contents of the system tables, it cannot be executed within a transaction.

Rules

Rules restrict the literal data values that can be stored in a user-defined data type, or in a table column and that are not data values covered by the column's data types. Rules function to ensure the accuracy of data stored in table columns. When a rule is present, every time data rows are inserted or updated, the SQL Server automatically checks the submitted data values against the data-integrity constraints embodied in the rule(s). In addition, rules cannot override the definition of a table column. Assume that you have a rule whose definition does not include a NULL value. If that rule is bound to a table column that is nullable, you can still insert the NULL value into that column.

Granting Permission to Create Rules

By default, users of a database do not have permission to create rules within that database. To grant permission to a user, a list of users, the groups (including the `public` group), or a role to create rules, log on to the SQL Server as an account with **dbo** or with **sa_role** privileges and enter these commands:

```
1>use NameOfDatabase
2>go
1>grant create rule
2>to {public | name_list | role_name}
3>go
```

where:

NameOfDatabase—the name of the database in which you want to grant permission to create rules to a user, a list of users, the groups (including the `public` group), or a role.

{public | name_list | role_name}—the user, list of users, group, or role to which you want to grant create-rule permission.

Once this command completes successfully, the login account is immediately capable of creating rules within the database. This command changes the database's system tables, so to ensure its recovery, be certain to dump its transaction log and then dump the database itself. Also, because this command changes the contents of the system tables, it cannot be executed within a transaction.

Creating a Rule

The right to create rules in a given database rests with the owner of the database. However, any Sybase account that is authorized to use a given database can be granted permission to create rules by the owner of that database. However, before you go ahead and create a rule in a given database, you should look to determine which rules already exist therein. To determine which, if any, rules exist in a given database, log on to the SQL Server as any Sybase account that is authorized to use that database and enter these commands:

```
1>use NameOfDatabase
2>go
1>sp_help
2>go
```

where:

NameOfDatabase—the name of the database from which you want a listing of principal database objects.

The command will display, for your inspection, a listing of all principal database objects contained within the current database, their type and their owner. On the left-hand side of the report above the listing of defaults and user-defined data types and immediately following the listing of stored procedures, the rules will be listed, if there are any present within the database. For each rule contained within the database the report will indicate the name of the rule and the name of the owner of the rule.

To examine the definition of a rule in a given database, log on to the SQL Server as any Sybase account that is authorized to use that database and enter these commands:

```
1>use NameOfDatabase
2>go
1>sp_helptext [loginame.]NameOfRule
2>go
```

where:

NameOfDatabase—the name of the database that contains the user-defined data type whose definition you want to inspect.

`[loginame.]`—the name of the Sybase account that owns the rule. If you are the owner of the rule, then you do not have to provide this parameter.

NameOfRule—the name of the rule whose definition you want to inspect.

To create a rule, log on to the SQL Server as a Sybase account authorized in the current database and issue the following commands:

```
1>use NameOfDatabase
2>go
1>create rule NameOfRule
2>as ConditionExpression
3>go
```

where:

NameOfDatabase—the name of the database in which you want to create the new rule.

NameOfRule—the name of the rule you want to create. The name of the rule must comply with the rules for identifiers, and it must be unique to the owner of the new rule within the current database. You will be the owner of this rule.

`as` *ConditionExpression*—after the `as`, you enter the condition expression. The condition expression contains the rule argument followed by the rule definition. There are a number of rules governing rule condition expressions:

1. The condition expression takes a single argument, called the *rule's argument*. While you can use any name or symbol for the rule argument, the first character of the name must be the "at" symbol (@). The rule argument refers to the column value that, when inserted or updated, is affected by the rule.
2. Enclose character and date constants in quotation marks.
3. You do not need to enclose floating point, integer, or money constants in quotation marks.
4. Binary data constants must have the "0x" prefix.
5. Money data constants must have the "$" prefix.
6. A rule definition can include any expression that is legal in a **where** clause (arithmetic operators, between, system functions,

like, relational operators, etc.) that does not reference another column in the table and that does not reference another database object (e.g., >=, getdate(), etc.).

This change will take effect immediately. This command changes the database, so to ensure its recovery, be certain to dump the database's transaction log, and then dump the database itself. As this command changes the contents of system tables, it cannot be executed within a transaction.

An account with **dbo** or **sa_role** privileges can create rules that will be owned by another Sybase account that is authorized to use a given database. To create a rule that will be owned by another Sybase account, log on to the SQL Server as an account with **dbo** or **sa_role** privileges and enter these commands:

```
1>use NameOfDatabase
2>go
1>create rule loginame. NameOfRule
2>as ConditionExpression
3>go
```

where:

NameOfDatabase—the name of the database in which you want to create the new rule.

`loginame.`—the name of the Sybase account that will own default you have created in the current database.

NameOfRule—the name of the rule you want to create. The name of the rule must comply with the rules for identifiers, and it must be unique to the owner of the new rule within the current database. You will be the owner of this rule.

`as` *ConditionExpression*—after the `as`, you enter the condition expression. The condition expression contains the rule argument followed by the rule definition. There are a number of rules governing rule condition expressions:

1. The condition expression takes a single argument, called the *rule's argument*. While you can use any name or symbol for the rule argument, the first character of the name must be the "at" symbol (@). The rule argument refers to the column value that, when inserted or updated, is affected by the rule.
2. Enclose character and date constants in quotation marks.
3. You do not need to enclose floating point, integer, or money constants in quotation marks.

4. Binary data constants must have the "0x" prefix.

5. Money data constants must have the "$" prefix.

6. A rule definition can include any expression that is legal in a **where** clause (arithmetic operators, between, system functions, like, relational operators, etc.) that does not reference another column in the table and that does not reference another database object (e.g., >=, getdate(), etc.).

This change will take effect immediately. This command changes the database, so to ensure its recovery, be certain to dump the database's transaction log, and then dump the database itself. As this command changes the contents of system tables, it cannot be executed within a transaction.

Now that the rule has been created, you will need to bind it to a user-defined data type or to a table column. When you do so, be certain to test the rule by inserting data into the table.

The SQL Server also allows you to create rules for table columns by using the **constraint** clause of the `create table` statement, or by using the **constraint** clause of the `alter table` statement. However, unlike the rules you create with the preceding technique, these column rules are limited to the specific table column they were created for. That is, you cannot bind these rules to any other table column, and you cannot bind them to user-defined data types.

Changing the Name of a Rule

The SQL Server provides you with a system procedure to change the name of a rule. If you are the owner of the rule and you want to change its name, log on to the SQL Server and enter these commands:

```
1>use NameOfDatabase
2>go
1>sp_rename NameOfRule, NewNameOfRule
2>go
```

where:

NameOfDatabase—the name of the database that contains the rule that you own whose name you want to change.

NameOfRule—the current name of the rule that you own whose name you want to change.

NewNameOfRule—the new name you want to assign to the rule that you own.

This change will take effect immediately. This command changes the database, so to ensure its recovery, be certain to dump the database's transaction log, and then dump the database itself. As this command changes the contents of system tables, it cannot be executed within a transaction.

An account with **dbo** or **sa_role** privileges can change the name of a rule that you own, as well as rules that are owned by any other Sybase account that is authorized to use your database. Just enter the `setuser` command before you execute the `sp_rename` command.

Rule and Default Conflicts

Before we explore binding rules to user-defined data types and table columns, we need to consider the relationship that exists between defaults and rules. Basically, rules take precedence over defaults.

If a user-defined data type or table column has both a default and a rule bound to it, then the default's constant data value must fall within the domain defined by the rule (a *domain* is a finite set of legal data values, all of the same data type). If the default's constant data value is not a member of the rule's domain, then the rule will automatically reject the default, an error will be raised, and the transaction will be rejected unless the column is nullable.

As we saw previously, when a default is bound to a table column it will replace the default bound to the user-defined data type on which the table column is based. However, when a default is bound to a table column it will not replace the rule bound to the user-defined data type on which the table column is based.

Binding a Rule to a User-Defined Data Type

A rule you own can be bound to one or more user-defined data types that you also own, just as long as the rule's domain does not conflict with the base data type of your user-defined data type. But, it is not possible for you to bind a rule you own either to a user-defined data type that you do not own, or to a SQL Server-supplied system data type.

Here are some important facts to understand about binding rules to user-defined data types:

1. If the user-defined data type already has a rule bound to it, then you must unbind the current rule, before you attempt to bind the new rule to it.

2. Rules are not applied to data already stored within table columns based on the user-defined data type to which you are presently binding the rule.

3. Rules are not tested on data values inserted into SQL Server variables that are based on the user-defined data type to which you have bound a rule.

4. Binding a rule to a user-defined data type will not replace a rule that is bound to a table column based on the user-defined data type.

When you bind a rule to a user-defined data type, you have two options:

1. Have the rule take immediate effect on all existing table columns that are based on the user-defined data type within the current database.

2. Prevent the rule from taking effect on all existing table columns based on the user-defined data type, and instead, have the default binding take effect only on future table columns that will be based on the user-defined data type within the current database.

The options are available to you except for the case where existing table columns based on the user-defined data type, within the current database, have previously had their rule changed.

To bind a rule you own to a user-defined data type that you own, and have that rule take immediate effect on all existing table columns that are based on that user-defined data type, log on to the SQL Server as a Sybase account that owns both the rule and the user-defined data type and enter these commands:

```
1>use NameOfDatabase
2>go
1>sp_bindrule NameOfRule, NameOfUserDefinedDataType
2>[futureonly]
3>go
```

where:

NameOfDatabase—the name of the database that contains the rule and user-defined data type that you own and which you want to bind to one another.

NameOfRule—the rule that you own and want to bind to the user-defined data type that you own.

NameOfUserDefinedDataType—the name of the user-defined data type that you own to which you want to bind the rule that you own.

[futureonly]—this optional parameter prevents existing table columns based on the user-defined data type from immediately inheriting the rule.

This change will take effect immediately. This command changes the database, so to ensure its recovery, be certain to dump the database's transaction log, and then dump the database itself. As this command changes the contents of system tables, it cannot be executed within a transaction.

An account with **dbo** or **sa_role** privileges can bind a rule to a user-defined data type that are both owned by another Sybase account (that is the same account) by logging on to the SQL Server as the Sybase account that owns the database. Just enter the setuser command before you execute the sp_bindrule command.

Binding a Rule to a Table Column

A rule can be bound to one or more columns in one or more tables, just so long as the:

1. Value of rule does not conflict with the table column's data type.
2. Table column's data type is not time stamp, text, or image.

If and only if you own a table, then you can bind defaults that you also own to columns in that table.

Here are some important facts to understand about binding rules to user-defined data types:

1. If the table column already has a rule bound to it, then you must unbind the current rule before you attempt to bind the new rule to it.
2. Rules are not applied to data already stored within table columns based on the user-defined data type to which you are presently binding the rule.

To bind a rule you own to a column in a table that you own, log on to the SQL Server as a Sybase account that owns both the rule and the table and enter these commands:

```
1>use NameOfDatabase
2>go
1>sp_bindrule NameOfRule, "NameOfTable.NameOfColumn"
2>go
```

where:

NameOfDatabase—the name of the database that contains the rule and table column that you own and want to bind to one another.

NameOfRule—the rule that you own and want to bind to the table column that you own.

NameOfTable.NameOfColumn—the name of the table column that you own, to which you want to bind a rule which you also own. Both the table and the column names are enclosed in quotes because they contained an embedded punctuation, the period (.) symbol. When you pass a parameter that contains an embedded punctuation to a SQL Server system procedure, it must be enclosed in quotation marks.

This change will take effect immediately. This command changes the database, so to ensure its recovery, be certain to dump the database's transaction log, and then dump the database itself. As this command changes the contents of system tables, it cannot be executed within a transaction.

An account with **dbo** or **sa_role** privileges can bind the rule to a column in that table as long as both the rule and the table are both owned by the same Sybase account. Just enter the `setuser` command before you execute the `sp_bindrule` command.

After the rule is bound to the table column, be certain to test it to ensure that the rule is achieving the desired effect.

Unbinding a Rule from a User-Defined Data Type

A rule you own can be unbound from a user-defined data type that you also own. When a rule is unbound, the link between it and the user-defined data type is merely broken (i.e., the rule is not destroyed) and remains within the current database, available for future use.

When you unbind a rule from a user-defined data type, you have two options:

1. Have the rule unbinding take immediate effect on all existing table columns that are based on the user-defined data type within the current database.

2. Prevent the rule unbinding from taking effect on all existing table columns based on the user-defined data type.

The options are available to you except for the case where existing table columns based on the user-defined data type within the current database have previously had their rule changed.

To unbind a rule you own from a user-defined data type that you own, and have that rule unbinding take immediate effect on all existing table columns that are based on that user-defined data type, log on to the SQL Server as a Sybase account that owns both the rule and the user-defined data type and enter these commands:

```
1>use NameOfDatabase
2>go
1>sp_unbindrule NameOfRule, NameOfUserDefinedDataType
2>[futureonly]
3>go
```

where:

NameOfDatabase—the name of the database that contains the rule and user-defined data type that you own and which you want to unbind from one another.

NameOfRule—the rule that you own and want to unbind from the user-defined data type that you also own.

NameOfUserDefinedDataType—the name of the user-defined data type that you own and from which you want to unbind the rule that you also own.

`[futureonly]`—this optional parameter prevents existing table columns based on the user-defined data type from having their rule unbound.

This change will take effect immediately. This command changes the database, so to ensure its recovery, be certain to dump the database's transaction log, and then dump the database itself. As this command changes the contents of system tables, it cannot be executed within a transaction.

An account with **dbo** or **sa_role** privileges can unbind the rule from the user-defined data type, just as long as both the rule and the user-defined data type are both owned by the same Sybase account. Just enter the `setuser` command before you execute the `sp_unbindrule` command.

Unbinding a Rule from a Table Column

If and only if you own a table, then you can unbind rules that you also own from columns in that table.

To unbind a rule you own from a column in a table that you also own, log on to the SQL Server as a Sybase account that owns both the rule and the table and enter these commands:

```
1>use NameOfDatabase
2>go
```

```
1>sp_unbindrule NameOfRule, "NameOfTable.NameOfColumn"
2>go
```

where:

NameOfDatabase—the name of the database that contains the rule and table column that you own, and which you want to unbind from one another.

NameOfRule—the rule that you own that you want to unbind from the table column that you also own.

NameOfTable.NameOfColumn—the name of the table column that you own from which you want to unbind a rule which you also own. Both the table and the column names are enclosed in quotes because they contained an embedded punctuation, the period (.) symbol. When you pass a parameter that contains an embedded punctuation to a SQL Server system procedure, it must be enclosed in quotation marks.

This change will take effect immediately. This command changes the database, so to ensure its recovery, be certain to dump the database's transaction log, and then dump the database itself. As this command changes the contents of system tables, it cannot be executed within a transaction.

An account with **dbo** or **sa_role** privileges can unbind the rule from a column in that table. Just enter the `setuser` command before you execute the `sp_unbindrule` command.

You will have to use the `alter table` statement to unbind rules bound using either the `create table` statement or the `alter table` statement.

Dropping a Rule

You can drop a rule that you own just so long as that rule is not already bound to a user-defined data type or table column in the current database. If you attempt to drop a rule that is being used, then the SQL Server will abort your instruction and display an error message indicating the context(s) in which the rule is presently being used in the current database. If you really want to drop the rule, then you must first unbind it from all user-defined data types and table columns that are presently using it.

To drop an unused rule that you own, log on to the SQL Server as a Sybase account authorized in the current database and issue the following commands:

```
1>use NameOfDatabase
2>go
1>drop rule NameOfRule
```

```
2>[,NameOfRule] ...
3>go
```

where:

NameOfDatabase—the name of the database from which you want to drop the rule.

NameOfRule—the name of the unused rule you own that you want to drop.

[,*NameOfRule*] ...—the list of names of other unused rules that you also own that you want to drop as well.

This change will take effect immediately. This command changes the database, so to ensure its recovery, be certain to dump the database's transaction log, and then dump the database itself. As this command changes the contents of system tables, it cannot be executed within a transaction.

An account with **dbo** or **sa_role** privileges can drop rules that are owned by another Sybase account that is authorized to use a given database. To drop a rule that is owned by another Sybase account, log on to the SQL Server as an account with **dbo** or **sa_role** privileges and enter these commands:

```
1>use NameOfDatabase
2>go
1>drop rule loginame.NameOfRule
2>[,loginame.NameOfRule] ...
3>go
```

where:

NameOfDatabase—the name of the database from which you want to drop the rule.

loginame.—the name of the Sybase account that owns the unused rule you want to drop from the current database.

NameOfRule—the name of the unused rule you want to drop.

[,loginame.*NameOfRule*] ...—the list of names of other unused rules you want to drop.

This change will take effect immediately. This command changes the database, so to ensure its recovery, be certain to dump the database's transaction log, and then dump the database itself. As this command changes the contents of system tables, it cannot be executed within a transaction.

Revoking Permission to Create Rules

To revoke permission to a user, a list of users, the groups (including the `public` group), or a role to create rules, log on to the SQL Server as an account with **dbo** or **sa_role** privileges and enter these commands:

```
1>use NameOfDatabase
2>go
1>revoke create rule
2>from {public | name_list | role_name}
3>go
```

where:

NameOfDatabase—the name of the database in which you want to revoke permission to create rules from a user, a list of users, the groups (including the `public` group), or a role.

`{public | name_list | role_name}`—the user, list of users, group, or role for which you want to revoke create-rule permission.

This change will take effect immediately. This command changes the database, so to ensure its recovery, be certain to dump the database's transaction log, and then dump the database itself. As this command changes the contents of system tables, it cannot be executed within a transaction.

8

Tables and Indexes

Tables

A table is a relational data structure that is composed of a finite set of columns in which data values are stored. Taken together, these columns constitute a data row. Each table will contain one or more rows of information. The number of rows a given table can contain is limited by the amount of available storage and the maximum size of a database. Each SQL Server database can contain up to 2 billion tables. While a table can contain up to 250 columns, the maximum width of any given table is just 1,962 bytes.

Within the SQL Server, each table is implemented as a doubly linked list of data pages. The SQL Server supports two types of tables: system tables that are automatically appended to the database (from the *model* system database) when the database is created, and user tables that are created by you.

Merely knowing the facts in this chapter does not constitute a proper understanding of how create tables for a System 11 SQL Server. Just because one successfully executes a `create table` statement (or a create index statement), does not mean that one has created a good table (or a good index). To be blunt, do the SQL Server engine and everyone who will have to use or support your tables (and indexes) a big favor, and do not create tables (or indexes) until you have a proper understanding of how to logically design tables to support the business and how to physically design tables (and indexes) for a System 11 SQL Server. If I had a dollar for every bad table (and index) I've come across in my career, I'd be able to pay off my family's share of the U.S.A.'s national debt.

SQL Server Kernel Configuration
for Table Partitioning

Unlike its predecessors, the System 11 SQL Server supports the partitioning of heap tables (a heap table is a table that does not have a clustered index). By default, a heap table has a single double-linked page chain. All insert operations take place in a serialized manner on the last page of the heap table's page chain. Completing an insert operation on a heap table requires an exclusive lock on its last page be taken and held for the life of the transaction (blocking all other processes from modifying the last page). As a consequence, the last page of an unpartitioned heap table can become a single point of contention (i.e., a performance bottleneck for multiple processes that are doing concurrent insert operations into the unpartitioned heap table).

When a heap table is partitioned, the SQL Server transparently creates multiple double-linked page chains for the partitioned heap table, each with its own last page. As a consequence, multiple insertion points exist within partitioned heap tables, thereby reducing insert operation contention and providing a real boost to performance for multiple processes that are doing concurrent insert operations into the partitioned heap table.

When supporting insert operations into the partitioned heap table, the SQL Server essentially selects an insertion point (a last page of one of the many page chains) at random. Within a given transaction, all insert operations will take place inside the same page chain, i.e., partition. If a segment containing the partitioned heap table spans multiple database devices, then insert operation performance will be further enhanced by the automatic distribution of simultaneous insert operations across multiple database devices.

When a heap table is partitioned, the SQL Server creates a control page for each page chain (partition). Within each partition's control page is stored information of the page chain's last page and the database devices that support the partition. To enhance performance, the SQL Server tries to keep information in the partitioned heap table control pages in cache.

It is possible to partition a heap table when it is created, while it is empty, and when it contains data. Partitioning a heap table does not move any data contained therein. To obtain the best level of performance, it is best to partition a heap table before you insert data into it. However, once you have partitioned the heap table, you cannot use the create clustered index, drop table, or truncate table commands, or the sp_placeobject system procedure on it. If you want to use these commands and this system procedure on a partitioned heap table, then you will first have to unpartition the table using the alter table command. At present, partitioned heap tables do not support parallel **bcp** or parallel table scans.

It is not possible to partition system tables, temporary tables, work tables, a user table that has a clustered index on it, or a heap table that is already partitioned. While you can partition a heap table that contains text or image columns, partitioning will have no effect on how the text or image data is stored (or continues to be stored on a single page chain) or captured during insert operations.

To get the greatest level of performance out of a partitioned heap table, follow this process:

1. Create a segment spanning multiple database devices on separate disk drives (optional). If the partitioned table resides on a default segment, then it will compete for space with other database objects.
2. When you create the table, specify that it will reside on the segments you have specifically created for its use (or use the `sp_placeobject` system command to move it onto the segment after the table is created).
3. Use the `alter table` command to partition the table and specify the number of partition groups the table will need.

The SQL Server has two configuration parameters in support of heap table partitioning:

1. `partition groups`
2. `partition spinlock ratio`

When you partition a heap table, or when you first access the partitioned heap table after the SQL Server is restarted, the SQL Server allocates partition groups to the partitioned heap table. Partition groups are internal structures that the SQL Server uses to control access to partitions. Each partition group contains sixteen partition caches, each of which stores information about an individual heap table partition. Processes use these caches when accessing the partition, such as the partition's last page. All partition caches in a given partition group are dedicated to a specific partitioned heap table. If the heap table to which a partition group is dedicated has fewer than sixteen partitions, then the unused partition caches are wasted. If a partitioned heap table has more than sixteen partitions, then multiple partition groups will be assigned to support it. The `partition groups` SQL Server configuration parameter establishes how many partition groups will be allocated for use by the SQL Server. If the count of partition groups is insufficient to support the needs of the SQL Server, users will be unable to access partitioned heap tables. The default value of the `partition groups` SQL Server configuration parameter is 64, which supports access to a maximum of 64 partitioned heap tables that have no more that sixteen partitions each. The range of values for the `partition groups` SQL Server configuration parameter is 1 through 2,147,483,647.

To determine the current value of the `partition groups` SQL Server configuration parameter, log on to the SQL Server as any Sybase account and enter these commands:

```
1>use master
2>go
1>sp_configure "partition groups"
2>go
```

To set the value of the `partition groups` SQL Server configuration parameter to 128, log on to the SQL Server as an account with **sa_role** privileges and enter these commands:

```
1>use master
2>go
1>sp_configure "partition groups", 128
2>go
```

As the `partition groups` SQL Server configuration parameter is a static parameter, the SQL Server must be shut down and restarted for the new setting to take effect. This command changes the *master* system database, so to ensure its recovery, be certain to dump the *master* system database. As this command changes the contents of system tables, it cannot be executed within a transaction.

When a process wants to gain access to a partition cache, it must acquire that partition cache's spinlock. Once the process has the partition cache's spinlock, it can access the information contained in the partition cache. Another process cannot access that partition cache, so it must wait (or spin) until the spinlock is released. Each partition cache spinlock consumes 256 bytes of memory. The `partition spinlock ratio` SQL Server configuration parameter establishes the ratio of spinlocks to partition caches, that is the number of partition caches that must share a single spinlock. The default value of the `partition spinlock ratio` SQL Server configuration parameter is 32. This means that there is one spinlock that protects 32 partition caches. The range of values for the `partition spinlock ratio` SQL Server configuration parameter is 1 through 2,147,483,647. The recommended number of partition cache spinlocks is ten percent of the total number of partitions that will be concurrently accessed by the SQL Server. Theory states that the least contention exists when each partition cache has its own spinlock.

To determine the current value of the `partition spinlock ratio` SQL Server configuration parameter, log on to the SQL Server as any Sybase account and enter these commands:

```
1>use master
2>go
1>sp_configure "partition spinlock ratio"
2>go
```

To set the value of the `partition spinlock ratio` SQL Server configuration parameter to 10, log on to the SQL Server as an account with **sa_role** privileges and enter these commands:

```
1>use master
2>go
1>sp_configure "partition spinlock ratio", 10
2>go
```

As the `partition spinlock ratio` SQL Server configuration parameter is a static parameter, the SQL Server must be shutdown and restarted for the new setting to take effect. This command changes the *master* system database, so, to ensure its recovery, be certain to dump the *master* system database. As this command changes the contents of system tables, it cannot be executed within a transaction.

SQL Server Kernel Configuration for Index Fill Factor

When you create a clustered or nonclustered index, you can establish the percentage of each index page (i.e., the index's fill factor) that will be populated with index rows. If you do not elect to specify the index's fill factor, then the index's fill factor will be determined by the value of the `default fill factor percent` SQL Server configuration parameter. You can always override the value of the `default fill factor percent` SQL Server configuration parameter by specifying the fill factor when creating an index.

If the table upon which the index is based contains data, then the newly created index's pages will be populated with data from the table, up to the (specified) fill factor. As new data is inserted into the base table, the SQL Server does not maintain the index page fill factor, and, eventually, the index pages will be populated with data up to their saturation point.

To determine the current value of the `default fill factor percent` SQL Server configuration parameter, log on to the SQL Server, and, as any Sybase account enter these commands:

```
1>use master
2>go
1>sp_configure "default fill factor percent"
2>go
```

Right out of the box, the default value of the `default fill factor percent` SQL Server configuration parameter is set to zero. Its legal range of values is 1 through 100. When a fill factor of 0 is used, the SQL Server will leave an adequate amount of space within the B-tree structure for expansion while completely filling the data pages of a clustered index and completely filling the leaf pages in nonclustered indexes.

When the value of the `default fill factor percent` SQL Server configuration parameter is set to 100 or when the fill factor is specified to be 100 when the index is created, then the SQL Server will not leave room for expansion within the B-trees, and it will completely fill pages in both clustered and nonclustered indexes. If you know that the table will not grow over time, then using a fill factor of 100 makes good sense, because you will minimize the number of data and index pages in the table and thereby minimize disk I/O overhead associated with the table.

When the value of the fill factor parameter, or the `default fill factor percent` SQL Server configuration parameter, is set somewhere between 1–99, the SQL Server will create indexes containing pages that are filled only to the specified percentage. As a consequence, the lower the value of the fill factor (except where it equals 0), the more pages are used, the more page splits may occur, and the more disk overhead is incurred.

Because you can always override the value of the `default fill factor percent` SQL Server configuration parameter when you create an index, it seldom makes sense to change the default value of this SQL Server configuration parameter. However, if you determine that the world would be a lot safer for democracy if you set this configuration parameter to 90 percent, for example, log on to the SQL Server as an account with **sa_role** privileges and enter these commands:

```
1>use master
2>go
1>sp_configure "default fill factor percent", 90
2>go
```

As the `default fill factor percent` SQL Server configuration parameter is a static parameter, the SQL Server must be shut down and restarted for the new setting to take effect. This command changes the *master* system database, so to ensure its recovery, be certain to dump the *master* system database. As this command changes the contents of system tables, it cannot be executed within a transaction.

Displaying Table Information

Before you go ahead and create a table in a given database, you should look in that database to determine which user tables already exist therein. Remember, when the database was created, the appropriate system tables were automatically created within the database.

To determine which user tables exist in a given database, log on to the SQL Server as any Sybase account that is authorized to use that database and enter these commands:

```
1>use NameOfDatabase
2>go
1>sp_help
2>go
```

where:

NameOfDatabase—the name of the database from which you want a listing of principal database objects.

The command will display a listing of all principal database objects contained within the current database, their types, and their owners. At the top of the report will be the listing of tables. For each table contained within the database, the report will indicate the name of the table, its type (i.e., system or user), and the name of the owner of that table.

To examine the definition of a given table in a given database, log on to the SQL Server as any Sybase account that is authorized to use that database and enter these commands:

```
1>use NameOfDatabase
2>go
1>sp_help [loginame.]NameOfTable
2>go
```

where:

NameOfDatabase—the name of the database that contains the table whose definition you want to inspect.

[loginame.]—the name of the Sybase account that owns the table. If you are the owner of the table, then you do not have to provide this parameter.

NameOfTable—the name of the table whose definition you want to inspect. If the table is not owned by you, then you will have to put the login name and table name inside quotes (" ").

The displayed report will provide you with information about the date the table was created, its type, the names of the columns contained in it, their data types and lengths, precision, and scale (where applicable); it will indicate whether the column allows the NULL value, the name of defaults that are bound to the columns (where applicable), and the name of the rules that are bound to the columns (where applicable). The report will also show whether the column has the IDENTITY property in effect, and you can monitor data cache bindings (if applicable), indexes and keys related to the table, other principal database objects that the table references, and table-partitioning information.

To obtain a report on a heap table's partitions, log on to the SQL Server as any Sybase account that is authorized to use that database and enter these commands:

```
1>use NameOfDatabase
2>go
1>sp_helpartition [loginame.]NameOfTable
2>go
```

where:

NameOfDatabase—the name of the database that contains the partitioned heap table you want to inspect.

[loginame.]—the name of the Sybase account that owns the table. If you are the owner of the table, then you do not have to provide this parameter.

NameOfTable—the name of the partitioned table whose partitions you want to inspect. If the table is not owned by you, then you will have to put the login name and table name inside quotes (" ").

The displayed report will provide you a list of the first page and the control page for each partition in the partitioned heap table.

Granting Permission to Create Tables

By default, users of a database do not have permission to create tables within that database. Be very careful about granting create table permission to users in a database (i.e., they can load data into these tables and consume disk space at a rate at which the **dbo** has no practical control).

To grant `create table` permission to a user, to a list of users, to the groups (including the **public** group), or to a role, log on to the SQL Server as an account with **dbo,** or **sa_role,** privileges and enter these commands:

```
1>use NameOfDatabase
2>go
1>grant create table
2>to {public | name_list | role_name}
3>[with grant option]
4>go
```

where:

NameOfDatabase—the name of the database in which you want to grant permission to create tables to a user, to a list of users, to the groups (including the **public** group), or to a role.

`{public | name_list | role_name}`—the user, list of users, group, or role to which you want to grant **create table** permission.

`[with grant option]`—this optional parameter is used to permit the owner of the table to grant access permissions on the table to other users within the database. However, you cannot extend this additional permission to any group or role.

Once this command completes successfully, the login account is immediately capable of creating tables within the database. This change takes effect immediately. This command changes the database's system tables; to ensure its recovery, be certain to dump its transaction log and then dump the database itself. As this command changes the contents of system tables, it cannot be executed within a transaction.

A user who creates a table owns that table and automatically obtains all permissions on it. All other users of the database, including the account(s) with **dbo** and **sa_role** privileges, are denied automatic access to a table they do not own unless the owner of the table explicitly grants access permissions to them (just as long as the accounts with **dbo** and **sa_role** privileges explicitly granted permission to the table owner to grant access permission to other database users when that table owner was granted permission to create tables).

Every table owner automatically has the exclusive right to execute these commands against the tables they own:

1. `alter table`
2. `drop table`
3. `create index`

4. create trigger

5. truncate table

6. update statistics

If when a user was granted permission to create tables, he or she was also granted permission to authorize access to this table, then a table owner can grant, revoke, insert, delete, select, and update permissions to users, groups, and roles within the database on any table they own.

Creating a Table

The right to create tables in a given database rests with the owner of the database. However, any Sybase account that is authorized to use a given database can be granted permission to create tables by an account with **dbo,** or **sa_role,** privileges.

To create a user table that you will own, log on to the SQL Server as a Sybase account authorized in the current database and issue the following commands:

```
1>use NameOfDatabase
2>go
1>create table [NameOfDatabase.[loginame].]NameOfTable (
2>NameOfColumn NameOfDatatype
3>[default {ConstantExpression | user | null}]
4>{[[{identity | null | not null}]
5>|[[constraint NameOfConstraint]
6>{{unique | primary key}
7>[clustered | nonclustered]
8>[with {fillfactor | max_rows_per_page}= x]
9>[on NameOfSegment]
10>references [[NameOfDatabase.]loginame.]NameOfReferencedTable
11>[(.NameOfReferencedColumn)]
12>| check (SearchCondition)}]}...
13>| [constraint NameOfConstraint]
14>{{unique | primary key}
15>[clustered | nonclustered]
16>(NameOfColumn [{, NameOfColumn}...])
17>[with {fillfactor | max_rows_per_page}= x]
18>[on NameOfSegment]
19>| foreign key (NameOfColumn[{,NameOfColumn}...])
20>references [[NameOfDatabase.] loginame.]
   NameOfReferencedTable
21>[(NameOfReferencedColumn[{,NameOfReferencedColumn}...])]
22>| check (SearchCondition)}
23>{, {NameOfNextColumn | NameOfNextConstraint}}...])
24>[with max_rows_per_page = x]
```

```
25>[on NameOfSegment]
26>go
```

where:

NameOfDatabase—the name of the database that will contain the table you are creating.

`create table [`*NameOfDatabase*`.[ loginame].]`*NameOfTable* (—it is possible to use one database and create a table in another database. It is also possible, if you logged on to the SQL Server as an account with **dbo** or **sa_role** privileges, to create a table that will be owned by another Sybase account.

where:

NameOfDatabase—the name of the database in which you want the table to be created. If you want the table to be created in the current database, then you do not have to provide this optional parameter.

`loginame`—the name of the Sybase account that will own the table. If you will be the owner of the table, then you do not have to provide this optional parameter.

NameOfTable—the name that you want the new table to have. The name must conform to the rules governing SQL Server identifiers, and must be unique, to the owner, in the given database. If, in your current session, you have entered the command `set quoted_ identifier on`, then you can use a delimited identifier for the name of the table. However, in that case you would have to enclose the table name in double quotes (`""`).

NameOfColumn NameOfDatatype

where:

NameOfColumn—the name of the new table column. The name of each column in a table must be unique within that table. The name must conform to the rules governing SQL Server identifiers. If, in your current session, you have entered the command `set quoted_identifier on`, then you can use a delimited identifier for the name of the column. However, in that case you would have to enclose the column name in double quotes (`""`).

NameOfDatatype—the name of the data type upon which the table column will be based. The data type can be a SQL Server system data type or a user-defined data type. Where applicable, you will have to indicate in parentheses the length, precision, and scale of the data type for this table column. If the IDENTITY property will be enabled for this column, then its data type must be numeric with a scale of zero. Remember, the use of variable-length data types degrades SQL Server performance relative to fixed-length data types.

[default {*ConstantExpression* | user | null}]—a column-level constraint.

where:

default—an optional parameter that indicates a default will be created and then bound to this particular table column.

ConstantExpression—the definition of the default for this table column. For instructions on how to specify a default's constant expression, refer to the preceding sections in this chapter that cover defaults.

user | null—these optional parameters are mutually exclusive. The user parameter instructs the SQL Server to use the name of the Sybase account that created a given row as the column's default data value. To use this parameter the column's data type must be either char(30), or varchar(30). The null parameter instructs the SQL Server to use the NULL value as the column's default data value. Remember, the use of the NULL value degrades SQL Server performance.

{[{identity | null | not null}]—a column-level constraint. You can choose only one of these three optional parameters for a given table column.

where:

identity—specifies that this table column will have the IDENTITY property enabled.

null—this optional parameter specifies that the SQL Server is to insert the NULL value into this column if a data value is not provided when the row is inserted.

not null—this optional parameter specifies that the SQL Server is not to allow the NULL value in this column. This is the default setting for the SQL Server. The transaction that inserts a row in this table must provide a data value for this column, if a default has not been bound to this column.

|[[constraint *NameOfConstraint*]—a column-level constraint.

where:

constraint—an optional parameter that indicates a constraint (e.g., rule, unique, primary key, referential, or check) will be bound to this particular table column.

NameOfConstraint—this optional parameter is the name of the constraint that you are linking to this table column. If the constraint is a rule, then the name of the constraint must be the name of the rule you are binding to this table column. You must own the rule that you intend to bind to your table column. If the constraint is to be either the unique or the primary key constraint, then you can choose to, or not to, provide a name for the constraint. If you elect to provide a name for the unique or the primary key constraint, then that name must be unique to the table owner within the current database, and that name must conform to the rules for SQL Server identifiers. If you elect not to provide a name for the unique or the primary key constraint, then the SQL Server will automatically generate an identifier that is structured in this manner: the first 10 characters of the table name, followed by an underscore symbol (_), then the first 5 characters of the column name, followed by an underscore symbol (_), and ending with the system-generated identifier for this constraint.

{{unique | primary key}—A column-level constraint. These optional parameters are mutually exclusive and are directly related to the constraint parameter.

where:

unique—this column constraint ensures that no two rows in the table will have the same literal data value stored in this table column. It is important to realize that one or more columns in a given table can have this type of column constraint specified. When more than one column has this constraint specified, the SQL Server manages them as a group of columns and ensures that the combination of literal data values stored in the group are always unique. When this column constraint has been specified, the SQL Server will automatically generate a unique index that is based on the column, or columns, that have been specified as being unique. Once a column has been specified as being unique, the only way you can change that specification is by using the alter table statement. By default, the SQL Server will create a unique nonclustered index for unique constraints.

primary key—this column constraint ensures that no two rows in the table will have the same literal data value stored in this table column and that the NULL data value will never be stored within a column so specified. It is important to realize that one or more columns in a given table can have this type of column constraint specified. When more than one column has this constraint specified, the SQL Server manages them as a group of columns and ensures that the combination of literal data values stored in the group are always unique and that none of the columns in the group will have a NULL data value stored within them. When this column constraint has been specified, the SQL Server will automatically generate a unique index that is based on the column, or columns, that have been specified as being unique. Once a column has been specified as being unique, the only way you can change that specification is by using the `alter table` statement. By default, the SQL Server will create unique clustered indexes for primary key constants.

[`clustered` | `nonclustered`]—these two optional parameters are mutually exclusive and are directly related to the unique and primary key constraint parameters.

where:

`clustered`—specifies that the unique index based on the unique or primary key constraint specifications for this table will be clustered. There can be one, and only one, clustered index for a given table. This is the default for the primary key constraint.

`nonclustered`—specifies that the unique index based on the unique or primary key constraint specifications for this table will be nonclustered. There can be 0, 1, or 249 nonclustered indexes for a given table. This is the default for the unique constraint.

[`with` {`fillfactor` | `max_rows_per_page`}= x]—these optional parameters are mutually exclusive and impact the indexes created by the unique and primary key constraint specifications.

`fillfactor` = x—this optional parameter specifies the percentage of each index page that will be filled with index rows when the index is first created using the data that currently exists within the table. If not supplied, then the fill factor value as determined by the `default fill factor percent` SQL Server configuration parameter will be used.

`max_rows_per_page` = x—this optional parameter establishes the maximum number of rows the SQL Server will store on leaf-level pages of indexes that support this table for (unlike `fillfactor`) the life of the table. If you do not specify a value for `max_rows_per_page`, then the SQL Server default (0) is used, and data pages of clustered indexes will be filled, and leaf pages of nonclustered indexes will be filled, but a suitable amount of space within the index B-tree structure will be retained in both clustered and nonclustered indexes. For leaf pages, the range of legal value for the `max_rows_per_page` parameter is 0 through 256. However, if only 50 rows can fit on a page, and you set the `max_rows_per_page` parameter to a value greater than 50, then the `create table` command will complete successfully, but once you insert 50 rows into the table, you will not be able to insert any more rows into the table. So be absolutely certain that the value of the `max_rows_per_page` parameter is not greater than the table row length dictates. For nonclustered indexes, the minimum value of the max_rows_per_page parameter is zero, while its maximum value depends on the size of the nonclustered index key. To determine the maximum value of the max_rows_per_page parameter for nonclustered indexes, use this formula: [(page size – page header size]/min. index row length). This parameter is typically used to decrease the number of rows per page. You may want to decrease the number of rows per page to minimize contention between transactions that modify the pages (inserts, deletes, and updates) and transactions that read pages by spreading the rows across more pages. In addition, decreasing the number of rows per page increases the chances of direct updates occurring within tables that contain columns of variable length. Also, when the value of the max_rows_per_page parameter is set to 1, you can simulate row level locking. (However, when deleting the last row on a page, locks will still be taken on the page and on the pages that surround it.) Decreasing the number of rows per page has its negative aspects. On the downside, the number of index levels will increase if there are a lot of insert and delete operations on this table, then page splits and page shrinks will increase, and more disk space will be consumed, driving up disk I/O rates and decreasing read and write operation performance. It is not a good idea to use the max_rows_per_page parameter if the table will be supporting only read operations, if table scans are being performed on the table, if multiple rows are typically referenced, or if the structure will support a lot of insert or delete transactions. The value of the max_rows_per_page parameter specified for a clustered index will override the value of the max_rows_per_page parameter specified at the end of the create table statement. If clustered index creation did not specify a value for the max_rows_per_page parameter, its value is inherited from the value of the max_rows_per_page parameter specified at end of the create table statement.

[on *NameOfSegment*]—this optional parameter specifies the segment upon which the index will be created. The specified segment must exist and must be added to the current database before it can be referenced here. If the index being created is a clustered index, then all data pages will reside on the same segment as the clustered index. If you do not use this optional parameter, then the object will be placed on the database's default segment.

references [[*NameOfDatabase*.] loginame.]*NameOfReferencedTable*

[(.*NameOfReferencedColumn*)]—this optional parameter is a column-level constraint that specifies a referential-integrity constraint on this table column. At the column level, you can specify one and only one column reference. When you state that the column references another column in another table, you are forcing the SQL Server to verify that any data value placed within this column must already exist in the other table column being referenced (or the referenced column must contain the NULL value, if appropriate). The referenced table column must exist at the point in time it is referenced, and it can exist within the current database or another database on the same SQL Server. For this to work, you must have select permission on the referenced table, and the referenced table column must be constrained by a unique index (if no column is specified, then the appropriate column in the referenced table must have a primary key constraint). You cannot reference a column in a temporary table, and the referenced table column must be the same as this column's data type. As if things weren't complicated enough, the plot thickens when you start to reference another table, so hold on to your hat. The SQL Server does not allow you to delete rows from or modify column values in a referenced table that matches rows or column values in the referencing table. In addition, the SQL Server will not allow you to drop the referenced table, rename the current database, or, if the referenced table is inside another database, you cannot drop or rename the other database that contains the referenced table. However, you can remove cross-database and cross-table reference constraints by using the `alter table` command on the respective tables. Every time you create or destroy a cross-database constraint, dump both impacted databases. Be absolutely certain not to load earlier dump images of either database, as this will certainly result in database corruption. However, you can still drop the referencing table and its database without wreaking havoc, because the SQL Server will automatically remove foreign key information from the referenced database for you.

| `check` (*SearchCondition*)}]}...—this optional column-level constraint defines a search condition that the SQL Server automatically enforces on all rows within the table. You can use check-integrity constraints as an alternative to rules and triggers. However, they are not as reusable as rules because they are limited to the table column for which they are created: they cannot be bound to columns in other tables; they cannot be bound to user-defined data types. And, unlike triggers, they cannot reference columns in other tables. But, you can create multiple check constraints on a given table column. Finally, the SQL Server does not support check constraints within temporary tables.

SearchCondition—can include a list of constant expressions introduced with the `in` keyword (that allows you to match any one value of a list of values) or a set of conditions (that may contain wild-card characters) introduced with the `like` keyword (used to match specified portions of a character string). However, the search condition cannot be a range of constant expressions introduced with the `between` keyword, nor can it include arithmetic operators or built-in spinlock functions.

| [[constraint *NameOfConstraint*]—a table-level constraint.

where:

> `constraint`—an optional parameter that indicates a constraint (e.g., rule, unique, primary key, referential, or check) will be bound to this particular table.
>
> *NameOfConstraint*—the constraint you are linking to this table. If the constraint is to be either the unique or the primary key constraint, then you may choose to provide a name for the constraint. If you elect to provide a name for the unique or the primary key constraint, then that name must be unique to the table owner within the current database, and that name must conform to the rules for SQL Server identifiers. If you elect not to provide a name for the unique or the primary key constraint, then the SQL Server will automatically generate an identifier that is structured in this manner: the first 10 characters of the table name, followed by an underscore symbol (_), then the first five characters of the column name, followed by an underscore symbol (_), and ending with the system-generated identifier for this constraint.

{{unique | primary key}—a table-level constraint. These optional parameters are mutually exclusive and are directly related to the constraint parameter.

where:

> `unique`—this column constraint ensures that no two rows in the table will have the same literal data value stored in this table column. It is important to realize that one or more columns in a given table can have this type of column constraint specified. When more than one column has this constraint specified, the SQL Server manages them as a group of columns and ensures that the combination of literal data values stored in the group are always unique. When this column constraint has been specified, the SQL Server will automatically generate a unique index that is based on the column, or columns, that have been specified as being unique. Once a column has been specified as being unique, the only way you can change that specification is by using the `alter table` statement. By default, the SQL Server will create a unique nonclustered index for unique constraints.

primary key—this column constraint ensures that no two rows in the table will have the same literal data value stored in this table column and that the NULL data value will never be stored within a column so specified. It is important to realize that one or more columns in a given table can have this type of column constraint specified. When more than one column has this constraint specified, the SQL Server manages them as a group of columns and ensures that the combination of literal data values stored in the group are always unique and that none of the columns in the group will have a NULL data value stored within them. When this column constraint has been specified, the SQL Server will automatically generate a unique index that is based on the column or columns that have been specified as being unique. Once a column has been specified as being unique, the only way you can change that specification is by using the alter table statement. By default, the SQL Server will create unique clustered indexes for primary key constraints.

[clustered | nonclustered]—these two optional parameters are mutually exclusive, and are directly related to the unique and primary key constraint parameters.

where:

clustered—specifies that the unique index based on the unique or primary key constraint specifications for this table will be clustered. There can be one and only one clustered index for a given table. This is the default for the primary key constraint.

nonclustered—specifies that the unique index based on the unique or primary key constraint specifications for this table will be nonclustered. There can be 0, 1, or 249 nonclustered indexes for a given table. This is the default for the unique constraint.

(*NameOfColumn* [{ , *NameOfColumn*}...])—this optional parameter specifies the rest of the names of the table columns that make up the index.

[with {fillfactor | max_rows_per_page}= x]—these optional parameters are mutually exclusive and impact the indexes created by the unique and primary key constraint specifications.

fillfactor = x—this optional parameter specifies the percentage of each index page that will be filled with index rows when the index is first created, using the data that currently exists within the table. If not supplied, then the fill factor value as determined by the default fill factor percent SQL Server configuration parameter will be used.

`max_rows_per_page` = x—this optional parameter establishes the maximum number of rows the SQL Server will store on leaf-level pages of indexes that support this table for the life of the table, unlike `fillfactor`. If you do not specify a value for `max_rows_per_page`, then the SQL Server default (0) is used and data pages of clustered indexes and leaf pages of nonclustered indexes will be filled, but a suitable amount of space within the index B-tree structure will be retained in both clustered and nonclustered indexes. For leaf pages, the range of legal value for the `max_rows_per_page` parameter is 0 through 256. However, if only 50 rows can fit on a page and you set the `max_rows_per_page` parameter to a value greater than 50, then the `create table` command will complete successfully, but once you insert 50 rows into the table, you will not be able to insert any more rows into the table. So be absolutely certain that the value of the `max_rows_per_page` parameter is not greater than the table row length dictates. For nonclustered indexes, the minimum value of the `max_rows_per_page` parameter is zero, while its maximum value depends on the size of the nonclustered index key. To determine the maximum value of the `max_rows_per_page` parameter for nonclustered indexes, use this formula: [(page size – page header size]/min. index row length). This parameter is typically used to decrease the number of rows per page. You may want to decrease the number of rows per page to minimize contention between transactions that modify the pages (inserts, deletes, and updates) and transactions that read pages by spreading the rows across more pages. In addition, decreasing the number of rows per page increases the chances of direct updates occurring within tables that contain variable length columns. Also, when the value of the `max_rows_per_page` parameter is set to one, you can simulate row level locking. (However, when deleting the last row on a page, locks will still be taken on the page and on the pages that surround it.) Decreasing the number of rows per page has its negative aspects. On the downside, the number of index levels will increase if there are a lot of inserts and deletes. Page splits and page shrinks will also increase, and more disk space will be consumed, driving up disk I/O rates and decreasing read and write operation performance. It is not a good idea to use the `max_rows_per_page` parameter if the table will be supporting only read operations, if table scans are being performed on the table, if multiple rows are typically referenced, or if the structure will support a lot of insert or delete transactions. The value of the `max_rows_per_page` parameter specified for a clustered index will override the value of the `max_rows_per_page` parameter specified at the end of the `create table` statement. If clustered index creation did not specify a value for the `max_rows_per_page` parameter, its value is inherited from the value of the `max_rows_per_page` parameter specified at end of the `create table` statement.

[`on` *NameOfSegment*]—this optional parameter specifies the segment upon which the index will be created. The specified segment must exist, and must be added to the current database, before it can be referenced here. If the index being created is a clustered index, then all data pages will reside on the same segment as the clustered index. If you do not use this optional parameter, then the object will be placed on the database's `default` segment.

| `foreign key` (*NameOfColumn*[{,*NameOfColumn*}...])—this optional table-level constraint states that a list of columns in this table are foreign keys whose source keys are those columns listed within the table-level reference constraint.

`references` [[*NameOfDatabase*.] `loginame`.] *NameOfReferencedTable* [(*NameOfReferencedColumn*[{,*NameOfReferencedColumn*} ...])]—this optional clause is a table-level constraint that compliments the foreign clause and specifies a referential-integrity constraint that exists on this table. The `foreign key` clause must be used when using this optional `references` clause. At the table level, you can specify one or more column references. When you state that the column references another column in another table, any data value placed within this column must already exist in the other table column it is referencing (or the referenced column must contain the NULL value, if appropriate). The referenced table can be the table itself, and it must exist at the point in time it is referenced within the current database or another database on this SQL Server. For this to work, you must have select permission on the referenced table, the referenced table column must be constrained by a unique index (if no column is specified, then the appropriate column in the referenced table must have a primary key constraint), it cannot be a column in a temporary table, and the referenced table column must be the same as this column's data type. Listing the referenced column names is only optional if the columns in the referenced tables are the columns in the referenced table's primary key as designated by the referenced table's primary key constraint. The SQL Server does not allow you to delete rows from or modify column values in a referenced table that matches rows or column values in the referencing table. In addition, the SQL Server will not allow you to drop the referenced table or rename the current database, or, if the referenced table is inside another database, you cannot drop or rename the other database that contains the referenced table. However, you can remove cross-database and cross-table reference constraints by using the `alter table` command on the respective tables. Every time you create or destroy a cross-database constraint, dump both of the impacted databases. Be absolutely certain not to load earlier dump images of either database, as this will certainly result in database corruption. However, you can still safely drop the referencing table and its database because the SQL Server will automatically remove foreign key information from the referenced database for you.

`|` `check` (*SearchCondition*)}]}...—this optional, table-level constraint defines a search condition that the SQL Server automatically enforces on all rows within the table. Table-level check constraints can reference any column in the table. You can use check-integrity constraints as an alternative to rules and triggers. However, they are not as reusable as rules because they are limited to the table column for which they are created: they cannot be bound to columns in other tables, and they cannot be bound to user-defined data types. And, unlike triggers, they cannot reference columns in other tables. But you can create multiple check constraints on a given table column. Finally, the SQL Server does not support check constraints within temporary tables.

SearchCondition—can include a list of constant expressions introduced with the `in` keyword (that allows you to match any one value of a list of values), or it can include a set of conditions (which may contain wild-card characters) introduced with the `like` keyword (used to match specified portions of a character string). However, the search condition cannot be a range of constant expressions introduced with the `between` keyword, nor can it include arithmetic operators or built-in spinlock functions.

{,{*NameOfNextColumn* | *NameOfNextConstraint*}}...])—this expression announces that the table will include multiple columns.

`[with max_rows_per_page = x]`—this optional parameter establishes the maximum number of rows the SQL Server will store on a data page and the leaf-level pages of indexes (which are the same thing as data pages) that support this table, for the life of the table unlike `fillfactor`. If you do not specify a value for `max_rows_per_page`, then the SQL Server default (0) is used, data pages of clustered indexes will be filled, and leaf pages of nonclustered indexes will be filled, but a suitable amount of space within the index B-tree structure will be retained in both clustered and nonclustered indexes. For data pages (and clustered leaf pages), the range of legal value for the `max_rows_per_page` parameter is 0 through 256. However, if only 50 rows can fit on a page and you set the `max_rows_per_page` parameter to a value greater than 50, then the `create table` command will complete successfully, but once you insert 50 rows into the table, you will not be able to insert any more. So be absolutely certain that the value of the `max_rows_per_page` parameter is not greater than the table row length dictates. For nonclustered indexes, the minimum value of the `max_rows_per_page` parameter is zero, while its maximum value depends on the size of the nonclustered index key. To determine the maximum value of the `max_rows_per_page` parameter for nonclustered indexes, use this formula: [(page_size − page header size)/min. index row length]. This parameter is typically used to decrease the number of rows per page. You may want to decrease the number of rows per page to minimize contention between transactions that modify the pages (inserts, deletes, and updates) and transactions that read pages by spreading the rows across more pages. In addition, decreasing the number of rows per page increases the chances of direct updates occurring within tables that contain columns of variable length. Also, when the value of the `max_rows_per_page` parameter is set to 1, you can simulate row-level locking (however, when deleting the last row on a page, locks will still be taken on the page and on the pages that surround it). Decreasing the number of rows per page has its negative aspects. On the downside, the number of index levels will increase, and if there are a lot of inserts and deletes, page splits and page shrinks will increase and more disk space will be consumed, driving up disk I/O rates and decreasing read and write operation performance. It is not a good idea to use the `max_rows_per_page` parameter if the table will be supporting only read operations, if table scans are being performed on the table, if multiple rows are typically referenced, or if the structure will support a lot of insert or delete transactions. The value of the `max_rows_per_page` parameter specified for a clustered index will override the value of the `max_rows_per_page` parameter specified at the end of the `create table` statement.

[`on` *NameOfSegment*]—this optional parameter specifies the segment upon which the table will be created. The specified segment must exist and must be added to the current database before it can be referenced here. If a clustered index is created for this table, then all data pages will reside on the same segment as the clustered index. If you do not use this optional parameter, then the object will be placed on the database's `default` segment.

Finally, if you are creating the *sysaudits* table used by the SQL Server security system to support auditing, then you must be the **sso_role** when you create it.

This change takes effect immediately. This command changes the database's system tables, so to ensure its recovery, be certain to dump its transaction log and then dump the database itself. As this command changes the contents of system tables, it cannot be executed within a transaction.

Creating a Schema

The SQL Server provides you with the ability to group multiple `create table`, `create view`, and `grant` and `revoke` permission statements (i.e., a database schema) in a single command. This technique of grouping these commands is a convenient way to ensure that collections of objects and their permissions are managed and deployed as a single unit. Also, as was explained in the `create table` syntax specific to referential integrity (i.e., a referenced table must exist at the time referential integrity constraint is created), this technique is the only way to simultaneously create two tables that reference one another.

Only database users who have permission to create tables and/or to create views and/or to grant or revoke permissions can create schema. In addition, unlike the `create table` and `create view` command syntax, schema can only be created in the current database. To create a schema, log on to the SQL Server as an authorized user account or as an account with **dbo** or **sa_role** privileges and enter these commands:

```
1>use NameOfDatabase
2>go
1>create schema authorization UserNameInDatabase
2>create_object_statement
3>[ create_object_statement ... ]
4>[ permission_statement ... ]
5>go
```

where:

NameOfDatabase—the name of the database that will contain the table you are creating.

UserNameInDatabase—the name of the user in this database who is creating the schema. If the login account has not been given a user name in the database, then this parameter will be set to the name of the login account.

`create_object_statement`—the first `create table` or a `create view` command statement.

`[ create_object_statement ... ]`—the optional additional `create table` or `create view` command statements.

[permission_statement ...]—the optional additional command statements that grant or revoke permission.

The create schema command can be terminated by your regular command terminator or by any command other than create table, create view, grant, or revoke commands. The entire create schema command completes in total, or it entirely fails. Also, tables, views, and permissions created within a schema can be individually dropped and revoked in the usual manner.

This change takes effect immediately. This command changes the database's system tables, so to ensure its recovery, first dump its transaction log and then the database itself. As this command changes the contents of system tables, it cannot be executed within a transaction.

Table Consistency Checking

Despite the best efforts put forward by the developers of the System 11 SQL Server, database consistency can be lost as a result of product bugs or as a result of the SQL Server crashing. The goal of Sybase is to make the need to check database consistency a thing of the past. But, while significant improvements have been made with System 11, we are not quite there yet at the time of this writing. Therefore, you may need to schedule times when you check the consistency of each and every system and user database that is managed by the SQL Server.

The SQL Server has a utility called the Database Consistency Checker (**dbcc**) that database owners can use to check the logical and physical consistency within the databases they own. It is important to understand that in order for the **dbcc** utility to do its work, it takes and locks hold on the database object it is checking. As a consequence of taking these locks, serious contention problems can arise within the database, and performance can grind to a halt. So, be certain to execute the **dbcc** utility when doing so avoids contention within the database.

The **dbcc** utility can detect and sometimes correct logical and physical inconsistencies within databases before (and after) these inconsistencies result in a database outage. Your goal should be to discover the database inconsistency as soon as possible, and then take the necessary steps to repair whatever damage occurred (if possible).

The **dbcc** utility has three facilities that the table owner (or an account with **dbo** or **sa_role** privileges that has taken on the identity of the table owner) can use to check (and repair) the consistency of tables:

1. `dbcc checktable ({ `*`NameOfTable`*` | table_id}[, skip_ncindex])`
2. `dbcc tablealloc ({`*`NameOfTable`*` | table_id [, {full | optimized | fast | null}[, fix | nofix]])`
3. `dbcc fix_text ({`*`NameOfTable`*` | table_id})}`

The **dbcc checktable** utility runs these checks on a table to ensure that it is consistent as regards:

1. Data page linkages (even across partitions).
2. Index page linkages.
3. Sort order of the index.
4. All pointers (e.g., allocation page pointers, OAM page pointers).
5. Data rows on every data page have an entry in the first OAM page to maps to their respective locations on the data page. If a data row is not accounted for on the OAM page, then the OAM page will be updated.
6. Index rows on every index page have an entry in the first OAM page to maps to their respective locations on the index page. If an index row is not accounted for on the OAM page, then the OAM page will be updated.

To run the **dbcc checktable** utility, log on to the SQL Server as the table owner (or as an account with **dbo** or **sa_role** privileges that has taken on the identity of the table owner) and enter this command in the current database:

```
1>dbcc checktable ({NameOfTable |table_id}[, skip_ncindex])
2>go
```

where:

{*NameOfTable* |`table_id`}—the name, or ID, of the table whose consistency you want to check. If an account with **dbo** or **sa_role** privileges is checking a table owned by another database user, then prefix the name or ID of the table with the table owner name and enclose this parameter in quotes (`""`). If you want to check a table that is not in the current database, then prefix the table name with the database name and the table owner name, and enclose this parameter in quotes (`""`). (To find the ID of the table, select id from sysobjects where name = *NameOfTable.*)

`skip_ncindex`—this optional parameter allows the **dbcc checktable** utility to skip the checking of nonclustered indexes on user tables in the current database. As it is possible to simply rebuild corrupted nonclustered indexes without fear of loss of data, using this option can decrease the time it takes to check the database. The default is to check all indexes.

The SQL Server will produce a report of this consistency check and will produce error messages of any inconsistency it encounters. If errors are reported, then read the Sybase Trouble Shooting Guide (and contact Sybase Technical Support, if need be) for assistance in recovering consistency.

If you have bound the tables the **dbcc checktable** utility is checking to a Named Data Cache with a 16K Memory Pool, then the **dbcc checktable** utility will use that 16K Memory Pool when checking the consistency of the tables. However, the **dbcc checktable** utility will always use a 2K Memory Pool when checking the consistency of the table indexes.

When working with large tables, or when working on a relatively underpowered host computer, using the **dbcc checktable** utility to verify the consistency of tables gives you flexibility that the **dbcc checkdb** utility does not provide. Unlike the **dbcc checktable** utility, when you execute the **dbcc checkdb** utility, you:

1. Have no control over the order in which tables are checked

2. Do not have the ability to check certain tables and not others

3. Do not have the ability to check multiple tables simultaneously (to a limited degree)

All the above features of the **dbcc checktable** utility can provide you with the ability to fit your database object consistency checks within the window you have to do your work in.

The **dbcc tablealloc** utility runs these checks on a table to ensure that it is consistent as regards:

1. All pages of all types are accurately allocated

2. No page is allocated that is not being used

3. No page that is being used is not allocated

To run the **dbcc tablealloc** utility, log on to the SQL Server as an account with **dbo** or **sa_role** privileges and enter these commands:

```
1>dbcc tablealloc({NameOfTable | table_id [ {, full |
  optimized | fast | null}[, fix | nofix]])
2>go
```

where:

{*NameOf Table* |table_id}—this is the name, or ID, of the table whose consistency you want to check. If an account with **dbo** or **sa_role** privileges is checking a table owned by another database user, then prefix the name, or ID, of the table with the table owner name, and enclose this parameter in quotes (""). If you want to check a table that is not in the current database, then prefix the table name with the database name and the table owner name and enclose this parameter in quotes (""). (To find the ID of the table, select id from sysobjects where name = *NameOf Table.*)

{full | optimized | fast | null}—this parameter specifies the type of report that the utility will create. A full report will contain all types of allocation errors. An optimized report will contain information about allocation pages in the table's OAM page(s). An optimized report does not report on extents on allocation pages that are not listed in an OAM page, nor will it automatically fix unreferenced extents. The optimized report is the default report that this utility produces if you do not specify a report type or if you use null. If you specify a fast report, this utility will produce an exception report that lists pages that are referenced but that are not allocated in an extent. Using the full report type will result in more repairs being done than if you specify optimized or fast report types. If you specify **fix,** then the report will contain the problems uncovered and the description of the actions taken to correct the problems.

fix | nofix—specifies whether or not this utility fixes allocation errors uncovered in this table. The default is to automatically fix all user tables but not system tables. If you are going to fix the corrupted tables, then the database must be in single-user mode, preferably for use only by the **dbo.** You can specify fix or nofix only if you also specify the type of report this utility produces.

The SQL Server will produce a report of this consistency check and will produce error messages of any inconsistency it encounters. If SQL Server memory has been configured to support extent I/O work buffers, then the **dbcc tablealloc** facility will use them to complete its work at a significantly faster rate.

When working with large tables, or when working on a relatively underpowered host computer, using the **dbcc tablealloc** utility to verify the consistency of tables gives you flexibility that the **dbcc checkalloc** utility does not provide. Unlike the **dbcc tablealloc** utility, when you execute the **dbcc checkalloc** utility, you:

1. Have no control over the order in which tables are checked
2. Do not have the ability to check only certain tables
3. Do not have the ability to check multiple tables simultaneously (to a limited degree)

All of the above features of the **dbcc tablealloc** utility can provide you with the ability to fit your database object consistency checks within the window in which you have to do your work.

If you change the SQL Server's character set from any character set to a new multibyte character set, you will have to run the **dbcc fixtext** utility on every table that contains a column of text data type, or else select, readtext, or writetext commands will fail against the text data.

To run the **dbcc fixtext** utility, log on to the SQL Server as the table owner (or as an account with **dbo** or **sa_role** privileges that has taken on the identity of the table owner) and enter this command in the current database:

```
1>dbcc fixtext({NameOfTable |table_id}
2>go
```

where:

{ *NameOfTable* |table_id}—the name, or ID, of the table that you want to convert to the new multibyte character set. If an account with **dbo** or **sa_role** privileges is checking a table owned by another database user, then prefix the name, or ID, of the table with the table owner name, and enclose this parameter in quotes (""). If you want to check a table that is not in the current database, then prefix the table name with the database name and the table owner name and enclose this parameter in quotes (""). (To find the ID of the table, select id from sysobjects where name = *NameOfTable*.)

When going to a multibyte character set, more information must be stored on text pages to handle characters that span page boundaries. The **dbcc fixtext** utility adds this additional information to the text pages in small update batches. However, the **dbcc fixtext** utility can generate large numbers of transaction log records and possibly fill the database's transaction log. If, when running the **dbcc fixtext** utility, you fill the transaction log, clear the transaction log and re-execute the **dbcc fixtext** utility on the table.

These commands change the database tables, so to ensure recovery, be certain to dump the transaction log and then the database itself.

Determining the Size of a Table

The SQL Server provides any user of a database with the means to determine the amount of space a given table (including its indexes) is taking up (i.e., its size as well as the amount of space that all tables and all indexes in the current database are taking up). To determine the size of a table in your current database, log on to the SQL Server as any valid database user and enter these commands:

```
1>use NameOfDatabase
2>go
1>sp_spaceused [NameOfTable [,1] ]
2>go
```

where:

NameOfDatabase—the name of the database that will contain the table whose size you want to determine.

NameOfTable—this optional parameter is the name of the table whose size you want to determine. If you do not provide this optional parameter, then a summary report for the entire database will be produced, governing all tables and indexes in the current database.

[,1]—this optional parameter is used to produce reports that contain separate metrics for each index associated with a table.

If you do not specify a table, a summary report will be produced that shows the name of the current database, its allocated size (in megabytes), the amount of space reserved for the database (in kilobytes), an estimate of the amount of space (in kilobytes) that is being used to store data, an estimate of the amount of space (in kilobytes) that is being used to store indexes, and an estimate of the amount of reserved space (in kilobytes) that is not currently being used.

If you specify a table name and do not also specify the "1" optional parameter, a report will be produced that shows the name of the table, an estimate of the count of rows in the table, an estimate of the amount of space reserved for the table (in kilobytes), an estimate of the amount of space (in kilobytes) that is being used to store the table's data, an estimate of the amount of space (in kilobytes) that is being used to store the table's indexes, and the amount of reserved space (in kilobytes) that is not currently being used by the table. The **sp_spaceused** system procedure calculates the count of rows in the table using the built-in **rowcnt** function. The **rowcnt** function uses a value from the table's allocation pages for the average count of rows per data page. In that only the **update statistics** command and the **dbcc checktable** and

checkdb utilities update this value from the table's allocation pages, the estimate of the count of rows in the table will not reflect the delete and insert activity that has taken place on the table since the last time a check was run. To produce a better estimate of the count of rows in the table, run the **sp_spaceused** command immediately after the value from the table's allocation pages has been updated.

If you specify both the name of a table and the "1" optional parameter, a report will be produced that shows, for each index on the table, the name of the index, an estimate (in kilobytes) of the size of the index, the amount of space (in kilobytes) reserved for the index, and an estimate of the size (in kilobytes) of reserved but unused space. Below the lists of indexes will appear the name of the table, an estimate of the count of rows in the table, an estimate of the amount of space reserved for the table (in kilobytes), an estimate of the amount of space (in kilobytes) that is being used to store the table's data, an estimate of the amount of space (in kilobytes) that is being used to store the table's indexes, and the amount of reserved space (in kilobytes) that is not currently being used by the table.

Predicting Table Size

As you deploy tables and indexes, it is extremely important to produce a capacity plan for each database managed by the SQL Server. The capacity plan should show how large the table and its indexes will be when the table is first populated with data and then how large it will be at future points in time. With a good capacity plan in hand, you will avoid taking a long walk off a short pier (or at least being in the position to tell management how much disk capacity they should have purchased ahead of time).

The SQL Server provides you with a tool, the **sp_estspace** system procedure, for planning table and index space consumption, cache space consumption, and memory resource consumption. If you want an estimate of a table's space usage, follow this procedure:

1. Create the table and all the indexes that will be based on this table. It is not necessary to load data into the table.

2. Log on to the SQL Server as any valid user of the current database and enter these commands:

```
1>use NameOfDatabase
2>go
1>sp_estspace NameOfTable, no_of_rows
2>[, fill_factor
3>[, cols_to_max
4>[, textbin_len
```

```
5>[, iosec]]]]
6>go
```

where:

NameOfDatabase—the name of the database that contains the table whose size you want to estimate.

NameOfTable—the name of the table whose size you want to estimate.

no_of_rows—the estimated number of rows that the table will contain at the point in time for which you want to produce an estimated size.

fill_factor—this optional parameter is the fill factor that will be applied to every index on this table. If you do not provide this optional parameter, then the SQL Server will use its configured default fill factor.

cols_to_max—this optional parameter is a comma-separated list of the variable-length columns in the table for which you want to use the maximum column length instead of the average column length. By default, the average column length will be used.

textbin_len—this optional parameter is used to specify the length, per row, of all text and image columns contained in the table. The default length, per row, of a text or image column is zero.

iosec—use this optional parameter to specify the number of disk I/Os per second of the disk drive on which the table and its indexes will reside. The default is 30 I/Os per second.

The report that will be produced will contain estimates for the total number of data pages and the space they will consume (in kilobytes), the total number of text and image pages and the space they will consume (in kilobytes), and for each index, the index level, the total number of index pages and the space they will consume (in kilobytes) for that index level, the total space the table and its indexes will consume (in kilobytes), and the time (in minutes) to create the table and each of its indexes.

While the **sp_estspace** is a useful tool, it does have these drawbacks:

1. The space usage is only an estimate. The estimate space does not account for different fill factors on different indexes, page splitting that may occur as data is inserted and deleted over time from the table, nor does it represent the actual length of variable length columns.

2. The estimate time it will take to create the table and its indexes does not take into account how you have configured the SQL Server

or the load on the SQL Server when the table and its indexes are created.

If these drawbacks are more than you are comfortable with, then it is recommended that you use the formula in the Sybase SQL Server Performance and Tuning manual for calculating the size of tables and indexes. While the formula is not an absolute predictor of the future, it does produce more robust estimates.

Altering a Table

The SQL Server provides a table owner (or an account with **dbo** or **sa_role** privileges that has taken on the identity of the table owner) to change a table by adding new columns; by adding, changing, or dropping column-level constraints; by replacing column defaults; by adding, changing, or dropping table-level constraints; and by partitioning and unpartitioning (heap tables).

To alter the definition of a table, log on to the SQL Server as the a table owner (or an account with **dbo** or **sa_role** privileges that has taken on the identity of the table owner), and enter these commands:

```
1>use NameOfDatabase
2>go
1>alter table [NameOfDatabase.[ loginame].]NameOfTable
2>{ add NameOfColumn NameOfDatatype
3>[default {ConstantExpression | user | null}]
4>{[{identity | null | not null}]
5>| [[constraint NameOfConstraint]
6>{{unique | primary key}
7>[clustered | nonclustered]
8>[with {fillfactor | max_rows_per_page}= x]
9>[on NameOfSegment]
10>references [[NameOfDatabase.] loginame.]
    NameOfReferencedTable
11>[( .NameOfReferencedColumn )]
12>| check (SearchCondition)}]]}...
13>{{, NameOfNextColumn]}...
14>| add [constraint NameOfConstraint]
15>{{unique | primary key}
16>[clustered | nonclustered]
17>(NameOfColumn [{, NameOfColumn}...])
18>[with {fillfactor | max_rows_per_page}= x]
19>[on NameOfSegment]
20>| foreign key (NameOfColumn[{,NameOfColumn }...])
21>references [[NameOfDatabase.] loginame.]
    NameOfReferencedTable
```

```
22>[(NameOfReferencedColumn[{,NameOfReferencedColumn}...])]
23>| check (SearchCondition)}
24>| drop constraint NameOfConstraint
25>| replace NameOfColumn default {default {ConstantExpression
   | user | null}
26>| partition NumberOfPartitions
27>| unpartition
28>go
```

where:

> *NameOfDatabase*—the name of the database that will contain the table you are creating.

> alter table [*NameOfDatabase*.[loginame].]*NameOfTable*—it is possible to use one database and to alter a table in another database. It is also possible, if you logged on to the SQL Server as an account with **dbo** or **sa_role** privileges, to alter a table that is owned by another Sybase Account.

> where:

>> *NameOfDatabase*—the name of the database that contains the table you want to alter. If the table to be altered is in the current database, then you do not have to provide this optional parameter.

>> loginame—the name of the Sybase account that owns the table. If you are the owner of the table, then you do not have to provide this optional parameter.

>> *NameOfTable*—the name of the table you want to alter.

> add *NameOfColumn NameOfDatatype*

> where:

>> *NameOfColumn*—the name that you want the new table column to have. The name of each column in a table must be unique within that table. The name must conform to the rules governing SQL Server identifiers. If, in your current session, you have entered the command set quoted_identifier on, then you can use a delimited identifier for the name of the column. However, in that case you would have to enclose the column name in double quotes ("").

>> *NameOfDatatype*—the name of the data type upon which the table column will be based. The data type can be a SQL Server system data type or a user-defined data type, except the bit-data type. Where applicable, you will have to indicate in parentheses the length, precision, and scale of the data type for this table column. If the IDENTITY property will be enabled for this column, then its data type must be numeric with a scale of zero. Remember, the use

of variable-length data types degrades SQL Server performance relative to fixed-length data types.

[default {*ConstantExpression* | user | null}]—a column-level constraint.

where:

default—an optional parameter that indicates a default will be created and then bound to this particular table column.

ConstantExpression—the definition of the default for this table column. For instructions on how to specify a default's constant expression, refer to the preceding sections in this chapter that cover defaults.

user | null—these optional parameters are mutually exclusive. The user parameter instructs the SQL Server to use the name of the Sybase account that created a given row as the column's default data value. To use this parameter the column's data type must be either char(30) or varchar(30). The null parameter instructs the SQL Server to use the NULL value as the column's default data value. Remember, the use of the NULL value degrades SQL Server performance.

{[{identity | null | not null}]—a column-level constraint. You can choose only one of these three optional parameters for a given table column.

where:

identity—specifies that this table column will have the IDENTITY property enabled. When you add an IDENTITY column to a table that contains data:

1. Make certain that the column precision is great enough to handle the number of rows that currently exist within the table.
2. The SQL Server will take a lock on the entire table, where it automatically generates values for the IDENTITY column. As this will produce contention on the table and may take a long amount of time, be certain that you add this IDENTITY column during the right period of time.
3. When the SQL Server assigns values to the IDENTITY column, a log record will be written to the database's transaction log, so be certain to dump the database's transaction log before adding the table, and be certain that the database's transaction log is large enough to handle all the related log records.

null—this optional parameter specifies that the SQL Server is to insert the NULL value into this column if a data value is not provided when the row is inserted.

`not null`—this optional parameter specifies that the SQL Server is not to allow the NULL value in this column. This is the default setting for the SQL Server. The transaction that inserts a row in this table must provide a data value for this column, if a default has not been bound to this column.

`|[[constraint` *NameOfConstraint*`]`—a column-level constraint.

where:

`constraint`—an optional parameter that indicates a constraint (e.g., rule, unique, primary key, referential, or check) will be bound to this particular table column.

NameOfConstraint—this optional parameter is the name of the constraint that you are linking to this table column. If the constraint is a rule, then the name of the constraint must be the name of the rule you are binding to this table column. You must own the rule that you intend to bind to your table column. If the constraint is to be either the unique or the primary key constraint, then you can choose to, or not to, provide a name for the constraint. If you elect to provide a name for the unique or the primary key constraint, then that name must be unique to the table owner within the current database, and that name must conform to the rules for SQL Server identifiers. If you elect not to provide a name for the unique or the primary key constraint, then the SQL Server will automatically generate an identifier that is structured in this manner: the first 10 characters of the table name, followed by an underscore symbol (_), then the first 5 characters of the column name, followed by an underscore symbol (_), and ending with the system generated identifier for this constraint.

`{{unique | primary key}`—a column-level constraint. These optional parameters are mutually exclusive and are directly related to the constraint parameter.

where:

`unique`—this column constraint ensures that no two rows in the table will have the same literal data value stored in this table column. It is important to realize that at least one column in a given table can have this type of column constraint specified. When more than one column has this constraint specified, the SQL Server manages them as a group of columns and ensures that the combination of literal data values stored in the group are always unique. When this column constraint has been specified, the SQL Server will automatically generate a unique index that is based on the column, or columns, that have been specified as being unique. Once a column has been specified as being unique, the only way you can change that specification is by using the `alter table` statement. By default, the SQL Server will create a unique non-clustered index for unique constraints.

`primary key`—this column constraint ensures that no two rows in the table will have the same literal data value stored in this table column and that the NULL data value will never be stored within a column so specified. It is important to realize that one or more columns in a given table can have this type of column constraint specified. When more than one column has this constraint speci-fied, the SQL Server manages them as a group of columns and ensures that the combination of literal data values stored in the group are always unique and that none of the columns in the group will have a NULL data value stored within them. When this column constraint has been specified, the SQL Server will automatically generate a unique index that is based on the col-umn, or columns, that have been specified as being unique. Once a column has been specified as being unique, the only way you can change that specification is by using the `alter table` statement. By default, the SQL Server will create unique clustered indexes for primary key constants.

`[clustered | nonclustered]`—these two optional parameters are mutually exclusive and are directly related to the unique and pri-mary key constraint parameters.

where:

`clustered`—specifies that the unique index based on the unique or primary key constraint specifications for this table will be clus-tered. There can be one and only one clustered index for a given table. This is the default for the primary key constraint.

`nonclustered`—specifies that the unique index based on the unique or primary key constraint specifications for this table will be non-clustered. There can be as many as 249 nonclustered indexes for a given table. This is the default for the unique constraint.

`[with {fillfactor | max_rows_per_page}= x]`—these optional param-eters are mutually exclusive and impact the indexes created by the unique and primary key constraint specifications.

`fillfactor = x`—this optional parameter specifies the percentage of each index page that will be filled with index rows when the index is first created, using the data that currently exists within the table. If not supplied, then the fill factor value as determined by the `default fill factor percent` SQL Server configuration parameter will be used.

`max_rows_per_page = x`—this optional parameter establishes the maximum number of rows the SQL Server will store on leaf-level pages of indexes that support this table for the life of the table, unlike `fillfactor`. If you do not specify a value for `max_rows_per_page`, then the SQL Server default (0) is used and data pages of clustered indexes and leaf pages of nonclustered indexes will be filled, but a suitable amount of space within the index B-tree structure will be retained in both clustered and nonclustered indexes. For leaf pages, the range of legal value for the `max_rows_per_page` parameter is 0 through 256. However, if only 50 rows can fit on a page and you set the `max_rows_per_page` parameter to a value greater than 50, then the `create table` command will complete successfully, but once you insert 50 rows into the table, you will not be able to insert any more. So be absolutely certain that the value of the `max_rows_per_page` parameter is not greater than the table row length dictates. For nonclustered indexes, the minimum value of the `max_rows_per_page` parameter is zero, while its maximum value depends on the size of the nonclustered index key. To determine the maximum value of the `max_rows_per_page` parameter for nonclustered indexes, use this formula: [(page_size – page header size)/min. index row length]. This parameter is typically used to decrease the number of rows per page. You may want to decrease the number of rows per page to minimize contention between transactions that modify the pages (inserts, deletes, and updates) and transactions that read pages by spreading the rows across more pages. In addition, decreasing the number of rows per page increases the chances of direct updates occurring within tables that contain variable length columns. Also, when the value of the `max_rows_per_page` parameter is set to one, you can simulate row-level locking. (However, when deleting the last row on a page, locks will still be taken on the page and on the pages that surround it.) Decreasing the number of rows per page has its negative aspects. On the downside, the number of index levels will increase, if there are a lot of inserts and deletes, then page splits and page shrinks will increase and more disk space will be consumed, driving up disk I/O rates and decreasing read and write operation performance. It is not a good idea to use the `max_rows_per_page` parameter if the table will be supporting only read operations, if table scans are being performed on the table, if multiple rows are typically referenced, or if the structure will support a log of insert or delete transactions. The value of the `max_rows_per_page` parameter specified for a clustered index will override the value of the `max_rows_per_page` parameter specified at the end of the `create table` statement. If clustered index creation did not specify a value for the `max_rows_per_page` parameter, its value is inherited from the value of the `max_rows_per_page` parameter specified at the end of the `create table` statement.

[on *NameOfSegment*]—this optional parameter specifies the segment upon which the index will be created. The specified segment must exist and must be added to the current database before it can be referenced here. If the index being created is a clustered index, then all data pages will reside on the same segment as the clustered index. If you do not use this optional parameter, then the object will be placed on the database's **default** segment. Because data rows move to the site where the clustered index resides, dropping and recreating a table's clustered index on a different segment is an easy way to move the table's data from its current location to a new home.

references [[*NameOfDatabase*.] loginame.]*NameOfReferencedTable* [(.*NameOfReferencedColumn*)]—this optional parameter is a column-level constraint that specifies a referential-integrity constraint that exists on this table column. At the column level, you can specify one, and only one, column reference. When you state that the column references another column in another table, any data value placed within this column must already exist in the other table column it is referencing (or the referenced column must contain the NULL value, if appropriate). The referenced table column must exist at the point in time it is referenced, and it can exist within the current database, or it can exist within another database on this SQL Server. For this to work, you must have select permission on the referenced table, the referenced table column must be constrained by a unique index (if no column is specified then the appropriate column in the referenced table must have a primary key constraint), it cannot be a column in a temporary table, and the referenced table column must be the same as this column's data type. Furthermore, the SQL Server does not allow you to delete rows from, or to modify column values in, a referenced table that matches rows or column values in the referencing table. In addition, the SQL Server will not allow you to drop the referenced table, rename the current database, or, if the referenced table is inside another database, you cannot drop or rename the other database that contains the referenced table. However, you can remove cross-database and cross-table reference constraints by using the alter table command on the respective tables. Every time you create or destroy a cross-database constraint, dump both of the impacted databases. Be absolutely certain not to load earlier dump images of either database, as this will certainly result in database corruption. However, you can still drop the referencing table and its database without doing harm, because the SQL Server will automatically remove foreign key information from the referenced database for you.

| check (*SearchCondition*)}]}...—this optional column-level constraint defines a search condition that the SQL Server automatically

enforces on all rows within the table. You can use check-integrity constraints as an alternative to rules and triggers. However, they are not as reusable as rules because they are limited to the table column for which they are created: they cannot be bound to columns in other tables and they cannot be bound to user-defined data types. And, unlike triggers, they cannot reference columns in other tables. But, you can create multiple check constraints on a given table column. Finally, the SQL Server does not support check constraints within temporary tables.

> *SearchCondition*—can include a list of constant expressions introduced with the `in` keyword (that allows you to match any one value of a list of values) or can include a set of conditions (that may contain wild-card characters) introduced with the `like` keyword (used to match specified portions of a character string). However, the search condition cannot be a range of constant expressions introduced with the `between` keyword, nor can it include arithmetic operators or built-in spinlock functions.

`{{, ` *NameOfNextColumn* `]}` `...`—this optional parameter is the list of other columns and their alterations.

`| add [[constraint ` *NameOfConstraint*`]`—a table-level constraint that you want to add.

where:

> `constraint`—an optional parameter that indicates a constraint (e.g., rule, unique, primary key, referential, or check) will be bound to this particular table.

> *NameOfConstraint*—this optional parameter is the name of the constraint that you are linking to this table. If the constraint is to be either the unique or the primary key constraint, then you can choose to, or not to, provide a name for the constraint. If you elect to provide a name for the unique or the primary key constraint, then that name must be unique to the table owner within the current database, and that name must conform to the rules for SQL Server identifiers. If you elect not to provide a name for the unique or the primary key constraint, then the SQL Server will automatically generate an identifier that is structured in this manner: the first 10 characters of the table name, followed by an underscore symbol (_), then the first 5 characters of the column name, followed by an underscore symbol (_), and ending with the system-generated identifier for this constraint.

`{{unique | primary key}`—a table-level constraint. These optional parameters are mutually exclusive and are directly related to the constraint parameter.

where:

unique—this column constraint ensures that no two rows in the table will have the same literal data value stored in this table column. It is important to realize that one or more columns in a given table can have this type of column constraint specified. When more than one column has this constraint specified, the SQL Server manages them as a group of columns and ensures that the combination of literal data values stored in the group are always unique. When this column constraint has been specified, the SQL Server will automatically generate a unique index that is based on the column or columns that have been specified as being unique. Once a column has been specified as being unique, the only way you can change that specification is by using the alter table statement. By default, the SQL Server will create a unique nonclustered index for unique constraints.

primary key—this column constraint ensures that no two rows in the table will have the same literal data value stored in this table column, and that the NULL data value will never be stored within a column so specified. It is important to realize that one or more columns in a given table can have this type of column constraint specified. When more than one column has this constraint specified, the SQL Server manages them as a group of columns and ensures that the combination of literal data values stored in the group are always unique and that none of the columns in the group will have a NULL data value stored within them. When this column constraint has been specified, the SQL Server will automatically generate a unique index that is based on the column or columns that have been specified as being unique. Once a column has been specified as being unique, the only way you can change that specification is by using the alter table statement. By default, the SQL Server will create unique clustered indexes for primary key constants.

[clustered | nonclustered]—these two optional parameters are mutually exclusive and are directly related to the unique and primary key constraint parameters.

where:

clustered—specifies that the unique index based on the unique or primary key constraint specifications for this table will be clustered. There can be one and only one clustered index for a given table. This is the default for the primary key constraint.

nonclustered—specifies that the unique index based on the unique or primary key constraint specifications for this table will be nonclustered. There can be zero, one, or many nonclustered indexes for a given table. This is the default for the unique constraint.

(*NameOfColumn* [{, *NameOfColumn*}...])—this optional parameter specifies the rest of the names of the table columns that make up the index.

[with {fillfactor | max_rows_per_page}= x]—these optional parameters are mutually exclusive and impact the indexes created by the unique and primary key constraint specifications.

fillfactor = x—this optional parameter specifies the percentage of each index page that will be filled with index rows when the index is first created using the data that currently exists within the table. If not supplied, then the fill factor value as determined by the default fill factor percent SQL Server configuration parameter will be used.

max_rows_per_page = x—this optional parameter establishes the maximum number of rows the SQL Server will store on leaf-level pages of indexes that support this table for the life of the table. If you do not specify a value for max_rows_per_page, then the SQL Server default (0) is used, and data pages of clustered indexes and leaf pages of nonclustered indexes will be filled, but a suitable amount of space within the index B-tree structure will be retained in both clustered and nonclustered indexes. For leaf pages, the range of legal value for the max_rows_per_page parameter is 0 through 256. However, if only 50 rows can fit on a page and you set the max_rows_per_page parameter to a value greater than 50, then the create table command will complete successfully, but once you insert 50 rows into the table, you will not be able to insert any more rows into the table. So be absolutely certain that the value of the max_rows_per_page parameter is not greater than the table row length dictates. For nonclustered indexes, the minimum value of the max_rows_per_page parameter is zero, while its maximum value depends on the size of the nonclustered index key. To determine the maximum value of the max_rows_per_page parameter for nonclustered indexes, use this formula: [(page size – page header size)/min index row length]. This parameter is typically used to decrease the number of rows per page. You may want to decrease the number of rows per page to minimize contention between transactions that modify the pages (inserts, deletes, and updates) and transactions that read pages by spreading the rows across more pages. In addition, decreasing the number of rows per page increases the chances of direct updates occurring within tables that contain variable-length columns. Also, when the value of the max_rows_per_page parameter is set to 1, you can simulate row-level locking. (However, when deleting the last row on a page, locks will still be taken on the page and on the pages that surround it.) Decreasing the number of rows per page has its negative aspects. On the downside, the number of index levels will increase; if there are a lot of inserts and deletes, then page splits and page shrinks will increase; and more disk space will be consumed, driving up disk I/O rates and decreasing read and write operation performance. It is not a good idea to use the `max_rows_per_page` parameter if the table will be supporting only read operations, if table scans are being performed on the table, if multiple rows are typically referenced, or if the structure will support a lot of insert or delete transactions. The value of the `max_rows_per_page` parameter specified for a clustered index will override the value of the `max_rows_per_page` parameter specified at the end of the `create table` statement. If clustered index creation did not specify a value for the `max_rows_per_page` parameter, its value is inherited from the value of the `max_rows_per_page` parameter specified at end of the `create table` statement. Existing page allocations are not effected by changes in the value of the `max_rows_per_page` parameter.

[on *NameOfSegment*]—this optional parameter specifies the segment upon which the index will be created. The specified segment must be added to the current database before it can be referenced here. If the index being created is a clustered index, then all data pages will reside on the same segment as the clustered index. If you do not use this optional parameter, then the object will be placed on the database's **default** segment.

| foreign key (*NameOfColumn*[{,*NameOfColumn*}...])—this optional table-level constraint states that a list of columns in this table are foreign keys whose source keys are those columns listed within the table-level reference constraint.

references [[*NameOfDatabase*.] loginame.] *NameOfReferencedTable* [(*NameOfReferencedColumn*[{,*NameOfReferencedColumn*} ...])]—this optional clause is a table-level constraint that compliments the foreign clause and specifies a referential-integrity constraint that exists on this table. The foreign key clause must be used when using this optional references clause. At the table level, you can specify one or more column references. When you state that the column references another column in another table, any data value placed within this column must already exist in the other table column it is referencing (or the referenced column must contain the NULL value, if appropriate). The referenced table can be the table itself. It must exist at the point in time it is referenced, and it can exist within the current database, or it can exist within another database on this SQL Server. For this to work, you must have select permission on the referenced table, the referenced table column must be constrained by a unique index (if no column is specified, then the appropriate column in the referenced table must have a primary key constraint), it cannot be a column in a temporary table, and the referenced table column must be the same as this column's data type. Listing the referenced column names is only optional if the columns in the referenced tables are the columns in the referenced table's primary key as designated by the referenced table's primary key constraint. Furthermore, the SQL Server does not allow you to delete rows from, or to modify column values in, a referenced table that matches rows, or column values, in the referencing table. In addition, the SQL Server will not allow you to drop the referenced table, rename the current database, or, if the referenced table is inside another database, you cannot drop or rename the other database that contains the referenced table. However, you can remove cross-database and cross-table reference constraints by using the `alter table` command on the respective tables. Every time you create or destroy a cross-database constraint, dump both impacted databases. Be absolutely certain not to load earlier dump images of either database, as this will certainly result in database corruption. However, you can still drop the referencing table and its database fairly cleanly because the SQL Server will automatically remove foreign key information from the referenced database for you.

| `check` (*SearchCondition*)}]}...—this optional, table-level, constraint defines a search condition that the SQL Server automatically enforces on all rows within the table. Table-level check constraints can reference any columns in the table. You can use check integrity constraints as an alternative to rules and triggers. However, they are not as reusable as rules because they are limited to the table column for which they are created: they cannot be bound to columns in other tables, and they cannot be bound to user-defined data types. And, unlike triggers, they cannot reference columns in other tables. But, you can create multiple check constraints on a given table column. Finally, the SQL Server does not support check constraints within temporary tables.

SearchCondition—can include a list of constant expressions introduced with the **in** keyword (that allows you to match any one value of a list of values) or can include a set of conditions (that may contain wild card characters) introduced with the **like** keyword (used to match specified portions of a character string). However, the search condition cannot be a range of constant expressions introduced with the **between** keyword, nor can it include arithmetic operators or built-in spinlock functions.

| `drop constraint` *NameOfConstraint*—this optional parameter is the table-level constraint you want to drop.

| replace *NameOfColumn* default {default {*ConstantExpression* | user | null}—this optional parameter is the column default you want to replace.

| partition *NumberOfPartitions*—this optional parameter is used to create partitions on a heap table. You can specify the number of partitions that the partitioned heap table will have. The number of partitions must be a whole number that is equal to or greater than 2.

| unpartition—this optional parameter is used to unpartition a partitioned heap table.

Here are a few important facts to understand about the alter table command:

1. It cannot be used to remove a column from a table.
2. If you want to change the number of partitions in a partitioned heap table, you must first unpartition the heap table.
3. A column added to a table cannot be referenced by a stored procedure that uses the select* statement on the altered table. To ensure that the new column is referenced by such a stored procedure, you must drop and re-create the stored procedure (don't forget to grant the appropriate execute permissions after the stored procedure is re-created).

This change takes effect immediately. This command changes the database's system tables; to ensure its recovery, be certain to dump its transaction log and then dump the database itself. As this command changes the contents of system tables, it cannot be executed within a transaction.

Changing Maximum Rows per Page of a Table or Index

As an alternative technique to the alter table command, The SQL Server provides you with the sp_chgattribute system procedure for changing max_rows_per_page value of an index. But, like the alter table command, it only effects future page allocations. In addition, the sp_chgattribute system procedure can also change the max_rows_per_page value of tables as well.

To change the table value of max_rows_per_page to 20, for example, log on to the SQL Server as the table owner (or as an account with **dbo** or **sa_role** privileges that has taken on the identity of the table owner), and enter these commands:

```
1>use NameOfDatabase
2>go
1>sp_chgattribute NameOfTable, "max_rows_per_page", 20
2>go
```

where:

NameOfDatabase—the name of the database that contains the table whose `max_rows_per_page` attribute you want to change.

NameOfTable—the name of the table whose `max_rows_per_page` attribute you want to change.

`max_rows_per_page`—establishes the maximum number of rows the SQL Server will store on a data page and leaf-level pages of indexes (which are the same thing as data pages) that support this table for the life of the table. If you do not specify a value for `max_rows_per_page`, then the SQL Server default (0) is used and data pages of clustered indexes and leaf pages of nonclustered indexes will be filled, but a suitable amount of space within the index B-tree structure will be retained in both clustered and nonclustered indexes. For data pages (and clustered leaf pages), the range of legal value for the `max_rows_per_page` parameter is 0 through 256. However, if only 50 rows can fit on a page and you set the `max_rows_per_page` parameter to a value greater than 50, then the `create table` command will complete successfully; but once you insert 50 rows into the table, you will not be able to insert any more. So be absolutely certain that the value of the `max_rows_per_page` parameter is not greater than the table row length dictates. For nonclustered indexes, the minimum value of the `max_rows_per_page` parameter is zero, while its maximum value depends on the size of the nonclustered index key. To determine the maximum value of the `max_rows_per_page` parameter for nonclustered indexes, use this formula: [(page_size – page header size)/min. index row length]. This parameter is typically used to decrease the number of rows per page. You may want to decrease the number of rows per page to minimize contention between transactions that modify the pages (inserts, deletes, and updates) and transactions that read pages by spreading the rows across more pages. In addition, decreasing the number of rows per page increases the chances of direct updates occurring within tables that contain columns of variable length. Also, when the value of the `max_rows_per_page` parameter is set to 1, you can simulate row-level locking. (However, when deleting the last row on a page, locks will still be taken on the page and on the pages that surround it.) Decreasing the number of rows per page has its negative aspects. On the downside, the number of index levels will increase; if there are a lot of inserts and deletes, then page splits and page shrinks will increase; and more disk space will be consumed, driving up disk I/O rates and decreasing read and write operation performance. It is not a good idea to use the `max_rows_per_page` parameter if the table will be supporting only read operations, if table scans are being performed on the table, if multiple rows are typically referenced, or if the structure will support a lot of insert or delete transactions. The value of the `max_rows_per_page` parameter specified for a clustered index will override the value of the `max_rows_per_page` parameter specified at the end of the `create table` statement.

This change takes effect immediately. This command changes the database's system tables; to ensure its recovery, be certain to dump its transaction log and then dump the database itself. As this command changes the contents of system tables, it cannot be executed within a transaction.

To change the index value of `max_rows_per_page` to 15, for example, log on to the SQL Server as the table owner (or as an account with **dbo** or **sa_role** privileges that has taken on the identity of the table owner) and enter these commands:

```
1>use NameOfDatabase
2>go
1>sp_chgattribute "NameOfTable.NameOfIndex", "max_rows_per_
  page", 15
2>go
```

where:

NameOfDatabase—the name of the database which contains the index whose `max_rows_per_page` attribute you want to change.

NameOfTable—the name of the table whose index's `max_rows_per_page` attribute you want to change.

NameOfIndex—the name of the index whose `max_rows_per_page` attribute you want to change.

`max_rows_per_page`—establishes the maximum number of rows the SQL Server will store on leaf-level pages of indexes that support this table for the life of the table. If you do not specify a value for `max_rows_per_page`, then the SQL Server default (0) is used and data pages of clustered indexes and leaf pages of nonclustered indexes will be filled, but a suitable amount of space within the index B-tree structure will be retained in both clustered and nonclustered indexes. For leaf pages, the range of legal value for the `max_rows_per_` page parameter is 0 through 256. However, if only 50 rows can fit on a page and you set the max_rows_per_page parameter to a value greater than fifty, then the create table command will complete successfully; but once you insert 50 rows into the table, you will not be able to insert any more. So be absolutely certain that the value of the max_rows_per_page parameter is not greater than the table row length dictates. For nonclustered indexes, the minimum value of the max_rows_per_page parameter is zero, while its maximum value depends on the size of the nonclustered index key. To determine the maximum value of the max_rows_per_page parameter for nonclustered indexes, use this formula: [(page size – page header size)/min. index row length]. This parameter is typically used to decrease the number of rows per page. You may want to decrease the number of rows per page to minimize contention between transactions that modify the pages (inserts, deletes, and updates) and transactions that read pages by spreading the rows across more pages. In addition, decreasing the number of rows per page increases the chances of direct updates occurring within tables that contain variable length columns. Also, when the value of the max_rows_per_page parameter is set to 1, you can simulate row-level locking. (However, when deleting the last row on a page, locks will still be taken on the page and on the pages that surround it.) Decreasing the number of rows per page has its negative aspects. On the downside, the number of index levels will increase; if there are a lot of inserts and deletes, then page splits and page shrinks will increase; and more disk space will be consumed, driving up disk I/O rates and decreasing read and write operation performance. It is not a good idea to use the max_rows_per_page parameter if the table will be supporting only read operations, if table scans are being performed on the table, if multiple rows are typically referenced, or if the structure will support a lot of insert or delete transactions. The value of the max_rows_per_page parameter specified for a clustered index will override the value of the max_rows_per_page parameter specified at the end of the create table statement. If clustered index creation did not specify a value for the max_rows_per_page parameter, its value is inherited from the value of the max_rows_per_page parameter specified at end of the create table statement.

This change takes effect immediately. This command changes the database's system tables, so to ensure its recovery, be certain to dump its transaction log and then dump the database itself. As this command changes the contents of system tables, it cannot be executed within a transaction.

Reporting on Table Constraints

To produce a report of check constraints, defaults, primary, unique key constraints, and referential constraints for a given table, log on to the SQL Server as any valid database user and enter these commands:

```
1>use NameOfDatabase
2>go
1>sp_helpconstraint NameOfTable [, detail]
2>go
```

where:

NameOfDatabase—the name of the database that contains the table for which you want a constraint report produced.

NameOfTable—the name of the table for which you want a constraint report produced.

[, detail]—if you use this optional parameter, then information about the constraint's user and error messages will be displayed.

The report produced by this command will show the name, definition, and user or error messages (if requested) of every constraint associated with this table.

Reporting on Primary Key Constraints

If, in all the hustle and bustle to get the database completed, you've forgotten where all the primary key constraints exist within the database, don't worry. The SQL Server provides you with a tool to report on primary key constraints created by the create table and the alter table commands. The only problem is you have to produce the report for each table in the current database.

To produce a report on the primary key constraints of a table within the current database, log on to the SQL Server as any valid database user and enter these commands:

```
1>use NameOfDatabase
2>go
1>sp_pkeys NameOfTable, loginame, NameOfDatabase
2>go
```

where:

NameOfDatabase—the name of the database that contains the table for which you want a primary key constraint report produced.

NameOfTable—the name of the table for which you want a primary key constraint report produced.

`loginame`—the name of the table owner.

When the `sp_pkeys` catalog stored procedure completes, the report will show the name of the current database, the name of the table owner, the name of the table, the name of each table column that participates in the primary key, and the sequence number, which indicates the location of the column within multicolumn primary keys. However, as the `sp_pkeys` catalog stored procedure updates the database system tables, it cannot be executed from within another transaction.

Reporting on Foreign Key Constraints

If you've also forgotten where all the foreign key constraints exist within the database, don't worry about this, either. The SQL Server provides you with a tool to report on foreign key constraints created by the `create table` and the `alter table` commands. The only problem is you have to produce the report for each table in the current database, and the table must have both a foreign key and primary key constraint defined.

To produce a report that shows tables that include a foreign key to a given table within the current database, log on to the SQL Server as any valid database user and enter these commands:

```
1>use NameOfDatabase
2>go
1>sp_fkeys NameOfPKTable, loginame, NameOfPkDatabase, NULL
2>[, NameOfFkTableOwner], NameOfFkDatabase
```

where:

NameOfPkDatabase—the name of the database that contains the table with the primary key constraint for which you want a foreign key constraint report produced.

NameOfPKTable—the name of the table with the primary key constraint for which you want a foreign key constraint report produced.

`loginame`—the name of the owner of the table with the primary key constraint.

NameOfFkTableOwner—optional parameter used to specify the owner of a table that contains a foreign key constraint that maps to the table with the primary key constraint. If you do not provide this optional parameter, then tables owned by the current log in account will be examined, and then tables owned by the **dbo** will be examined. To complete this analysis, you'll have to work you way through all other accounts in the current database that have **create table** permissions.

NameOfFkDatabase—the name of the database that contains the table with the foreign key constraint.

When the **sp_fkeys** catalog stored procedure completes, the report will show the name of the current database, the name of the owner of the table with the primary key constraint, the name of the table with the primary key constraint, the name of each table column that participates in the primary key, the name of the database that contains the table with the foreign key constraint (this will be the current database as well), the name of the owner of the table with the foreign key constraint, the name of the column that participates in the foreign key constraint, and the sequence number indicating the location of the column within multicolumn foreign keys. If there is action to be taken upon an update, then UPDATE will be displayed; if not, then zero will be displayed, and if there is action to be taken upon a delete, then DELETE will be displayed. If not, then zero will be displayed. However, as the **sp_fkeys** catalog stored procedure updates the database system tables, it cannot be executed from within another transaction.

To produce a report that shows all tables that are related by a primary key/foreign key relationship to a foreign key in a foreign key table within the current database, log on to the SQL Server as any valid database user and enter these commands:

```
1>use NameOfDatabase
2>go
1>sp_fkeys NULL, loginame, NameOfPkDatabase, NameOfFKTable
2>[, NameOfFkTableOwner] , NameOfFkDatabase
```

where:

NameOfPkDatabase—the name of the database that contains the table with the foreign key constraint for which you want a foreign key constraint report produced.

loginame—the name of the owner of the table with the primary key constraint.

NamOfFKTable—the name of the table with the foreign key constraint for which you want a primary key/foreign key relationship constraint report produced.

NameOfFkTableOwner—this optional parameter is used to specify the owner of a table that contains a foreign key constraint that maps to the table with the primary key constraint. If you do not provide this optional parameter, then tables owned by the current log in account will be examined, and then tables owned by the **dbo** will be examined. To complete this analysis, you'll have to work your way through all other accounts in the current database that have **create table** permissions.

NameOfFkDatabase—the name of the database that contains the table with the foreign key constraint.

When the **sp_fkeys** catalog stored procedure completes, the report will show the name of the current database, the name of the owner of the table with the primary key constraint, the name of the table with the primary key constraint, the name of each table column that participates in the primary key, the name of the database that contains the table with the foreign key constraint (this will be the current database as well), the name of the owner of the table with the foreign key constraint, the name of the column that participates in the foreign key constraint, and the sequence number indicating the location of the column within multicolumn foreign keys. If there is action to be taken upon an update, then UPDATE will be displayed; if not, then zero will be displayed, and if there is action to be taken upon a delete, then DELETE will be displayed. If not, then zero (0) will be displayed. However, as the **sp_fkeys** catalog stored procedure updates the database system tables, it cannot be executed from within another transaction.

On-Line Documentation of Table Primary, Foreign, and Common Keys

It is possible, when using the `create table` and `alter table` commands syntax, to construct tables that contain primary and foreign keys without explicitly stating so. For example, you could create a table that implicitly contains a foreign key but not state that referential integrity constraint within the `create table` statement. As a consequence, there would be nothing in the database's system tables that would tell someone that this referential integrity constraint exists within the database. To enhance communication among database users, the SQL Server supports the documentation of primary, foreign, and common keys, as well as the production of reports containing such information.

To document the existence of a primary key constraint that was not explicitly stated in a `create table` or `alter table` command, log on to the SQL Server as the table owner (or as an account with **dbo** or **sa_role** privileges that has taken on the identity of the table owner) and enter these commands:

```
1>use NameOfDatabase
2>go
1>sp_primarykey NameOfTable, NameOfColumn [, NameOfColumn,
  ..., NameOfColumn]
2>go
```

where:

NameOfDatabase—the name of the database that contains the table whose primary key you want to document.

NameOfTable—the name of the table whose primary key you want to document.

NameOfColumn[, NameOfColumn, ..., NameOfColumn]—the list of one or more column names that make up the table's primary key.

Once this command completes successfully, the table's primary key will be recorded within the *syskeys* system table, and it can then be examined by all database users. It is important to realize that the SQL Server will not enforce this primary key constraint on the table. You are merely documenting the fact that it exists. This change takes effect immediately. This command changes the database's system tables, so to ensure its recovery, be certain to dump its transaction log and then dump the database itself. As this command changes the contents of system tables, it cannot be executed within a transaction.

To document the existence of a foreign key constraint that was not explicitly stated in a `create table` or `alter table` command, log on to the SQL Server as the table owner (or as an account with **dbo** or **sa_role** privileges that has taken on the identity of the table owner) and enter these commands:

```
1>use NameOfDatabase
2>go
1>sp_foreignkey NameOfFKTable, NameOfPKTable, NameOfColumn
2>[, NameOfColumn, ..., NameOfColumn]
3>go
```

where:

NameOfDatabase—the name of the database that contains the table whose foreign key you want to document.

NameOfFKTable—the name of the table whose foreign key you want to document.

NameOfPKTable—the name of the table with primary key to which the foreign key corresponds.

NameOfColumn [, *NameOfColumn* , . . . , *NameOfColumn*]—the list of one or more column names that make up the table's foreign key. The foreign key column data types, data type length, order, and count must exactly match the primary key to which they correspond. However, their nullability need not match the primary key.

Once this command completes successfully, the table's foreign key will be recorded within the *syskeys* system table, and it can then be examined by all database users. It is important to realize that the SQL Server will not enforce this foreign key constraint on the table. You are merely documenting the fact that it exists. This change takes effect immediately. This command changes the database's system tables, so to ensure its recovery, be certain to dump its transaction log and then dump the database itself. As this command changes the contents of system tables, it cannot be executed within a transaction.

A common key contains one or more columns that support a join between two tables. To document the existence of a common key constraint, log on to the SQL Server as the table owner (or a **dbo** or an **sa_role** that has taken on the identity of the table owner) and enter these commands:

```
1>use NameOfDatabase
2>go
1>sp_commonkey NameOfTable1, NameOTable2, NameOfColumn1A,
  NewOfColumn2A
2>[, ... NewOfColumn1N, NameOfColumn2N]
3>go
```

where:

NameOfDatabase—the name of the database that contains the common key you want to document.

NameOfTable1—the name of the first table that supports the join.

NameOTable2—the name of the second table that supports the join.

NameOfColumn1A, NewOfColumn2A [, . . . *NewOfColumn1N* , *NameOfColumn2N*]—the list of column pairs that make up the common key.

Once this command completes successfully, the common key will be recorded within the *syskeys* system table, and it can then be examined by all database users. This change takes effect immediately. This command changes the database's system tables; to ensure its recovery, be certain to dump its transaction log and then dump the database itself. As this command changes the contents of system tables, it cannot be executed within a transaction.

Reporting on Primary, Foreign, and Common Keys

Once you've documented these implicit primary, foreign, and common keys, then every user of the database will be able to produce a report of these keys. These reports will go a long way towards helping them (developers in particular) understand the integrity constraints implicit in the database. To produce a report about documented primary, foreign, and common keys, log on to the SQL Server as any valid login account and enter these commands:

```
1>use  NameOfDatabase
2>go
1>sp_helpkey  [NameOfTable]
2>go
```

where:

NameOfDatabase—the name of the database for which you want a primary, foreign, and common key report produced.

[NameOfTable]—use this optional parameter to specify a particular table for which you want a primary, foreign, and common key report produced. If you do not use this optional parameter, then a report that covers all tables (and views) in the database will be produced.

When the command completes, the SQL Server will produce a report containing the primary, foreign, and common keys in the database.

Consider the situation where you'd like to join two tables in a query, but you are uncertain about the common key that may exist between them. To determine which columns to use to support your join, log on to the SQL Server as any valid login account, and enter these commands:

```
1>use  NameOfDatabase
2>go
1>sp_helpjoin  NameOfTable1, NameOfTable2
2>go
```

where:

NameOfDatabase—the name of the database that contains the two tables between which you want to determine if a common key exists.

NameOfTable1—the name of the first table that might support the join.

NameOfTable2—the name of the second table that might support the join.

When the command completes, the SQL Server will produce a report based on documented foreign and common keys in the database, listing the columns that you might be able to use to support your join.

Dropping a Primary, Foreign, or Common Key

Over time, you'll probably have to purge the syskeys of incorrectly documented primary, foreign, and common keys. To accomplish this task, log on to the SQL Server as the table owner (or as an account with **dbo** or **sa_role** privileges that has taken on the identity of the table owner), and enter these commands:

```
1>use  NameOfDatabase
2>go
1>sp_dropkey { primary | foreign | common },     NameOfTable
   [, NameOfFKTable]
2>go
```

where:

NameOfDatabase—the name of the database that contains the documented key you want to purge from the *systypes* system table.

{ primary | foreign | common }—this parameter has three (3) valid choices: primary, foreign, or common. You must choose one.

NameOfTable—if you are dropping a primary key, then this is the name of the table that contains the primary key. The SQL Server will automatically purge any documented foreign key that corresponds to this primary key.

[, *NameOfFKTable*]—if you are dropping a primary key, then you do not use this optional parameter. If you dropped a foreign or a common key, then this is the name of the second table in the relationship. If you are dropping a foreign key, then this is the name of the table that contains the corresponding primary key. If you are dropping a common key, then this will be the second table as reported in the **sp_helpkey** report.

Once this command completes successfully, the key will be purged from the *syskeys* system table. This change takes effect immediately. This command changes the database's system tables; to ensure its recovery, be certain to dump its transaction log and then dump the database itself. As this command changes the contents of system tables, it cannot be executed within a transaction.

Changing the Name of a Table Column

If you do not like the name of a table column, don't worry; you can always change it—carefully, that is. If you change the name of a table column, then all triggers, stored procedures, and views that reference the table column will continue to work until the point in time when they are recompiled. So before you go ahead and change the name of a table column, log on to the SQL Server and enter these commands:

```
1>use NameOfDatabase
2>go
1>sp_depends [loginame.]NameOfTable
2>go
```

where:

NameOfDatabase—the name of the database that contains the table whose dependencies you want to inspect.

[loginame.]—the name of the Sybase account that owns the table. If you are the owner of the table, then you do not have to provide this parameter.

NameOfTable—the name of the table whose dependencies you want to inspect. If the table is not owned by you, then you will have to put the login name and table name inside quotes (" ").

The displayed report will list the triggers, stored procedures, and views within the current database that depend on the table whose column name you intend to change, or it will notify you that there are no such dependencies. Each object that depends on this table will have to be dropped, modified to reference the new column name, and re-created, and then have appropriate permissions granted once again. This report will not inform you of objects that depend on this table but that were created before the table was created, nor will it inform you of objects outside the current database that depend on this table. The SQL Server does not eliminate the need for good database documentation.

So, after you have completed your impact assessment, if you want to change the name of a table column, log on to the SQL Server as the table owner (or as an account with **dbo** or **sa_role** privileges that has taken on the identity of the table owner) and enter these commands:

```
1>use NameOfDatabase
2>go
1>sp_rename "NameOfTable.NameOfColumn", NewNameOfColumn
2>go
```

where:

NameOfDatabase—the name of the database that contains the table whose column name you want to change.

NameOfTable—the name of the table whose column name you want to change.

NameOfColumn—this is the name that you want to change. The table name and column names must be enclosed in quotes ("").

NewNameOfColumn—the new name that you want the table column to have. The name of each column in a table must be unique within that table. The name must conform to the rules governing SQL Server identifiers. If, in your current session, you have entered the command `set quoted_identifier on`, then you can use a delimited identifier for the name of the column. However, in that case you would have to enclose the column name in double quotes ("").

Once this command completes successfully, the table column can only be referenced by its new name. This change takes effect immediately. This command changes the database's system tables; to ensure its recovery, be certain to dump its transaction log and then dump the database itself. As this command changes the contents of system tables, it cannot be executed within a transaction.

Changing the Name of a Table

You can always change the name of a table. If you change the name of a table, then all triggers, stored procedures, and views that reference the table will continue to work until the point in time when they are recompiled. So before you go ahead and change the name of a table, log on to the SQL Server and execute these commands:

```
1>use NameOfDatabase
2>go
1>sp_depends [loginame.]NameOfTable
2>go
```

where:

NameOfDatabase—the name of the database that contains the table whose dependencies you want to inspect.

[loginame.]—the name of the Sybase account that owns the table. If you are the owner of the table, then you do not have to provide this parameter.

NameOfTable—the name of the table whose dependencies you want to inspect. If the table is not owned by you, then you will have to put the login name and table name inside quotes (" ").

The displayed report will list the triggers, stored procedures, and views within the current database that depend on the table whose name you intend to change, or it will notify you that there are no such dependencies. Each object that depends on this table will have to be dropped, modified to reference the new table name, and re-created and then have appropriate permissions granted once again. This report will not inform you of objects that depend on this table but that were created before the table was created, nor will it inform you of objects outside the current database that depend on this table. The SQL Server does not eliminate the need for good database documentation.

So, after you have completed your impact assessment, if you want to change the name of a table, log on to the SQL Server as the table owner (or as an account with **dbo** or **sa_role** privileges that has taken on the identity of the table owner), and enter these commands:

```
1>use  NameOfDatabase
2>go
1>sp_rename  NameOfTable ,  NewNameOfTable
2>go
```

where:

NameOfDatabase—the name of the database that contains the table whose name you want to change.

NameOfTable—the name of the table whose name you want to change.

NewNameOfTable—this is the new name that you want the table to have. The name of each table in a database must be unique to the owner within that database. The name must conform to the rules governing SQL Server identifiers and cannot begin with the "#" symbol. If, in your current session, you have entered the command set quoted_identifier on, then you can use a delimited identifier for the name of the column. However, in that case you would have to enclose the column name in double quotes (" ").

Once this command completes successfully, the table can only be referenced by its new name. This change takes effect immediately. This command changes the database's system tables; to ensure its recovery, be certain to dump its transaction log and then dump the database itself. As this command changes the contents of system tables, it cannot be executed within a transaction.

Granting Access Permission to a Table

If you are an account with **dbo** or **sa_role** privileges, you can grant permission to database users, groups, or roles to access a table you own. If you are a database user and you have permission to both create tables and grant access permissions, then you can grant permission to other database users, groups, or roles to access tables that you own.

The SQL Server supports five table-access permissions:

1. *Delete.*   Lets you delete data rows from the table.
2. *Insert.*   Lets you insert new data rows into the table.
3. *References.*   Lets you create referential integrity constraints on another table that reference any column in this table.
4. *Select.*   Lets you read data rows.
5. *Update.*   Lets you update the literal data values of data contained in data rows.

The SQL Server supports three table-access permissions that are specific to a subset of table columns:

1. *References.*   Lets you create referential integrity constraints on another table that reference a subset of columns in this table.
2. *Select.*   Lets you read a subset of columns in this table.
3. *Update.*   Lets you update the literal data values of data contained in a subset of columns in this table.

To grant access permission to a table, log on to the SQL Server as the owner of the table (or as an account with **dbo** or **sa_role** privileges that has taken on the identity of the table owner) and enter these commands:

```
1>use NameOfDatabase
2>go
1>grant {all | permission_list}
2>on { NameOfTable
3>to {public | name_list | role_name}
4>[with grant option]
5>go
```

where:

NameOfDatabase—the name of the database that contains the table for which you want to grant access permission.

{all | permission_list}—if you specify "all," then you will be granting delete, insert, references, select, and update permissions. If you want to grant a subset of these permissions, then specify a comma-delimited list of permissions you are granting.

on { *NameOfTable*—the name of the table for which you want to grant access permissions.

to {public | name_list | role_name}—you can grant access permissions to the public group, to a list of database users and groups, or to a list of roles.

[with grant option]—this optional parameter allows a user (not a group or role) to grant the access permissions to other users, groups, or roles.

Once this command completes successfully, the login account is immediately capable of exercising its access rights within the database. This change takes effect immediately. This command changes the database's system tables; to ensure its recovery, be certain to dump its transaction log and then dump the database itself. As this command changes the contents of system tables, it cannot be executed within a transaction.

To grant access permission to a subset of columns in a table, log on to the SQL Server as the owner of the table (or as an account with **dbo** or **sa_role** privileges that has taken on the identity of the table owner) and enter these commands:

```
1>use NameOfDatabase
2>go
1>grant {all | permission_list}
2>on { NameOfTable (column_list)
3>to {public | name_list | role_name}
4>[with grant option]
5>go
```

where:

NameOfDatabase—the name of the database that contains the table for which you want to grant access permission.

{all | permission_list}—if you specify "all," then you will be granting references, select, and update permissions. If you want to grant a subset of these permissions, then specify a comma-delimited subset of permissions.

on { *NameOfTable* (column_list)—the list of columns in the table for which you want to grant access permissions. If you want to grant access to more than one column, then specify a comma-delimited subset of column names.

to {public | name_list | role_name}—you can grant access permissions to the public group, to a list of database users and groups, or to a list of roles.

[with grant option]—this optional parameter allows a user (not a group or role) to grant the access permissions to other users, groups, or roles.

Once this command completes successfully, the login account is immediately capable of exercising its access rights within the database. This change takes effect immediately. This command changes the database's system tables, so to ensure its recovery, be certain to dump its transaction log and then dump the database itself. As this command changes the contents of system tables, it cannot be executed within a transaction.

Reporting on Table Permissions

The SQL Server provides you with three tools to report on table permission on a given table:

1. **sp_helprotect**
2. **sp_table_privileges**
3. **sp_column_privileges**

To produce a report of all permissions on a table, log on to the SQL Server as any valid login account and enter these commands:

```
1>use NameOfDatabase
2>go
1>sp_helprotect NameOfTable [, loginame]
2>go
```

where:

NameOfDatabase—the name of the database that contains the table for which you want a report on access permission.

NameOfTable—the name of the table for which you want a report on access permission.

[, loginame]—this optional parameter is the name of a given user of the database. If you elect to use this optional parameter, then the report will contain only this user's access permissions to the specified table.

When the **sp_helprotect** system procedure completes, the report will show the name of the grantor, the grantee, whether the permission is granted or revoked, the access privilege for each table column, the name of the table, the name of each column, and whether or not the grantee can grant access permission in turn.

To produce a report of all permissions on a table, log on to the SQL Server as any valid login account and enter these commands:

```
1>use NameOfDatabase
2>go
1>sp_table_privileges NameOfTable, loginame, NameOfDatabase
2>go
```

where:

NameOfDatabase—the name of the database that contains the table for which you want a report on access permission.

NameOfTable—this is the name of the table for which you want a report on access permission. This cannot be a temporary table.

loginame—the name of the table owner.

When the sp_table_privileges catalog stored procedure completes, the report will show the name of the grantor, the grantee, whether the permission is granted or revoked, the access privilege for each table column, the name of the table, the name of each column, and whether or not the grantee can grant access permission in turn. However, as the sp_table_privileges catalog stored procedure updates the database system tables, it cannot be executed from within another transaction.

To produce a report of all permissions on a table column, log on to the SQL Server as any valid login account and enter these commands:

```
1>use NameOfDatabase
2>go
1>sp_column_privileges NameOfTable, loginame, NameOfDatabase,
  NameOfColumn
2>go
```

where:

NameOfDatabase—the name of the database that contains the table for which you want a report on access permission.

on { *NameOfTable* (column_list)—the list of columns in the table for which you want to revoke access permissions. If you want to revoke access to more than one column, then specify a comma-delimited subset of column names.

to {public | name_list | role_name}—you can revoke access permissions to the public group, to a list of database users and groups, or to a list of roles.

[cascade]—if a user has been granted permission to grant access privileges to tables they own, then this optional parameter revokes access privileges they have granted on their tables to other users, groups, or roles.

Once this command completes successfully, the login account is immediately incapable of exercising its previous access rights within the database. This change takes effect immediately. This command changes the database's system tables; to ensure its recovery, be certain to dump its transaction log and then dump the database itself. As this command changes the contents of system tables, it cannot be executed within a transaction.

ting an Unpartitioned Table

The SQL Server provides you with two methods for purging data rows from a table:

1. The delete command without a **where** clause. When you run the delete command, a log record for each data row is written into the database's transaction log. Depending on the amount of data rows in the table and the size of the database's transaction log, this method can fill a transaction log with delete log records. This command will work on both partitioned and unpartitioned tables.

2. The truncate table command. When you run the truncate table command, data-row-log records are not written to the transaction log. Instead, deallocation log records for data and index pages are written to the transaction log. As a consequence, the truncate table command will run significantly faster than the delete command without the risk of filling the transaction log. However, because deleted data-row log records are not written to the transaction log, the truncate table command cannot fire a table's delete trigger. This command will only work on unpartitioned tables.

To truncate a table, log on to the SQL Server as the table owner (or a **dbo** or an **sa_role** that has taken on the identity of the table owner) and enter these commands:

```
1>use NameOfDatabase
2>go
1>truncate table [[NameOfDatabase.] loginame.] NameOfTable
2>go
```

where:

NameOfDatabase—this optional parameter is the name of the database that contains the table that you want to truncate. If the table is located in the current database, then you do not have to provide this parameter.

`loginame`—this optional parameter is the name of the table owner. If you are the owner of the table, then you do not have to provide this parameter.

NameOfTable—the name of the table that you want to truncate.

If you intend to truncate the *sysaudits* table, then you must be the **sso_role.**

Dropping an Unpartitioned User Table

When an unpartitioned user table is no longer needed, it can be destroyed. When you destroy a table, you also destroy all indexes, triggers, and permissions based on it, and links between it and defaults and rules are broken. If the table is referenced by another table, then you must destroy such references using the `alter table` command. If you wish to destroy a partitioned table, then you must unpartition it first, using the `alter table` command.

To drop an unpartitioned user table (or collection of unpartitioned user tables), log on to the SQL Server as the table owner (or as an account with **dbo** or **sa_role** privileges that has taken on the identity of the table owner) and enter these commands:

```
1>use NameOfDatabase
2>go
1>drop table [[NameOfDatabase.] loginame.] NameOfTable [,
2>[[NameOfDatabase.] loginame.] NameOfTable ]...
3>go
```

where:

NameOfDatabase—this optional parameter is the name of the database that contains the table that you want to drop. If the table is located in the current database, then you do not have to provide this parameter.

loginame—this optional parameter is the name of the table owner. If you are the owner of the table, then you do not have to provide this parameter.

NameOf Table—the name of the table that you want to drop.

Once this command completes successfully, the table will be dropped from the database. This change takes effect immediately. This command changes the database's system tables; to ensure its recovery, be certain to dump its transaction log and then dump the database itself. As this command changes the contents of system tables, it cannot be executed within a transaction.

Revoking Permission to Create Tables

To revoke the permission to create tables to a user, a list of users, the groups (including the **public** group), or a role, log on to the SQL Server as an account with **dbo** or **sa_role** privileges and enter these commands:

```
1>use NameOf Database
2>go
1>revoke create table
2>from {public | name_list | role_name}
3>[cascade]
4>go
```

where:

NameOf Database—the name of the database in which you want to revoke permission to create tables from a user, from a list of users, from the groups (including the public group), or from a role.

{public | name_list | role_name}—the user, list of users, group, or role for which you want to revoke create table permission.

[cascade]—this optional parameter is to be used only if the permission that granted table creation also permitted the table owners to grant access permissions to their tables to other users in the database. When used, this parameter will revoke access permission to other users in the database that were granted to them by the user, list of users, group, or role whose permission to create tables is being revoked.

Once this command completes successfully, the login account is immediately incapable of creating tables within the database. This change takes effect immediately. This command changes the database's system tables; to ensure its recovery, be certain to dump its transaction log and then dump the database itself. As this command changes the contents of system tables, it cannot be executed within a transaction.

Indexes

Indexes are distinct storage structures that allow rapid access to information stored on data pages. An index can speed up data access because, fundamentally, it is a logical pointer to the exact data page that contains the information you are searching for (this is the case with a clustered index; however, a nonclustered index also includes the data row identifier).

It is on the index pages where index rows are recorded or entered. Each index row, or entry, contains the literal data values of the key columns that make up the index, the associated data page logical pointer, and, where applicable, the data row identifiers. A key column is a column within a table that declares or participates in the declaration of a given index. At minimum, the declaration of an index includes one or more table column names.

Internally, the SQL Server builds a dedicated B-Tree (binary tree) structure to store and manage each user-defined index. The B-Tree structure has been enhanced to support the growth of the index and is populated with index pages. The SQL Server uses B-Tree search algorithms to scan index pages for matching data page identifiers (and data row identifiers when applicable) based on the literal data values of key columns addressed by a submitted query.

Whenever a B-Tree search is conducted, the SQL Server analyzes the index row located in the middle of the index page. If that row is a match, then the search stops. However, if the row is not a match, then the index page is halved and the B-Tree search continues in the direction indicated by the key column comparison.

An index B-Tree is a special type of balanced, multileveled data structure that is comprised of three separate sections:

1. A single index root page that is your entry way into the index. The index root page contains the first and last entry in the index. The page identifier of the index root page is stored within `sysindexes.. root`. Each database you create contains its own *sysindexes* system table.

2. The index node pages make up the binary tree itself. The index node pages are sometimes called intermediate pages because they exist between the top of the B-Tree, which is the index root page, and bottom of the B-Tree, which are the index leaf pages. Every entry in an

index node page contains the number of the previous and the next index page in the page chain; these numbers are the index page pointers. Therefore, each index node page participates in a (doubly linked) index page chain. Each given index page chain, within a given index, is called an index level. By default, the SQL Server automatically assigns the number 0 to the bottom, or lowest, index level. As the index is traversed from the bottom level to the top level, or root, the numbers automatically assigned to the index level increase monotonically (i.e., 0, 1, 2, 3, . . .). The page identifier of the first index node page of the lowest level index page chain is stored within *sysindexes..first*.

3. The index leaf pages are index pages at the lowest index level. Index leaf pages are always stored in index sequence sort order.

A B-Tree is a "balanced" data structure because all index leaf pages are the same distance from the index root page. The distance between the index root page and all associated index leaf pages is automatically maintained by the SQL Server whenever a new index row is added to the index or whenever an existing index row is deleted from the index.

Without getting into a discussion of the use of indexes, two basic types of indexes are supported by the SQL Server.

1. *Clustered*—enforces a user-defined physical sorted order to the placement of data rows within data pages. As a consequence of the clustered index's ability to impose by force the placement of data rows, there can be one and only one clustered index per table. If a table lacks a clustered index, then its data rows are not distributed across a B-Tree structure but are, instead, stored in a heap structure. Every table that has a clustered index will have a data row in *sysindexes* where the *indid* column's literal data value has been set to 1. The intermediate level index pages, or index leaf pages, contain logical pointers to data pages. Within the intermediate level index pages of a clustered index, there is one and only one entry for each data page in the table. At the leaf level of the clustered index are data pages. In that only the first data row of each data page in the table has a logical pointer in an index page, a clustered index is sometimes referred to as a sparse index.

2. *Nonclustered*—enforces a user-defined physical sorted order to the key columns that make up the nonclustered index. However, the placement of data rows within the data pages is *not* physically ordered by a nonclustered index. A given table can have up to 249 nonclustered indexes associated with it. Every table that has a nonclustered index will have a data row in *sysindexes* where the *indid* column's literal data value has been set to be greater than 1. The lowest level index pages, or index leaf pages, contain logical pointers to each data row within the

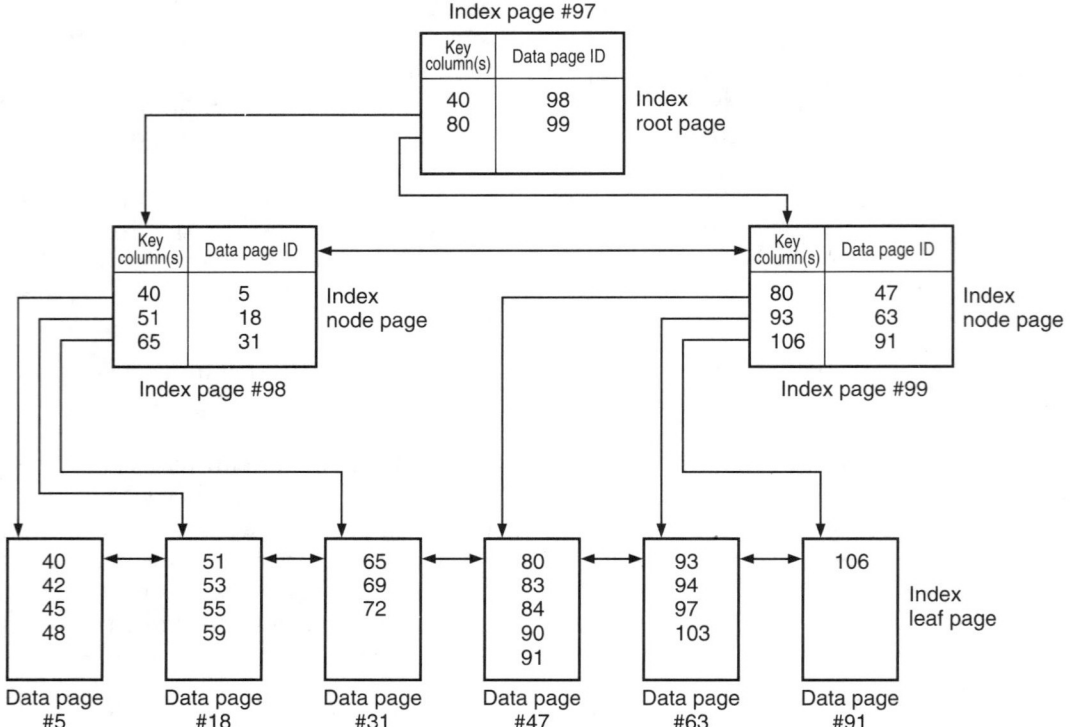

Figure 8.1 Detail of unique clustered index.

table's data pages. In that each data row on each data page in the table has a logical pointer in an index page, a nonclustered index is sometimes referred to as a dense index.

In addition to their ability to regulate (in the case of clustered indexes) the distribution of data rows within data pages, indexes can be used to impose data row uniqueness within a table. When you define an index to be unique, the SQL Server ensures that two or more data rows with identical key columns will not be placed within a given table. When used in this way, indexes serve as a data integrity tool.

To simplify scanning, space on the index page is used contiguously. If an index row is deleted or inserted on an index page, other index rows will be moved to keep the space contiguous.

Like all database servers, your choice of data type has a significant impact on performance. Specifically, the use of variable length data types, such as varchar, seriously extends index search time for the SQL Server. Index pages, unlike the data page, do not contain an offset table

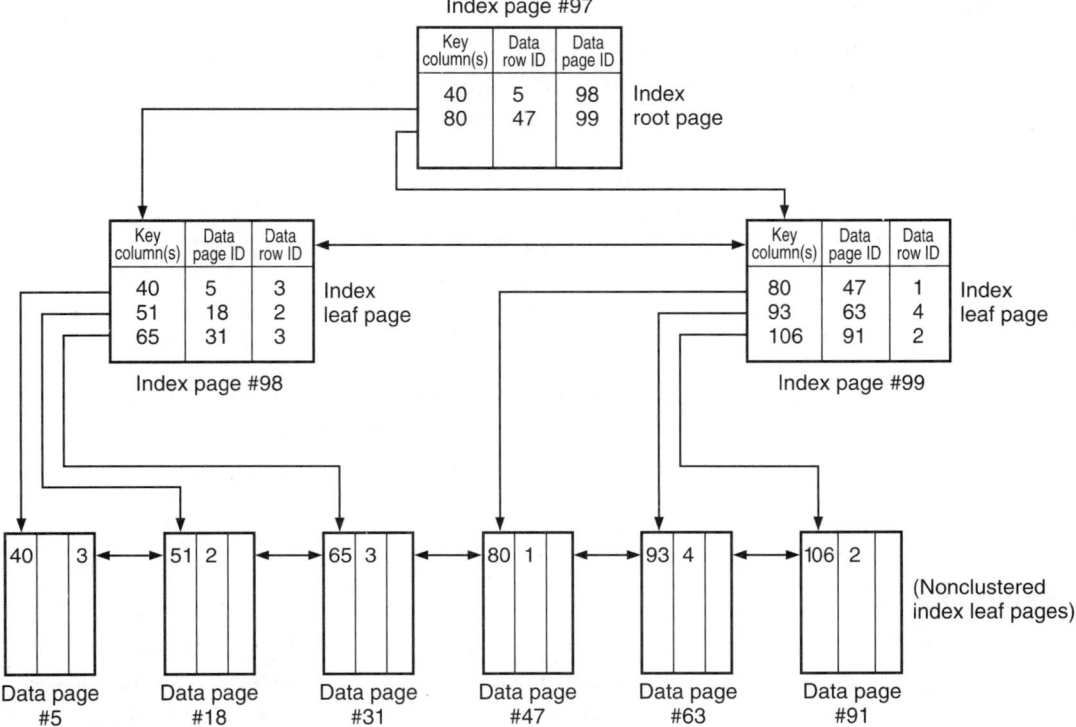

Figure 8.2 Detail of unique nonclustered index.

of index row numbers. As a result, whenever an index contains variable length key columns, the SQL Server must use a sliding binary search. With this variation of a binary search, if there is space available on the index page located in the cache, then the bottom of that index page is used to store a binary search table. But, if that index page does not have space available on it, then the SQL Server has to create an internal index row offset table within which it performs a binary search. It is the run-time construction of these offset tables that significantly contributes to query performance degradation.

In that nonclustered indexes contain the data page and data row identifiers, any inserting or deleting of data rows forces the updating of nonclustered index leaf pages. Updating of the nonclustered index must take place, or else the nonclustered index would become inconsistent, thereby totally defeating its purpose. Therefore, because of the need to maintain consistency, the use of nonclustered indexes will, whenever row insertion or deletion occurs, introduce (potentially significant) SQL Server overhead.

Reporting on Table Indexes

The SQL Server can provide you with a report of all indexes associated with a specific table. To examine a table's indexes, log on to the SQL Server as any valid login account and enter these commands:

```
1>use NameOfDatabase
2>go
1>sp_helpindex NameOfTable
2>go
```

where:

NameOfDatabase—the name of the database that contains the table for which you want a report of its indexes produced.

NameOfTable—the name of the table for which you want a report of its indexes produced.

Creating an Index

The SQL Server provides an alternative method to the `create table` and the `alter table` commands for creating clustered and nonclustered indexes called the `create index` command. Now, before you go ahead and create an index, keep these thoughts in mind:

1. Index common keys that support active joins.

2. While indexes do significantly speed up select statements, they also have a dark side to them (i.e., the SQL Server has to manage keeping the indexes up to date when inserts, deletes, and update statements change the tables they are based on). As a consequence, the performance of insert, delete, and update statements can degrade.

3. When possible, create nonclustered indexes on segments (and disk drives) that are physically separate from the table (and its clustered index, if applicable). Doing this will give you the highest possible level of performance.

4. When a clustered index is created, the SQL Server automatically makes a duplicate copy of the data, builds the clustered index using that duplicate copy, and, when the clustered index is finished being built, deletes the original data. So, if your table contains data, use the `sp_spaceused` system procedure to determine its current size. Then make certain that you have allocated and unused database device resources that are at least 120 percent of the reserved table space to support the creation of the clustered index.

5. When you create a clustered index, all nonclustered indexes on the table will automatically be re-created by the SQL Server. So, if you are going to create a suite of indexes on the same table, create the clustered index first.

6. Consider creating a 16K Memory Pool to speed up the creation of the index.

7. Don't forget, you cannot create a clustered index on a partitioned table (and you cannot partition a table that has a clustered index).

To create a table index, log on to the SQL Server as the table owner (or as an account with **dbo** or **sa_role** privileges that has taken on the identity of the table owner) and enter these commands:

```
1>use NameOfDatabase
2>go
1>create [unique]
2>[clustered | nonclustered]
3>index NameOfIndex
4>on [[NameOfDatabase.] loginame.] NameOfTable (NameOfColumn
5>[,NameOfColumn]...)
6>[with {{fillfactor | max_rows_per_page}= x,
7>ignore_dup_key,
8>sorted_data,
9>[ignore_dup_row | allow_dup_row]}]
10>[on NameOfSegment]
11>go
```

where:

NameOfDatabase—the name of the database that will contain the index you are creating.

create [unique]—this optional parameters ensures that no two rows in the table will have the same literal data value stored in this table. It is important to realize that one or more columns in a given table can have this type of column constraint specified. When more than one column has this constraint specified, the SQL Server manages them as a group of columns and ensures that the combination of literal data values stored in the group are always unique. By default, the SQL Server will create a unique nonclustered index when this optional parameter is used. If you specify that the index is unique, then none of the columns of which the index is composed can allow the NULL value. If any one of them allows the NULL value, the create index command will fail when unique is specified. Also, if the table contains data and if there are duplicate rows in that table, then any attempt to create a unique index will fail when the first duplicate row is encountered.

[clustered | nonclustered]—these two optional parameters are mutually exclusive.

where:

clustered—specifies that the unique index based on the unique constraint specification for this index will be clustered. There can be one and only one clustered index for a given table.

nonclustered—specifies that the unique index based on the unique constraint specification for this table will be nonclustered. There can be up to 249 nonclustered indexes for a given table. This is the default for the unique constraint.

index *NameOfIndex*—the name that you want the new index to have. The name must conform to the rules governing SQL Server identifiers and must be unique to the table.

on [[*NameOfDatabase*,] loginame.] *NameOfTable* (*NameOfColumn*—it is possible to use one database and create an index in another database. It is also possible, if you logged on to the SQL Server as an account with **dbo** or **sa_role** privileges, to create a table that will be owned by another Sybase Account.

where:

NameOfDatabase—the name of the database in which you want the index to be created. If you want the index to be created in the current database, then you do not have to provide this optional parameter.

loginame—the name of the Sybase account that owns the table. If you are the owner of the table, then you do not have to provide this optional parameter.

NameOfTable—the name of the table for which you are creating the new index.

NameOfColumn—the name of the first column that makes up the index. Columns of data type bit, text, or image cannot be used to create an index.

[,*NameOfColumn*]...)—this is the sorted order list of the other column's names of which the new index is composed. An index can be composed of one through sixteen columns. However, the maximum length of an index row cannot exceed 256 bytes.

[with {{fillfactor | max_rows_per_page}= x,—these optional parameters are mutually exclusive and impact the indexes created by the unique constraint specifications.

fillfactor = x—this optional parameter specifies the percentage of each index page that will be filled with index rows when the index is first created using the data that currently exists within the table. If not supplied, then the fill factor value as determined by the default fill factor percent **SQL Server configuration** parameter will be used.

max_rows_per_page = x—this optional parameter establishes the maximum number of rows the SQL Server will store on leaf-level pages of indexes that support this table for the life of the table. If you do not specify a value for max_rows_per_page, then the SQL Server default (0) is used and data pages and leaf pages of nonclustered indexes will be filled, but a suitable amount of space within the index B-tree structure will be retained in both clustered and nonclustered indexes. For leaf pages, the range of legal values for the max_rows_per_page parameter is 0 through 256. However, if only 50 rows can fit on a page and you set the max_rows_per_page parameter to a value greater than 50, the create table command will complete successfully; but once you insert 50 rows into the table, you will not be able to insert any more. So be absolutely certain that the value of the max_rows_per_page parameter is not greater than the table row length dictates. For nonclustered indexes, the minimum value of the max_rows_per_page parameter is zero, while its maximum value depends on the size of the nonclustered index key. To determine the maximum value of the max_rows_per_page parameter for nonclustered indexes, use this formula: [(page size − page header size)/min. index row length]. This parameter is typically used to decrease the number of rows per page. You may want to decrease the number of rows per page to minimize contention between transactions that modify the pages (inserts, deletes, and updates) and transactions that read pages by spreading the rows across more pages. In addition, decreasing the number of rows per page increases the chances of direct updates occurring within tables that contain variable length columns. Also, when the value of the max_rows_per_page parameter is set to one, you can simulate row-level locking. (However, when deleting the last row on a page, locks will still be taken on the page and on the pages that surround it.) Decreasing the number of rows per page has its negative aspects. On the downside, the number of index levels will increase; if there are a lot of inserts and deletes, then page splits and page shrinks will increase; and more disk space will be consumed, driving up disk I/O rates and decreasing read and write operation performance. It is not a good idea to use the max_rows_per_page parameter if the table will be supporting only read operations, if table scans are being performed on the table, if multiple rows are typically referenced, or if the structure will support a lot of insert or delete transactions. The value of the `max_rows_per_page` parameter specified for a clustered index will override the value of the `max_rows_per_page` parameter specified at the end of the `create table` statement.

`ignore_dup_key`—if you use this optional parameter, and you have specified that the index will be unique, then any insert that contains a duplicate key will be allowed to complete successfully. However, the SQL Server will return a message to that effect. If you use this optional parameter, and you have specified that the index will be unique, then any update that produces a duplicate key will not be allowed to complete successfully, and the SQL Server will return an error message to that effect.

`sorted_data`—use this optional parameter to speed up the insertion of data that is in the sorted order specified in the index column listing. If you use this optional parameter to create the index and then try to load unsorted data into the table, that load will fail.

`[ignore_dup_row | allow_dup_row]}]`—these options are mutually exclusive and can only be used if you are creating a nonunique clustered index.

where:

`ignore_dup_row`—this optional parameter is used to remove duplicate rows from a batch of data being inserted into the table. When this optional parameter is used on nonunique clustered indexes, any insert or update statement that would create a duplicate data row is canceled, but the rest of the batch can continue on.

`allow_dup_row`—this optional parameter allows you to create a nonunique clustered index on a table that does not already have a unique index and that contains duplicate data rows. When this optional parameter is used, you insert and update statements that will create duplicate data rows.

`[on NameOfSegment]`—this optional parameter specifies the segment upon which the index will be created. The specified segment must exist and must be added to the current database before it can be referenced here. If the index being created is a clustered index, then all data pages will reside on the same segment as the clustered index. If you do not use this optional parameter, then the index will be created on the **default** segment. Because data rows move to the site where the clustered index resides, dropping and recreating a table's clustered index on a different segment is an easy way to move the table's data from its current location to a new home.

This change takes effect immediately. This command changes the database's system tables; to ensure its recovery, be certain to dump its transaction log and then dump the database itself. As this command changes the contents of system tables, it cannot be executed within a transaction.

Maintaining Index Statistics

The SQL Server uses a statistical query optimizer to determine the "best" access method to your data. To enhance query optimizer performance, the SQL Server produces key value distribution statistics for indexes. Each index has a distribution page linked to it, on which key value distribution statistics are stored. The query optimizer examines these key value distribution statistics on the indexes distribution page when determining which index to use to support a given query. However, the only key values for which distribution statistics are produced by the SQL Server are those for the first column in the key. So, for those indexes that are composite keys, there are no distribution statistics available to the query optimizer for columns two through N (bummer).

When you create an index on a table that contains data, the SQL Server automatically produces the key value distribution statistics for that index. Unfortunately, as data is subsequently inserted, deleted, and updated, the key value distribution statistics are not automatically updated by the SQL Server. As a consequence, the quality of the key value distribution statistics deteriorates over time. Just how well your query is optimized is directly dependent on the quality of these key value distribution statistics. When you consider the fact that it takes machine cycles and likely disk I/O to keep the key value distributions statistics up to date, if they were maintained in a real-time manner, the performance of your insert and delete transactions would degrade (remember, the relational model states do not update key values).

Periodically, the need will arise to update key value distribution statistics for the first column of an index. To accomplish this maintenance task, log on to the SQL Server as the table owner (or as an account with **dbo** or **sa_role** privileges that has taken on the identity of the table owner) and enter these commands:

```
1>use NameOfDatabase
2>go
1>update statistics NameOfTable [NameOfIndex]
2>go
```

where:

NameOfDatabase—the name of the database that contains the indexes whose statistics you want to update.

NameOfTable—the name of the table whose index statistics you want to update.

[*NameOfIndex*]—this optional parameter is the name of the index for which you want key value distribution statistics updated. If you do not use this optional parameter, then all indexes for the specified table will have their key value distribution statistics updated.

When this command completes successfully, a new index distribution page will be constructed, and the distribution column in the database's *sysindexes* system table will be updated to point the index's new distribution page. In addition, the internal allocation page value that is used to estimate the count of rows contained in a table will be updated as well. This change takes effect immediately. This command changes the database's system tables, so, to ensure its recovery, be certain to dump its transaction log and then the database itself. As this command changes the contents of system tables, it cannot be executed within a transaction.

Checking the Consistency of an Index

Just like a system table and a user table, the consistency of an index needs to be verified periodically. The **dbcc indexalloc** utility runs these checks on a user table index to ensure that it is consistent as regards:

1. All pages, of all types, are accurately allocated.

2. No page is allocated that is not being used.

3. No page that is being used is not allocated.

As system table indexes are automatically checked and rebuilt if necessary, when the SQL Server is started, you do not check system table index consistency. To run the **dbcc indexalloc** utility on user tables, log on to the SQL Server as an account with **dbo** or **sa_role** privileges, and enter these commands:

```
1>dbcc indexalloc({NameOfTable | table_id} index_id [, {
  full | optimized | fast | null}[, fix | nofix]])
2>go
```

where:

{*NameOfTable* |table_id}—the name, or ID, of the table whose consistency you want to check. If an account with **dbo** or **sa_role** privileges is checking a table owned by another database user, then prefix the name, or ID, of the table with the table owner name and enclose this parameter in quotes (""). If you want to check an index that is not in the current database, then prefix the table name with the database name and the table owner name, and enclose this parameter in quotes (""). (To find the ID of the table, select id from sysobjects where name = *NameOfTable*.)

index_id—the ID of the index whose consistency you want to check. To find the ID of the index, select indid from sysindexes where name = *NameOfIndex*.

{full | optimized | fast | null}—this parameter specifies the type of report that the utility will create. A full report will contain all types of allocation errors. An optimized report will contain information about allocation pages in the index's OAM pages. An optimized report does not report on extents on allocation pages that are not listed in an OAM page, nor will it automatically fix unreferenced extents. The optimized report is the default report that this utility produces if you do not specify a report type or use NULL. If you specify a fast report, this utility will produce an exception report that lists pages that are referenced but that are not allocated in an extent. Using the full report type will result in more repairs being done than if you specify optimized or fast report types. If you specify fix, then the report will contain the problems uncovered and the description of the actions taken to correct the problems.

fix | nofix—specifies whether or not this utility fixes allocation errors uncovered in this index. The default is to fix automatically all user table indexes but not system table indexes. If you are going to fix the corrupted index, then the database must be in single user mode. You can specify fix or nofix only if you also specify the type of report this utility produces.

The SQL Server will produce a report of this consistency check, and it will produce error messages of any inconsistency it encounters. If SQL Server memory has been configured to support extent I/O work buffers, the **dbcc indexalloc** facility will use them to complete its work at a significantly faster rate. This change takes effect immediately. This command changes the database's system tables; to ensure its recovery, be certain to dump its transaction log and then dump the database itself. As this command changes the contents of system tables, it cannot be executed within a transaction.

Changing the Name of an Index

If you do not like the name of an index, no problem; you can always change it. So, if you want to change the name of an index, log on to the SQL Server as the table owner (or as an account with **dbo** or **sa_role** privileges that has taken on the identity of the table owner) and enter these commands:

```
1>use  NameOfDatabase
2>go
1>sp_rename  "NameOfTable.NameOfIndex" ,  NewNameOfIndex
2>go
```

where:

NameOfDatabase—the name of the database that contains the index whose name you want to change.

NameOfTable.NameOfIndex—the name of the index whose name you want to change.

NewNameOfIndex—the new name that you want the index to have. The name of each index for a table must be unique for that table. The name must conform to the rules governing SQL Server identifiers.

This change takes effect immediately. This command changes the database's system tables; to ensure its recovery, be certain to dump its transaction log and then dump the database itself. As this command changes the contents of system tables, it cannot be executed within a transaction.

Dropping an Index

Over time, you may need to destroy an index on a user table. But, before you go ahead and destroy an index, keep these facts in mind:

1. You cannot drop an index that is being used by an open cursor. So, before you try to drop an index, execute the **sp_cursorinfo** system procedure to get a report on all active cursors.

2. If the index was created as a `unique constraint` via the `create table` or the `alter table` commands, then the only way it can be destroyed is by using the **drop constraint** clause of the `alter table` command (or by dropping the table itself).

3. You cannot drop indexes on system tables.

4. When you drop an index, the `max_rows_per_page` value reverts to zero.

To drop a user table index (or collection of indexes), log on to the SQL Server as the table owner (or as an account with **dbo** or **sa_role** privileges that has taken on the identity of the table owner) and enter these commands:

```
1>use NameOfDatabase
2>go
1>drop index [[NameOfDatabase.] loginame.] NameOfTable.
  NameOfIndex[,
2>[[NameOfDatabase,] loginame.] NameOfTable.NameOfIndex]...
3>go
```

where:

NameOfDatabase—this optional parameter is the name of the database that contains the index that you want to drop. If the index is located in the current database, then you do not have to provide this parameter.

`loginame`—this optional parameter is the name of the table owner. If you are the owner of the table, then you do not have to provide this parameter.

NameOfTable.*NameOfIndex*—the name of the index that you want to drop.

Once this command completes successfully, the index will be dropped from the database, and all the space it used will become available to other objects in the database. This change takes effect immediately. This command changes the database's system tables; to ensure its recovery, be certain to dump its transaction log and then dump the database itself. As this command changes the contents of system tables, it cannot be executed within a transaction.

Advanced Techniques for Placing Data on User-Defined Segments

In this section we will explore two advanced techniques for explicitly locating data on user-defined segments:

1. The partial load technique.
2. The isolation of text and image data chains.

The partial load technique is used to spread different collections of data or index rows (horizontal table fragments) across different segments to enhance data access to large data sets (when you hang the underlying disk drives off of separate disk controllers, you take this technique to its limit—take it to the limit if you can afford it because you will then be able to handle simultaneous disk I/O across different controllers and different disk drives). There are limitations to using this technique:

1. Only the table owner, or an account with **dbo** or **sa_role** privileges, can use the partial load method.

2. Placing data or index rows on separate segments does not affect the placement of existing data or index rows. They will remain in their current locations. Only data and index rows allocated in the future will have space allocated to them from the new segments they are associated with.

3. You cannot influence the future space allocations of system tables. The SQL Server ensures that all system tables reside on a **system** segment. The only exception to this constraint is the capability of the sp_logdevice command to move the *syslogs* table.

4. You cannot influence the future space allocations of partitioned heap tables. To use this technique on them, you will have to unpartition the heap table.

5. This technique requires that distinct user-defined segments be created to store specific horizontal fragments.

6. Tables and indexes that would be subject to frequent insert transactions after they have been placed are most likely not good candidates for use with this technique. If you use this technique on such tables, performance will degrade, and you will periodically have to drop the table and re-create it using the partial load technique to regain lost performance levels. On the other hand, tables that are used to archive static historical data make excellent candidates for use with this technique (e.g., you can place January's data on one segment, February's data on another segment, and so on).

7. After placing horizontal fragments onto distinct user-defined segments, the **dbcc checkalloc** utility will produce this error message:

```
Extent not within segment: Object object_name, indid index_
    id includes extents on allocation page page_number which is
    not in segment segment_name.
```

This is a false alarm. You can safely ignore this message.

To apply the partial load technique, follow these steps in their exact order:

1. Correctly allocate multiple logical database devices to the target database. The best results will be attained when each of these log-

ical database devices reside on separate disk drives that are each managed by separate disk controllers.

2. Create a user-defined segment for each logical database device allocated to the target database.

3. Unmap the default and system segments from all but the first allocated logical database device.

4. Create the table and its clustered index on the first segment.

5. Correctly separate the table's source data into its horizontal fragments, such that one horizontal fragment maps to one operating system flat file. This will ensure that data and index rows from different horizontal fragments will not subsequently be placed on the wrong segment. Be certain that each target segment is large enough to store its horizontal fragment.

6. Sort each horizontal fragment in the exact sorted order as specified by the table's clustered index so that the batch load runs at top speed.

7. As the owner of the table or the holder of an account with **dbo** or **sa_role** privileges, load the first ordered horizontal fragment into the table using the **bcp** utility.

8. As the owner of the table or the holder of an account with **dbo** or **sa_role** privileges, enter this command:

```
1>sp_placeobject NameOfSecondSegment, NameOfTable
2>go
```

where:

NameOfSecondSegment—the name of the second segment into which you want to load the second horizontal fragment.

NameOfTable—the name of the table for which you are using the partial load technique.

9. Load the second ordered horizontal fragment into the target table using the **bcp** utility.

10. Repeat steps 8 and 9 for each successive ordered horizontal fragment.

The partial load technique can be used to control future space allocations for nonclustered indexes as well. Instead of passing the name of the table as a parameter to the `sp_placeobject` command, you pass the "*NameOfTable NameOfNonClusteredIndex*" parameter to it.

As was explained in the chapter on physical resources, the SQL Server stores text and image data on separate data page chains. To access text or image data, the table is read to obtain the text or image pointer, and then an additional read operation is required to access the text or image data page chain. By default, these text and image data page chains reside on the same segment as the table that contains the text or image columns. By isolating text and image data page chains on separate disk drives (and separate disk drive controllers) from the base table, enhanced disk I/O performance can be achieved. To isolate future text and image data space allocations to separate disk drives, pass the "*NameOf Table . NameOf TextColumn*" parameter to the `sp_placeobject` command.

Binding Objects to Named Data Caches

When it comes to explaining the appropriate manner by which to bind database objects to Named Data Caches, a clear understanding of the caching strategies used by the applications that the SQL Server supports is mandatory. The appropriate manner includes the techniques of binding database objects as well as the sound reasons for doing so. In this section we will consider the techniques for binding database objects to Named Data Caches.

When approaching the techniques for binding database objects to Named Data Cache, an understanding of the data cache hierarchy that the System 11 SQL Server follows is necessary. Starting at the top of the hierarchy and by working its way down from there, the SQL Server makes its data cache binding decisions accordingly:

1. If the database object has been explicitly bound to a given Named Data Cache, then that database object binding will be used.

2. If the database object has not been explicitly bound to a given Named Data Cache, but the database to which that database object belongs has been explicitly bound to a Named Data Cache, then this database binding will be used. If this seems confusing, then keep in mind that you can bind a database to one Named Data Cache and also bind its individual tables, indexes, text object and image objects to a different Named Data Cache.

3. If neither the database object nor the database to which this data object belongs has been bound to a Named Data Cache, then it will be brought into the Default Data Cache.

Just like any good cook, before you prepare the meal you will want to study the materials at hand. So, to start off, you will need to view all data caches and their bindings that currently exist within your SQL Server. To accomplish this task, log on to the SQL Server as any valid Sybase account and enter these commands:

```
1>use master
2>go
1>sp_helpcache
2>go
```

Once the command completes executing, all information about all data caches and all related bindings will be displayed.

If you want to view the bindings of a specific Named Data Cache, then log on to the SQL Server as any valid Sybase account and enter these commands:

```
1>use master
2>go
1>sp_helpcache NameOfDataCache
2>go
```

where:

NameOfDataCache—the Named Data Cache for which you want to view all binding information. The `sp_helpcache` command is capable of supporting string matching on the name of the data cache. To take advantage of this command capability, pass this argument to the command `%string%`, where `string` is any legal byte sequence of your choosing.

Once the command completes executing, all related binding information about the Named Data Cache will be displayed.

If you want to view the bindings of a specific database to a specific Named Data Cache, then log on to the SQL Server as any valid Sybase account and enter these commands:

```
1>use master
2>go
1>sp_helpcache NameOfDataCache, NameOfDatabase
2>go
```

where:

NameOfDataCache—the name of the Named Data Cache for which you want to view the binding information of a specific database. The `sp_helpcache` command is capable of supporting string matching on the name of the data cache. To take advantage of this command capability pass this argument to the command `%string%`, where `string` is any legal byte sequence of your choosing.

NameOfDatabase—the name of the database for which you want to view all related binding information.

Once the command completes executing, all related database binding information about the Named Data Cache will be displayed.

Whether you elect to view information about data caches and their bindings individually or collectively, here are some important facts to keep in mind when executing the sp_helpcache command:

1. The Status column of the sp_helpcache report shows a cache binding as being either valid ("V") or invalid ("I"). If you had previously created a Named Data Cache, bound a database or its database objects to it, and then subsequently dropped that Named Data Cache, the related binding information is still stored in the system catalogs, but the bindings are marked invalid. In most cases, unless you plan to re-create the dropped Named Data Cache, the appropriate technique to follow is to unbind all related databases or database objects before you dropped the Named Data Cache. If you planned to re-create the dropped Named Data Cache, then once it is re-created (using the same name), the related database or database object bindings will automatically be marked as valid once the status of the Named Data Cache becomes active. If the databases and database object bindings are marked as invalid, then the related databases and database objects will be supported by the Default Data Cache.

2. The sp_helpcache command can only report binding information about databases that are currently on-line. If a database is off-line, then none of its binding information will be reported.

Binding information can be obtained about specific databases, tables, and indexes. To view binding information (as well as other information) about a given database, log on to the SQL Server as any valid Sybase account and enter the following commands:

```
1>use NameOfDatabase
2>go
1>sp_helpdb NameOfDatabase
2>go
```

where:

NameOfDatabase—the name of the database for which you want to view all related binding information.

Once the command completes executing, all related database binding information about the database (as well as many other types of information about the database) will be displayed.

To determine the database objects that are contained within a given database, log on to the SQL Server as any valid Sybase account and enter the following commands:

```
1>use NameOfDatabase
2>go
1>sp_help
2>go
```

where:

NameOfDatabase—the name of the database for which you want to view the listing of all database objects it contains.

Once the command completes executing, the list of all database objects that the database contains will be displayed.

To view binding information (as well as other information) about a given table, log on to the SQL Server as any valid Sybase account and enter the following commands:

```
1>use NameOfDatabase
2>go
1>sp_help NameOfTable
2>go
```

where:

NameOfTable—the name of the table for which you want to view all related binding information.

Once the command completes executing, all related binding information about the table (as well as many other types of information about the table) will be displayed.

To view binding information (as well as other information) about a given index, log on to the SQL Server as any valid Sybase account and enter these commands:

```
1>use NameOfDatabase
2>go
1>sp_helpindex NameOfIndex
2>go
```

where:

NameOfIndex—the name of the index for which you want to view all related binding information.

Once the command completes executing, all related binding information about the index (as well as many other types of information about the index) will be displayed.

There are different techniques for binding different types of database objects:

1. Transaction logs.

2. System tables and indexes on system tables that are not contained within the *master* system database.

3. Database objects that are owned by you.

4. Databases objects that are not owned by you, but you have an account with **dbo** or **sa_role** privileges.

The appropriate techniques for binding transaction logs to Named Data Caches will be covered in its own section that immediately follows this section. In this current section, we will address the appropriate techniques for the last three types of database objects.

Before you use any technique for explicitly binding a specific database object to a specific Named Data Cache, you need to know the present size of the database object in question, and you need to have an estimate of its likely size in the future. This information is critically important because you do not want to bind the database object to a Named Data Cache that is too small to handle the binding.

To determine the present size of the database object that you want to explicitly bind to a Named Data Cache, log on to the SQL Server as any valid Sybase account and enter these commands:

```
1>use NameOfDatabase
2>go
1>sp_spaceused NameOfDatabaseObject
2>go
```

where:

NameOfDatabaseObject—the name of the table or index, the present size of which you need to know.

Once the command completes executing, all related size information about the database object will be displayed.

To obtain an estimate of the future size of the table or index, the **sp_estspace** system procedure is used. To understand how to use the **sp_estspace** system procedure, refer to the chapter on tables. As long as you know the present size of the database object in question and its estimated size in the future, you are in a position to bind the database object to a Named Data Cache that is not too small to handle the binding.

Binding a User Table to a Named Data Cache

It seems that every database has at least one heavily used table. Significant performance gains can be obtained by binding such "hot" tables to a Named Data Cache, such that they reside (entirely) in cache, and related disk I/O overhead is minimized. To bind a database table to a mixed Named Data Cache, log on to the SQL Server as an account with **sa_role** privileges and enter these commands:

```
1>use NameOfDatabase
2>go
1>sp_bindcache NameOfDataCache, NameOfDatabase, NameOfTable
2>go
```

where:

NameOfDataCache—the name of the mixed Named Data Cache to which you want to exclusively bind the database table. This Named Data Cache must exist before you execute the sp_bindcache command. Be certain that the data cache is type "mixed," since you cannot bind the database table to a data cache of type "logonly." Also, the status of this data cache must be active; that is, the SQL Server must have been restarted since the point in time when this data cache was created or else the database table cannot be bound to it.

NameOfDatabase—the name of the database that contains the table you want to bind to a mixed data cache. This database must exist before you can bind any of its tables to a Named Data Cache.

NameOfTable—the name of the table that you want to bind to the Named Data Cache.

Here are a few important facts to keep in mind when binding a database table to mixed Named Data Caches:

1. When you bind a database table to a mixed Named Data Cache you must be in the database that contains the system table.

2. Binding the table to a Named Data Cache takes effect immediately (i.e., you do not have to restart the SQL Server).

3. If the table is already bound to another Named Data Cache, the old binding is dropped and the new one is created (i.e., you do not have to unbind the table before you create its new binding).

4. When you bind the table to a Named Data Cache, any of its pages in memory are flushed to disk. They will be located in the Named Data Cache to which they are bound once a user process needs to access them.

5. You cannot bind the table to a Named Data Cache if either of these two conditions are present:

5.1 There is an isolation level zero taking place on the table.

5.2 The user process that is doing the database binding also has a cursor open on the table.

6. The named data cache to which the system table is being bound must be of type "mixed."

7. When you bind the table to a mixed Named Data Cache, the SQL Server must acquire exclusive locks on all related table, index, and log pages residing in data cache. The SQL Server will cause the binding process to sleep until these exclusive locks can be acquired. In addition, these exclusive locks will degrade the performance of any transaction that requires locks on the affected table, index, or log pages. Once these exclusive locks are acquired, the SQL Server will flush all related dirty pages to disk and drop all related clean pages from the data cache. When these pages are needed once again to support a query, they are read into the mixed Named Data Cache to which they have been bound. As a consequence, the performance of the queries that first read the pages back into the data cache will degrade.

8. If a Named Data Cache to which the table is currently bound is dropped, the data cache binding records remain within the system catalogs but are marked as invalid. As a consequence, warning messages about the table binding will be written to the SQL Server error log each time the SQL Server boots. If you subsequently re-created the Named Data Cache (using exactly the same name), the bindings will automatically take effect and be marked as valid once the status of the Name Data Cache becomes active. So, unless you intend to re-create a dropped Named Data Cache to which a database object is bound, you should unbind the table from the Named Data Cache before you drop the Named Data Cache.

9. In this scenario, it is not necessary to specify the table owner name because it is owned by **dbo.**

10. You can bind nonsystem tables and their indexes contained within the master system database to Named Data Cache.

11. When you bind a table to a Named Data Cache, all the stored procedures and triggers that reference it are recompiled the next time they are executed.

12. When you drop a table or index that is bound to a Named Data Cache, all the data cache binding associated with it are also dropped automatically by the SQL Server.

13. In that the `sp_bindcache` command modifies system tables, you cannot execute this command from within a transaction.

The technique for binding a table that you do not own involves a slight variation of the technique for binding tables that you do own. To bind a database table that you do not own to a mixed Named Data Cache, log on to the SQL Server as an account with **sa_role** privileges and enter these commands:

```
1>use NameOfDatabase
2>go
1>sp_bindcache NameOfDataCache, NameOfDatabase,
  "NameOfObjectOwner.NameOfTable"
2>go
```

where

NameOfDataCache—the name of the mixed Named Data Cache to which you want to exclusively bind the database table. This Named Data Cache must exist before you execute the `sp_bindcache` command. Be certain that the data cache is type "mixed," since you cannot bind the database table to a data cache of type "logonly." Also, the status of this data cache must be active; that is, the SQL Server must have been restarted since the point in time when this data cache was created or else the database table can be bound to it.

NameOfDatabase—is the name of the database that contains the table you want to bind to a mixed data cache. This database must exist before you can bind any of its tables to a Named Data Cache.

"NameOfObjectOwner.NameOfTable"—this parameter comes in three parts: the first part is the name of the Sybase account that owns the table, the second part is a period (.), and the third part is the name of the table that you want to bind to the Named Data Cache (i.e., `"bsmith.product"`. You must enclose this parameter in quotation marks, because the period in the parameter is a special character as far as the SQL Server is concerned.

When binding a table that you do not own to a Named Data Cache, be certain to keep in mind the same set of important facts related to binding a table to a mixed Named Data Cache.

Binding User Tables with Text/Image Data Types to Named Data Caches

The technique for binding a table that contains text or image data types involves a slight variation of the technique for binding "normal" tables. To bind a database table that contains text or image data types to a mixed Named Data Cache, log on to the SQL Server as an account with **sa_role** privileges and enter these commands:

```
1>use NameOfDatabase
2>go
1>sp_bindcache NameOfDataCache, NameOfDatabase, NameOfTable,
2>"text only"
3>go
```

where:

NameOfDataCache—the name of the mixed Named Data Cache to which you want to exclusively bind the database table. This Named Data Cache must exist before you execute the `sp_bindcache` command. Be certain that the data cache is type "mixed," since you cannot bind the database table to a data cache of type "logonly." Also, the status of this data cache must be active; that is, the SQL Server must have been restarted since the point in time when this data cache was created or else the database table can be bound to it.

NameOfDatabase—the name of the database that contains the table you want to bind to a mixed data cache. This database must exist before you can bind any of its tables to a Named Data Cache.

NameOfTable—the name of the table that contains the text or image data types that you want to bind to the Named Data Cache.

`"text only"`—this parameter effectively binds the text or image pages associated with the table to the Named Data Cache as a separate data structure. When the `"text only"` parameter is used, you cannot give the name of a table index in the same command statement.

When binding a table that contains text or image data types to a Named Data Cache, be certain to keep in mind the same set of important facts related to binding a table to a mixed Named Data Cache.

Binding a User Table Index to a Named Data Cache

To bind a database table's index to a mixed Named Data Cache, log on to the SQL Server as an account with **sa_role** privileges and enter these commands:

```
1>use NameOfDatabase
2>go
1>sp_bindcache NameOfDataCache, NameOfDatabase, NameOfTable,
2>NameOfTableIndex
3>go
```

where

NameOfDataCache—the name of the mixed Named Data Cache to which you want to exclusively bind the database table. This Named Data Cache must exist before you execute the `sp_bindcache` command. Be certain that the data cache is type "mixed," since you cannot bind the database table to a data cache of type "logonly." Also, the status of this data cache must be active; that is, the SQL Server must have been restarted since the point in time when this data cache was created or else the database table can be bound to it.

NameOfDatabase—the name of the database that contains the table index you want to bind to a mixed data cache. This database must exist before you can bind any of its table indexes to a Named Data Cache.

NameOfTable—the name of the table whose index you want to bind to the Named Data Cache.

NameOfTableIndex—the name of the table index that you want to bind to the Named Data Cache.

When binding a table's index to a Named Data Cache, be certain to keep in mind the same set of important facts related to binding a table to a mixed Named Data Cache.

The technique for binding an index that you do not own involves a slight variation of the technique for binding indexes that you do own. To bind an index that you do not own to a mixed Named Data Cache, log on to the SQL Server as an account with **sa_role** privileges and enter these commands:

```
1>use NameOfDatabase
2>go
1>sp_bindcache NameOfDataCache, NameOfDatabase,
  "NameOfObjectOwner.NameOfTable"
2>NameOfTableIndex
3>go
```

where

NameOfDataCache—the name of the mixed Named Data Cache to which you want to exclusively bind the database table. This Named Data Cache must exist before you execute the `sp_bindcache` command. Be certain that the data cache is type "mixed," since you cannot bind the database table to a data cache of type "logonly." Also, the status of this data cache must be active; that is, the SQL Server must have been restarted since the point in time when this data cache was created or else the database table can be bound to it.

NameOfDatabase—the name of the database that contains the table you want to bind to a mixed data cache. This database must exist before you can bind any of its tables to a Named Data Cache.

"*NameOfObjectOwner.NameOfTable*"—this parameter comes in three parts: the first part is the name of the Sybase account that owns the table, the second part is a period (.), and the third part is the name of the table that you want to bind to the Named Data Cache (i.e., `"bsmith.product"`). You must enclose the parameter in quotation marks, because the period in the parameter is a special character as far as the SQL Server is concerned.

NameOfTableIndex—the name of the table index you do not own that you want to bind to the Named Data Cache.

When binding an index that you do not own to a Named Data Cache, be certain to keep in mind the same set of important facts related to binding a table to mixed Named Data Cache.

Unbinding Database Objects from a Named Data Cache

There are different techniques for unbinding different types of individual database objects from a specific Named Data Cache:

1. Transaction logs.
2. System tables and indexes on system tables that are not contained within the *master* system database.
3. Database objects that are owned by you.
4. Databases objects that are not owned by you, but you have **dbo** or **sa_role** privileges.

Unbinding User Tables from Named Data Caches

To unbind a database table from a mixed Named Data Cache, log on to the SQL Server as an account with **sa_role** privileges and enter these commands:

```
1>use NameOfDatabase
2>go
1>sp_unbindcache NameOfDatabase, NameOfTable
2>go
```

where:

NameOfDatabase—the name of the database that contains the table you want to unbind from a mixed data cache.

NameOfTable—the name of the table that you want to unbind from the Named Data Cache.

Here are a few important facts to keep in mind when unbinding a database table from a mixed Named Data Cache:

1. When you unbind a database table from a mixed Named Data Cache, you must be in the database that contains the table.

2. Unbinding the table from Named Data Cache takes effect immediately (i.e., you do not have to restart the SQL Server).

3. When you unbind the table from a Named Data Cache, any of its pages in memory are flushed to disk. They will be located in the Default Data Cache once a user process needs to access them.

4. You cannot unbind the table from a Named Data Cache if either of these two conditions are present:

4.1. There is an isolation level zero taking place on the table.

4.2. The user process that is doing the database unbinding also has a cursor open on the table.

5. When you unbind the table from a mixed Named Data Cache, the SQL Server must acquire exclusive locks on all related table, index, and log pages residing in data cache. The SQL Server will cause the `sp_unbindcache` process to sleep until these exclusive locks can be acquired. In addition, these exclusive locks will degrade the performance of any transaction that requires locks on the effected table, index, or log pages. Once these exclusive locks are acquired, the SQL Server will flush all related dirty pages to disk and drop all related clean pages from the data cache. When these pages are needed once again to support a query, they are read into the Default Data Cache. As a consequence, the performance of the queries that first read the pages back into data cache will degrade.

6. In this scenario, it is not necessary to specify the table owner name because it is owned by **dbo.**

7. You can unbind nonsystem tables and their indexes contained within the master system database to Named Data Caches.

8. When you unbind a table from a Named Data Cache, all the stored procedures and triggers that reference it are recompiled the next time they are executed.

9. When you drop a table or index that is bound to a Named Data Cache, all the data cache binding associated with it are also dropped automatically by the SQL Server.

10. In that the `sp_unbindcache` command modifies system tables, you cannot execute this command from within a transaction.

The technique for unbinding a table that you do not own involves a slight variation of the technique for unbinding tables that you do own. To unbind a database table that you do not own from a mixed Named Data Cache, log on to the SQL Server as an account with **sa_role** privileges and enter these commands:

```
1>use NameOfDatabase
2>go
1>sp_unbindcache NameOfDatabase, "NameOfObjectOwner.
  NameOfTable"
2>go
```

where:

NameOfDatabase—the name of the database that contains the table you want to unbind from a mixed data cache.

"NameOfObjectOwner.NameOfTable"—this parameter comes in three parts: the first part is the name of the Sybase account that owns the table, the second part is a period (.), and the third part is the name of the table that you want to unbind from the Named Data Cache (i.e., `"bsmith.product"`). You must enclose this parameter in quotation marks because the period in the parameter is a special character as far as the SQL Server is concerned.

When unbinding a table that you do not own from a Named Data Cache, be certain to keep in mind the same set of important facts related to unbinding a table you do own from a mixed Named Data Cache.

Unbinding User Tables with Text/Image Data Types from a Named Data Cache

The technique for unbinding a table that contains text or image data types involves a slight variation of the technique for unbinding "normal" tables. To unbind a database table that contains text or image data types from a mixed Named Data Cache, log on to the SQL Server as an account with **sa_role** privileges and enter these commands:

```
1>use NameOfDatabase
2>go
1>sp_unbindcache NameOfDatabase, NameOfTable,
2>"text only"
3>go
```

where:

>*NameOfDatabase*—the name of the database that contains the table you want to unbind from a mixed data cache.

>*NameOfTable*—the name of the table that contains the text or image data types that you want to unbind from the Named Data Cache.

>`"text only"`—this parameter effectively unbinds the text or image pages associated with the table from the Named Data Cache as a separate data structure. When the `"text only"` parameter is used, you cannot give the name of a table index in the same command statement.

When unbinding a table that contains text or image data types from a Named Data Cache, be certain to keep in mind the same set of important facts related to unbinding a table from a mixed Named Data Cache.

Unbinding a User Table's Index from a Named Data Cache

To unbind a database table's index from a mixed Named Data Cache, log on to the SQL Server as an account with **sa_role** privileges and enter these commands:

```
1>use NameOfDatabase
2>go
1>sp_unbindcache NameOfDatabase, NameOfTable,
2>NameOfTableIndex
3>go
```

where:

>*NameOfDatabase*—the name of the database that contains the table index you want to unbind from a mixed data cache.

>*NameOfTable*—the name of the table whose index you want to unbind from the Named Data Cache.

>*NameOfTableIndex*—the name of the table index that you want to unbind from the Named Data Cache.

When unbinding a table's index from a Named Data Cache, be certain to keep in mind the same set of important facts related to unbinding a table from a mixed Named Data Cache.

The technique for unbinding an index that you do not own involves a slight variation of the technique for unbinding indexes that you own.

To unbind an index that you do not own from a mixed Named Data Cache, log on to the SQL Server as an account with **sa_role** privileges and enter these commands:

```
1>use NameOfDatabase
2>go
1>sp_unbindcache NameOfDatabase, "NameOfObjectOwner.
  NameOfTable"
2>NameOfTableIndex
3>go
```

where:

NameOfDatabase—the name of the database that contains the table you want to unbind from a mixed data cache.

"NameOfObjectOwner.NameOfTable"—this parameter comes in three parts: the first part is the name of the Sybase account that owns the table, the second part is a period (.), and the third part is the name of the table that you want to unbind from the Named Data Cache (i.e., `"bsmith.product"`). You must enclose this parameter in quotation marks because the period in the parameter is a special character as far as the SQL Server is concerned.

NameOfTableIndex—The name of the table index you do not own that you want to unbind from the Named Data Cache.

When unbinding an index that you do not own from a Named Data Cache, be certain to keep in mind the same set of important facts related to unbinding a table you do own from a mixed Named Data Cache.

Unbinding All Database Objects from a Named Data Cache

When it comes to unbinding databases or database objects from a Named Data Cache, you have two options:

1. Unbind individual databases and individual database objects from a specific Named Data Cache (as has been demonstrated).

2. Unbind all databases and all database objects from a specific Named Data Cache.

To unbind all database objects from a specific Named Data Cache, the SQL Server provides you with the `sp_unbindcache_all` system procedure. However, the `sp_unbindcache_all` system procedure is only capable of opening eight databases simultaneously. If there are more than eight databases, or if there are database objects from more than eight separate databases simultaneously bound to this Named Data Cache, the `sp_unbindcache_all` system procedure will not work. If this is the case, then your only recourse is to use the `sp_unbindcache` system procedure to reduce the numbers of bound databases and objects to a level manageable by the `sp_unbindcache_all` system procedure.

To unbind all databases and database objects from Named Data Cache, log on to the SQL Server as an account with **sa_role** privileges and enter these commands:

```
1>use master
2>go
1>sp_unbindcache_all  NameOfDataCache
2>go
```

where:

NameOfDataCache—the name of the named data cache from which you want to unbind all databases and database objects.

Here are a few important facts to keep in mind when executing the `sp_unbindcache_all` system command:

1. All databases that are presently bound to the Named Data Cache must be placed in single user mode before you execute the `sp_unbindcache_all` system command.

2. When you unbind a database from a Named Data Cache you must be in the *master* system database.

3. Unbinding of databases and database objects from a Named Data Cache takes effect immediately (i.e., you do not have to restart the SQL Server).

4. When a database or a database object is unbound from a Named Data Cache, all compiled objects that reference database objects contained within the bound database are recompiled the next time they are executed by a user process.

5. If you drop a database that is bound to a Named Data Cache, then all its related bindings are automatically dropped by the SQL Server.

6. When you unbind a database from a mixed Named Data Cache, the SQL Server must acquire exclusive locks on all table, index, and log pages residing in the data cache. The SQL Server will cause the `sp_unbindcache_all` command to sleep until these exclusive locks can be acquired. In addition, these exclusive locks will degrade the performance of any transaction that requires locks on the effected table, index, or log pages. Once these exclusive locks are acquired, the SQL

Server will flush all related dirty pages to disk and drop all related clean pages from the data cache. When these pages are needed once again to support a query, they are read into the Default Data Cache. As a consequence, the performance of the queries that first read the pages back into data cache will degrade.

7. You cannot unbind a database from a Named Data Cache if either of these two conditions are present:

7.1. There is an isolation level zero taking place on any table in the databases.

7.2. The user process that is doing the database unbinding also has a cursor open on any table contained within the databases being bound.

8. In that the `sp_unbindcache_all` command modifies system tables, you cannot execute this command from within a transaction.

Bulk Loading Data into Tables

The SQL Server provides you with a utility called bulk copy (**bcp**) for loading batch data from an operating system flat file into a table and for copying the entire contents or portions of a table to an operating system flat file. When loading batch data into a table, the data is appended to the table, and when copying data from a table to a flat file, anything in the target file will be overwritten.

To use the **bcp** utility requires:

1. An operating system login account.

2. Appropriate permissions in the operating system for reading and writing flat files.

3. A SQL Server login account.

4. Your SQL Server login account must be a user of the database in which you will be working.

5. To copy data from a table, your login account must have select permission on the user table.

6. To insert data into a table, your login account must have insert permission on the user tables, and it must have select permission on the *syscolumns, sysindexes,* and *sysobjects* system tables.

When loading batch data into a table, the **bcp** utility executes in either of two modes:

Fast.   The **bcp** utility is optimized for loading data into tables that do not have indexes or triggers. With fast **bcp,** insert records are not written into the transaction log; only page allocations are logged. You are trading off performance for database recoverability. To use fast **bcp,** the "select into/bulkcopy" database option must be set in the database. If this database option is not set on, and you **bcp** data into a table that does not have indexes or triggers, the load will fail, and then the SQL Server will respond with an error message. To regain database recoverability, you must dump the database (not the transaction log) after the fast **bcp** completes.

Slow.   Used to load batch data into tables that have indexes or triggers. With slow **bcp,** insert records are logged. To use slow **bcp,** the "select into/bulkcopy" database option does not have to be set in the database. When using slow **bcp,** be aware that the transaction log can easily be filled. When the slow **bcp** completes, dump the database and then truncate its transaction log.

In that the **bcp** utility can take advantage of the number of preallocated extents SQL Server configuration parameter, if you want your **bcp** jobs to run at their fastest possible rate, and if you want to decrease the possibility of **bcp** page allocations from filling the database's transaction log, then you should consider turning this SQL Server configuration parameter.

When loading batch data into a table, the **bcp** utility does not cause any triggers to fire, nor can the SQL Server enforce rules defined for the target table. You will have to query the loaded data to verify if it complies with rules and triggers bound to the table. However, the **bcp** utility does observe defaults bound to columns and to user-defined data types.

To use the **bcp** utility, log on to the host computer and enter this command:

```
bcp [[NameOfDatabase,]loginame.]NameOfTable {in | out}
    NameOfFile
[-U loginame] [-P passwd] [-S NameOfSQLServer] [-I
    NameOfInterfacesFile]
[-y SybaseDirectory] [-X] [-b batchsize] [-A NetworkPacketSize]
[-m maxerrors] [-e NameOfErrorFile]
[-F firstrow] [-L lastrow] [-c [-N]] [-E] [-n] [-f format
    file]
[-t field_terminator] [-r row_terminator] [-T text_or_
    image_size]
[-a NameOfDisplayCharacterSet] [-q][-J ClientCharacterConversionS]
[-z language] [-v]
```

where:

[[*NameOfDatabase.*]loginame.]*NameOfTable*

where

> *NameOfDatabase*—the name of the database that contains the table from which or into which you want to copy data. If the table is within your login account's default database, then you do not have to provide this parameter.

> loginame—the name of the Sybase account that owns the table. If you are the owner of the table, then you do not have to provide this optional parameter.

> *NameOfTable*—the name of the table from which or into which you want to copy data.

{in | out}—these parameters indicate the direction of the bulk copy and are mutually exclusive. Use in to indicate that data from a file will be loaded into a table. Use out to indicate that data from a table will be copied to a file.

NameOfFile—the name of the operating system file from which the data will be read or to which data will be written. The maximum length of the name of the operating system file is 255 characters. To reduce network traffic, this file should reside on the same host computer that the SQL Server is running on. Also, you cannot use named pipes to redirect **bcp** data to files.

U loginame—this optional parameter is the name of the Sybase login account that is logging into the SQL Server. If this optional parameter is not supplied, then the SQL Server will prompt you for it.

P passwd—this optional parameter is the password of the Sybase login account that is logging into the SQL Server. If this optional parameter is not supplied, then the SQL Server will prompt you for it.

S *NameOfSQLServer*—this optional parameter is the name of the SQL Server to which you want to log on. If you use the "-S" parameter and do not specify the name of the SQL Server, **bcp** will assume that you want to connect to the SQL Server named SYBASE. If you do not use this optional parameter at all, then the **bcp** will connect to the SQL Server specified by the DSQUERY operating system environment variable.

I *NameOfInterfacesFile*—this optional parameter specifies the **interfaces** file that **bcp** will use when connecting to the target SQL Server. If you do not specify this optional parameter, then **bcp** will use the interfaces file in the directory specified by the SYBASE operating system environment variable.

y *SybaseDirectory*—this optional parameter specifies the SYBASE directory that **bcp** will use. If you do not provide this optional parameter, then **bcp** will use the SYBASE directory specified by the SYBASE operating system environment variable.

X—if the **bcp** software crashes while you are using it, a core image of the **bcp** software will be created. In that core image will be your password. To secure your password against this risk exposure, you can pass this optional parameter to the SQL Server. When the SQL Server receives this parameter, it will send an encryption key back to **bcp, bcp** will use this key to encrypt the login password, and the SQL Server will use the encryption key to authenticate the login password when it is sent.

[-b batchsize]—by default, **bcp** copies all records into the target table as a single insert transaction that is committed at the end of the batch. As a consequence, if the batch load fills up the database's transaction log, then the entire batch will fail and be rolled back. The purpose of this optional parameter is to give you control over the count of records that make up a single insert transaction that is committed. It has no effect when copying data out of a table.

A *NetworkPacketSize*—this optional parameter is used to set the network packet size that **bcp** and the SQL Server will use to transmit data to one another. When there is a lot of data to move between the two software components, be sure to use this parameter to enhance performance. The value you set for this parameter must fall between the default network packet size and the max network packet size. SQL Server configuration parameters must be one-third the size of the additional network memory SQL Server configuration parameter and must be a multiple of 512. If there is not enough memory available, then the SQL Server will use the packet size closest to 512.

[-m maxerrors]—this optional parameter is used to specify the maximum number of nonfatal errors that will be permitted per batch before the **bcp** utility aborts the insert transaction. The default value of this parameter is 10. When handling nonfatal errors, the **bcp** utility discards each record it cannot insert, counting each failed record as an individual error.

[-e *NameOfErrorFile*—this optional parameter designates the name of the file that the **bcp** utility will use to store records (in character format) that it was unable to insert into the target table or cannot copy out of the source table.

[-F firstrow]—this optional parameter allows you to indicate the number of the first record to copy. The default is to start copying from the first record.

[-L lastrow]—this optional parameter allows you to indicate the number of the last record to copy. The default is to stop copying when the last record is retrieved.

[-c]—this optional parameter is used to designate that the copy/ load operation will be using the character data type format. This

option should be used to format data moved between dissimilar host computers. If you do not use this or the "n" option, then **bcp** will prompt you to define the data's format interactively. Character format is the default **bcp** format.

[-N]—this optional parameter is used in conjunction with the "c" parameter. If you use this optional parameter when copying data out of a table that contains an IDENTITY column, then the IDENTITY column will be skipped. Use this optional parameter when loading data into a table that contains an IDENTITY column, where your source file does not contain a placeholder for the IDENTITY column values.

[-E]—Use this optional parameter when loading data into a table that contains an IDENTITY column, where your source file contains the IDENTITY column values.

[-n]—this optional parameter is used to designate that the copy/load operation will be using the host computer's native data type format. This option can be used to format data that is being moved between similar host computers, as the file sizes will be significantly smaller than character format files. If you do not use this or the "c" option, then **bcp** will prompt you to define the data's format interactively.

[-f formatfile]—this optional parameter is the name of the file that stores format information that the **bcp** utility uses when copying data from and to a given table. When this custom format file is first built, it is created interactively by prompting you to answer data type formatting questions. The default name for this file will be bcp.fmt.

[-t field_terminator]—this optional parameter is used to indicate the field record terminator that will be used to differentiate individual record fields. A field record terminator can be up to 30 bytes of characters, and you must enclose it in quotation marks (""). By default, character formatted files use the tab as a field terminator. Native formatted files do not contain field terminators. If you intend to designate a field terminator, be certain not to designate one that appears within the data you are moving and does not conflict with your operating system. Using this optional parameter is not necessary if you are going to create a file format interactively.

[-r row_terminator]—this optional parameter is used to indicate the record terminator that will be used to differentiate individual records. By default, character-formatted files use the newline symbol as a record terminator. Native formatted files do not contain record terminators. If you intend to designate a record terminator, be certain not to designate one that appears within the data you are moving and does not conflict with your operating system. Using this optional parameter is not necessary if you are going to create a file format interactively.

[-T text_or_image_size]—this optional parameter is used to designate, in bytes, the maximum length of text of image data that the SQL Server will pass back to the **bcp** utility. The default maximum length of text of image data that the SQL Server will pass back is just 32 bytes. If the text or image data is longer than 32 bytes, then the SQL Server will only send the first 32 bytes and will not raise an error to the **bcp** utility. So, if you want all the text and image data, then be certain to use this optional parameter to specify its actual length in bytes.

a *NameOfDisplayCharacterSet*—this optional parameter is related to the -J and -q optional parameters. You will use this optional parameter when **bcp** will display on a terminal whose character set is different from the character set of the host computer on which **bcp** is executing. Use this optional parameter with the -J optional parameter to specify the character-set translation file that supports the character conversion. Use this optional parameter without using the -J optional parameter only if the **bcp** character set is the same as the default SQL Server character set.

q—when you are using **bcp** in a Japanese language environment, this optional parameter is used to translate Hankaku Katakana (half-width characters) into Zenkaku Katakana (full-width characters). With this optional parameter, use the argument "zenkaku" and the -J flag to indicate **bcp**'s Japanese character set (sjis or eucjis). The zenkaku conversion file will only translate from the **bcp** terminal display to the SQL Server and not from the SQL Server to the **bcp** terminal display.

J *ClientCharacterConversionSet*—this optional parameter is used to instruct the SQL Server to convert to and from the character set in use on the host computer where **bcp** is executing. Use the -J parameter to specify that the host computer where **bcp** is executing, and the SQL Server it is connecting to, are using the same Japanese environment character set.

z *AlternateIsqlLanguage*—if you do not use this optional parameter, then **bcp** will display prompts and messages using the SQL Server's default language. If you do not want to use the SQL Server default language, then you can use this optional parameter to specify an alternate language that the SQL Server supports.

v—this optional parameter prints the version (and copyright statement) of the **bcp** software you are using and then ends the session by disconnecting from the SQL Server.

When the **bcp** job completes, a report showing the total number of records copied, the number of records that could not be copied, the elapsed clock time of the copy, the average amount of time it took to copy a single record, and the count of records copied per second will be displayed to you.

Finally, if you are going to **bcp** data into partitioned tables, it is recommended that you run half as many concurrent **bcp** jobs as there are table partition groups. This is a good place to start, and you can always increase or decrease the count of concurrent **bcp** jobs if contention occurs within the partitioned table because of the **bcp** jobs.

Segments and Thresholds

Segments

A segment is a label, or name, used to point to one or more logical database devices. Each time a database is created on a logical database device, the SQL Server automatically creates three segments on the logical database device that support the new database:

1. system—automatically used by the SQL Server to store system-catalog tables.
2. default—automatically used by the SQL Server to store user tables or indexes.
3. logsegment—automatically used by the SQL Server to store the database's *syslogs* system table (i.e., its transaction log).

The function of a segment is to map the future allocations of different types of data in a given database to different areas of logical database devices. For example, tables and indexes are, by default, assigned to the default segment. Each time a new logical database device is added to database (via the alter database command), the SQL Server automatically extends the system and default segments to the new logical database device that supports the database:

Segments are limited in the following ways:

1. The total number of segments that an individual SQL Server database can have is limited to no more than 32.
2. Segments can be defined only on logical database devices used by a given database.
3. Segments are mapped to the entire database device and not just to the space fragments.

4. While a logical database device can contain more than one type of segment, a segment can contain only one type of data. While different types of data can be on the same database device, only one type of data can be stored in a given segment (e.g., `logsegments` hold only the *syslogs* system table, `system` segments hold only system catalog tables, etc.

Segments and System Tables

Three system tables hold information about segments:

1. `master..sysusages` - `sysusages..segmap` provides bit maps to the segments in the database for each logical database device.

2. `syssegments`—one in each database lists the segments in a database.

3. `sysindexes`—one in each database. When you create a table or index, SQL Server adds a new row to `sysindexes`. The `sysindexes...segment` column holds the segment number, indicating where the SQL Server will allocate new space for the table or index object. If you create a table containing text or image columns, a second row is also added to `sysindexes` for the linked list of text pages.

Creating a User-Defined Segment

While the SQL Server will automatically place system tables, user tables and indexes, and transaction logs on the appropriate segments, you can take the use of segments a step further. You can create user-defined segments and then, for performance reasons, purposely place user tables and indexes on them to minimize disk I/O contention. To take this technique to its furthest limit, given multiple disk drives, each supporting a logical disk drive, you can create a user-defined segment that spans across multiple disk drives.

While the SQL Server automatically creates `default` and `system` segments of databases, and automatically extends them to each new logical database device that is added to the database, the SQL Server does not optimally determine which tables or indexes will occupy which logical database device to which the `default` segment is mapped.

As new tables and indexes are created, the SQL Server populates the `default` segment on the database's first logical database device, and when that first and then second logical database device is filled the SQL Server proceeds to work its way across any remaining logical database devices assigned to the database. As a consequence, it is possible for points of contention to develop (i.e., collections of heavily used tables and indexes end up on the same logical database device, instead of being spread out to minimize disk I/O contention).

User-defined segments provide you with the means to control the placement of tables and indexes such that disk I/O contention is kept to a minimum and adequate amounts of restricted disk space are available to specific objects. You can, when you create or alter a user table or index, specifically place that object on a user-defined segment and effectively isolate it from other user tables and indexes. The use of segments to control the placement of user tables and indexes is covered in Chap. 8, "Tables And Indexes."

Before you create a user-defined segment for a user database, that user database and the logical database device(s) it uses, must exist. There are two preliminary steps to creating a user-defined segment within a database:

1. Initialize the physical device with the `disk init` command.
2. Make the database device available to the database by using the `on` clause to the `create database`, or `alter database`, commands.

To create a new user-defined segment, you must be the owner of the database within which the segment will be created or you must be as an account with **sa_role** privileges. To create a user-defined segment, log on to the SQL Server as an account with **dbo** or **sa_role** privileges, and enter these commands:

```
1>use NameOfDatabase
2>go
1>sp_addsegment NameOfSegment, NameOfDatabase,
   NameOfDatabaseDevice
2>go
```

where:

NameOfSegment—the name of the segment to be created. The name of the segment must conform to the Sybase rules for identifiers. Segment names are added to the *syssegments* table within the current database you are using, and must be unique within that database.

NameOfDatabase—the name of the database for which you want to create a user-defined segment.

NameOfDatabaseDevice—the name of a database device that is being used by the current database on which you want to locate the new segment. You cannot use the name of the database device that is being used by a *syslogs* system table, or by a dump device.

When the command completes successfully, the new user-defined segment will be immediately available for use by the **dbo.** In that the **sp_addsegment** system procedure modifies system tables (i.e., *sysseg-*

ments), it cannot be executed within a transaction. This command changes the user database, so to ensure its recovery, be certain to dump its transaction log and then dump the database itself.

Reporting on Segments within a Database

To check the space you have available on a segment, or to list the database devices to which a given segment is mapped, use the **sp_helpsegment** system procedure. By default, anyone can execute the **sp_helpsegment** system procedure. To check on space available on a segment, log on to the SQL Server as any valid Sybase account and enter these commands:

```
1>use NameOfDatabase
2>go
1>sp_helpsegment [NameOfSegment]
2>go
```

where:

NameOfDatabase—the name of the database for which you want a segment report produced.

NameOfSegment—the name of the segment for which you want a segment report produced. If you want a report on the default segment, then be certain to enclose its name in quotes (""). If you do not use this optional parameter, then all segments in the database will be reported on.

The report will show the name(s) and status of the segment(s), the names and sizes of the logical database devices the segment is mapped to, the list of tables and indexes placed on the segment, and the count of free pages in the segment.

For an alternative tool for gathering information about segments for a given database, use the **sp_helpdb** system procedure. And, if you want information about the segment placement of a table or index, then use the **sp_help** or the **sp_helpindex** system procedure.

Extending a Segment

Over time, a segment can become full and need more space. A segment can be extended over one or more database devices. However, before you can extend a segment:

1. The database device must be listed within the *sysdevices* table.

2. The database device must be in use by the current database.

3. The segment must exist in the current database.

To increase the size of a segment you must be the owner of the database within which the segment will be created, or you must be as an account with **sa_role** privileges. To increase the size of a segment, log on to the SQL Server as an account with **dbo** or **sa_role** privileges and enter these commands:

```
1>use NameOfDatabase
2>go
1>sp_extendsegment NameOfSegment, NameOfDatabase,
   NameOfDatabaseDevice
2>go
```

where:

NameOfSegment—the name of the segment to be extended. If you want to increase the size of the `default` segment, then be certain to enclose its name in quotes (`" "`).

NameOfDatabase—the name of the database that is mapped to the segment whose size you are increasing.

NameOfDatabaseDevice—the name of a database device that is being used by the current database on which you want to extend the segment. You cannot use the name of the database device that is being used by a *syslogs* system table or by a dump device. In addition, you cannot extend a segment onto the only or last database device that has free space available to the current database for creating new database objects.

When the command completes successfully, the new space allocated to the segment will be immediately available for use by the **dbo.** In that the **sp_extendsegment** system procedure modifies system tables (i.e., *syssegments*), it cannot be executed within a transaction. This command changes the user database, so to ensure its recovery, be certain to dump its transaction log and then dump the database itself.

Unmapping a Segment

As was previously mentioned, the `default` and `system` segments are automatically extended by the SQL Server over all logical database devices that a database uses. Given the automatic behavior of the SQL Server in relation to new user tables and indexes (i.e., it will automatically place them on the `default` segment), you may need to remove the `default` and `system` segments from certain logical database devices that a database uses so that you can gain greater control over the placement of user tables and indexes. If you intend to reduce the scope of the database's `default` or `system` segments, then be extremely careful that you do not leave insufficient space for system-table growth, or for the growth of user tables and indexes that you do not plan to explicitly place on a user-defined segment.

When you reduce the scope of a `default`, `system`, or user-defined, segment you are unmapping that segment from a specific logical database device. When a segment is unmapped from a database device, the segment no longer references that specific database device. Therefore, that specific logical database device can no longer be used by the segment for storing data or log information. However, bear in mind that an unmapped segment is also not dropped from a database, nor can you unmap a segment that is currently supporting a table or an index (you will have to place them somewhere else before you unmap the segment).

To unmap a segment, log on to the SQL Server as an account with **dbo** or **sa_role** privileges and enter these commands:

```
1>use NameOfDatabase
2>go
1>sp_dropsegment NameOfSegment, NameOfDatabase
  [, NameOfDatabaseDevice]
2>go
```

where:

NameOfSegment—the name of the segment to be unmapped. If you want to unmap a `default`, a `system`, or a `logsegment` segment, then be certain to enclose its name in quotes (`""`). Also, you cannot dereference the last remaining segment.

NameOfDatabase—the name of the database whose segment you want to unmap.

NameOfDatabaseDevice—the name of a database device from which the segment is being unmapped. If you are unmapping a `default`, `system` or `logsegment` segment, then this parameter is not optional; it is mandatory. Also, you can not drop the last logical database device reference for a segment (when you work your way down to the last reference, you just drop the entire segment).

When the command completes successfully, the segment will no longer be associated with the logical database device. In that the **sp_dropsegment** system procedure modifies system tables (i.e., *syssegments*), it cannot be executed within a transaction. This command changes the user database, so to ensure its recovery, be certain to dump its transaction log and then dump the database itself.

Keep these three facts in mind when we examine thresholds:

1. Unmapping a segment drops all thresholds, associated with that segment, that exceed the total space on the segment.

2. The SQL Server will recalculate the last-chance threshold whenever you unmap a `logsegment` from one or more database devices.

Dropping a Segment

When you drop a segment, it will no longer exist with the current database. If the segment to be dropped is the last segment that references a specific database device, then that database device is no longer available for use by the current database. However, you cannot drop a segment if it is referenced by any table or index in the current database. Therefore, to drop such a segment, you must first move the objects that reside on it somewhere else.

To drop a segment, log on to the SQL Server as an account with **dbo** or **sa_role** privileges and enter these commands:

```
1>use NameOfDatabase
2>go
1>sp_dropsegment NameOfSegment, NameOfDatabase
2>go
```

where:

NameOfSegment—the name of the segment to be dropped. Be certain not to drop the last `default`, `system`, or `logsegment` segment.

NameOfDatabase—the name of the database whose segment you want to drop.

When the command completes successfully, the segment will no longer exist within the database. Also, dropping a segment drops all thresholds associated with it as well. In that the **sp_dropsegment** system procedure modifies system tables (i.e., *syssegments*), it cannot be executed within a transaction. This command changes the user database, so to ensure its recovery, be certain to dump its transaction log and then dump the database itself.

The Database Transaction Log and Segments

The logical database device or the segment on which you place the *syslogs* system table is used exclusively by that table. You cannot create additional segments on a logical database device that is dedicated to a transaction log.

Always place the database transaction log on a separate logical database device and segment from the actual data. If the data and transaction log are on the same segment:

1. You cannot use `dump transaction` to copy the transaction log and truncate it.
2. You cannot use `dump transaction with no_truncate` to copy the transaction log without truncating it.
3. You must use `dump transaction with truncate_only` to remove committed transactions from the log without making a backup copy.
4. You cannot determine the amount of log space used.
5. The log segment cannot have a last-chance threshold.

The Threshold Manager

Another major benefit of segments is that they allow you to use thresholds. A *threshold* monitors how much free space remains on a particular segment. A given segment can have zero, one, or many thresholds associated with it. Over time, as tables and indexes are stored on a segment, and as transactions are recorded within the log segment, they consume that segment's free space. When the amount of free space on a given segment falls below a given threshold, the SQL Server will automatically execute the stored procedure associated with that given threshold.

In effect, the threshold acts as a detection device that fires off a stored procedure. However, Sybase does not provide you with any threshold's stored procedure. You must create every threshold's stored procedure. For example, you may want a data segment's threshold stored procedure to write a message into the SQL Server's error log and then request an Open-Server-based application to send an electronic-mail message to (or to page) the database Administrator, notifying them that the threshold has been crossed.

Alternatively, you might want a log segment's threshold stored procedure to execute the `dump transaction` Transact-SQL command. Just what type of behavior you want a threshold's stored procedure to exhibit is up to you.

A predefined global variable called the `@@thresh_hysteresis` represents the change in free space required to fire a threshold's stored procedure. This amount, also known as the hysteresis value, is measured in 2K pages. Once a threshold stored procedure is executed, the threshold is turned off. It will remain turned off until the amount of free space in the segment increases `@@thresh_hysteresis` pages beyond the threshold. This internal governor prevents thresholds from repeatedly executing their procedures in response to insignificant oscillations in free space.

In that multiple thresholds can be associated with a given segment, the @@thresh_hysteresis global variable serves another purpose: it is used to determine how closely multiple thresholds can be placed on a segment.

Log Segment Thresholds

For each new database, the SQL Server automatically creates a **last-chance** threshold for the logsegment. In addition, you can create other thresholds for the logsegment.

The **last-chance** threshold is an estimate of the number of free log pages within the transaction log that are required to record the dump transaction command. To successfully back up a transaction log, it must contain enough free log pages on which to record the dump transaction Transact-SQL command. If there are not enough free log pages within the transaction log, then the dump transaction command will fail.

When the amount of free space in the log segment falls below the **last-chance** threshold, SQL Server automatically executes a special stored procedure called **sp_thresholdaction** (but remember, the SQL Server does not provide you with the **sp_thresholdaction** stored procedure). Generally, you will implement this **sp_thresholdaction** stored procedure to execute the dump transaction command. In this way, the **last-chance** threshold and the **sp_thresholdaction** stored procedure work together to free space within the log segment so that the transaction log does not run out of space while supporting active transactions. Just be sure that the dump device that is to hold the transaction log dump image always has sufficient space to accept the generated dump image. When correctly implemented, these deployed facilities should ensure that you never have to execute the dump transaction .. with no_log command.

When the **last-chance** threshold is crossed, SQL Server automatically suspends active user processes and displays an error message. If the SQL Server is unable to put a given transaction to sleep, it will abort that transaction. You will have to rerun any such aborted transaction. Only commands that are not recorded in the transaction log can be executed, such as fast bcps, readtext and writetext commands, read-only queries, and certain variations of the dump transaction command can be executed when the **last-chance** threshold is crossed. Once sufficient log-segment space is freed, suspended processes are automatically awakened and complete. However, the account with **sa_role** privileges may have to increase the size of the transaction log to provide sufficient free space on the log segment. If user processes are suspended due to reaching a **last-chance** threshold on a log segment, extending to the log segment will awaken the processes. Finally, if a database has the `abort tran on log full` database option set to `true`, the SQL Server will roll back all transactions that have not yet been logged when the **last-chance** threshold is crossed. You will have to rerun any such rolled-back transaction.

As has been explained, the space allocated to a log segment can be increased over time. To ensure that the **last-chance** threshold remains viable, the SQL Server automatically adjusts the **last-chance** threshold whenever you allocate more space to the log segment.

As you might have inferred, due to the behavior that takes over whenever a **last-chance** threshold is crossed (i.e., transactions are put to sleep, aborted, or rolled back), this is not the type of product feature you want to automatically kick in within a production environment. Therefore, to minimize the chance of encroaching upon the **last-chance** threshold, adding a second well-placed threshold (on `logsegment`) that precedes it is fundamentally a good practice.

The purpose of this second log segment threshold is to dump the transaction log with such frequency as to avoid crossing the **last-chance** threshold. However, the second log segment threshold should not make so many transaction log dumps that restoring the production database involves loading an exorbitant count of transaction log dumps. In a word, the second log segment threshold is a double-edged sword. But then again, don't leave home without it.

The general rule of thumb is to place the second log segment threshold in the middle of the log segment, and then keep a close eye on its behavior for a reasonable period of time. If you are lucky, the behavior of your database is consistent, so finding the appropriate resting place for the second log segment threshold will take a short amount of time and effort. If you are not so lucky, because the behavior of your database is too chaotic, then finding the placement of the second log segment may require ongoing maintenance.

Data Segment Thresholds

As with log segments, free space within data segments is consumed over time. While the problem being managed is the same (i.e., the progressive loss of free space on a segment), the behavior of stored procedures associated with data segment threshold stored procedures are distinctly different from log segment threshold stored procedures. Also, the rules governing the placement of data segment thresholds are not similar to log segment thresholds.

The behavior of data segment threshold stored procedures should follow an escalation formula that is in harmony with the manner in which free space on data segments is being consumed by the application. The key here is the behavior of the application that the database supports.

Case in point, the behavior of an on-line transaction processing (OLTP) application is distinctly different from a batch process-based database, like a Decision Support System (DSS), or a Data Warehouse.

The volume of new data loads for databases that are dominated by batch processes, with the exception of their initial data-load run, tend not to fluctuate to any significant degree (i.e., usually the initial data load is vastly greater than the daily delta feeds). For example, the initial data load could be three months of operational data, while the delta feeds merely address a single day's new data volume. Given this tendency toward stability, it is relatively straightforward to predict the rate at which free space will be consumed over a given period for this type of database. The first challenge is to allocate sufficient data space to hold the initial data load. And, the second challenge is to allocate additional data space that is adequate to support the data volumes that will be assimilated over three-, six-, nine-, and twelve-month periods. The data segment threshold stored procedure you establish for the initial data load will attempt to ensure that the database Administrator is notified when it appears that the initial data load allocation is inadequate to support the initial data load. After the initial data load has completed successfully, then the data segment threshold stored procedure should fire off when it looks like you will be unable to support the delta feeds sometime in the short, near, and long terms. Basically, this second set of thresholds should be capable of notifying the database Administrator so that deviation from the free data space capacity plan is known early enough so that disk drives can be deployed well ahead of the point in time in which they are needed to support day-to-day operations.

For batch-based data segment thresholds, it may be sufficient to have the data segment threshold stored procedure write an error message into the SQL Server error log stating that free space is predicted to be gone at a certain point in the future. Your custom-built script that monitors the SQL Server error log should then scan these messages from the error log and send, at minimum, an e-mail message to the responsible parties (i.e., the database Administrator and the system Administrator). As that point the future gets closer to the present, then the data segment threshold stored procedure should be paging the responsible parties, and their supervisors.

Thresholds for OLTP-based databases require an approach that differs from their batch cousins, as volumes of new data of OLTP-based databases can fluctuate radically when the business processes they support are highly volatile. With this type of system, a week's new data volume can be entered in a single day, and continue for many consecutive days. Therefore, the data segment threshold stored procedure should escalate warning messages up through the organization structures at a high rate. Instead of settling for messages being printed just to the SQL Server error log, the data segment threshold stored procedure should send a request to an Open-Server-based application that pages the responsible parties and their supervisors as soon as the threshold has been crossed.

Threshold Stored Procedures

When a threshold is crossed, an internal SQL Server process executes the stored procedure, and uses one user connection for as long as it takes to execute it. However, the stored procedure run as background processes.

The SQL Server executes threshold stored procedures with the permissions of the Sybase account that created the threshold (at the time the Sybase account created the threshold) minus any permissions that have been revoked from that Sybase account since the point in time when the threshold was created.

At execution time, the SQL Server follows this path in search of the threshold stored procedure:

1. If the threshold stored procedure name does not specify a database, the SQL Server looks in the current database (i.e., the database in which the threshold was crossed).

2. If the threshold stored procedure is not found in the current database, and the threshold stored procedure name has an `sp_` prefix, then the SQL Server looks in the *sybsystemprocs* system database.

3. If the threshold stored procedure is not found in either the current database or in the *sybsystemprocs* system database, then the SQL Server sends an error message to the SQL Server error log.

The internal SQL Server process passes four parameters to a threshold stored procedure:

1. `@dbname`—the data type and length is varchar(30). This parameter identifies the current database.

2. `@segmentname`—the data type and length is varchar(30). This parameter identifies the current segment.

3. `@space_left`—the data type is int. This parameter indicates the number of free pages associated with the crossed threshold.

4. `@status`—the data type is int. This parameter has a value of 1 for **last-chance** thresholds and 0 for other thresholds.

As these parameters are passed by position rather than by name, a threshold stored procedure can use other names for its parameters, however they must be declared in the order shown in the previous list and with the same data types and lengths (where applicable).

Any Sybase account with `create procedure` permission granted to the current database can create a threshold stored procedure in that database.

It is not absolutely necessary that you create a unique stored procedure for each threshold. You can create a single threshold stored procedure in the *sybsystemprocs* system database and associate it with all the thresholds you create in a given SQL Server. This approach does tend to decrease your maintenance overhead, but in most installations, the creation of multiple threshold stored procedures is generally required. And, finally, it is generally good practice to include `print` and `raiserror` statements in the threshold stored procedure so that appropriate messages are sent to the SQL Server error log.

Examining Segment Thresholds

To examine thresholds in the current database or all thresholds for a particular segment in the current database, log on to the SQL Server as any valid Sybase account (that has permissions to use the database you want to examine), and enter these commands:

```
1>use NameOfDatabase
2>go
1>sp_helpthreshold [NameOfSegment]
2>go
```

where:

NameOfDatabase—the name of the database whose segment thresholds you want to examine.

[NameOfSegment]—This is the name of a segment within the current database. If you use this optional parameter, then a list of thresholds for that particular segment is produced. Be certain to use quotes when specifying the "default" segment (i.e., as default is a SQL Server reserved word you must use quotes). If you do not specify a segment, then information for all segments within the current database is reported.

When the **sp_helpthreshold** completes executing, the following information will be displayed:

`name`—the name of the segment within the current database.

`free_space`—the count of 2K pages that represents the individual threshold's free space high-water mark.

last-chance—basically status information. If the value displayed equals 1, then you are looking at the **last-chance** threshold, else the value display will be 0, indicating that it is not the **last-chance** threshold.

proc_name—the name of the stored procedure associated with a given threshold.

Creating a Segment Threshold

A SQL Server database can have up to 256 thresholds. To create a threshold, log on to the SQL Server as an account with **dbo** or **sa_role** privileges and enter these commands:

```
1>use NameOfDatabase
2>go
1>sp_addthreshold NameOfDatabase, NameOfSegment,
2>CountOfFreePages, NameOfStoredProcedure
3>go
```

where:

NameOfDatabase—the name of the database whose segment you want to add a threshold to.

NameOfSegment—the name of the segment to which you want to add a threshold.

CountOfFreePages—the number of free pages at which the threshold is crossed. When free space in the segment falls below this level, SQL Server executes the associated stored procedure. There must be at least two times @@thresh_hysteresis pages from the closest threshold on this segment.

NameOfStoredProcedure—the name of the stored procedure to execute when the amount of free space on segment drops below the free pages high-water mark. Thresholds can execute a stored procedure in the same database, in another user database, in the *sybsystemprocs* system database, or in the *master* system database. The stored procedure can be located on the current SQL Server. However, thresholds cannot execute stored procedures on remote SQL Servers. The sp_addthreshold command does not verify that the specified stored procedure exists. Therefore, as it is possible to add a threshold before creating the stored procedure it executes, be absolutely certain to create the associated stored procedure before you create the new threshold. The stored procedure has the permissions of the user who created the threshold, less any permissions that have been revoked on that Sybase account since that point in time when the threshold was created.

When the command completes successfully, the segment threshold will take effect immediately. In that the **sp_addthreshold** system procedure modifies system tables (i.e., *syssegments*), it cannot be executed within a transaction. This command changes the user database, so to ensure its recovery, be certain to dump its transaction log and then dump the database itself.

Modifying a Database Threshold

It is possible to modify an existing threshold. But whenever you modify a threshold, the existing threshold is dropped and a new one is created in its place. There are three ways to modify a threshold:

1. Associate a threshold with a new threshold stored procedure.
2. Associate a threshold with a new free-space value.
3. Associate a threshold with a new segment.

However, you cannot modify the amount of free space or the segment name for the **last-chance** threshold from a log segment. But, you can change the name of the threshold stored procedure that will execute when the **last-chance** threshold is crossed.

To modify a threshold, log on to the SQL Server as an account with **dbo** or **sa_role** privileges and enter these commands:

```
1>use NameOfDatabase
2>go
1>sp_modifythreshold NameOfDatabase, NameOfSegment,
2>CountOfFreePages, [,NameOfNewStoredProcedure]
3>[,CountOfNewFreePages][,NameOfNewSegment]
4>go
```

where:

NameOfDatabase—the name of the database whose threshold you want to modify.

NameOfSegment—the name of the segment whose threshold you want to modify.

CountOfFreePages—the number of free pages at which the threshold is crossed. When free space in the segment falls below this level, SQL

Server executes the associated stored procedure. There must be at least two times @@thresh_hysteresis pages from the closest threshold on this segment.

NameOfNewStoredProcedure—this optional parameter is the name of the new stored procedure to execute when the amount of free space on the segment drops below the free page's high-water mark. Thresholds can execute a stored procedure in the same database, in another user database, in the *sybsystemprocs* system database, or in the *master* system database. The stored procedure can be located on the current SQL Server. However, thresholds cannot execute stored procedures on remote SQL Servers. The `sp_addthreshold` command does not verify that the specified stored procedure exists. Therefore, as it is possible to add a threshold before creating the stored procedure it executes, be absolutely certain to create the associated stored procedure before you create the new threshold. The stored procedure has the permissions of the user who created the threshold, less any permissions that have been revoked on that Sybase account since that point in time when the threshold was created. If you will not be associating a new stored procedure to this threshold, then enter the character string NULL.

[,*CountOfNewFreePages*]—this optional parameter is the new free-space value you want to associate with the threshold. However, you cannot modify the amount of free space of a **last-chance** threshold of a log segment. If you will not be associating a new free-space value for this threshold, then enter the character string NULL.

[,*NameOfNewSegment*]—this optional parameter is the name of the new segment you want to associate with the threshold. You cannot modify the name of the segment of a **last-chance** threshold of a log segment.

Use of the `sp_modifythreshold` system command has these constraints:

1. The command does not verify that the stored procedure exists at the time you modify the threshold.
2. Each time a Sybase account modifies a threshold, that Sybase account becomes the threshold owner. When the threshold is crossed, SQL Server executes the threshold with the permissions of the owner at the time the Sybase account modified the threshold, minus any permissions that have been revoked from that Sybase account after the threshold was modified.
3. You cannot change the free-space value or segment name associated with the **last-chance** threshold.

4. You can modify thresholds only in the database you are currently using.

When the command completes successfully, the segment change(s) to the threshold will take effect immediately. In that the **sp_modify-threshold** system procedure modifies system tables (i.e., *syssegments*), it cannot be executed within a transaction. This command changes the user database, so to ensure its recovery, be certain to dump its transaction log and then dump the database itself.

Enabling Segment Free-Space Accounting

By default, the no free space acctg database option is set to true in all databases, and free-space accounting, and the execution of threshold actions for nonlog segments, are disabled. As a consequence, the rows-per-page value for each table is not automatically kept up to date by the SQL Server. As a result, system procedures that estimate nonlog segment usage by the database will likely produce incorrect information. When the value of this option is set to false, database recovery is significantly increased because during the recovery process free-space counts are recalculated for every nonlog segment associated with the database. However, you cannot disable free-space accounting on log segments.

To set the no free space acctg database option to false, log on to the SQL Server as an account with **dbo** or **sa_role** privileges, verify that no one is using the target database (kill any offending processes if need be), and enter these commands:

```
1>use master
2>go
1>sp_dboption NameOfDatabase, "no free space acctg", false
2>go
1>checkpoint
2>go
```

where:

NameOfDatabase—the name of the user database in which you want to set the no free space acctg database option to false.

checkpoint—the new database option setting will not take effect until this command is issued (or until the SQL Server is restarted).

This command changes the *master* system database, so to ensure its recovery, be certain to dump the *master* system database.

There are some constraints associated with the **sp_dboption** system procedure:

1. No one can be using the database when you set one of its database options.

2. During SQL Server run time, the change in a database option takes place only after running the `checkpoint` Transact-SQL command.

Dropping a Database Threshold

You can destroy, or drop, an existing threshold. To drop a threshold, log on to the SQL Server as an account with **dbo** or **sa_role** privileges, and enter these commands:

```
1>use NameOfDatabase
2>go
1>sp_dropthreshold NameOfDatabase, NameOfSegment,
2>CountOfFreePages
3>go
```

where:

NameOfDatabase—the name of the database whose threshold you want to drop.

NameOfSegment—the name of the segment whose threshold you want to drop.

CountOfFreePages—the number of free pages at which the threshold is crossed (of the threshold you want to drop).

You cannot use the **sp_dropthreshold** system command to drop the **last-chance** threshold from a log segment. When the command completes successfully, the segment threshold will be immediately purged from the database. In that the **sp_dropthreshold** system procedure modifies system tables (i.e., *syssegments*), it cannot be executed within a transaction. This command changes the user database, so to ensure its recovery, be certain to dump its transaction log and then dump the database itself.

Threshold Limitations

Thresholds operate under these constraints:

1. Recall that tasks initiated by the threshold stored procedure execute as background processes (i.e., these tasks do not have an associated terminal or user session), and that this background process requires a user connection to the SQL Server. As a result, if there are no available user connections, the threshold stored procedure will not exe-

cute and an error message will be written into the SQL Server error log by the internal SQL Server process.

2. If there is not enough space within the internal SQL Server procedure cache to execute the threshold stored procedure, the threshold stored procedure will not execute and an error message will be written into the SQL Server error log by the internal SQL Server process.

3. Each database can have, at most, 256 thresholds, including the **last-chance** threshold.

4. Multiple thresholds can be created within a given segment. However, each new threshold must be at least two times `@@thresh_hysteresis` pages from the next closest threshold.

5. You can only execute a threshold stored procedure to dump the transaction log where `the trunc log on chkpt` database option is set to `false` within the current database.

6. If unlogged transactions were running between the point in time when the last database dump was taken and when the **last-chance** threshold is crossed, then the `dump transaction` Transact-SQL command cannot be executed. When this happens, you must first execute the `dump database` Transact-SQL command and then execute the `dump transaction` Transact-SQL command.

Stored Procedures, Triggers, and Views

Stored Procedures

A stored procedure is an extension to the Transact-SQL language. With stored procedures you can:

1. Combine a wide variety of Transact-SQL commands with control-of-flow constructs.

2. Define one or more parameters to be passed to the stored procedure when it is executed. You can provide a constant default value to a given parameter, which the SQL Server will use if you do not provide a value for that given parameter at the point in time when you execute the stored procedure.

3. Define one or more local variables that can be assigned literal data values within the stored procedure, while the given stored procedure is executing.

4. Define one or more values to be returned from the executed stored procedure to its caller.

5. Define return status from the executed stored procedure to its caller.

6. Execute a stored procedure on a remote SQL Server via a logical unit of work that is executing on your local SQL Server. This is referred to as making a remote procedure call. This is possible if and only if the local SQL Server and the remote SQL Server are both configured to allow remote login. It is important to understand that remote procedure calls are not treated as a part of the logical unit of work that is executing within the local SQL Server. If your local logical unit of work executes a remote procedure call,

and then you subsequently roll back your local logical unit of work, the database operation produced on the remote SQL Server is not rolled back.

7. Execute other stored procedures from within a given stored procedure. This includes executing a stored procedure from within a trigger.

8. Grant permission to SQL Server users, other than the owner of the stored procedure, to execute a stored procedure. This permission can be granted even if the SQL Server user lacks permissions to read or modify the underlying table(s) or view(s) the stored procedure acts upon.

9. Decrease the transaction execution time (relative to Transact-SQL command statements) because a stored procedure is precompiled and its query execution plan is saved and reused whenever the stored procedure is executed. In this way, the processing step to produce the query execution plan is skipped after the first time the stored procedure runs.

10. Instruct explicitly the SQL Server not to save the stored procedure's query execution plan, but, instead, have the query execution plan generated each and every time the stored procedure is executed.

11. Place a collection of stored procedures into a given group and destroy that collection with a single command.

12. Create and then use temporary tables within a given stored procedure.

13. Invoke system functions within stored procedures.

Optimization Stages

When a process submits a transaction to the SQL Server, three tasks are undertaken by the optimizer before the transaction is executed:

1. The transaction statement is cast, using a resolution process, into a proprietary internal format called a *query tree*. This internal format is a canonical representation (of the transaction) expressed in relational algebra. During this step, the transaction statement's syntax is also checked, and all referenced principal database object identifiers are verified. If any of the referenced principal database objects is a view, then a relational algebraic expression that computes the view is assimilated into the canonical representation of the transaction statement.

2. A suite of alternate, equivalent expressions is produced, and one alternate is found to be the most efficient to execute.

3. The best access path to the data is determined. This step is known as *query optimization.*

For noncompiled transactions, these query trees exist only for the life of the transaction. But for compiled objects, like stored procedures and triggers, query trees are permanently stored in the database's *sysprocedures* system table, reused, and maintained as need be. And, when a stored procedure or trigger is created, the ASCII text of the procedure is stored in the *syscomments* table of the database in which it was created. The ASCII text of the procedure or trigger cannot exceed 16 MB.

The Statistical Query Optimizer

As Transact-SQL is based on relational algebra, a stored procedure's transaction statements are merely prescriptive (i.e., they simply represent one particular sequence of operations). Within relational algebra, it is possible to express an operation in many equivalent, alternate ways. However, even though two or more ways of expressing a relational algebra operation may be equivalent, one of the expressions might execute with greater efficiency, relative to the alternates.

The main function of the statistical query optimizer is to determine which alternate expression will execute that quickest. The statistical query optimizer makes these determinations by using information about the target database, and by applying the research findings by computer scientists who study database access methods.

For the most part, the information about the target database that the optimizer uses is readily available to you (e.g., the number of rows in a table, the number of pages in a table, etc.). As for the application of computer-science expertise in the field of database access methods by Sybase, this matter is a highly guarded trade secret which this author is not privileged to know (as the old joke goes, "Don't ask. I can't tell you. Because, if I told you, I'd have to shoot you.").

The Problem of Too Many Data Access Paths

Any query optimizer that can quickly recognize and discard the inefficient expressions, and then turn and focus on the minimal number of promising alternates, provides a DBMS vendor with a significant competitive advantage. However, finding the best possible path to the data is not an easy matter, particularly when the transaction involves a three-table join.

Each table has at least one associated data access path. For each index that a table has, it has associated with it another data access path. For example, a table that has one index will have two access paths to the data stored within it, if a table has two indexes then there will be three access paths, and so on. To give you an idea of just how large the count of data access paths can easily grow to, let's consider a couple of examples. First, let's join two tables that have one index each. Looking at this transaction we can see that:

1. There are two data access paths for each of the two tables ($2 * 2 = 4$).
2. A two-table join can be performed in two different orders: AB, BA ($2 * 1 = 2$).
3. For each join order there is one kind of join.

Next, let's examine a three-table join where each of the tables, participating in the join, has two indexes. Looking at this transaction we can see that:

1. There are three data access paths for each of the three tables ($3 * 3 * 3$), or 27 total.
2. A three-table join can be performed in six different orders; XYZ, XZY, YZX, YXZ, ZXY, ZYX ($3 * 2 * 1 = 6$).
3. For each join, there are two different kinds of joins ($2 * 2 = 4$).
4. There are ($27 * 6 * 4$) or 648 possible data access paths for this three-table join.

To appreciate just how rapidly the total number of data access paths can increase, imagine that each of the preceding tables had three indexes. If it were the case that they did have three indexes each, then the total number of data access paths would jump to 1536.

Information Examined by the Optimizer

When you send a SQL statement to the SQL Server, the request first goes to a cost-based query optimizer whose job it is to find the most efficient data access path to fulfill the request. To determine which of the most promising data access paths is likely to execute the quickest, the optimizer examines the following information:

1. The physical structure and type of indexes for all relevant tables (as represented in the query tree).
2. The coverage of the relevant indexes (i.e., can the query be satisfied by retrieving data just from the available indexes or must data pages be referenced).

3. The distribution of literal data values stored within the individual columns that makes up all relevant indexes (i.e., the distribution statistics and their density).

4. The number of rows in the table(s) involved.

5. The number of data pages used by the table(s) involved.

6. The specified caching strategy (or will, when it is not explicitly stated, determine the best caching strategy).

7. The amount of available data cache, and the Buffer Mass size supported by the data cache.

8. The total number of data pages being used by all tables involved in the transaction.

9. The amount of physical disk I/O involved in reading pages from disk.

10. The amount of logical I/O involved in repeatedly reading pages within data cache.

11. The best join order, if applicable.

12. If there are no indexes to support the query, then the overhead of building work tables within the *tempdb* system database to support the join columns will be determined and a comparison to doing repeated table scans will be conducted.

13. Search arguments within the query statement will be examined to determine if existing indexes can be used to support the query.

14. If the statement contains a **max** or **min** scalar aggregate, then it will determine if an existing index can be used to find the value without having to scan the relevant table.

15. If the statement contains an **order by, group by,** or **distinct** clause, then the additional physical and logical I/O costs for performing sorts within the *tempdb* system database will be determined.

And, when determining the best access method for a stored procedure, the query optimizer will consider the literal data values of any parameters passed to the procedure on its first execution.

When you consider the types of information that the optimizer examines to find the most suitable access path, it is clear that the manner in which you configure your SQL Server; implement your physical database, and maintain your distribution statistics has a significant impact on the performance of the optimizer, and on the efficiency of any given data access path. As the quality of these aspects of your computing system is directly under your control, the better you control their quality, the better the statistical optimizer will perform. Conversely, poor-quality statistics and bad physical-database design will significantly degrade the performance of the optimizer.

Collecting Statistics

The performance of the optimizer is heavily dependent upon the accuracy of the distribution statistics for all the indexes under its examination. Distribution statistics are statistics on the distribution of literal data values stored within individual columns (sometimes referred to as *keys*) that make up a given index. The optimizer uses these distribution statistics to determine which index(es) to use when processing your transaction.

Whenever you create an index for a table that contains data, the SQL Server automatically runs the `update statistics` command. This command updates information about the distribution of the literal data values stored within individual columns that make up a given index. The `update statistics` command also updates allocation page values that are used by the query optimizer to estimate the number of rows in the specified table.

To execute the `update statistics` command you must be the owner of the specified table. Or, if you are the owner of the database that contains the specified table, you can execute this command after you have impersonated the table owner (by using the `setuser` command). The distribution statistics are stored in a distribution page. Each index has its own distribution page. The `master..sysindexes` system table in each database stores a pointer to the distribution page for each index in the database. You will need to rerun the `update statistics` command as the literal data values of the index keys change noticeably, or as (relatively) large-volume rows are inserted in or deleted from the underlying table.

Because of its negative impact on distribution statistics, special consideration must be given to the use of the `truncate table` command. As previously explained, the `truncate table` command deallocates all of the pages that support an index. The `truncate table` command also, because of its effect on indexes, also deallocates all of the distribution pages for all impacted indexes. Therefore, to ensure efficient data access to a truncated table, be sure to run the `update statistics` command after you have added the new rows to a truncated table.

Query Plan

With this information in hand, the statistical query optimizer calculates which access path would require the least amount of I/O, and therefore would be the fastest. Once the optimal access path is calculated, it is stored in a query plan within the procedure cache. This process of building a query plan is called *compilation.* Since query plans are held only in procedure cache and not on disk, stored procedure and trigger query plans must be recompiled (i.e., rebuilt) each time SQL Server is started. On the first execution of a stored procedure, the corresponding query tree is read from the *sysprocedures* table and loaded into the procedure cache.

Stored procedures are reusable, not reentrant. This means that only one user may be executing a given copy of a procedure's query plan at one time. If two or more users try to execute the same procedure at the same time, SQL Server will create an additional query plan based on the parameters used on the latter execution. When a user finishes using the procedure, the query plan is then available for reuse, in cache, for anyone else with execute permissions. The additional query plans stay in procedure cache until they are swapped out, and could cause one execution to run very differently from another, though the returned results are the same. The end user has no control or knowledge of which query plan he will get for a given execution.

Here are two other interesting facts about stored procedure (and trigger) query plans:

1. Dropping and recreating the compiled object will cause all existing query plans to be flushed out of procedure cache.

2. Dropping an index or table referenced by a compiled object will invalidate all existing cached copies of the query plan.

Creating a Show Plan

The showplan command is provided to allow you to view the plan the optimizer has chosen and to follow each step that the optimizer took to determine the execution path. This command causes SQL Server to display query plan information for every SQL statement executed within the scope of the SQL Server session. Since your procedures and triggers will persist over time, it is extremely important that you ensure that their query plans are suitable for the tasks you intend them to undertake.

Since the determination of a query plan is performed independently from the actual data retrieval or modification, it is possible to examine and tune query plans without actually executing the SQL statements. To examine a transaction's query plan without causing the transaction to actually manipulate any data, log on to the SQL Server and enter this command before you submit your transaction to the SQL Server:

```
1>set showplan on, noexec
2>go
```

After you submit your query to the SQL Server it will not be executed, but a report, called a *show plan,* outlining each step in the transaction's query plan will be produced.

Reresolution of Stored Procedures

The process of updating the existing query tree in the *sysprocedures* table and invalidating any query plans in procedure cache is called reresolution. Reresolution can be triggered by various activities, most of which are controlled by SQL Server, not the procedure owner or the System Administrator. SQL Server reresolves procedures after any of the following:

1. Executing a load database on the database containing the procedure.
2. A table used/referred to by the procedure is dropped and re-created.
3. A load database of a database where a referenced table resides.
4. A database containing a referenced table is dropped and re-created.
5. A rule is bound or unbound to a table referred to by a query in the procedure.
6. A default is bound or unbound to a table referred to by a query in the procedure.
7. An index which is referred to by a procedure is dropped and re-created.

When reresolution occurs the SQL Server must rebuild some parts of the query tree. Unfortunately, the old parts of the query tree cannot be deallocated and the query will grow, slightly. So, to keep the size of your query trees (and query plans) in procedure cache to their absolute minimum size, it is important to drop and re-create affected compiled objects on a routine basis.

Granting Permission to Create
Stored Procedures

By default, users of a database do not have permission to create stored procedures within that database. Be very careful about granting `create procedure` permission to users in a database (i.e., they can easily corrupt data and destroy the integrity of the database).

To grant permission to a user, a list of users, the groups (including the `public` group), or a role, log on to the SQL Server as an account with **dbo** or **sa_role** privileges, and enter these commands:

```
1>use NameOfDatabase
2>go
1>grant create procedure
2>to {public | name_list | role_name}
3>[with grant option]
4>go
```

where:

NameOfDatabase—the name of the database in which you want to grant permission to create procedures to a user, a list of users, the groups (including the `public` group), or a role.

{public | name_list | role_name}—the user, list of users, group, or role to which you want to grant `create procedure` permission.

[with grant option]—this optional parameter is used to permit the owner of the table to grant execute permissions on the stored procedure to other users within the database. However, you can not extend this additional permission to any group or role.

Once this command completes successfully, the login account is immediately capable of creating stored procedures (and triggers) within the database. This command changes the database's system tables, so to ensure its recovery, be certain to dump its transaction log and then dump the database itself. Also, because this command changes the contents of the system tables, it cannot be executed within a transaction.

A user who creates a table owns that stored procedure and automatically obtains all permissions on it. All other users of the database, including an account with **dbo** and **sa_role** privileges, are denied automatic access to a stored procedure they do not own, unless the owner of the table explicitly grants access permissions to them (just as long the account with **dbo** or **sa_role** privileges explicitly granted permission to the table owner to grant access permission to other database users, when that table owner was granted permission to create tables).

Reporting on Stored Procedures

The SQL Server provides you with three means by which to produce reports on stored procedures in a database:

1. `sp_help`—(refer to Chap. 6, "Databases," for an explanation of this system procedure).

2. `sp_helptext`—(refer to Chap. 7, "User-Defined Data Types, Defaults and Rules," for an explanation of this system procedure).

3. `sp_depends`—(refer to Chap. 8, "Tables and Indexes," for an explanation of this system procedure).

Creating a Stored Procedure

To create a good stored procedure, a thorough knowledge of Transact-SQL is a prerequisite. Providing you with that knowledge is outside the scope of this book. To create a stored procedure, log on to the SQL Server as an authorized account, as an account with **dbo** or **sa_role** privileges and enter these commands:

```
1>use NameOfDatabase
2>go
1>create procedure [loginame.]NameOfStoredProcedure[; number]
2>[[ (] @NameOfParameter NameOfDataType [(length) | (precision
  [, scale])]
3>[ = default] [output]
4>[,@NameOfParameter NameOfDataType[(length) | (precision [,
  scale])]
5>[ = default][output]] ... [) ]]
6>[with recompile]
7>as TransactSQLStatements
8>go
```

where:

NameOfDatabase—the name of the database in which you want to create a stored procedure.

`[loginame.]`—the name of the login account that will own the stored procedure. If you will own the stored procedure, then you do not have to provide this parameter.

NameOfStoredProcedure—the name of the stored procedure you want to create. The name of the stored procedures must conform to the rules for Sybase identifiers.

`[;number]`—this optional parameter is used to group together procedures with the same name. Procedures in a group cannot be individually dropped. They can only be dropped as an entire group.

@NameOfParameter—this optional parameter is the name of an argument of the stored procedure. The name of the stored procedure

arguments must begin with the @ symbol, and must conform to the rules for Sybase identifiers. The length of an argument, including the @ symbol, cannot exceed 30 characters. Argument names must be unique within a given stored procedure. A stored procedure can have more than one argument. An alphanumeric value assigned to a stored procedure argument must be enclosed in quotes (" "). A stored procedure can have at most 255 arguments.

NameOfDataType [(length) | (precision [, scale])]—the data type of the stored procedure parameter. Text and image data types are not allowed. Each stored procedure parameter must have its data type defined.

[= default]—this optional parameter specifies the constant default value of the stored procedure parameter. If the stored procedure is executed without passing a value to this stored procedure parameter, then the value of the default will be used. The default can be a wild-card character if the procedure is implemented to handle the parameter with the "like" keyword. The default can also be a NULL if the procedure is implemented to handle the NULL value.

[output]—this optional parameter is used to indicate that the stored procedure parameter is a value that will be returned by the stored procedure to the process that executes it.

[with recompile]—this optional parameter is used to instruct the SQL Server to create a new query plan every time the stored procedure is executed. The effort to create a new query plan will degrade the performance of the stored procedure.

as   *TransactSQLStatements*—the Transact-SQL command language statements that define the action(s) the stored procedure will undertake. Within a stored procedure you cannot include the create default, the create procedure, the create rule, the create trigger, the create view, or the use commands. You can reference other principal database objects from within a stored procedure (such as another stored procedure, a table, or a view), but those objects must exist at the time the stored procedure is first compiled. For example, you cannot create a table and then insert data into that table from within a stored procedure because that table does not exist at the time the stored procedure is first compiled. Also, along these same lines, you cannot create an object, drop it, and then re-create that object within a stored procedure. If a login account, other than the owner of the stored procedure, is to use the stored procedure, then all object names used with the alter table, the create index, the create table, any **dbcc,** the drop index, the drop table, and the update statistics commands must be qualified with the login account that owns the object. From within a stored procedure you can create and reference a temporary table only if it is truly temporary (i.e., it disappears at the end of the stored procedure's execution). You can also incorporate the `set` command within a stored procedure and invoke any system function.

This command changes the database's system tables, so to ensure its recovery, be certain to dump its transaction log and then dump the database itself. Also, because this command changes the contents of the system tables, it cannot be executed within a transaction.

When a stored procedure that accesses the current database is created, the SQL Server does not verify that the owner of the stored procedures has the necessary permissions of the objects referenced in the stored procedure's Transact-SQL statements. The necessary permissions on the referenced objects are verified when the stored procedure executes. As a consequence, the stored procedure will fail if the necessary permissions are not in place. However, when you create a stored procedure that accesses another database, the SQL Server determines whether or not you are an authorized user of that other database.

Granting Permission to Execute a Stored Procedure

If you are an account with **dbo** or **sa_role** privileges, then you can grant permission to database users, groups, or roles to execute a stored procedure you own. If you are a database user and you have permission to both create procedures and grant execute permissions, then you can grant permission to other database users, groups, or roles to execute stored procedures that you own.

To grant execute permission on a stored procedure, log on to the SQL Server as the owner of the stored procedure (or an account with **dbo** or **sa_role** privileges that has taken on the identity of the table owner) and enter these commands:

```
1>use NameOfDatabase
2>go
1>grant execute
2>on NameOfStoredProcedure
3>to {public | name_list | role_name}
4>[with grant option]
5>go
```

where:

NameOfDatabase—the name of the database that contains the stored procedure for which you want to grant execute permission.

on *NameOfStoredProcedure*—the name of the stored procedure for which you want to grant execute permissions.

to {public | name_list | role_name}—the parameter which grants execute permissions to the public group, a list of database users and groups, or a list of roles.

[with grant option]—optional parameter that allows a user (not a group or role) to grant the execute permission(s) to other users, groups, or roles.

Once this command completes successfully, the login account is immediately capable of executing the stored procedure. This command changes the database's system tables, so to ensure its recovery, be certain to dump its transaction log and then dump the database itself. Also, because this command changes the contents of the system tables, it cannot be executed within a transaction.

Executing a Stored Procedure

Except for that fact that permissions on referenced objects are not checked until the stored procedure is run, executing a stored procedure is a pretty straightforward matter. Log on to the SQL Server as the owner of the stored procedure, as an account that has been granted execute permission, or as an account with the **dbo** or **sa_role** privileges and enter these commands:

```
1>use NameOfDatabase
2>go
1>[execute] [@return_status = ]
2>[[[NameOfSQLServer.]NameOfDatabase.]loginame.]
   NameOfStoredProcedure
3>[;number]
4>[[@NameOfParameter =] value |
5>[@NameOfParameter =] @ NameOfVariable[output]
6>[,[@NameOfParameter =] value |
7>[@NameOfParameter =] @ NameOfVariable[output]...]]
8>[with recompile]
9>go
```

where:

NameOfDatabase—the name of the database in which the stored procedure is located.

[execute]—the reserved keyword that instructs the SQL Server to run the stored procedure. It is optional if the stored procedure invocation is the first statement in a batch.

[@return_status =]—this optional parameter is an integer variable that is used to hold the return status of the stored procedure. It must be declared within the stored procedure before it can be used.

[*NameOfSQLServer.*]—this optional parameter is the name of the remote SQL Server at which you want the stored procedure to execute.

NameOfDatabase.]—this optional parameter is the name of the database in which you want the stored procedure to execute. In general, if you provide the name of the database, then you must also provide the name of the login account that owns the stored procedure. If the owner of the stored procedure is also the **dbo,** then you do not have to provide the login account name of the owner of the stored procedure.

loginame.]—this optional parameter is the name of the login account that is the owner of the stored procedure. If you are the owner of the stored procedure, then you do not have to provide this optional parameter.

NameOfStoredProcedure—the name of the stored procedure you want to execute.

[;number]—this optional parameter is the number of the grouped stored procedure you want to execute.

[[@*NameOfParameter* =] value |—this optional parameter is the name of an argument to the stored procedure.

value |—the literal data value you are assigning to the argument.

@NameOfVariable—the variable that will be used to store data returned by the stored procedure.

[output]—designates that this argument is a return parameter.

[with recompile]—this optional parameter tells the SQL Server to produce a new query plan when the stored procedure is invoked.

Run-Time Verification of Stored Procedure Permissions

Coming to grips with how the SQL Server verifies referenced object permissions during run time can be frustrating, but it is not a mess, nor will it torture you soul and induce manic depression. Just keep these rules in mind:

1. If the login account that executes the stored procedure is the owner of the stored procedure and also owns all referenced objects, and all referenced objects are in the same database, then the SQL Server does not verify permissions at run time.

2. If the login account that executes the stored procedure is the owner of the stored procedure and also owns all referenced objects, but all referenced object are not in the same database, then the SQL Server verifies that the login account is a valid or a guest user of each database containing a referenced object.

3. If the login account that executes the stored procedure is the owner of the stored procedure, but does not also own all referenced objects, and all referenced objects are in the same database, then the SQL Server verifies that the login account has been granted the correct permission(s) on the referenced objects it does not own.

4. If the login account that executes the stored procedure is the owner of the stored procedure but does not also own all referenced objects, and all referenced objects are not in the same database, then the SQL Server verifies that the login account has been explicitly granted the correct permission(s) on the referenced objects it does not own and verifies that the login account is a valid or a guest user of each database containing a referenced object.

5. If the login account that executes the stored procedure is not the owner of the stored procedure, then the stored procedure executes as if it were being run by the login account that owns the stored procedure. As such, manipulation of referenced objects can take place through stored procedures without needing to explicitly grant access permissions on the referenced objects to all login accounts that execute the stored procedure. In this way a store procedure can be used as an effective security mechanism.

6. When a stored procedure that must only be executed by a specific role (e.g., **sa_role**) is created, the SQL Server does not verify that the login account to which execute permission has been granted also has that role privilege. To stop the incorrect login accounts from executing, a stored procedure is created only for use executed by a specific role, use the **proc_role** ( ) system function to validate the login account's role privileges. If the login account does not have the appropriate role privileges, the stored procedure will automatically abort its execution.

Nested Stored Procedures

The nesting of stored procedures occurs when one stored procedure executes another stored procedure. However, their are two constraints that must be observed when nesting stored procedures:

1. The levels of stored-procedure nesting cannot exceed 16 levels. The stored procedure's current nesting level is stored within the

@@nestlevel global variable. Each procedure that is called increments this global variable and decrements it when it finishes executing.

2. If a lower-level stored procedure is to return a parameter, then each impacted stored procedure must use the output option with the returned parameter, including the stored procedure at the top level.

On the plus side, an invoked stored procedure can manipulate any object created by the invoking stored procedure.

Recompiling a Stored Procedure

The process of creating a new query plan from an existing query tree is called *recompilation*. Recompilation of a stored procedure takes place whenever one of the following events occurs:

1. The stored procedure is loaded from disk to the procedure cache.
2. An index on any table referred to in the stored procedure is dropped.
3. All copies of the query plan in cache are currently in use.
4. A stored procedure is created using the recompile option.
5. A stored procedure is recompiled because someone has used the **sp_recompile** system procedure against a table that is referenced by the stored procedure.

Adding an index to a referenced table or updating statistics of a referenced index does not force recompilation. To recompile the stored procedure that references the table with the new index, or that uses an index against which the update statistics command has been run, log on to the SQL Server as the owner of the referenced table (or an account with **dbo** or **sa_role** privileges that has taken on the identity of the table owner) and enter these commands:

```
1>use NameOfDatabase
2>go
1>sp_recompile NameOfTable
2>go
```

where:

NameOfDatabase—the name of the database that contains the table that the stored procedure references.

NameOfTable—the name of the table that is referenced by the stored procedure that you want to have recompiled the next time it is executed. This table cannot be a system table.

Changing the Name of a Stored Procedure

If you do not like the name of a stored procedure, don't worry; you can always change it—carefully, that is. If you change the name of a stored procedure, then all triggers, stored procedures, and views that reference it will continue to work, until the point in time when they are recompiled. So before you go ahead and change the name of a stored procedure, log on to the SQL Server and execute these commands:

```
1>use NameOfDatabase
2>go
1>sp_depends [loginame.] NameOfStoredProcedure
2>go
```

where:

NameOfDatabase—the name of the database that contains the stored procedure whose dependencies you want to inspect.

`[loginame.]`—the name of the Sybase account that owns the stored procedure. If you are the owner of the stored procedure, then you do not have to provide this parameter.

NameOfStoredProcedure—the name of the stored procedure whose dependencies you want to inspect. If the stored procedure is not owned by you, then you will have to put the login name and stored procedure name inside quotes (`""`).

The displayed report will list the triggers, stored procedures, and views within the current database that depend on the stored procedure whose name you intend to change, or it will notify you that there are no such dependencies. Each object that depends on this stored procedure will have to be dropped, modified to reference the new stored procedure name, re-created, and then have appropriate permissions granted once again. This report will not inform you of objects that depend on this stored procedure, but which were created before the stored procedure, nor will it inform you of objects outside the current database that depend on this stored procedure. The SQL Server does not eliminate the need for good database documentation.

So, after you have completed your impact assessment, if you want to change the name of a stored procedure, log on to the SQL Server as the stored procedure owner (or an account with **dbo** or **sa_role** privileges that has taken on the identity of the table owner) and enter these commands:

```
1>use NameOfDatabase
2>go
1>sp_rename NameOfStoredProcedure, NewNameOfStoredProcedure
2>go
```

where:

NameOfDatabase—the name of the database that contains the stored procedure whose name you want to change.

NameOfStoredProcedure—the name of the stored procedure whose name you want to change.

NewNameOfStoredProcedure—the new name that you want the stored procedure to have. The name of each stored procedure in a database must be unique, to the owner, within that database. The name must conform to the rules governing SQL Server identifiers.

Once this command completes successfully, the stored procedure can be referenced only by its new name. This command changes the database's system tables, so to ensure its recovery, be certain to dump its transaction log and then dump the database itself. Also, because this command changes the contents of the system tables, it cannot be executed within a transaction.

Creating Threshold Stored Procedures

The SQL Server does not provide the **sp_thresholdaction** stored procedure, or any other threshold stored procedure. You must create these procedures yourself to ensure that they are tailored to you particular needs. Any user with `create procedure` permission can create a threshold procedure in a database. When a threshold is crossed, SQL Server searches for the stored procedure in the database where the threshold event occurs. If it doesn't exist in that database, SQL Server searches for it in the *sybsystemprocs* system database. If SQL Server does not find the stored procedure, it sends an error message to the SQL Server error log.

SQL Server passes four parameters to a threshold procedure:

1. `@dbname`, varchar(30)—contains the name of the database.
2. `@segmentname`, varchar(30)—contains the name of the segment.
3. `@space_left`, int—contains the space-left value for the threshold.
4. `@status`, int—a Boolean indicator that has a value of 1 for **last-chance** thresholds and 0 for all other thresholds.

These parameters are passed by position, rather than by name. Your stored procedure can use other names for these parameters, but you must declare them in the order shown and with the data types shown.

Your stored procedure should include a `print` or `raiserror` statement so that the error log will contain a record of the threshold event. Also, it is possible for one or more thresholds to execute the same stored procedure.

User-Created System Procedures

Login accounts with **sa_role** privileges can create new system procedures. Unlike a normal stored procedure:

1. The name of a system procedure beings with the "sp_" prefix.
2. It resides within the *sybsystemprocs* system database.
3. It can be executed from within any database, without need to qualify the name of the system procedure with the name of its database.
4. A system procedure that modifies a system table cannot be executed within a transaction, as this would compromise recovery of the database.

Other than these differences they are just like a user-created stored procedure.

Revoking Permission to Create Stored Procedures

To revoke permission to a user, a list of users, the groups (including the public group), or a role, to create stored procedures, log on to the SQL Server as an account with **dbo** or **sa_role** privileges and enter these commands:

```
1>use NameOfDatabase
2>go
1>revoke create procedure
2>from {public | name_list | role_name}
3>[cascade]
4>go
```

where:

NameOfDatabase—the name of the database in which you want to revoke permission to create stored procedures from a user, a list of users, the groups (including the public group), or a role.

{public | name_list | role_name}—the user, list of users, group, or role for which you want to revoke create-procedure permission.

[cascade]—optional parameter used only if the granting create-procedure permission permitted the stored procedure owner to grant execute permissions to their stored procedures to other users in the database. When used, this parameter will revoke execute permission to other users in the database that was granted to them by the user, list of users, group, or role whose create-procedure permission is being revoked.

Once this command completes successfully, the login account is immediately incapable of creating stored procedures within the database. This command changes the database's system tables, so to ensure its recovery, be certain to dump its transaction log and then dump the database itself. Also, because this command changes the contents of the system tables, it cannot be executed within a transaction.

Dropping a Stored Procedure

When a stored procedure is no longer needed, it can be destroyed. To drop a stored procedure (or a group of stored procedures), log on to the SQL Server as the stored procedure owner (or an account with **dbo** or **sa_role** privileges that has taken on the identity of the stored-procedure owner) and enter these commands:

```
1>use NameOfDatabase
2>go
1>drop proc[edure] [[NameOfDatabase.] loginame.]
  NameOfStoredProcedure[,
2>[[NameOfDatabase,] loginame.] NameOfStoredProcedure]...
3>go
```

where:

NameOfDatabase—this optional parameter is the name of the database that contains the stored procedure that you want to drop. If the stored procedure is located in the current database then you do not have to provide this parameter.

`loginame`—this optional parameter is the name of the stored-procedure owner. If you are the owner of the stored procedure, then you do not have to provide this parameter.

NameOfStoredProcedure—the name of the stored procedure (or group of stored procedures) that you want to drop.

Once this command completes successfully, the stored procedure will be dropped from the database. This command changes the database's system tables, so to ensure its recovery, be certain to dump its transaction log and then dump the database itself. Also, because this command changes the contents of the system tables, it cannot be executed within a transaction.

Triggers

A trigger is simply a special kind of stored procedure, linked to a specific-user table, that is used to protect referential integrity (to enforce rules about the relationships among data in different columns in the same table or in different tables, or tables in different databases). Triggers can enforce constraints that are more complex than those defined with rules, because unlike rules, triggers can reference columns or database objects in the same database or in multiple databases. Triggers are frequently used to handle cascading updates and deletes throughout a database schema. Triggers can perform simple "what if" analyses.

Triggers kick in when a transaction attempts to modify data by using an `insert`, `delete`, or `update` command. By default, a trigger fires only once per data modification statement. The condition for which you have implemented the trigger will determine whether the `insert`, `update` or `delete` command causes the trigger action(s) to be carried out. However, the SQL Server checks referential-integrity constraints before any trigger fires, so a data modification statement that violates an explicit-table constraint does not also fire the trigger.

Just like stored procedures, triggers are an extension to the Transact-SQL language. With triggers you can:

1. Combine a wide variety of Transact-SQL commands with control-of-flow constructs.

2. Define one or more local variables that can be assigned literal data values within the trigger, while the given trigger is executing.

3. Execute a stored procedure on a remote SQL Server via a logical unit of work that is executing on your local SQL Server. This is referred to as making a remote procedure call. This is possible if and only if the local SQL Server and the remote SQL Server are both configured to allow remote login. It is important to understand that remote procedure calls are not treated as a part of the logical unit of work that is executing within the local SQL Server. If your trigger executes a remote procedure call and you subsequently roll back your local logical unit of work, the database operation produced on the remote SQL Server is not rolled back.

4. Execute stored procedures from within a given trigger.

5. Create and then use temporary tables within a given trigger.

6. Invoke system functions within triggers.

7. Permanently store query trees in the database's *sysprocedures* system table reusing and maintaining as need be.

8. Store the ASCII text of the trigger in the *syscomments* table of the database in which it was created. The ASCII text of the trigger cannot exceed 16 MB.

9. Recompile the trigger the next time it is executed if the **sp_ recompile** system procedure is run against the table the trigger is linked to.

10. Automatically recompile the trigger when it is first loaded from disk into procedure cache, and when all copies of the triggers in the cache query plan are currently in use.

11. Execute another trigger if allowed. A maximum of 16 levels are allowed. If this limit is exceeded, then the initiating transaction (and all spawned transactions) will be rolled back. If you are going to allow nested triggers then be certain to implement them such that they correctly reference the @@nestlevel global variable.

Unlike stored procedures, it is recommended that triggers not include select statements that return results to a use process. If a trigger does return a result set, then every process that kicks off the trigger action will have to be coded such that it explicitly handles the returned result set.

SQL Server Kernel Configuration for Nested Triggers

The allow nested triggers SQL Server configuration parameter is a toggle that controls whether a trigger can kick off other triggers. By default, the value of the allow nested triggers SQL Server configuration parameter is set to 1 (i.e., on), thereby allowing a trigger to execute other triggers. To prohibit triggers from executing other triggers, log on to the SQL Server as an account with **sa_role** privileges and enter these commands:

```
1>use master
2>go
1>sp_configure "allow nested triggers",0
2>go
```

As the allow nested triggers SQL Server configuration parameter is a static parameter, the SQL Server must be shut down and restarted for the new setting to take effect. This command changes the *master* system database, so to ensure its recovery, be certain to dump the *master* system database.

Gathering Information about a Trigger

The SQL Server provides you with three means by which to produce reports on triggers in a database:

1. **sp_help** (refer to Chap. 5, "Databases," for an explanation of this system procedure).

2. **sp_helptext** (refer to Chap. 7, "User-Defined Data Types, Defaults and Rules," for an explanation of this system procedure).

3. **sp_depends** (refer to Chap. 8, "Tables and Indexes," for an explanation of this system procedure).

Creating a Trigger

As the owner of a table, you can create two general types of triggers: those that do not have an `if update` clause associated with a specific table column, and those that do. The purpose to the `if update` clause is to test whether the corresponding column is modified by an `update` or `insert` statement. Let's consider triggers in the former category first.

To create a trigger, log on to the SQL Server as the table owner (or an account with **dbo** or **sa_role** privileges that has taken on the identity of the table owner) and enter these commands:

```
1>use NameOfDatabase
2>go
1>create trigger [loginame.]NameOfTrigger
2>on [loginame.]NameOfTable
3>for {insert , update , delete}
4>as TransactSQLStatements
5>go
```

where:

NameOfDatabase—the name of the database that contains the table for which you are creating a trigger. You can create a trigger only in the current database.

`loginame`—this optional parameter is the name of the owner of the table for which you are creating a trigger. If you are the owner of the table, then you do not have to provide this parameter.

NameOfTrigger—the name of the trigger. The name of the trigger must comply with the rules for SQL Server identifiers and must be unique within the database for the table owner.

NameOfTable—the name of the table for which you are creating a trigger. A given table can have, at most, three triggers linked to it; `insert`, `update` and `delete`. However, a given trigger can be linked to only one table. You cannot create a trigger on a system table or on a temporary table (or on a view for that matter).

`for {insert , update , delete}`—this parameter can include one, two, or all three options. They refer to the individual types of transactions (i.e., conditions) that will cause the trigger to undertake an action after the modification statement has completed. If an error is detected by the SQL Server, then the trigger and the modification statement are rolled back.

`as` *TransactSQLStatements*—defines the conditions under which the trigger will fire, and the action(s) the trigger will take per condition (e.g., a subquery, execute a stored procedure, examine the table's "test" tables, etc.). You can reference other principal database objects inside and outside the current database from within a trigger. The same trigger action can be defined for more than one condition. If the trigger is going to reference identifiers that do not comply with the SQL Server's rules for identifiers, then you must enter the `"set quoted_identifier on"` command before you create the trigger, and enclose all such referenced identifiers in double quotes (`" "`). Within a trigger you cannot include the following commands: `alter database`, `alter table`, `create`, `disk`, `drop`, `grant`, `revoke`, `load database`, `load transaction`, `reconfigure`, `sp_configure`, `select into ...`, `truncate table`, `update statistics`, or the `use` command. You can incorporate the `set` command within a trigger (which stays in effect while the trigger is executing) and can invoke any system function. If the `allow nested triggers` SQL Server configuration parameter is toggled on, then you can use the `"set self_recursion on"` command. This setting can cause the trigger to fire repeatedly, based on a specific condition being satisfied. However, be very careful when setting this feature on inside a trigger, as the condition may very well cause the maximum trigger-nesting level to be exceeded. Also, avoid using `select` statements that return result sets.

To create a trigger that uses the `if update` clause, log on to the SQL Server as the table owner (or an account with **dbo** or **sa_role** privileges that has taken on the identity of the table owner) and enter these commands:

```
1>use NameOfDatabase
2>go
1>create trigger [loginame.]NameOfTrigger
2>on [loginame.]NameOfTable
3>for {insert , update}
4>as [if update (NameOfColumn) [{and | or} update
  (NameOfColumn)]...]
5>TransactSQLStatements
6>[if update (NameOfColumn)[{and | or} update
  (NameOfColumn)]...
7>TransactSQLStatements]...
8>go
```

where:

if update—used to determine whether or the not the associated column is referenced in an update or insert statement. This approach allows you to implement triggers that are limited to conditions for a given column or columns verses the entire tables.

Not all transactions that modify the contents of a table, or of columns in that table, can result in a trigger being fired off:

1. The truncate table command does not cause a delete trigger to fire.
2. The writetext command, whether it is logged or is not logged, does not cause a trigger to fire.

Trigger Test Tables

As pointed out in Chap. 6 "Transaction Log Subsystem," linking a trigger on a table causes deferred updates to take place on the table. In addition, when a trigger is linked to a table, the SQL Server creates two cached virtual tables (that are structurally similar to the base table), for the table to which the trigger is linked:

1. *Deleted test table.*   Used to hold rows that would be removed from the table due to a delete or update statement (recall that an update statement is implemented internally by the SQL Server as a delete followed by an insert). The deleted row is actually physically removed from the base table, and transferred into the deleted test table. For this reason, the base table and the deleted test table never contain the same data row.
2. *Inserted test table.*   Used to hold rows that would be added to the table due to an insert or an statement. The row to be inserted is written simultaneously into the base and the inserted test tables.

The trigger examines the data written to these internal cache test tables to determine whether and how the trigger action(s) should be undertaken.

Run-Time Verification of Trigger Permissions

The rules for run-time verification of trigger permissions are identical to those for stored procedures:

1. If the login account that executes the trigger is the owner of the trigger, and also owns all referenced objects, and all referenced objects

are in the same database, then the SQL Server does not verify permissions at run time.

2. If the login account that executes the trigger is the owner of the trigger, and also owns all referenced objects, but all referenced objects are not in the same database, then the SQL Server verifies that the login account is a valid or `guest` user of each database containing a referenced object.

3. If the login account that executes the trigger is the owner of the trigger, but does not also own all referenced objects, and all referenced objects are in the same database, then the SQL Server verifies that the login account has been granted the correct permission(s) on the referenced objects it does not own.

4. If the login account that executes the trigger is the owner of the trigger, but does not also own all referenced objects, and all referenced objects are not in the same database, then the SQL Server verifies that the login account has been explicitly granted the correct permission(s) on the referenced objects it does not own, and verifies that the login account is a valid or `guest` user of each database containing a referenced object.

5. If the login account that executes the trigger is not the owner of the trigger, then the stored procedure executes as if it were being run by the login account that owns the trigger. As such, manipulation of referenced objects can take place through triggers without needing to explicitly grant access permissions on the referenced objects to all login accounts that execute the trigger. In this way a stored procedure can be used as an effective security mechanism.

Changing the Name of a Trigger

If you do not like the name of a trigger, don't worry; you can always change it—carefully, that is. If you change the name of a trigger, then all triggers, stored procedures, and views that reference the trigger will continue to work until the point in time when they are recompiled. So, before you go ahead and change the name of a trigger, log on to the SQL Server and execute these commands:

```
1>use NameOfDatabase
2>go
1>sp_depends [loginame.] NameOfTrigger
2>go
```

where:

NameOfDatabase—the name of the database that contains the trigger whose dependencies you want to inspect.

`[loginame.]`—the name of the Sybase account that owns the trigger. If you are the owner of the trigger, then you do not have to provide this parameter.

NameOfTrigger—the name of the trigger whose dependencies you want to inspect. If the trigger is not owned by you, then you will have to put the login and trigger names inside quotes (`" "`).

The displayed report will list the triggers, stored procedures, and views within the current database that depend on the trigger whose name you intend to change or will notify you that there are no such dependencies. Each object that depends on this trigger will have to be dropped, modified to reference the new trigger name, recreated, and then have appropriate permissions granted once again. This report will not inform you of objects that depend on this trigger, but which were created before the trigger, nor inform you of objects outside the current database that depend on this trigger. The SQL Server does not eliminate the need for good database documentation.

So, after you have completed your impact assessment, if you want to change the name of a trigger, log on to the SQL Server as the trigger owner (or an account with **dbo** or **sa_role** privileges that has taken on the identity of the table owner), and enter these commands:

```
1>use NameOfDatabase
2>go
1>sp_rename NameOfTrigger, NewNameOfTrigger
2>go
```

where:

NameOfDatabase—the name of the database that contains the trigger whose name you want to change.

NameOfTrigger—the name of the trigger whose name you want to change.

NewNameOfTrigger—the new name that you want the trigger to have. The name of each trigger in a database must be unique (to the owner) within that database. The name must conform to the rules governing SQL Server identifiers.

Once this command completes successfully, the trigger can be referenced only by its new name. This command changes the database's system tables, so to ensure its recovery, be certain to dump its transaction log and then dump the database itself. Also, because this command changes the contents of the system tables, it cannot be executed within a transaction.

Dropping a Trigger

When a trigger is no longer needed, it can be destroyed. To drop a trigger, log on to the SQL Server as the a table owner (or an account with **dbo** or **sa_role** privileges that has taken on the identity of the table owner) and enter these commands:

```
1>use NameOfDatabase
2>go
1>drop trigger [loginame.] NameOfTrigger[,
2>[loginame.] NameOfTrigger]...
3>go
```

where:

NameOfDatabase—the name of the database that contains the trigger that you want to drop.

loginame—this optional parameter is the name of the trigger owner. If you are the owner of the trigger, then you do not have to provide this parameter.

NameOfTrigger—the name of the trigger that you want to drop.

Once this command completes successfully, the trigger will be dropped from the database. This command changes the database's system tables, so to ensure its recovery, be certain to dump its transaction log and then dump the database itself. Also, because this command changes the contents of the system tables, it cannot be executed within a transaction.

Views

Views are virtual tables that are composed of columns derived from one or more tables (and, or, one or more views). Views provide a focused and customized perception of data in your database. No separate copies of the data from the view's underlying table are stored in the database. Only the definition of the view is stored (within the database's *syscomments* system table). A view looks to a process just like a table, and can be accessed like a table, but there are some restrictions on how the view's underlying data can be manipulated.

Granting Permission to Create Views

By default, users of a database do not have permission to create views within that database. Be very careful about granting `create view` permission to users in a database (i.e., they can load data into the underlying tables and consume disk space at a rate at which the **dbo** has no practical control).

To grant `create view` permission to a user, a list of users, the groups (including the `public` group), or a role, log on to the SQL Server as an account with **dbo** or **sa_role** privileges and enter these commands:

```
1>use NameOfDatabase
2>go
1>grant create view
2>to {public | name_list | role_name}
3>[with grant option]
4>go
```

where:

NameOfDatabase—the name of the database in which you want to grant permission to create views to a user, a list of users, the groups (including the `public` group), or a role.

`{public | name_list | role_name}`—the user, list of users, group, or role to which you want to grant `create view` permission.

`[with grant option]`—this optional parameter is used to permit the owner of the view to grant access permissions on the view to other users within the database. However, you cannot extend this additional permission to any group or role.

Once this command completes successfully, the login account is immediately capable of creating views within the database. This command changes the database's system tables, so to ensure its recovery, be certain to dump its transaction log and then dump the database itself. Also, because this command changes the contents of the system tables, it cannot be executed within a transaction.

A user who creates a view owns that view and automatically obtains all permissions on it. All other users of the database, including an account with **dbo** or **sa_role** privileges, are denied automatic access to a view they do not own, unless the owner of the view explicitly grants access permissions to them (just as long the **dbo** or the **sa_role** explicitly granted permission to the view owner to grant access permission to other database users when that view owner was granted permission to create views). Every view owner automatically has the exclusive right to drop the view. If, when the user was granted permission to create views, permission was also granted to authorize outside access to those views, then a view owner can `grant`, `revoke`, `insert`, `delete`, `select` and `update` permissions to users, groups, and roles within the database on any view owned.

Creating Views

The right to create views in a given database rests with the owner of the database. However, any Sybase account that is authorized to use a given database, can be granted permission to create views by the owner of that database.

To create a view that you will own, log on to the SQL Server as a Sybase account authorized in the current database as an account with **dbo** or **sa_role** privileges and issue the following commands:

```
1>use NameOfDatabase
2>go
1>create view [loginame.]NameOfView
2>[(NameOfColumn [,NameOfColumn]...)]
3>as select [distinct] select_statement
4>[with check option]
5>go
```

where:

NameOfDatabase—the name of the database in which you want to create the view.

`[loginame.]`—the name of the login account that will own the view. If you will own the view, then you do not have to provide this parameter.

NameOfView—the name that you want the new view to have. The name must conform to the rules governing SQL Server identifiers and must be unique to the owner in the given database. If, in your current session, you have entered the command `set quoted_identifier on`, then you can use a delimited identifier for the name of the view. However, in that case you would have to enclose the view name in double quotes (`""`).

`[(NameOfColumn [,NameOfColumn]...)]`—this optional parameter is the name that you want the new view's column to have. If no column names are specified, then the view's column names will be taken from the name of the columns in the view's `select` statement. When a view's column is derived from Transact-SQL arithmetic express, system function, string concatenation, or constant value, then you must provide the view's column name. The name of columns must conform to the rules governing SQL Server identifiers, and must be unique to the view. If, in your current session, you have entered the command `set quoted_identifier on`, then you can use a delimited identifier for the name of the view's column. However, in that case you would have to enclose the view's column name in double quotes (`""`). A view cannot contain more that 250 columns.

`as select [distinct]`—this optional parameter is used to ensure that rows in a view are unique. However, in that the SQL Server applies the `distinct` requirement when the underlying table is first accessed, then, if the view is composed of a projection of an underlying table, it is possible for the view to contain duplicate rows even if rows in the underlying table are unique. Also, you can specify the `distinct` reserved keyword more than once in a view's `select` statement.

`select_statement`—this parameter defines the view. You must have `select` permission on all referenced tables, columns, and views. Your `select` statement can be very simple, or can be as complex as Transact-SQL allows (such as joins, outer joins, and subqueries) with these restrictions: it cannot reference a temporary table; it cannot include the `into` reserved keyword, it cannot include the `union` operator, it cannot include `readtext` and `writetext` commands, and it cannot include a **compute** clause or an **order by** clause.

`[with check option]`—if this optional parameter is used, then all rows inserted or updated through the view must meet the view's selection criteria. This will insure that an `update` will not result in a row disappearing from the view.

Once this command completes successfully the view can be used immediately by its owner. This command changes the database's system tables, so to ensure its recovery, be certain to dump its transaction log and then dump the database itself. Also, because this command changes the contents of the system tables, it cannot be executed within a transaction.

Run-Time Verification of View Permissions

To understand how the SQL Server verifies referenced-object permissions during run time for a view, keep these rules in mind:

1. If the login account that accesses the view is the owner of the view, and also owns all referenced objects, and all referenced objects are in the same database, then the SQL Server does not verify permissions at run time.

2. If the login account that accesses the view is the owner of the view, and also owns all referenced objects, but all referenced objects are not in the same database, then the SQL Server verifies that the login account is a valid or `guest` user of each database containing a referenced object.

3. If the login account that accesses the view is the owner of the view, but does not also own all referenced objects, and all referenced objects are in the same database, then the SQL Server verifies that the login account has been granted the correct permission(s) on the referenced objects it does not own.

4. If the login account that accesses the view is the owner of the view, but does not also own all referenced objects, and all referenced objects are not in the same database, then the SQL Server verifies that the login account has been explicitly granted the correct permission(s) on the referenced objects it does not own, and verifies that the login account is a valid or `guest` user of each database containing a referenced object.

5. If the login account that accesses the view is not the owner of the view, then the stored procedure executes as if it were being run by the login account that owns the view. As such, manipulation of referenced objects can take place through view without needing to explicitly grant access permissions on the referenced objects to all login accounts that access the view. In this way, a view can be used as an effective security mechanism.

View Resolution

Every time the view is accessed, it is cast into a proprietary internal format called a query tree using a process called *resolution*. This internal format is a canonical representation (of the transaction) expressed in relational algebra. During this step, the transaction statement's syntax is also checked, and all referenced principal database object identifiers are verified. If any of the referenced principal database objects is a view, then a relational algebraic expression that computes the view is assimilated into the canonical representation of the transaction statement. If the resolution process is successful, then a query plan will be produced, and the view will execute its `select` statement.

Restrictions on Modifying Data through Views

While the SQL Server places a few restrictions on select data through a view, it places quite a number of restrictions on modifying data through views:

1. You cannot `insert` or `update` an IDENTITY column in an underlying table.

2. If a view does not reference all not-null columns in underlying tables or views, then it cannot `insert` data.

3. If the view includes a computed column, a column created by a system function, or an aggregated column, then you cannot `insert`, or `delete` data.

4. If the view includes a **group by** clause, then an `update` statement cannot be used.

5. If the view includes a computed column or an aggregated column, then an `update` statement cannot modify the computed or aggregated column.

6. If the view was created with the optional `distinct` or `check` option, then `insert` or `update` that do not satisfy the selection criteria are not allowed.

7. If the view was created with the optional `distinct` or `check` option, then it cannot `insert`, `update`, or `delete` data.

8. If the view is a join view, then you can only `insert` or `update` data when all affected columns belong to the same underlying table.

9. If a view references more than one table, then it cannot `delete` data.

10. If a view references more than one table, and was created with the check option, then its `insert` and `update` statements are not allowed.

11. If a view references more than one table, and was created with the **distinct** option, then `insert` statements are not allowed.

Granting Permissions on a View

If you are an account with **dbo** or **sa_role** privileges, then you can grant permission to database users, groups, or roles to access a view you own. If you are a database user and you have permission to both create views and grant access permissions, then you can grant permission to other database users, groups, or roles to access views that you own.

The SQL Server supports four view-access permissions:

1. `delete`—this permission lets you `delete` data rows from the view.

2. `insert`—this permission lets you `insert` new data rows into the view.

3. `select`—this permission lets you read data rows.

4. `update`—this permission lets you update the literal data values of data contained in data rows.

The SQL Server supports two view-access permissions that are specific to a subset of view columns:

1. `select`—this permission lets you read a subset of columns in this view.

2. `update`—this permission lets you update the literal data values of data contained in a subset of columns in this view.

To grant access permission to a view, log on to the SQL Server as the owner of the table (or an account with **dbo** or **sa_role** privileges that has taken on the identity of the view owner) and enter these commands:

```
1>use NameOfDatabase
2>go
1>grant {all | permission_list}
2>on { NameOfView
3>to {public | name_list | role_name}
4>[with grant option]
5>go
```

where:

NameOfDatabase—the name of the database that contains the view for which you want to grant access permission.

{all | permission_list}—if you specify `all`, then you will be granting `delete`, `insert`, `references`, `select`, and `update` permissions. If you want to grant a subset of these permissions, then specify a comma-delimited subset of permissions.

on { *NameOfView*—the name of the view for which you want to grant access permissions.

to {public | name_list | role_name}—you can grant access permissions to the `public` group, a list of database users and groups, or a list of roles.

[with grant option]—this optional parameter allows a user (not a group or role) to grant the access permission(s) to other users, groups, or roles.

Once this command completes successfully, the login account is immediately capable of exercising its access rights within the database. This command changes the database's system tables, so to ensure its recovery, be certain to dump its transaction log and then dump the database itself. Also, because this command changes the contents of the system tables, it cannot be executed within a transaction.

To grant access permission to a subset of columns in a view, log on to the SQL Server as the owner of the table (or an account with **dbo** or **sa_role** privileges that has taken on the identity of the view owner) and enter these commands:

```
1>use NameOfDatabase
2>go
1>grant {all | permission_list}
2>on { NameOfView (column_list)
3>to {public | name_list | role_name}
4>[with grant option]
5>go
```

where:

NameOfDatabase—the name of the database that contains the view for which you want to grant access permission.

{all | permission_list}—if you specify all, then you will be granting references, select, and update permissions. If you want to grant a subset of these permissions, then specify a comma-delimited subset of permissions.

on { *NameOfView* (column_list)—the list of columns in the view for which you want to grant access permissions. If you want to grant access to more than one column, then specify a comma-delimited subset of column names.

to {public | name_list | role_name}—you can grant access permissions to the public group, a list of database users and groups, or a list of roles.

[with grant option]—this optional parameter allows a user (not a group or role) to grant the access permission(s) to other users, groups, or roles.

Once this command completes successfully, the login account is immediately capable of exercising their access rights within the database. This command changes the database's system tables, so to ensure its recovery, be certain to dump its transaction log and then dump the database itself. Also, because this command changes the contents of the system tables, it cannot be executed within a transaction.

Views versus Stored Procedures

In this chapter we have examined the capabilities of both stored procedures and views. It has been shown that:

1. There are a number of data access and manipulation restrictions with views that are not applicable to stored procedures.

2. Unlike when executing a stored procedure, every time a view is accessed the process incurs the overhead of view resolution.

3. Views are limited to the database in which they are created.

For these reasons, it seldom makes sense to use views when a stored procedure will accomplish the same task.

Changing the Name of a View

If you do not like the name of a view, you can always change it—carefully, that is. If you change the name of a view, then all stored procedures and views that reference the view will continue to work until the point in time when they are recompiled. So, before you go ahead and change the name of a view, log on to the SQL Server and execute these commands:

```
1>use NameOfDatabase
2>go
1>sp_depends [loginame.] NameOfView
2>go
```

where:

NameOfDatabase—the name of the database that contains the view whose dependencies you want to inspect.

[loginame.]—the name of the Sybase account that owns the view. If you are the owner of the view, then you do not have to provide this parameter.

NameOfView—the name of the view whose dependencies you want to inspect. If the view is not owned by you, then you will have to put the login name and view name inside quotes (" ").

The displayed report will list the stored procedures and views within the current database that depend on the view whose name you intend to change, or it will notify you that there are no such dependencies. Each object that depends on this view will have to be dropped, modified to reference the new view name, and recreated, and then have appropriate permissions granted once again. This report will not inform you of objects that depend on this view but which were created before the view was created; nor will it inform you of objects outside the current database that depend on this view. The SQL Server does not eliminate the need for good database documentation.

So, after you have completed your impact assessment, if you want to change the name of a view, log on to the SQL Server as the a stored procedure owner (or an account with **dbo** or **sa_role** privileges that has taken on the identity of the view owner) and enter these commands:

```
1>use NameOfDatabase
2>go
1>sp_rename NameOfView, NewNameOfView
2>go
```

where:

NameOfDatabase—the name of the database that contains the view whose name you want to change.

NameOfView—the name of the view whose name you want to change.

NewNameOfView—the new name that you want the view to have. The name of each view in a database must be unique to the owner within that database. The name must conform to the rules governing SQL Server identifiers.

Once this command completes successfully, the view can be referenced only by its new name. This command changes the database's system tables, so to ensure its recovery, be certain to dump its transaction log and then dump the database itself. Also, because this command changes the contents of the system tables, it cannot be executed within a transaction.

Revoking Access Permissions to a View

To revoke access permission to a view, log on to the SQL Server as the owner of the view (or an account with **dbo** or **sa_role** privileges that has taken on the identity of the view owner) and enter these commands:

```
1>use NameOfDatabase
2>go
1>revoke [grant option for]
2>{all | permission_list}
2>on { NameOfView
3>to {public | name_list | role_name}
4>[cascade]
5>go
```

where:

NameOf Database—the name of the database that contains the view for which you want to revoke access permission.

[grant option for]—if a user has been granted permission to grant access privileges to views they own, then this optional parameter revokes this permission. If this user has granted access privileges on their views to other users, groups, or roles, then you must also use the cascade option to revoke permissions from those users, groups, and roles as well.

{all | permission_list}—if you specify all, then you will be revoking delete, insert, references, select, and update permissions. If you want to revoke a subset of these permissions, then specify a comma-delimited subset of permissions.

on {*NameOfView*—the name of the view for which you want to revoke access permissions.

to {public | name_list | role_name}—you can revoke access permissions to the public group, a list of database users and groups, or a list of roles.

[cascade]—if a user has been granted permission to grant access privileges to views owned, then this optional parameter revokes those access privileges to other users, groups, or roles.

Once this command completes successfully, the login account is immediately incapable of exercising any previous access rights within the database. This command changes the database's system tables, so to ensure its recovery, be certain to dump its transaction log and then dump the database itself. Also, because this command changes the contents of the system tables, it cannot be executed within a transaction.

To revoke access permission to a subset of columns in a view, log on to the SQL Server as the owner of the view (or an account with **dbo** or **sa_role** privileges that has taken on the identity of the view owner) and enter these commands:

```
1>use NameOf Database
2>go
1>revoke [grant option for]
2>{all | permission_list}
3>on { NameOfView (column_list)
4>to {public | name_list | role_name}
5>[cascade]
6>go
```

where:

NameOfDatabase—the name of the database that contains the view for which you want to revoke access permission.

`[grant option for]`—if a user has been granted permission to grant access privileges to views owned, then this optional parameter revokes this permission. If this user has granted access privileges on their views to other users, groups, or roles, then you must also use the `cascade` option to revoke permissions from those users, groups, and roles as well.

`{all | permission_list}`—if you specify `all`, then you will be revoking references, `select`, and `update` permissions. If you want to revoke a subset of these permissions, then specify a comma-delimited subset of permissions.

`on {`*NameOfView*`(column_list)`—this is the list of columns in the view for which you want to revoke access permissions. If you want to revoke access to more than one column, then specify a comma delimited subset of column names.

`to {public | name_list | role_name}`—you can revoke access permissions to the public group, a list of database users and groups, or a list of roles.

`[cascade]`—if a user has been granted permission to grant access privileges to views owned, then this optional parameter revokes those access privileges to other users, groups, or roles.

Once this command completes successfully, the login account is immediately incapable of exercising its previous access rights within the database. This command changes the database's system tables, so to ensure its recovery, be certain to dump its transaction log and then dump the database itself. Also, because this command changes the contents of the system tables, it cannot be executed within a transaction.

Dropping a View

When a view is no longer needed, it can be destroyed. To drop a view (or collection of views), log on to the SQL Server as the a view owner (or an account with **dbo** or **sa_role** privileges that has taken on the identity of the view owner) and enter these commands:

```
1>use NameOfDatabase
2>go
1>drop view [loginame.] NameOfView[,
2>[loginame.] NameOfView]...
3>go
```

where:

NameOfDatabase—the name of the database that contains the view that you want to drop.

`loginame`—this optional parameter is the name of the view owner. If you are the owner of the view, then you do not have to provide this parameter.

NameOfView—the name of the view that you want to drop.

Once this command completes successfully, the view will be dropped from the database. All references to the view in the database's *sysobjects, syscolumns, syscomments, sysdepends, sysprocedures* and *sysprotects* system tables will be purged. This command changes the database's system tables, so to ensure its recovery, be certain to dump its transaction log and then dump the database itself. Also, because this command changes the contents of the system tables, it cannot be executed within a transaction.

Revoking Permission to Create Views

To revoke permission to a user, a list of users, the groups (including the `public` group), or a role to create views, log on to the SQL Server as an account with **dbo** or **sa_role** privileges and enter these commands:

```
1>use NameOfDatabase
2>go
1>revoke create view
2>from {public | name_list | role_name}
3>[cascade]
4>go
```

where:

NameOfDatabase—the name of the database in which you want to revoke permission to create views from a user, a list of users, the groups (including the `public` group), or a role.

`{public | name_list | role_name}`—the user, list of users, group, or role for which you want to revoke create-view permission.

`[cascade]`—this optional parameter is to be used only if the granting create-view permission permitted the view owner to grant access permissions to the views to other users in the database. When used, this parameter will revoke access permission to other users in the database that were granted to them by the user, list of users, group, or role whose create-view permission is being revoked.

Once this command completes successfully, the login account is immediately incapable of creating views within the database. This command changes the database's system tables, so to ensure its recovery, be certain to dump its transaction log and then dump the database itself. Also, because this command changes the contents of the system tables, it cannot be executed within a transaction.

The Parallel Lock Manager

Introduction

The System 11 SQL Server uses a Parallel Lock Manager (PLM) to manage effectively the simultaneous access of data resources in a multiuser environment. Through the use of locks, the PLM automatically ensures that individual processes acquire restricted access to, and modification of, specific sections of data without interfering with one another. The goal of the PLM is to maintain data consistency by restricting the manipulation of data in a manner that does not seriously constrain the availability of data. The PLM handles locking in a manner that is transparent to the user, but there are techniques that we will explore that enable you to manage locking within your transactions.

Lock Granularity

Lock granularity refers to the volume of data that can be locked for a given period of time. The SQL Server automatically supports table-level and page-level locking, but if you undertake the necessary steps to ensure that a single data row resides on a page, then you can simulate row-level locking within the SQL Server. When the statistical query optimizer produces a transaction's query plan, lock granularity is determined; however, in your transaction statement, you can force the SQL Server to increase or decrease lock granularity.

When lock granularity is course, the amount of processing overhead the SQL Server incurs to manage locking is minimized, but less data is available to other concurrent processes, and overall performance degrades as these other processes are forced to wait until the locks being held on the data they want to manipulate are released.

When lock granularity is fine, the amount of processing overhead the SQL Server incurs to manage locking is maximized, but there is more data available to other concurrent processes. Overall performance can degrade as CPU cycles are consumed to manage the locking, instead of managing transaction logs, memory caches, disk I/O, and the like.

Types of Locks

The SQL Server has two intrinsic lock levels: table locks and page locks. Table-level locks lock all pages in a table, while page-level locks lock all rows on a given page. By default, to reduce data access contention among concurrent processes, the SQL Server will use page locks wherever possible. However, if, during run-time, the SQL Server detects that a transaction statement will acquire more locks that the internal lock promotion threshold allows, the SQL Server attempts to take a table-level lock. If the table-level lock can be acquired, then the page-level locks are released. If the query optimizer determines that most or all of the pages in a table need to be locked, then, for efficiency reasons, a table-level lock will be taken. Table-level locks are also used to avoid page-level lock collisions between concurrent processes.

Page Locks

Attempts to acquire page locks are taken when a transaction begins to be executed by the SQL Server. The SQL Server supports three types of page locks:

Shared (S) page lock. When a shared page lock is taken, the transaction can read the page and other transactions can also acquire and concurrently read a shared page lock on the page, but no transaction can acquire exclusive (page or table) locks on that page until all shared page locks are released. A transaction that needs an exclusive lock must wait until the shared page locks are released before the exclusive lock is acquired. In this way, no transaction can modify to a page while another transaction is reading that same page. By default, the SQL Server releases a shared page lock after the index or table scan completes on a given page. A shared page lock is not, by default, held on a page until the associated transaction completes (i.e., until it commits or aborts).

Update (U) page lock. This is an internal lock that the SQL Server acquires during the initial steps of an update, a delete, or a fetch (for cursors that are declared for update) as insurance against deadlocks. When an update page lock is acquired, other transactions can still acquire a shared page lock on that page, but these other transactions are prohibited from taking their own update page lock or any type of exclusive lock until the transaction that holds the lock completes. In subsequent steps of an update, a delete, or a fetch, if the lock page must be modified and if no shared page or table locks exist on the affected page, then this internal update lock is automatically promoted by the SQL Server to an exclusive page lock.

Exclusive (X) page lock.   These locks are used to change data on a page. One and only one transaction can acquire an exclusive page lock. All other transactions that need a lock on the same page must wait until the exclusive lock is released (when the transaction completes) before any other lock type is acquired.

In general, the query optimizer will specify that read operations are to acquire shared locks and that write operations are to acquire exclusive locks. However, exclusive page locks and update page locks are specified only if the columns in the predicate expression (i.e., the statement's **where** clause) are part of an index. If the query optimizer determines that an update or delete statement has no useful index, then a table scan will be undertaken, and the SQL Server is instructed to acquire a table-level lock. If the query optimizer determines that an update or delete statement has a useful index, then the SQL Server is instructed to begin by acquiring page-level locks and will attempt to acquire a table-level lock if need be. However, any type of statement that accumulates 200 page locks (or the amount of page locks specified in the lock promotion threshold SQL Server configuration parameter), the SQL Server will attempt to acquire a table-level lock.

Table Locks

The SQL Server supports these three types of table-level locks:

Intent table lock.   An intent-shared table lock is used to indicate at a table level that an attempt to acquire a shared page lock on a certain table will be made, and an intent exclusive table lock is used to indicate at a table level that an attempt to acquire an exclusive page lock on a certain table will be made. Intent table locks are an internal mechanism that is used to tell the SQL Server what table-level locks can possibly be obtained on a specific table. The SQL Server issues intent table locks right after the query optimizer builds a query plan and before the page-level locks are taken. These intent locks do not, in effect, lock a table; they merely prevent other transactions from acquiring a shared table or exclusive table lock on a table that currently has shared or exclusive page locks being held by another transaction. Intent locks are held as long as the existing page-level locks are in effect.

Shared (S) table lock.   A shared table lock is similar to a shared page lock, but it affects the entire table. The SQL Server will take a shared table lock when a nonclustered index is being built, or when a select statement contains the **holdlock** reserved keyword and does not use an index.

Exclusive (X) table lock.   An exclusive table lock is similar to an exclusive page lock, but it affects the entire table. The SQL Server will take an exclusive table lock when a clustered index is being built or when an update or delete statement's predicate expression does not reference indexed columns.

Demand Locks

The SQL Server uses an internal mechanism, called a *demand lock,* to prevent live lock situations from arising. A live lock situation is where read transactions are acquiring overlapping shared locks and monopolizing a table or page, and thereby causing write transactions to wait for extensive periods of time for an exclusive lock. The SQL Server uses demand locks as a placeholder to demarcate that a given transaction is next in line to lock a page or table. As soon as the preceding read transaction completes, the SQL Server allows the write transaction to proceed.

ANSI Isolation Levels

The American National Standards Institute (ANSI) SQL Standard establishes four transaction isolation levels: 0, 1, 2 and 3 (with 0 being the lowest isolation level and 3 being the highest isolation level). The higher the isolation level, the lower the probability that data inconsistency will arise and the lower the transaction concurrency. Higher isolation levels include the constraints imposed by the lower levels. The SQL Server only supports isolation levels 0, 1, and 3, and its default isolation level is 1.

Isolation level 0

Isolation level 0 is known as read uncommitted or dirty reads allowed. At isolation level 0, other transactions can read data that has been changed by another transaction but that has not yet been committed (i.e., doing a dirty read), but transactions are prevented from changing data that is currently being changed by another uncommitted transaction (i.e., other subsequent write transactions on that changed data are blocked until the changed data is committed and the exclusive page or table locks are released) and serialized access to that data is then allowed.

At isolation level 0, shared page or table locks are not taken by read statements, but write statements (and utilities like **dbcc**) still acquire shared locks for their reads. The SQL Server supports dirty reads by making in-cache copies of dirty pages that an isolation level 0 transaction needs to read.

Isolation level 0 is often used in on-line transaction processing (OLTP) SMP environments where approximate data consistency in query results is acceptable and where concurrent access to the same data, without encountering deadlock situations, is needed. While isolation level 0 allows readers and writers access to the same data that has exclusive page or table locks on it, reading uncommitted data is risky business (e.g., you could read the data changed by the uncommitted process only to have the transaction abort or roll back, thus invalidating your read). Avoid using isolation level 0 in cases where data consistency is required.

By default, any table that is supporting an isolation level 0 read must have a unique index (unless the database is in read-only mode). In that shared page or table locks are not taken by read statements, index and data rows that are being scanned can move as a result of write transactions by other processes. As a consequence, such scans will have to be restarted, and performance will degrade to handle the compensatory logical and physical I/O. The unique index is needed to support the restart of the scan. However, if you want to walk on the wild side, you can force the query to perform a table scan or to use a nonunique index (by using the **forceindex** option), but if you do, and there is a lot of update activity on the affected table, then an error message will be raised and the restarted scans will abort. Ouch!

Isolation level 1

Isolation level 1, the SQL Server's default isolation level, prevents dirty reads and is also known as the read-committed isolation level. Read transactions cannot access data that is changed but not committed. As a consequence, if a transaction reads the same page twice within a transaction, you may get different query results each time.

At isolation level 1, exclusive locks are acquired to support data modification and are not released until the transaction commits. Also, shared locks are taken on all pages being searched and then released after the page is read.

Isolation level 2

Isolation level 2 is known as the repeatable-read level and is currently not supported by the SQL Server. Basically, a repeatable read happens when a transaction reads a page more than once and the query results are identical across reads. A nonrepeated read can happen when one transaction reads a data row and another transaction modifies that same row. If the write transaction commits, then subsequent reads by the first transaction will produce a result set that is not identical to the original read. Also, nonrepeated reads can happen when a transaction scans a table and another transaction inserts a row into the table that would otherwise have qualified for the first transaction's query result set. This phenomenon is known as the phantom insert.

Isolation level 3

Isolation level 3 prevents nonrepeatable reads by a given transaction. The ANSI SQL Standard specifies level 3 as the default isolation level. The SQL Server enforces this level through explicit use of the `hold-lock` reserved keyword in a select statement, the `at isolation` clause of the select or readtext statement for just the query, and the `set transaction isolation level {3| serializable}` command. When these product features are used correctly, the SQL Server acquires exclusive locks on all pages or tables being written. These exclusive locks are held until the write transaction completes. Also, the SQL Server acquires shared locks on all pages or tables being read. These shared locks are held until the read transaction completes, i.e., the page lock is not released immediately after the page is read. As a consequence, data concurrency decreases and locking contention increases. As locking contention increases, the probability of deadlocking increases.

Choosing Isolation Levels

The SQL Server allows you to choose the isolation level for a given session or for a specific transaction within your session. To set the isolation level for your session, which will affect all transactions within your session, log on to the SQL Server and enter this command:

```
1>set transaction isolation level { 0 | 1 | 3 }
2>go
```

where:

0—isolation level 0. Instead of specifying "0," you can substitute the character string `read uncommitted`.

1—isolation level 1. Instead of specifying "1," you can substitute the character string `read committed`.

3—isolation level 3. Instead of specifying "3," you can substitute the character string `serializable`.

To choose an isolation level for a given transaction, you can specify the isolation level clause at the end of the select statement (e.g., `select ... at isolation ( read uncommitted | read committed | serializable )`).

If your session isolation level is either level 0 or 1 and you want a given query to execute at isolation level 3, then you can also use the `holdlock` reserved keyword (e.g., `select ... holdlock`).

If your session isolation level 3 and you want a given query to execute at isolation level 1, then you can also use the `noholdlock` reserved keyword (e.g., `select ... noholdlock`).

Other than the problems that were already mentioned about isolation level 0, some commands are not allowed against a table when an isolation level 0 scans is occurring on that table: `alter table`; `drop index`; `drop table`.

Also, when at isolation level 0, using a statement level 1 is illegal where you are combining it with `for browse`, `select ... into` in a `create view` statement, and `insert ... select`.

Finally:

1. System-stored procedures always execute at isolation level 1 and system-stored procedures created by users will run at the isolation level established in the stored procedure statement.

2. Stored procedures run at the isolation level established in the stored procedure statement. But, it the stored procedure is compiled at one level, and is then invoked from another level, the stored procedure will be recompiled.

3. Triggers execute at the level of the transaction that fires them, or at isolation level 1, whichever is higher. However, is an trigger is compiled at a specific isolation level, it will execute at that level.

SQL Server Kernel Configuration for Locks

The SQL Server has a fair number of kernel configuration parameters that control the Parallel Lock Manager, and we will examine each of these configuration parameters. The first SQL Server kernel configuration parameter to consider is the `number of locks` SQL Server configuration parameter that specifies the total count of table and page locks available to all active transactions at any given point in time.

By default, the SQL Server has 5000 locks. The range of legal settings for the `number of locks` SQL Server configuration parameter is 1000 through 2,147,483,647. Each lock consumes 72 bytes of memory. The total count of locks your SQL Server requires depends on the number of concurrent transactions it supports, as well as the mix of tasks these transactions are undertaking. If and when you run out of available locks, the SQL Server will raise an error message and abort the transaction that could not acquire required locks. If this event happens, then you could increase the total number of locks by 1000. Remember, each lock consumes memory that is taken away from data cache, so don't overkill this configuration parameter.

To reset the value of the `number of locks` SQL Server configuration parameter, log on to the SQL Server as a login account with **sa_role** privileges and enter these commands:

```
1>use master
2>go
1>sp_configure "number of locks", 6000
2>go
```

For this change to take effect, you will have to shut down, and then restart the SQL Server. As this command changes system tables, it cannot be run within a transaction. This command changes the *master* system database, so to ensure its recovery, be certain to dump the *master* system database.

SQL Server Kernel Configuration for Lock Manager Spinlocks

For SQL Servers running on SMP platforms, the SQL Server takes full advantage of the PLM. On single CPU platforms, the Lock Manager's resources are protected by a single spinlock. This architecture has been shown to limit the ability of the SQL Server to scale as the number of SQL Server engines increases. To eliminate that shortcoming on SMP platforms, the System 11 SQL Server supports multiple spinlocks to the Lock Manager's resources.

While it is strongly advised that you use the default Lock Manager's resources spinlock settings, you can tune three SQL Server configuration parameters that control the Lock Manager's resource spinlocks:

1. `page spinlock ratio`

2. `address spinlock ratio`

3. `table spinlock ratio`

Also, if you choose to create more spinlocks, remember that each spinlock consumes 256 bytes of memory, which is taken from memory that is allocated to data cache.

The `page lock spinlock ratio` SQL Server configuration parameter specifies the number of rows in the internal page lock hash table (i.e., hash bucket) that are protected by a single spinlock for SQL Servers configured to run multiple engines. If your installation is configured to run one engine, then there is only one spinlock for all internal page lock hash buckets (regardless of how you attempt to tune this parameter), and the `page lock spinlock ratio` SQL Server configuration parameter is always set to 100.

The SQL Server use the 1031 data rows in the internal page lock hash table to manage the acquisition and release of page locks. The spinlocks on this internal page lock hash table are used to serialize access to this table by concurrent processes executing on different SQL Server engines. By default, the value of the `page lock spinlock ratio` SQL Server configuration parameter on an SMP SQL Server is configured with eleven spinlocks. Each of the first ten spinlocks protect 100 rows within the internal page lock hash table. The eleventh spinlock protects the remaining 31 data rows within the internal page lock hash table.

The range of values for this configuration parameter is 1 through 2,147,483,647. If you increase the value of the `page lock spinlock ratio` SQL Server configuration parameter on an SMP SQL Server, then you will be increasing the number of data rows in the internal page lock hash table that are protected by a given spinlock. If you decrease the value of the `page lock spinlock ratio` SQL Server configuration parameter on an SMP SQL Server, then you will decrease the number of data rows in the internal page lock hash table that are protected by a given spinlock.

To set the value of the `page lock spinlock ratio` SQL Server configuration parameter on an SMP SQL Server to, for example, 25, log on to the SQL Server as an account that has **sa_role** privileges and enter these commands:

```
1>use master
2>go
1>sp_configure"page lock spinlock ratio", 25
2>go
```

For this change to take effect, you will have to shut down and then restart the SQL Server. As this command changes system tables, it cannot be run within a transaction. This command changes the *master* system database, so, to ensure its recovery, be certain to dump the *master* system database.

The `address lock spinlock ratio` SQL Server configuration parameter specifies the number of rows in the internal address lock hash table (i.e., the hash bucket) that are protected by a single spinlock for SQL Servers configured to run multiple engines. If your installation is configured to run one engine, then there is only one spinlock for all internal address lock hash buckets (regardless of how you attempt to tune this parameter), and the `address lock spinlock ratio` SQL Server configuration parameter is always set to 100.

The SQL Server use the 1031 data rows in the internal address lock hash table to manage the acquisition and release of address locks. The spinlocks on this internal address lock hash table are used to serialize access to this table by concurrent processes executing on different SQL Server engines. By default, the value of the `address lock spinlock ratio` SQL Server configuration parameter on an SMP SQL Server is configured with 11 spinlocks. Each of the first ten spinlocks protect 100 rows within the internal address lock hash table. The eleventh spinlock protects the remaining 31 data rows within the internal address lock hash table.

The range of values for this configuration parameter is 1 through 2,147,483,647. If you increase the value of the `address lock spinlock ratio` SQL Server configuration parameter on an SMP SQL Server, then you will be increasing the number of data rows in the internal address lock hash table that are protected by a given spinlock. If you decrease the value of the `address lock spinlock ratio` SQL Server configuration parameter on an SMP SQL Server, then you will decrease the number of data rows in the internal address lock hash table that are protected by a given spinlock.

To set the value of the `address lock spinlock ratio` SQL Server configuration parameter on an SMP SQL Server to, for example, 25, log on to the SQL Server as an account that has **sa_role** privileges and enter these commands:

```
1>use master
2>go
1>sp_configure"address lock spinlock ratio", 25
2>go
```

For this change to take effect, you will have to shut down and then restart the SQL Server. As this command changes system tables, it cannot be run within a transaction. This command changes the *master* system database, so to ensure its recovery, be certain to dump the *master* system database.

The `table lock spinlock ratio` SQL Server configuration parameter specifies the number of rows in the internal table lock hash table (i.e., the hash bucket) that are protected by a single spinlock for SQL Servers configured to run multiple engines. If your installation is configured to run one engine, then there is only one spinlock for all internal table lock hash buckets (regardless of how you attempt to tune this parameter), and the `table lock spinlock ratio` SQL Server configuration parameter is always set to 100.

The SQL Server uses the 101 data rows in the internal table lock hash table to manage the acquisition and release of table locks. The spinlocks on this internal table lock hash table are used to serialize access to this table by concurrent processes executing on different SQL Server engines. By default, the value of the `table lock spinlock ratio` SQL Server configuration parameter on an SMP SQL Server is configured with six spinlocks. Each of the first five spinlocks protect twenty rows within the internal table lock hash table. The sixth spinlock protects the last data row within the internal table lock hash table.

The range of values for this configuration parameter is 1 through 2,147,483,647. If you increase the value of the `table lock spinlock ratio` SQL Server configuration parameter on an SMP SQL Server, then you will be increasing the number of data rows in the internal table lock hash table that are protected by a given spinlock. If you decrease the value of the `table lock spinlock ratio` SQL Server configuration parameter on an SMP SQL Server, then you will decrease the number of data rows in the internal table lock hash table that are protected by a given spinlock.

To set the value of the `table lock spinlock ratio` SQL Server configuration parameter on an SMP SQL Server to, for example, 10, log on to the SQL Server as an account that has **sa_role** privileges and enter these commands:

```
1>use master
2>go
1>sp_configure "table lock spinlock ratio", 10
2>go
```

For this change to take effect, you will have to shut down and then restart the SQL Server. As this command changes system tables, it cannot be run within a transaction. This command changes the *master* system database, so to ensure its recovery, be certain to dump the *master* system database.

SQL Server Kernel Configuration for the Lock Manager Freelock Cache

On the SMP platform, where the SQL Server has been configured to run multiple engines, each engine has a list of lock structures stored in its configurable engine freelock cache. When the SQL Server needs to acquire a lock for a given transaction, it grabs one from the engine freelock cache of the engine within which the transaction is executing. If there are no more free lock structures in the engine's freelock cache, then the SQL Server will acquire a spinlock on the global freelock list and allocate a configurable count of free list structures from the global freelock list (residing in shared memory) to the engine's free-lock cache. The total number of locks in the global freelock list is established by the value of the `number of lock` SQL Server configuration parameter. When lock resources are allocated from the global freelock list to an engine freelock cache, nothing is physically moved from one memory location to another. Instead, the lock structures remain in the global freelock list, but the pointers that link the lock structures together are changed to reference the engine freelock cache to which they are allocated. As a consequence, they are no longer referenced as part of. the global freelock list. When the transaction releases the locks it acquired, the lock structures are automatically returned to the engine freelock cache. For single engine SQL Servers, the entire global freelock list is allocated to the engine when the server boots.

The SQL Server allocates a variety of lock resources from its single global freelock list that are shared across engines. Because the single global freelock list can become a point of contention across engines, the SQL Server has two configuration parameters you can tune:

1. `maximum engine freelocks`

2. `freelock transfer block size`

The `max engine freelocks` SQL Server configuration parameter is used to specify the maximum number of locks in each engine's freelock cache as a percentage of the `number of lock` SQL Server configuration parameter.

The default value of the `max engine freelocks` SQL Server configuration parameter is 10. The range of values for this configuration parameter is 1 through 50. Be very careful about setting the value of this configuration parameter. If you set it too low you will increase contention on the global freelock list. Also, if you set it too high, then most lock resources will end up within each engine, and when a given engine needs more lock resources, it may not be able to acquire them from the global freelock list because they are all spoken for. When this phenomena arises, the SQL Server will raise a 1279 error message.

To ensure that the use of lock resources is optimal, the SQL Server will move a count of lock structures from the engine freelock cache back to the global freelock list when the count of lock structures in the engine freelock cache exceeds the `max engine freelocks` SQL Server configuration parameter.

To set the value of the `max engine freelocks` SQL Server configuration parameter on an SMP SQL Server to, for example, 22, log on to the SQL Server as an account that has **sa_role** privileges and enter these commands:

```
1>use master
2>go
1>sp_configure "max engine freelocks", 22
2>go
```

This change will take effect immediately. As this command changes system tables, it cannot be run within a transaction. This command changes the *master* system database, so to ensure its recovery, be certain to dump the *master* system database.

The `freelock transfer block size` SQL Server configuration parameter is used to specify the count of lock structures that are to be allocated from the global freelock list to an engine freelock cache (and vice versa). The default value of the `freelock transfer block size` SQL Server configuration parameter is 30. The minimum allowed value is 1, and the maximum allowed value is determined according to this formula: [(max. engine freelocks × number of locks)(max online engines)/2]. If you increase the value of this configuration parameter, you will be decreasing contention on the global freelock list, but you will be running the risk of allocating more lock resources then are needed by the acquiring transaction.

To set the value of the `freelock transfer block size` SQL Server configuration parameter on an SMP SQL Server to 15, for example, log on to the SQL Server as an account that has **sa_role** privileges and enter these commands:

```
1>use master
2>go
1>sp_configure "freelock transfer block size", 15
2>go
```

This change will take effect immediately. As this command changes system tables, it cannot be run within a transaction. This command changes the *master* system database, so, to ensure its recovery, be certain to dump the *master* system database.

Reporting on Blocked Processes

To determine which processes are being blocked, log on to the SQL Server as any valid account and enter the `sp_who` command. The process report's status column will display `lock sleep` for blocked processes, and the report's `blk` column will show the process ID of the process that holds the locks blocking the other process that needs to acquire locking resources.

To determine how many locks are in use, log on to the SQL Server as any valid account and enter this command:

```
1>sp_lock [spid1 [, spid2]]
2>go
```

where:

[spid1—this optional parameter is the SQL Server process ID number for which you want a lock report produced.

[, spid2]]—this optional parameter is the second SQL Server process ID number for which you want a combination lock report produced.

If you do not provide one or both of the optional process IDs, then the SQL Server will report lock utilization by all active processes. Keep in mind that this report is a snapshot, and, as such, the active locks may change over the course of producing and displaying the report. The report will display the process IDs, the lock type and the identifier of the process that is blocking, the identifier of the table or page identifier on which the lock is held, and the name of the database in which the lock is held. The last column indicates if the lock is being held by a cursor. If applicable, the identifier of the cursor that holds the lock will be displayed in the last column.

Lock Promotion

As was previously explained, the SQL Server prefers to take page-level locks, but, past certain thresholds, the SQL Server will escalate from page-level locking to table-level locking for a given transaction. The SQL Server provides a mechanism, called lock promotion, that enables you to manage the escalation of lock resources on a SQL-Server-wide, database-wide, or table-wide basis.

SQL Server Configuration for Lock Promotion

To manage lock promotion, the SQL Server provides three configuration parameters that can be set at a SQL-Server-wide basis, at a database level, and at a table level:

1. lock promotion HWM
2. lock promotion LWM
3. lock promotion PCT

Taken together, the SQL Server uses these configuration parameters to establish the count of page locks that a given transaction can acquire during a single scan of a table or index before the SQL Server attempts to escalate from page-level locking to table-level locking for that given transaction.

As regards the precedence of these configuration parameters, server-wide settings are inherited by a database unless the configuration parameter is specified for a given database. Tables inherit database settings unless the configuration parameter is specified for a given table.

The `lock promotion HWM` (high-water mark) configuration parameter establishes the maximum number of page level locks that can be acquired by a transaction before lock promotion is attempted. Once this number is exceeded, the SQL Server escalates locking by attempting to acquire a table-level lock for the transaction. Whether you are setting the value of this configuration parameter on a serverwide basis, a database basis, or a table basis, in all cases the value of the `lock promotion HWM` configuration parameter must never exceed the value of the `number of locks` SQL Server configuration parameter.

The default value of the `lock promotion HWM` configuration parameter on a server-wide basis is 200. The range of values for this configuration parameter is 2 through 2,147,483,647. When you increase the value of this configuration parameter, you are decreasing the probability of a transaction acquiring a table-level lock and increasing transaction concurrency, which is preferable. By decreasing the value of this configuration parameter, you are increasing the probability of a transaction acquiring a table-level lock and reducing transaction concurrency. For most installations, the default value of the `lock promotion HWM` configuration parameter should work out just fine. However, if your database contains a large number of small tables that have clustered indexes, setting the `lock promotion HWM` configuration parameter to 80 percent of the value of the `number of locks` SQL Server configuration parameter may be more suitable.

To set the value of the `lock promotion HWM` configuration parameter on a serverwide basis to 230, for example, log on to the SQL Server as an account with **sa_role** privileges and enter these commands:

```
1>use master
2>go
1>sp_configure "lock promotion HWM", 230
2>go
```

Alternatively, you can log on to the SQL Server as an account with **sa_role** privileges and enter these commands:

```
1>use master
2>go
1>sp_setpglockpromote "server", NULL, NULL, 230, NULL
2>go
```

Either way, this change will take effect immediately. As these commands change system tables, they cannot be executed from within a transaction. These commands change the *master* system database, so to ensure its recovery, be certain to dump the *master* system database.

If you intend to specify the `lock promotion HWM` configuration parameter for a database, then you must first create a row for that database in the `master..sysattributes` table. To play it safe, create the row with the default values for the `lock promotion HWM`, `lock promotion LWM`, and the `lock promotion PCT` configuration parameters. To create that required row in the `master..sysattributes` table, log on to the SQL Server as an account with **sa_role** privileges and enter these commands:

```
1>use master
2>go
1>sp_setpglockpromote "database", NameOfDatabase, 200, 200, 100
2>go
```

where:

NameOfDatabase—the name of the database for which you intend to adjust the lock promotion high-water mark.

As this command changes system tables, it cannot be executed from within a transaction. This command changes the *master* system database, so, to ensure its recovery, be certain to dump the *master* system database.

To set the value of the `lock promotion HWM` configuration parameter on a database basis to 230, for example, log on to the SQL Server as an account with **sa_role** privileges and enter these commands:

```
1>use master
2>go
1>sp_setpglockpromote "database", NameOfDatabase, NULL, 230,
  NULL
2>go
```

where:

NameOfDatabase—the name of the database for which you want to the adjust the lock promotion high-water mark.

The change will take effect immediately. As this command changes system tables, it cannot be executed within a transaction. This command changes the *master* system database, so to ensure its recovery, be certain to dump the *master* system database.

If you intend to specify the `lock promotion HWM` configuration parameter for a table, you must first create a row for that table in the database's *sysattributes* table. To play it safe, create the row with the default values for the `lock promotion HWM`, the `lock promotion LWM`, and the `lock promotion PCT` configuration parameters. To create that required row in the database's *sysattributes* table, log on to the SQL Server as an account with **sa_role** privileges and enter these commands:

```
1>use NameOfDatabase
2>go
1>sp_setpglockpromote "table",[loginame.]NameOfTable, 200,
  200, 100
2>go
```

where:

NameOfDatabase—the name of the database for which you intend to adjust the lock promotion high-water mark for a given table.

`[loginame.]`—the name of the Sybase account that owns the table. If you are the owner of the table, then you do not have to provide this optional parameter.

NameOfTable—the name of the table for which you intend to adjust the lock promotion high-water mark. This table cannot be a system table.

As this command changes system tables, it cannot be executed within a transaction. This command changes the database's system table, so to ensure its recovery, be certain to dump the database's transaction log and then dump the database itself.

To set the value of the `lock promotion HWM` configuration parameter on a table basis to 230, for example, log on to the SQL Server as an account with **sa_role** privileges and enter these commands:

```
1>use NameOfDatabase
2>go
1>sp_setpglockpromote "table",[loginame.]NameOfTable, NULL,
  230, NULL
2>go
```

where:

NameOfDatabase—the name of the database that contains the table for which you want to the adjust lock promotion high-water mark.

`[loginame.]`—the name of the Sybase account that owns the table. If you are the owner of the table, then you do not have to provide this optional parameter.

NameOfTable—the name of the table for which you want to adjust the lock promotion high-water mark. This table cannot be a system table.

The change will take effect immediately. As this command changes system tables, it cannot be executed within a transaction. This command changes the database's system table, so to ensure its recovery, be certain to dump the database's transaction log and then dump the database itself.

The `lock promotion LWM` (low-water mark) configuration parameter establishes the minimum number of page-level locks that can be acquired by a transaction before lock promotion is attempted. The SQL Server will never attempt to acquire a table-level lock for the transaction until the value of this configuration parameter is matched.

The default value of the `lock promotion LWM` configuration parameter on a serverwide basis is 200. The range of values for this configuration parameter is 2 through less than or equal to the value of the `lock promotion HWM` configuration parameter. When you increase the value of this configuration parameter, you are decreasing the probability of a transaction acquiring a table-level lock and increasing transaction concurrency, which is preferable, but you also consume more page locks, which exposes you to the risk of running out of locks. By decreasing the value of this configuration parameter, you are increasing the probability of a transaction acquiring a table-level lock and reducing transaction concurrency. For most installations, the default value of the `lock promotion LWM` configuration parameter should work out just fine.

To set the value of the `lock promotion LWM` configuration parameter on a serverwide basis to 230, for example, log on to the SQL Server as an account with **sa_role** privileges and enter these commands:

```
1>use master
2>go
1>sp_configure "lock promotion LWM", 230
2>go
```

Alternatively, you can log on to the SQL Server as an account with **sa_role** privileges and enter these commands:

```
1>use master
2>go
1>sp_setpglockpromote "server", NULL, 230, NULL, NULL
2>go
```

Either way, this change will take effect immediately. As these commands changes system tables, they cannot be executed from within a transaction. These commands change the *master* system database, so to ensure its recovery, be certain to dump the *master* system database.

If you intend to specify the `lock promotion LWM` configuration parameter for a database, you must first create a row for that database in the `master..sysattributes` table. To play it safe, create the row with the default values for the `lock promotion HWM`, the `lock promotion LWM`, and the `lock promotion PCT` configuration parameters. To create that required row in the `master..sysattributes` table, log on to the SQL Server as an account with **sa_role** privileges and enter these commands:

```
1>use master
2>go
1>sp_setpglockpromote "database", NameOfDatabase, 200, 200, 100
2>go
```

where:

NameOfDatabase—the name of the database for which you intend to adjust the lock promotion low-water mark.

As this command changes system tables, it cannot be executed within a transaction. This command changes the *master* system database, so to ensure its recovery, be certain to dump the *master* system database.

To set the value of the `lock promotion LWM` configuration parameter on a database basis to 230, for example, log on to the SQL Server as an account with **sa_role** privileges and enter these commands:

```
1>use master
2>go
1>sp_setpglockpromote "database", NameOfDatabase, 230, NULL,
  NULL
2>go
```

where:

NameOfDatabase—the name of the database for which you want to the adjust lock promotion low-water mark.

The change will take effect immediately. As this command changes system tables, it cannot be executed from within a transaction. This command changes the *master* system database, so to ensure its recovery, be certain to dump the *master* system database.

If you intend to specify the `lock promotion LWM` configuration parameter for a table, you must first create a row for that table in the database's *sysattributes* table. To play it safe, create the row with the default values for the `lock promotion HWM`, the `lock promotion LWM`, and the `lock promotion PCT` configuration parameters. To create that required row in the database's *sysattributes* table, log on to the SQL Server as an account with **sa_role** privileges and enter these commands:

```
1>use NameOfDatabase
2>go
1>sp_setpglockpromote "table", [loginame.]NameOfTable, 200,
  200, 100
2>go
```

where:

NameOfDatabase—the name of the database for which you intend to adjust the lock promotion low-water mark for a given table.

`[loginame.]`—the name of the Sybase account that owns the table. If you are the owner of the table, then you do not have to provide this optional parameter.

NameOfTable—the name of the table for which you intend to adjust the lock promotion low-water mark. This table cannot be a system table.

As this command changes system tables, it cannot be executed within a transaction. This command changes the database's system table, so to ensure its recovery, be certain to dump the database's transaction log and then dump the database itself.

To set the value of the `lock promotion LWM` configuration parameter on a table basis to 230, for example, log on to the SQL Server as an account with **sa_role** privileges and enter these commands:

```
1>use NameOfDatabase
2>go
1>sp_setpglockpromote "table", [loginame.]NameOfTable, 230,
  NULL, NULL
2>go
```

where:

NameOfDatabase—this is the name of the database that contains the table for which you want to the adjust lock promotion low-water mark.

`[loginame.]`—the name of the Sybase account that owns the table. If you are the owner of the table, then you do not have to provide this optional parameter.

NameOfTable—the name of the table for which you want to adjust the lock promotion low-water mark. This table cannot be a system table.

The change will take effect immediately. As this command changes system tables, it cannot be executed within a transaction. This command changes the database's system table, so to ensure its recovery, be certain to dump the database's transaction log and then dump the database itself.

The `lock promotion PCT` (percentage) configuration parameter establishes the percentage of page locks based on the table's page count, above which the SQL Server will attempt to escalate to a table lock when the count of page locks is between the value of the `lock promotion LWM` configuration parameter and the value of the `lock promotion HWM` configuration parameter. Internally, the SQL Server computes lock promotion using this formula: (`lock promotion PCT` configuration parameter × table's page count)/100.

The default value of the `lock promotion PCT` configuration parameter, on a serverwide basis, is 100 percent. The range of values for this configuration parameter is 1 through 100 percent. When you decrease the value of this configuration parameter, you are increasing the probability of a transaction acquiring a table-level lock and reducing transaction concurrency. For most installations, the default value of the `lock promotion PCT` configuration parameter should work out just fine.

To set the value of the `lock promotion PCT` configuration parameter on a serverwide basis to 90, for example, log on to the SQL Server as an account with **sa_role** privileges and enter these commands:

```
1>use master
2>go
1>sp_configure "lock promotion PCT", 90
2>go
```

Alternatively, you can log on to the SQL Server as an account with **sa_role** privileges and enter these commands:

```
1>use master
2>go
1>sp_setpglockpromote "server", NULL, NULL, NULL, 90
2>go
```

Either way, this change will take effect immediately. As these commands change system tables, they cannot be executed within a transaction. These commands change the *master* system database, so to ensure its recovery, be certain to dump the *master* system database.

If you intend to specify the *lock promotion PCT* configuration parameter for a database, then you must first create a row for that database in the `master..sysattributes` table. To play it safe, create the row with the default values for the `lock promotion HWM`, the `lock promotion LWM`, and the `lock promotion PCT` configuration parameters. To create that required row in the `master..sysattributes` table, log on to the SQL Server as an account with **sa_role** privileges and enter these commands:

```
1>use master
2>go
1>sp_setpglockpromote "database", NameOfDatabase, 200, 200, 100
2>go
```

where:

> *NameOfDatabase*—the name of the database for which you intend to adjust the lock promotion percentage.

As this command changes system tables, it cannot be executed within a transaction. This command changes the *master* system database, so to ensure its recovery, be certain to dump the *master* system database.

To set the value of the `lock promotion PCT` configuration parameter on a database basis to 90, for example, log on to the SQL Server as an account with **sa_role** privileges and enter these commands:

```
1>use master
2>go
1>sp_setpglockpromote "database", NameOfDatabase, NULL, NULL, 90
2>go
```

where:

> *NameOfDatabase*—the name of the database for which you want to the adjust lock promotion percentage.

The change will take effect immediately. As this command changes system tables, it cannot be executed within a transaction. This command changes the *master* system database, so to ensure its recovery, be certain to dump the *master* system database.

If you intend to specify the `lock promotion PCT` configuration parameter for a table, then you must first create a row for that table in the database's *sysattributes* table. To play it safe, create the row with the default values for the `lock promotion HWM`, the `lock promotion LWM`, and the `lock promotion PCT` configuration parameters. To create that required row in the database's *sysattributes* table, log on to the SQL Server as an account with **sa_role** privileges and enter these commands:

```
1>use NameOfDatabase
2>go
1>sp_setpglockpromote "table", [loginame.]NameOfTable, 200,
  200, 100
2>go
```

where:

NameOfDatabase—the name of the database for which you intend to adjust the lock promotion percentage for a given table.

`[loginame.]`—the name of the Sybase account that owns the table. If you are the owner of the table, then you do not have to provide this optional parameter.

NameOfTable—the name of the table for which you intend to adjust the lock promotion percentage. This table cannot be a system table.

As this command changes system tables, it cannot be executed within a transaction. This command changes the database's system table, so to ensure its recovery, be certain to dump the database's transaction log and then dump the database itself.

To set the value of the `lock promotion PCT` configuration parameter on a table basis to 90, for example, log on to the SQL Server as an account with **sa_role** privileges and enter these commands:

```
1>use NameOfDatabase
2>go
1>sp_setpglockpromote "table",[loginame.]NameOfTable, NULL,
  NULL, 90
2>go
```

where:

NameOfDatabase—the name of the database that contains the table for which you want to the adjust lock promotion percentage.

`[loginame.]`—the name of the Sybase account that owns the table. If you are the owner of the table, then you do not have to provide this optional parameter.

NameOfTable—the name of the table for which you want to adjust the lock promotion percentage. This table cannot be a system table.

The change will take effect immediately. As this command changes system tables, it cannot be executed within a transaction. To ensure its recovery, be certain to dump the database's transaction log and then dump the database itself.

Dropping Database Lock Promotion Settings

If the adjustment you made to lock promotion parameters for a given database is not working out, then you can revert to the serverwide settings for that database. However, table-level settings of lock promotion parameters, if present, will still take precedence over the server-wide settings.

To drop the lock promotion parameters for a given database, log on to the SQL Server as an account with **sa_role** privileges and enter these commands:

```
1>use master
2>go
1>sp_dropglockpromote "database", NameOfDatabase
2>go
```

where:

NameOfDatabase—the name of the database for which you want to drop its lock promotion parameter settings.

The change will take effect immediately. As this command changes system tables, it cannot be executed from within a transaction. This command changes the *master* system database, so to ensure its recovery, be certain to dump the *master* system database.

Dropping Table Lock Promotion Settings

If the adjustment you made to lock promotion parameters for a given table is not working out, then you can revert to the database settings, where present, or to the serverwide settings.

To drop the lock promotion parameters for a given table, log on to the SQL Server as an account with **sa_role** privileges and enter these commands:

```
1>use NameOfDatabase
2>go
1>sp_dropglockpromote "table", [loginame.]NameOfTable
2>go
```

where:

NameOfDatabase—the name of the database that contains the table for which you want to drop its lock promotion parameter settings.

[loginame.]—the name of the Sybase account that owns the table. If you are the owner of the table, then you do not have to provide this optional parameter.

NameOfTable—the name of the table for which you want to drop its lock promotion parameter settings. This table cannot be a system table.

The change will take effect immediately. As this command changes system tables, it cannot be executed within a transaction. This command changes the database's system table, so to ensure its recovery, be certain to dump the database's transaction log and then dump the database itself.

Simulating Row-Level Locking

As mentioned in the introduction to this chapter, you can simulate row-level locking within the SQL Server. Despite the drawbacks of simulating row-level locking, you can approximate this behavior by taking advantage of the **fillfactor** and **max_rows_per_page** options when creating or altering your tables and indexes. For a detailed discussion of using these two table and index options to simulate row-level locking, refer to the chapter on tables and indexes.

Deadlocking

We have already discussed blocking (i.e., a process has a locked a page or table for which another process wants to acquire a lock but cannot). Deadlocking occurs when two processes each hold exclusive locks on separate resources that the other needs to access to complete the transaction. The processes deadlock when the first task waits for the second task to release its lock, but the second task will not release its lock until the first task's lock is released.

Internally, the SQL Server tries to reduce the possibility of deadlock events from occurring by using intent, update, and exclusive locks. Nonetheless, when the SQL Server automatically detects that a deadlock has occurred (after waiting a configured period of time for any sleeping process that is waiting on a lock to be released), it holds spinlocks on the lock structures in memory while it looks for the deadlock, then it chooses the deadlocked process that has accumulated the least amount of CPU time, aborts that process, and raises a 1205 error message.

To handle deadlocking, your application code will have to check for 1205 error messages, and when detected, restart the aborted transaction. The best solution to deadlocking, however, is to design the application such that the possibility of deadlocking is kept to a minimum. Here are some of the time-proven methods for minimizing the occurrence of deadlocking in your application:

1. When you are going to update multiple tables, always perform the update in the same order, (e.g., if a number of transactions update table *A* and table *B,* try to use the same update order in each transaction; update table *A* first and then table *B*). Using and reusing stored procedures can go a long way to enforcing updating in the same order.

2. As your application traverses through the database schema, travel through it along the same pathways where possible.

3. Avoid the use of isolation level 3 at a session transaction level.

4. Avoid long-running transactions.

SQL Server Kernel Configuration Parameters for Deadlocking

With System 11, the SQL Server no longer incurs the performance degradation of deadlock checking as soon as a process goes to sleep because it is waiting on a blocking process to release its lock resources. Frequently, before the deadlock checking would finish, the blocking transaction would complete and relinquishes its lock resources. Instead, with System 11 SQL Server, you are able to configure the amount of time, in milliseconds, a process delays before it initiates a deadlock check.

The `deadlock checking period` SQL Server configuration parameter is used to specify the minimum amount of time a block process will wait until it initiates a deadlock check. The default value of this configuration parameter is 500, and the range of values for it is 0 through 2,147,483,647 milliseconds. To turn off delayed deadlock checking, you would set the value of this configuration parameter to 0. Because the deadlock checking process holds spinlock on the lock resources in memory while it searches for the deadlock process to kill, do not turn off delayed deadlock checking for OLTP applications. If you set this configuration parameter too high, then blocked processes will have to wait too long to resolve deadlock situations. If you set this configuration parameter too low, then overall performance will degrade due to needless deadlock checking overhead.

To set the value of the `deadlock checking period` SQL Server configuration parameter to, for example, five hundred and fifty 550 milliseconds, log on to the SQL Server as an account that has **sa_role** privileges and enter these commands:

```
1>use master
2>go
1>sp_configure "deadlock checking period", 550
2>go
```

This change will take effect immediately. As this command changes system tables, it cannot be run within a transaction. This command changes the *master* system database, so to ensure its recovery, be certain to dump the *master* system database.

As was previously explained, the deadlock checking process identifies a deadlock "victim" that the SQL Server kills. The SQL Server grants the victim transaction a temporary reprieve by giving it a fix count of attempts it can make to acquire the lock resources it needs before it is killed. If it acquires the lock resources it needs before it is killed, then the SQL Server executes the transaction (no, this is not a paradox; after all, paradoxes only exist in language, not in nature). The `deadlock retries` SQL Server configuration parameter is used to specify the number of times the victim transaction can try to acquire the lock resources it needs before it is terminated by the SQL Server. The default value of this configuration parameter is 5, and the range of values for this configuration parameter is 0 through 2,147,483,647.

To set the value of the `deadlock retries` SQL Server configuration parameter to, for example, 6, log on to the SQL Server as an account that has **sa_role** privileges and enter these commands:

```
1>use master
2>go
1>sp_configure "deadlock retries", 6
2>go
```

This change will take effect immediately. As this command changes system tables, it cannot be run within a transaction. This command changes the *master* system database, so to ensure its recovery, be certain to dump the *master* system database.

Finally, if you are having serious problems with deadlocking processes and you need more information about these events to address the underlying causes of the problem you can instruct the SQL Server to print deadlock information to its error log. However, be forewarned, doing so can seriously degrade overall SQL Server performance. The `print deadlock information` SQL Server configuration parameter is used to turn on and turn off deadlock error reporting. By default it is turned off.

To turn on deadlock error reporting, log on to the SQL Server as an account that has **sa_role** privileges and enter these commands:

```
1>use master
2>go
1>sp_configure "print deadlock information", on
2>go
```

This change will take effect immediately. As this command changes system tables, it cannot be run within a transaction. This command changes the *master* system database, so to ensure its recovery, be certain to dump the *master* system database. To turn it off, then just pass this command the character string `off`.

Glossary

allocation unit A grouping of 256 contiguous 2K logical database pages. Each allocation unit contains 32 extents.

allocation unit page Within each allocation unit, the very first page of the very first extent is always the allocation unit page. It is used to hold information about the data stored within that allocation unit. The information held on the allocation unit page is an array data structure that records how the remaining 255 2K pages are being used by the occupying database.

Buffer An individual Buffer contains a Buffer Header linked to a page. The SQL Server Cache Manager ensures that each data, index, or transaction log page in Data Cache, and each stored procedure, trigger, and so on in Procedure Cache, is paired off with a Buffer that is dedicated to the referenced principal database object. The Buffer points to a specific page and serves to regulate its stay within Data Cache, or within the Procedure Cache, as the case may be. When the SQL Server boots, a Buffer Header is linked to a page. While the SQL Server is running, that linkage is maintained. However, it is information within the page (data and index information) that changes during run time.

Buffer Mass With System 11 SQL Server, a Buffer is actually a block of individual Buffers equal to the disk I/O size of the Memory Pool in which they reside. The disk I/O size of a Memory Pool can be one page (2K), two pages (4K), four pages (8K), and a single extent consisting of eight pages (16K). A Buffer is managed as a unit of disk I/O called a Buffer Mass, that is, all pages in a Buffer are read from disk, written to disk, or flushed from the cache simultaneously, in mass.

Buffer Wash Marker Contained within each MRU/LRU chain is a Buffer Wash Marker. The Buffer Wash Marker's purpose in life is to demarcate the position within the MRU/LRU chain where Buffers, following after the marker toward the LRU side of the chain, are either in the process of being written to disk by the Cache Manager or are clean.

check constraints Limit the literal data values that can be inserted into a table column. They define the search condition which any literal data value must satisfy before it is permitted by the SQL Server to be inserted into a table column.

Checkpoint process Responsible for ensuring that if the SQL Server must be restarted, the recovery of databases can be accomplished in a suitable period of time (this time quantum is user-configurable). Once per minute, the sleeping

Checkpoint process wakes up and examines the total number of changes to each database and, when it determines that the recovery of an individual database will take longer than the configured time period, it scans the data cache(s) and flushes any dirty pages out of data cache(s), out of UTL Caches, and out of *syslogs,* to disk.

clustered index   Enforces a user-defined physical-sorted order to the placement of data rows within data pages. As a consequence of the clustered index's ability to impose by force the placement of data rows, there can be one and only one clustered index per table. If a table lacks a clustered index, then its data rows are not distributed across a B-Tree structure, but are, instead, stored in a heap structure. The intermediate-level index pages, or index leaf pages, contain logical pointers to data pages. Within the intermediate-level index pages of a clustered index, there is one and only one entry for each data page in the table. At the leaf level of the clustered index are data pages. In that only the first data row of each data page in the table has an logical pointer in an index page, a clustered index is sometime referred to as sparse index.

database   An organized collection of data structures and executable processes that share a causal relationship. Whenever you create, modify, destroy, or read information being managed by a SQL Server, you are doing so within the context of a databases. A given SQL Server is capable of supporting up to 32,727 databases.

database device   A logical construct that the SQL Server uses to set aside an entire disk drive, a given section of a disk drive (i.e., a raw partition), or an operating system file.

Data Cache   A section of cache used to store data, index, and transaction log pages in memory.

defaults   Specify the default literal data value of a particular table column.

Default Data Cache   When you install the System 11 SQL Server right out of the box it comes with a single, mandatory Default Data Cache that contains a 2K Memory Pool. When the SQL Server is booted after all mandatory memory-resource requirements are satisfied, the remaining memory resources are assigned to Data Cache, and then, a specific percentage of the Data Cache is allocated to Procedure Cache. By default, the remaining memory resources are the reserve of the mandatory Default Data Cache. The minimum size of the Default Data Cache is 512K. Basically, the Default Data Cache mimics the pre-System 11 Data Cache. And, like its ancestors, it always has a 2K Memory Pool, and is always a "mixed" data cache.

distribution page   Contains information about index key values that are used by the statistical query optimizer.

d_master   A special database device that is made during SQL Server installation, via the **buildmaster** utility. The device number of **d_master** is always 0. At SQL Server installation time, the *master, model,* and *tempdb* system databases are, by default, stored on the **d_master** database device.

execution stack region   The memory area in which the SQL Server keeps track of the context, as well as the local data, of each user connection supported by an individual stack. The memory address space, the user's query, and the

SQL Server data structures corresponding to a user connection, are the context of the user connection.

extent   A contiguous block of eight 2K doubly linked pages.

global allocation map (GAM)   A bit map that records the allocation units belonging to a given database. Each bit in the map corresponds to an individual allocation unit. GAM page bit maps have 16,128 bits (from the 2048 byte page subtract 32 bytes for the page header, then, as there are 8 bits in a byte, multiply the result times 8), where each bit represents an individual allocation unit. As such, each individual GAM page can hold allocation unit information for, at maximum, 8 GB of data space allocated to that database.

group   A mechanism that allows database owners to create a name for a collection of users of their databases. Creating groups in a database is an advantageous way to grant and revoke permissions to principal database objects to a single entity, instead of to individual users of a database.

hash function   The purpose of the hash function is to grab a free Buffer Mass (according to the invoked caching strategy and the determined-target Memory Pool), place the Buffer Mass on the Kept chain, and then hash it. If the target is a 2K Memory Pool, then the Buffer Mass will be hashed on a single page identifier. If the target is a 4K, an 8K or a 16K Memory Pool, then the Buffer Mass will be hashed on the extent identifier and allocation page identifier. When reading pages into memory, a gain in overall system throughput is achieved because the SQL Server first scans the hash table for the referenced page, instead of searching the MRU/LRU chain, or instead of searching the Kept chain. If the requested page is found within a Buffer Mass in the hash table, then the SQL Server will take and hold a resource lock on the page while rows within the requested page are referenced on behalf of the user's transaction. If the requested page(s) does not exist within the hash table, and space is needed, then a Buffer Mass on the Memory Pool's MRU/LRU chain will be unhashed and the corresponding reference bits will be reset to "unreferenced" on all pages within the Buffer Mass.

hash table   A bit map that contains the list of Buffer Masses currently residing within a cache. The hash table (sometimes referred to as the hash bucket) enables the SQL Server to rapidly determine whether a given page is within a cache or whether the Cache Manager must undertake a disk I/O read to bring a copy of that page into a cache. Each Memory Pool has its own hash table. When an individual page in a Buffer Mass in the hash table is referenced by a user transaction, its reference bit is set to "referenced," and when a Buffer in the hash table is no longer referenced by a user transaction, its reference bit is set to "unreferenced."

HouseKeeper   An internal System 11 SQL Server function that washes Buffers contained within data caches (of type "mixed," only as the House-Keeper does not do any Buffer washing in data caches of type "logonly"), that is, it writes dirty pages to disk during idle CPU cycles.

identifier   Nothing more than the name that you assign to SQL Server objects.

IDENTITY property   User-defined data types and table columns have a property called IDENTITY, that, if you so choose, can be enabled. A table can have one and only one IDENTITY column. When the IDENTITY property is enabled, the SQL Server will automatically insert a unique, linearly sequential number into the column each time a new row is inserted into the table. In this way, the literal data value of the IDENTITY column uniquely identifies each row in a table.

index   A distinct storage structure that allows rapid access to information stored on data pages. An index can speed up data access because, fundamentally, it is a logical pointer to the exact data page that contains the information you are searching for (this is the case with a clustered index, however, a nonclustered index also includes the data row identifier).

interfaces file   The information these software components need to interoperate is stored within an interfaces file that has been distributed to them.

isql   When you purchase a SQL Server, you also get a client application, Interactive SQL (isql) parser, that enables you to create a session with the SQL Server (i.e., log on to the SQL Server).

Kept chain   A circular queue that contains the list of Buffer Masses that are currently in use by end-user processes. Each Memory Pool has its own Kept chain. The Buffer Masses in this list are not currently available for replacement by the Cache Manager. After the Buffer Mass is placed on the Kept chain, it is hashed.

LRU replacement strategy   When the Cache Manager follows the LRU replacement strategy, pages are read sequentially, replacing Buffers on the LRU portion of the MRU/LRU chain within the target Memory Pool. The LRU portion of the queue is the set of Buffers that are actually available to the Cache Manager so that it can allocate a Buffer to support reading a required page from disk. When a page is first read into cache, it is paired off with a Buffer from the LRU side of the LRU/MRU chain. Once the Buffer Mass is obtained by the Cache Manager it is placed on the MRU end of the MRU/LRU chain and hashed. In this way, the most commonly referenced data pages tend to remain in data cache. As more pages are read into cache, and as the page is aged over time, the Buffer Mass will migrate toward the LRU end of the MRU/LRU chain.

master system database   Contains system tables that keep track of information about the SQL Server as a whole and the *master* system database itself.

Memory Pool   Also referred to as a Buffer Pool, this is a circular linked list of Buffer Masses. Memory Pools come in just four sizes: 2K, 4K, 8K, and 16K. Every Data Cache, whether it is the Default Data Cache or a user-created Named Data Cache, always contains one (default) mandatory 2K Memory Pool. Each Memory Pool has its own MRU/LRU chain.

Memory Pool Wash Area   The portion of the MRU/LRU chain, between the Buffer Wash Marker and the end of the LRU chain is referred to as the Memory Pool Wash Area.

model system database   Within the model system database are the system tables, principal database objects, and user-defined data types required for each SQL Server user database. The model system database is used as a template for constructing user databases.

most recently used/least recently used (MRU/LRU) chain   A circular queue consisting of a doubly linked list of Buffer Masses that are currently available to the Cache Manager so that it can read new pages from disk into cache. Each Memory Pool has its own MRU/LRU chain.

named data cache   With the System 11 SQL Server, the consumer has the ability to improve performance by dividing the Default Data Cache into one or more separate Named Data Caches, and by then binding databases and database objects to these Named Data Caches. By default, all database and database objects reside within the Default Data Cache. So, it is important to realize that the SQL Server will use these Named Data Caches only after you have expressly bound databases or database objects to them. Like the Default Data Cache, each Named Data Cache contains a default 2K Memory Pool, and can be configured to contain a 4K, an 8K, and a 16K Memory Pool that will support larger disk I/O units.

nonclustered index   Enforces a user-defined physical sorted order to the key columns that make up the nonclustered index. However, the placement of data rows within the data pages is *not* physically ordered by a nonclustered index. A given table can have up to 249 nonclustered indexes associated with it. The lowest-level index pages, or index leaf pages, contain logical pointers to each data row within the table's data pages. In that each data row on each data page in the table has a logical pointer in an index page, a nonclustered index is sometimes referred to as a *dense index.*

NULL   A distinct value that is used to denote that the data value of the column is unknown. When you declare a column's data type, you can specify whether the SQL Server should assign a NULL value to that column if a user transaction does not provide an explicit data value for that column during insertion, and when nonnull default has not been explicitly bound to the column.

object allocation map (OAM)   The function of the OAM is to hold usage information about the pages that have been allocated to a given table or to a given index. In so doing, the OAM provides a precise representation of the allocation information for a given principal database object.

oper_role   The Operator role has the capability to dump and load any database or transaction log on a SQL Server, and these are the only capabilities of this role.

page   The SQL Server uses the page construct as the *unit of disk I/O* for accessing or modifying data. Each page is 2K in size.

parallel lock manager (PLM)   Used to effectively manage the simultaneous access of data resources in a multiuser environment. Through the use of locks, the PLM automatically ensures that individual processes acquire restricted access to and modification of specific sections of data without interfering with one another. The goal of the PLM is to maintain data consistency by restricting the manipulation of data in a manner that does not seriously constrain its availability.

procedure cache   A section of cache used to store active, compiled objects (using at least one buffer per object), for example, rules, defaults, views, check constraints, triggers, stored procedures, active query plans, and query trees.

query plan   An optimized series of steps requisite to executing a query, including the specific methods chosen by the SQL Server for access to each table within the query tree. The process of constructing a query plan is called *compilation*. A query plan is built when a Transact-SQL statement executes, or whenever a stored procedure (or trigger) is first executed. When a stored procedure executes, the SQL Server reads its query tree from the *sysprocedures* system table and places it within Procedure Cache. Next, the SQL Server creates a query plan and places it in Procedure Cache as well. The SQL Server uses the following information to construct the query plan: the query tree, the statistics corresponding to each table and index referenced within the procedure, and the literal data values of the parameters passed to the procedure when it is first executed. It is important to realize that query plans are held only in the Procedure Cache during run time, and are not written out to permanent storage. As a consequence, a stored procedure's query plan must be rebuilt if the SQL Server has been rebooted since the procedure was last executed.

query tree   An internal "normalized" representation of a Transact-SQL statement, stored procedure, view, trigger, rule, or default. Query trees are stored within the database's *sysprocedures* system table. When a compiled object (stored procedure, view, trigger, rule, or default) is executed, its query tree is read from disk, and brought into Procedure Cache. Query trees are constructed through a process called *resolution*. Query resolution is the process of validating the existence and accuracy of the definition of the related columns and tables (or views), converting table names into their object IDs, column names into their column IDs, and then transforming the query into an internal representation. A query tree is built whenever a Transact-SQL statement executes (keep this fact in mind if your application uses ad-hoc queries or submits Transact-SQL statements) or a compiled object is first created (keep this fact in mind if your application periodically re-creates stored procedures).

rules   Constrain the literal data values that can be entered into a particular table's column, or into table columns of a specific user-defined data type.

sa   This account is analogous to the root account of an operating system. When the SQL Server was installed, the **sa** account was automatically created by the SQL Server installation script, given ownership of all SQL Server system databases, and granted the System Administrator (**sa_role**), the System Security Officer (**sso_role**), and the Operator (**oper_role**) roles.

sa_role   The SQL Server System Administrator role.

segment   A label, or name, used to point to one or more logical database devices. Each time a database is created on a logical database device, the SQL Server automatically creates three segments on the logical database device that support the new database: system, default, and logsegment.

SQL Server engine   An executable heavyweight thread scheduled and dispatched by the operating system to run on a CPU that communicates with other SQL Server engines and shares databases and internal structures such as memory, disk, and lock resources through shared memory. In that each SQL Server engine is functionally identical, each engine can perform any user-of-system task such as physical and logical I/O or the acquisition of locking resources.

sso_role The responsibilities of login accounts with the SQL Server System Security Officer are all related to security matters.

stored procedure A compiled assortment of Transact-SQL statements saved within the SQL Server under an identifier (i.e., a name). In addition to the collection of SQL Server-supplied stored procedures (called system procedures), authorized Sybase accounts can create stored procedures within user databases. When a stored procedure is created the ASCII text of the procedure it is inserted into the database's *syscomments* system table. The stored procedure's query tree is inserted into the database's *sysprocedures* system table.

***sybsecurity* system database** Used to store its audit-trail information.

***sybsystemprocs* system database** Within the SQL Server, all system commands are implemented as stored procedures whose identifiers are prefixed with sp_ character string. All SQL Server system commands now reside within the *sybsystemprocs* system database.

table A relational data structure that is composed of a finite set of columns, in which data values are stored. Taken together, these columns constitute a data row. Each table will contain zero, one, or more rows of information. The number of rows a given table can contain is limited by the amount of available storage and the maximum size of a database. Each SQL Server database can contain up to 2 billion tables. While a table can contain up to 250 columns, the maximum width of any given table is just 1962 bytes. Within the SQL Server, each table is implemented as a doubly linked list of data pages. The SQL Server supports two types of tables: system tables that are automatically appended to the database (from the *model* system database) when the database is created, and user tables that are created by you.

tempdb system database Each time the SQL Server boots, it creates the *tempdb* system database, using the *model* system database as its template. The *tempdb* system database is shared by all login accounts to create temporary tables, and the SQL Server uses the *tempdb* system database to store, manage, and modify internal work tables.

temporary table Client process can explicitly create temporary tables within the *tempdb* system database in two different ways: prefix the temporary table identifier with the "#" symbol (this type of temporary table can only be accessed by the session that created it, i.e., other SQL Server sessions cannot read or write to such a table) and prefix the temporary table identifier with the tempdb.. character string (this type of temporary table exists either until its owner explicitly drops it, or until the SQL Server is rebooted. The same user can access the temporary table across successive sessions). Temporary tables are not recoverable, nor does the SQL Server take locks on temporary tables because they are always used by a single process.

threshold Monitors how much free space remains on a particular segment.

transaction log To facilitate database recovery, every database has its own individual write-ahead transaction log. When you create a user database, the transaction log, the spinlock for the transaction log, the segment on which the transaction log will reside, as well as the **last-chance** threshold for that log segment, are automatically created by the SQL Server for that database. The write-ahead transaction log is implemented as a heap table, called *syslogs* (in that it is a heap structure, it does not have any indexes). Every time you insert, update or delete data, you are (eventually) writing log records into *syslogs*.

trigger   A special type of stored procedure bound to a specific table that executes when a user process causes a change in the contents of the table such as when data is inserted, deleted, or updated.

user-defined data type   Within the SQL Server, Sybase accounts can construct their own data types that are based upon the provided SQL Server system data types.

user transaction log cache   Each user connection is allocated its own region in memory, called User Transaction Log (UTL) Cache (also called Private Log Cache), in which the user connection consolidates and buffers the transaction log records its transactions create.

view   A virtual table whose definition is usually founded upon a subset of columns in one or more underlying tables (or other views). The literal definition of a view is stored within the system catalogs of the database in which they are created. However, each time the view is invoked by a user connection it must be resolved. View resolution is the process of validating the existence and accuracy of the definition of the underlying columns and tables (or other views), of converting table names into their object IDs and column names into their column IDs, and then translating the query of the view into a query on the underlying tables. FYI—view resolution is a significant performance overhead.

work table   The query optimizer creates its own temporary tables called work tables. The work table holds all the intermediate results of queries that are ordered and/or grouped, and then the final select is done. When all results are returned, the table is dropped automatically. A work table is a system-generated temporary table, created for intermediate results for certain types of queries, or for certain processing strategies.

Index

abort tran on log full, 193, 259
additional network memory, 9
address spinlock ratio, 504–506
aggregate functions, 178
allocation page value, 406
allocation unit page, 84, 86, 525
allocation units, 75, 85, 525
allow_dup_row, 404
allow nested triggers, 476
allow nulls by default, 193
allow remote access, 52–53
allow sql server async, 57–58
allow updates to system tables, 170–171
alter database, 116, 143, 148, 174,
        220–223, 267–269
    for load, 190
alter table, 214–215, 307, 320, 326,
        330–331, 337, 360–372
ANSI Isolation Levels, 500
Approximate numeric, 288
at isolation clause, 502
Audit Queue, 94, 107, 108
auto identity, 193, 295–296

bcp utility, 75–76, 91, 102, 103, 144, 244,
        411, 428–434
Begin transaction record, 245, 254
binary, 289
binary tree, 78
bit, 290
B-Tree search algorithm, 78
Buffer, 109, 525
Buffer Header, 109
Buffer Mass, 109, 110, 116, 525
Buffer Mass replacement strategy, 111
Buffer Pool, 142
Buffer Wash Marker, 110, 145, 153, 525

Cache Manager, 109, 111–116
Chained Transaction Mode, 254
chained transactions, 9
char, 289
Character, 288–289
chargeback accounting, 21–26

Cheap direct updates, 248
check, 344–345
check constraints, 138, 345, 525
checkpoint command, 200
Checkpoint log record, 247
Checkpoint processing, 97, 116, 196, 197,
        256, 525–526
client character conversion set, 12
clustered index, 79–82, 400, 526
clustered index row, 82
column separator, 10
command line editor, 12
command statement syntax, 1
command terminator, 10
command timeout, 12
common key, 381, 400
compilation, 139
configuration file, 7, 97
Configured Memory, 96
constraint clause, 320, 340–341, 363, 367
control-flow constructs, 455, 475
cost-based query optimizer, 458
cpu accounting flush interval, 21–23
create database command, 116, 143, 148,
        173, 187–191, 197–198
create default command, 306–307
create index command, 101, 102, 143, 148,
        330, 337, 400–405
create procedure command, 464–466
create rule command, 318–320
create schema command, 351–352
create table command, 176, 307, 320, 326,
        338–351
create trigger command, 338, 477–479
create view command, 484–485

database consistency checker (dbcc),
        210–214
database devices, 59–74, 97, 526
database options, 193–196
Database owner, 3, 200–201
database recovery, 148, 175–176
databases, 169–242, 526
database size, 63, 188

database transaction log, 192
Data Cache, 94, 108–113, 141–142, 526
data page, 76–78, 114
data page allocation, 88–90
data rows, 77–78
data segment thresholds, 444–446
dataserver command, 7
datetime, 289
data type, 82, 287–290
data type hierarchy, 291–292
dbcc, 20, 102, 103, 143, 200, 210–214,
    352–353, 501
dbcc checkalloc, 85–86, 143, 211, 213–214,
    355–356, 410
dbcc checkcatalog, 211–213
dbcc checkdb, 143, 144, 211–212, 354, 357
dbcc checktable, 143, 144, 353–354, 356,
    357
dbcc dbrepair, 241
dbcc fixtext, 356
dbcc indexalloc, 406–408
dbcc log, 281–282
dbcc memusage, 96
dbcc tablealloc, 143, 354–355
dbcc traceon (3604), 96
dbo, 200–201
dbo login account, 3, 32–34
dbo use only, 193, 210, 213
ddl in tran, 176, 193–194, 197
deadlock, 23, 502, 521–524
deadlock checking period, 522–523
deadlock retries, 523
decimal(p,s), 288
dedicated B-Tree, 78
default database, 18
default database devices, 70–72
default database size, 185–186
Default Data Cache, 108, 111, 141–142,
    156–159, 526
default fill factor percent, 333–335
default language, 19
default network packet size, 9, 44, 46–47,
    98–100, 133
defaults, 138, 170, 173, 176, 304–316, 321,
    429, 526
default segment, 435
Deferred data row delete log record, 246
Deferred data row insert log record, 246
deferred index inserts, 252
Deferred index row delete log record, 246
Deferred index row insert log record, 246
deferred updates, 250–251, 290, 479
Deleted test table, 479
demand lock, 500
Direct data row delete log record, 245
Direct data row insert log record, 245
Direct index row delete log record, 246
Direct index row insert log record, 246
direct updates, 248–249, 290

dirty pages, 59, 136
dirty reads allowed, 500–501
Discretionary Access Control (DAC)
    system, 2
disk fragments, 74
disk init command, 62–64, 73–74, 143,
    148
disk i/o structures, 57–58
disk mirror, 66
disk refit, 74
disk reinit, 72–74
disk remirror, 67–68
disk unmirror, 66–67
display character set, 11
distribution page, 91, 405–406, 526
distribution statistics, 405, 459–460
d_master, 7, 62, 70–73, 172, 174, 180, 183,
    187, 526
domain, 293, 321
double precision, 288
drop constraint, 408
drop database command, 190, 200,
    240–241
drop default command, 314–315
drop index command, 409
drop rule command, 326–327
drop table command, 143, 148, 330, 337,
    394–395
drop trigger command, 482
drop view command, 493–494
drop proc[edure] command, 474
dump database command, 175, 184, 189,
    190, 195–196, 200, 224–225
dump tran[saction] command, 175, 184,
    189, 195, 200, 259, 269–271
dump tran[saction] with no_log command,
    244, 271
dump tran[saction] with truncate_only
    command, 270

encryption key, 9
End transaction log record, 245
engine freelock cache, 507–508
environment variable $DSQUERY, 10,
    430
environment variable $EDITOR, 11
environment variable $SYBASE, 8, 10,
    430
error log, 7, 97
error message severity level, 12
Exact numeric decimals, 287–288
Exact numeric integers, 287
exclusive locks, 418, 501
exclusive page lock, 499, 500
exclusive table lock, 500
execute, 467–468
Execution Stack Region, 94, 104–107,
    526–527
Expensive direct updates, 249

Extent allocation, 247
Extent deallocation, 247
extent i/o buffer memory overhead, 103
Extent Object Allocation Map (OAM)
    page, 87–89
extents, 75, 527

fast bulk copy, 116, 195
Fetch-And-Discard Buffer Mass
    replacement strategy, 111,
    114–115, 117–123
file descriptors, 97–98
fill factor, 333, 342, 403, 521
FIPS flagger, 9
float, 288
forceindex, 501
free extent, 85
freelock transfer block size, 508–509
free-space accounting, 451–452
free-space threshold, 189, 221

Generic Object Allocation Map (OAM)
    page, 87, 90
Generic page allocation, 247
Global allocation map (GAM) page, 84–85,
    527
global freelock list, 507–508
GAM page bit map, 85
grant command, 200, 201, 387–389,
    488–489
grant create database, 197–198
grant create default, 201, 304
grant create index, 201
grant create procedure, 201, 462–463
grant create rule, 201, 316–317
grant create table, 201, 336–338
grant create view, 201, 483
group commit, 252
groups, 201–202, 209–210, 527
guardword, 106
guest login account, 174, 204–205,
    208–209

Hash Function, 110, 527
Hash Table, 109–110, 527
Heap table, 78, 114, 243
holdlock, 502
housekeeper free write percent, 136–137
HouseKeeper process, 97, 135–138, 527

identifier, 14, 527
IDENTITY, 14, 293–299, 308, 310, 339,
    432, 527–528
identity burning set factor, 297–298
identity grab size, 297–299
identity in nonunique index, 194, 295–296
ignore_dup_key, 404
ignore_dup_row, 404
image, 289, 331

image page, 83, 144–145, 258–259
index, 78, 170, 176, 396–399, 528
index leaf page, 79, 113, 115
index node page, 79
index page, 78–83, 114
index page allocation, 88–90
index page splits, 253
index root page, 78, 113
index row, 81–82
Inner table, 113, 114, 115
In-place updates, 249
Inserted test table, 479
int, 287
Intent table lock, 499
Interactive SQL, 8–13
interfaces file, 5, 97, 528
intermediate-level index pages, 79
i/o accounting flush interval, 21–24
Isolation level 0, 500–501
Isolation level 1, 501
Isolation level 2, 501–502
Isolation level 3, 502, 522
isql, 8–13, 528

Join Query, 113, 114, 115

Kept Chain, 110, 528
Kernel Structures, 96
keywords, 1
kill, 20

last chance threshold, 260, 267, 441, 442,
    443–444, 446, 452
load database command, 116, 157, 190,
    201, 225
load transaction command, 157, 201, 271
local variables, 455, 475
lock granularity, 497–498
lock levels, 498
Lock Manager, 23
lock promotion, 510–521
lock promotion HWM, 510–519
lock promotion LWM, 510–519
lock promotion PCT, 510–519
lock promotion threshold, 499
locks, 497
lock sleep, 509
log data, 245
log header, 245
logical unit of work (LUW), 244, 248, 455
login account, 37–38
login account defaults, 26–27
login timeout, 12
Logonly Data Cache, 156–157, 271–273
logsegment, 435, 441, 443–444
log segment threshold, 443–444
LRU Buffer Mass replacement strategy,
    111, 113–114, 115–116, 528
LRU Chain, 145

master system database, 170–173, 180,
183, 187, 528
max async i/os per engine, 41, 43–44
max async i/os per server, 41, 43–44
maximum engine freelocks, 508–509
max network packet size, 9, 44, 46–47
max number network listeners, 44–46
max online engines, 41–42
max_rows_per_page, 342–343, 364–365,
372–375, 403–404, 408, 521
memory alignment boundary, 131–132
Memory Pool, 109–112, 142, 145–156, 528
2K, 112–113, 148–149
4K, 112–113
8K, 112–113
16K, 115, 143, 401
Memory Pool Buffer Masses, 112–113
Memory Pool Wash Area, 110, 145,
151–154, 528
min online engines, 41–42
mirror, 65
Mixed Caches, 142
Mixed Data Cache, 156–157, 180–181
model system database, 63, 73, 170,
173–176, 191, 197, 528
money, 289
Most Recently Used/Least Recently Used
(MRU/LRU) Chain, 109–112, 113,
136, 138, 139, 145, 529

Named Data Cache, 111, 141–143,
159–167, 179, 225–238, 412–428,
529
nchar, 289
net password encryption, 50–51
new chargeback interval, 25–26
no chkpt on recovery, 194, 259
no free space acctg, 194, 451–452
nonclustered index, 79–82, 115, 400, 529
nonclustered index row, 82
nonserial write operation, 65
NULL, 290–291, 529
number of devices, 60–61, 133
number of extent i/o buffers, 97, 101–103,
133, 143
number of index trips, 131, 133–134
number of locks, 133, 503–504
number of oam trips, 131, 134–135
number of open databases, 97, 100–101,
133, 185–186
number of open objects, 133, 185–187
number of preallocated extents, 75–76,
429
number of remote connections, 47–48
number of remote logins, 52–53
number of remote sites, 47–48
number of user connections, 133
numeric(p,s), 288
nvarchar, 289

Object allocation map (OAM) page, 84,
86–88, 90, 113, 114, 281, 407, 529
On-line Transaction Processing (OLTP),
72, 151, 445, 501, 522
oper_role, 2, 3, 30, 200–201, 529
Operator Role, 2, 3, 30–31, 34–35
Outer table, 115
overflow pages, 84, 253

Page Cache, 96
Page deallocation, 247
page lock, 498–499
pages, 76, 109, 529
page shrinking, 84
page spinlock ratio, 504–505
page splitting, 83
page utilization percent, 90–91
Parallel Lock Manager (PLM), 497–524,
529
partial load technique, 409–412
partition chain, 330
partitioned heap table, 330, 434
partition groups, 331–332
partition spinlock ratio, 331–333
passwd, 18
password, 18
password expiration, 27–28
phantom insert, 502
physical data storage hierarchy, 58–59
precision, 287
prefetch, 124–131
primary key, 341–342, 364
Principal database object, 3, 169–170
Principal database object owner, 3
print deadlock information, 524
print recovery information, 223–224
Private Log Caches, 243, 252
probe login account, 25
Proc Buffers, 96
Procedure Cache, 94, 96, 108–113,
138–140, 529
procedure cache percent, 133, 138,
140–141
Proc Headers, 96

query optimization, 457
Query Optimizer, 111–112
query plan, 138, 139, 456, 460–462, 470,
530
query tree, 113, 138, 139, 456–457, 462,
470, 475, 530

read committed, 501
read only, 194
read uncommitted, 500–501
real, 288
recompilation, 470
recovery interval in minutes, 223–224,
256–257

references, 343–344, 366
reformatting, 178–179
remote login accounts, 47, 52–56
remote server pre-read packets, 47–49
remote SQL Servers, 47–52
repeatable read, 501–502
reresolution process, 462
reserved keywords, 1, 15–16
reset command, 13
resolution process, 139
revoke command, 201, 391–393, 491–493
revoke create database, 197–198
revoke create default, 201, 315–316
revoke create index, 201
revoke create procedure, 201,
    473–474
revoke create rule, 201, 328
revoke create table, 201, 395–396
revoke create view, 201, 494–495
role, 3
rollback, 501
rowcnt, 357
row level locking, 497, 521
row offset table, 77
rule constraints, 170
rules, 138, 173, 176, 316–328, 429, 530

sa, 2, 4, 530
sa_role, 2–4, 35, 200–201, 215, 530
scalar aggregates, 459
scale, 287
segments, 435–442, 530
select . . . group by, 178
select @@max_connections, 98
select . . . order by, 178
select @@timeticks, 22
select . . . where not exists, 178
select . . . where . . . or . . . 178
select distinct, 178
select into, 116, 144, 178, 182, 195, 244
select into/bulkcopy, 176, 195, 258, 260,
    429
serial write operation, 65
Server Structures, 96
set prefetch, 131
set quoted_identifier system command,
    15, 339
set role command, 30–32
set string truncation command, 309
set transaction isolation level, 502–503
setuser command, 33–34, 201
shared memory, 94
shared memory files, 8
shared page lock, 498, 500
shared table lock, 500, 501
showplan, 461–462
show_role(), 17
showserver system command, 6
shutdown system command, 13

shutdown with no_wait command, 294,
    297
single-user mode, 7, 181, 195, 215
size of auto identity column, 295, 297–298
smalldatetime, 289
smallint, 287
smallmoney, 289
sorted_data, 404
sp_addalias system command, 201, 205
sp_addgroup system command, 201, 202
sp_addlogin system command, 18–19
sp_addremotelogin system command, 54
sp_addsegment system command,
    437–438
sp_addserver system command, 50
sp_addthreshold system command,
    448–449
sp_addtype system command, 301–302
sp_adduser system command, 201, 203,
    204
sp_bindcache system command, 181–183,
    226–232, 273–275, 417–422
sp_bindefault system command, 309–312
sp_bindrule system command, 322–324
sp_cacheconfig system command,
    157–167, 272–273
sp_cachestrategy system command,
    117–130
sp_changedbowner system command,
    198–200
sp_changegroup system command, 201,
    206
sp_checkreswords system command, 175,
    184
sp_chgattribute system command,
    372–373
sp_clearstats system command, 26
sp_column_privileges system command,
    389–391
sp_commonkey system command, 381
sp_configure system command, 22–24, 28,
    42, 44–49, 52, 53, 58, 61, 76, 91, 95,
    98, 99, 101–, 103, 105–107, 132–137,
    140, 171, 185–187, 224, 255–257,
    297–299, 332–334, 476, 504–507,
    509, 511, 514, 517, 523, 524
sp_dboption system command, 196–197,
    296
sp_depends system command, 215, 384,
    385–386, 464, 471, 480–481, 490
sp_diskdefault system command, 71–72
sp_displaylogin system command, 16–17
sp_dropalias system command, 199–200,
    201, 206
sp_dropdevice system command, 68–69
sp_dropgockpromote system command,
    520–521
sp_dropgroup system command, 201,
    209–210

sp_dropkey system command, 383
sp_droplogin system command, 38
sp_dropremotelogin system command,
    55–56
sp_dropsegment system command, 400,
    441
sp_dropserver system command, 51–52
sp_dropthreshold system command, 452
sp_droptype system command, 303–304
sp_dropuser system command, 199, 201,
    207–209
sp_estspace system command, 358–360,
    416
sp_extendsegment system command, 439
sp_fkeys system command, 377–379
sp_foreignkey system command, 380–381
sp_helppartition system command, 336
sp_helpcache system command, 162,
    413–414
sp_helpconstraint system command, 376
sp_helpdb system command, 198,
    217–218, 264, 414, 438
sp_helpdevice system command, 69–70
sp_helpindex system command, 400, 415,
    438
sp_helpjoin system command, 382–383
sp_helpkey system command, 382, 383
sp_helpremotelogin system command, 53
sp_helpprotect system command, 207,
    389–390
sp_helpsegment system command, 174,
    438
sp_helpserver system command, 49
sp_help system command, 217, 335
sp_helptext system command, 300–301,
    317–318, 464
sp_helpthreshold system command,
    447–448
sp_helpuser system command, 203
sp_locklogin system command, 36–37
sp_lock system command, 509–510
sp_logdevice system command, 265, 410
sp_logiosize system command, 275–278
sp_modifylogin system command, 204
sp_modify system command, 26–27
sp_modifythreshold system command,
    449–451
sp_password system command, 28–30
sp_pkeys system command, 376–377
sp_placeobject system command, 330, 411
sp_poolconfig system command, 146–156
sp_primarykey system command, 380
sp_recompile system command, 470, 475
sp_remoteoption system command, 55
sp_rename system command, 302–303,
    308, 320–321, 385, 386, 408, 471,
    481, 491
sp_renamedb system command, 216–217
sp_role system command, 30–35

sp_serveroption system command, 51
sp_setpglockpromote system command,
    511–519
sp_spaceused system command, 218–219,
    226, 357–358., 416
sp_table_privileges system command,
    389–390
sp_thresholdaction system command, 443,
    472
sp_unbindcache_all system command,
    237–238, 426–428
sp_unbindcache system command,
    233–236, 278–279, 422–426
sp_unbindefault system command,
    311–314
sp_unbindrule system command, 325–326
sp_who system command, 20
spid, 19, 20
spinlock, 85, 109, 161, 243, 254–256, 332,
    507–508
Split page allocation for a data page,
    246–247
Split page allocation for a index page, 247
SQL Server configuration file, 7, 97
SQL Server Engine, 40
SQL Server Error Log, 7, 97, 445
SQL Server Executable Code Region,
    95–96
SQL Server failure events, 244–245
SQL Server N_Engine, 40–41
SQL Server X_Engine, 40–41
SQL Server standard output file, 97
SQLSTATE, 309, 310
sso_role, 2–5, 531
stack guard area size, 99, 105–107
stack size, 99–100, 105–106, 131, 133
startserver system command, 6
statistical query optimizer, 405, 4547
stored procedure, 138, 169, 173, 384, 442,
    444, 455–474, 503, 531
suid, 18
swap space, 94–95
syb_identity, 295
sybsecurity system database, 107–108,
    170, 175, 185–186, 531
sybsystemprocs system database, 170,
    175, 183–184, 200, 446, 531
symmetrical multiprocessor (SMP), 39,
    161, 253, 501, 507–509
sysalternates system table, 191
sysattributes system table, 192
sysauditoptions system table, 108
sysaudits system table, 108
syscharsets system table, 172
syscolumns system table, 192, 229
syscomments system table, 138, 192
sysconfigures system table, 172
sysconstraints system table, 192
sysdatabases system table, 172

sysdepends system table, 192
sysdevices system table, 172
sysengines system table, 172
sysindexes system table, 192, 228, 436
syskeys system table, 192
syslanguages system table, 172
syslisteners system table, 172
syslocks system table, 173
syslogins system table, 173
sysloginroles system table, 173
syslogs, 192, 243, 253, 279–281
syslogshold, 282–285
sysmessages system table, 173
sysname, 293
sysobjects system table, 192, 229
syspartitions system table, 192
sysprocedures system table, 138, 139, 140,
        192
sysprocesses system table, 173
sysprotects system table, 192, 229
sysreferences system table, 192
sysremotelogins system table, 173
sysroles system table, 192
sysegments system table, 192, 436
sysservers system table, 173
syssrvroles system table, 173
System Administrator Role, 2–4, 31–32, 35
system databases, 170
system functions, 456
System Security Officer Role, 2–4, 8, 30
system segment, 435
system stored procedures, 503
systemwide password expiration, 27–28
systhresholds system table, 173, 192
systypes system table, 192
sysusages system table, 173, 436
sysusermessages system table, 193
sysusers system table, 193

table, 329–396, 531
table columns, 310–312, 313–314, 384
table locks, 498, 499–500
tables, 169, 173
table scan, 115
table spinlock ratio, 504–507
Tabular Data Stream (TDS), 40–41
tcp no delay, 44–45
tempdb system database, 60, 142, 161,
        170, 173, 174, 175, 176–183, 531
tempdb transaction log, 179
temporary tables, 176–177, 456, 531
text, 289, 331
text page, 83, 144–145, 258–259
three-table join, 457–458
@@threshold_hysteresis, 442–443
threshold manage, 442–443
threshold monitor, 442
thresholds, 440–453, 531
threshold stored procedures, 444–447

timeouts, 50–51
timestamp, 293, 310
tinyint, 287
total data cache size, 131–133
total memory, 97, 103–104, 107, 133
transaction abort, 501
transaction isolation level command, 502
transaction log, 148, 192, 243, 262–263,
        531
Transaction Log Caches, 243
transaction log records, 245–248
Transaction Log Subsystem, 243–285,
        252, 441–442
Transmission Control Protocol (TCP),
        44–45
triggers, 138, 139, 170, 384, 429, 474–482,
        503, 532
truncate table command, 330, 338,
        393–394, 460, 479
trun log on chkpt, 179, 195, 197, 256, 260
trusted, 54–55
Two-Phase Commit, 25

unique, 341, 363–364
UNIX File Management Subsystem, 59
unpinned, 253
update page lock, 498–499
update statistics, 144, 338, 405–406, 460,
        470
usage statistics, 24–25
user connections, 97–100, 104, 140
user databases, 170, 187–241
user database system tables, 191–193
user log cache size, 254–255
user log cache spinlock ratio, 254–256
user-defined data types, 173, 176, 293,
        299–304, 308–310, 312, 321–323,
        429, 532
user-defined segments, 436–438
User Transaction Log (UTL) Cache,
        252–256, 532

varbinary, 289
varchar, 289
variable length data types, 290
Vertical Server Architecture (VSA), 39
view resolution, 138, 486
views, 138, 170, 173, 384, 482–495, 532
virtual device number, 62–64

Wash Area, 145
Wash Marker, 111
Wash Point, 116
Work Buffers, 8K, 143
Work table, 115, 177–179, 181, 532
write-ahead transaction log, 243–244
writetext, 195, 244, 258–259, 479

Xact Logging Subsystem (XLS), 243

ABOUT THE AUTHOR

In 1987 Mr. Clifford earned his M.S. in Information Systems and Management Science from the University of Colorado. His thesis work centered on end user interfaces to UNIX systems. While still in graduate school, he went to work at a telecommunications research facility where he focused on End User Architecture, software productivity in distributed UNIX environments, and object-oriented methods and languages.

Since leaving the research facility, he has applied himself to the design and development of large-scale distributed computing systems for the telecommunication and capital market industries. While a Principle Consultant with Sybase, he worked as an architect and Replication Server specialist and won awards in service excellence and worldwide corporate innovation for his work on enterprise-wide systems. Recently, he has worked as a lead data architect and managed of a team of DBAs for a very large data warehouse project for a major U.S. firm on Wall Street.

Mr. Clifford is also the author of *Sybase Replication Server Primer* (McGraw-Hill). At present, he lives with his family in Rye, New York, and is working as an independent consultant. He can be reached via the Internet at ccliffor@ix.netcom.com

What's on the CD-ROM

Included with this book is a CD-ROM that contains all the chapters contained in the book. Each chapter has been converted into an individual HTML page.

SOFTWARE AND INFORMATION LICENSE

The software and information on this diskette (collectively referred to as the "Product") are the property of The McGraw-Hill Companies, Inc. ("McGraw-Hill") and are protected by both United States copyright law and international copyright treaty provision. You must treat this Product just like a book, except that you may copy it into a computer to be used and you may make archival copies of the Products for the sole purpose of backing up our software and protecting your investment from loss.

By saying "just like a book," McGraw-Hill means, for example, that the Product may be used by any number of people and may be freely moved from one computer location to another, so long as there is no possibility of the Product (or any part of the Product) being used at one location or on one computer while it is being used at another. Just as a book cannot be read by two different people in two different places at the same time, neither can the Product be used by two different people in two different places at the same time (unless, of course, McGraw-Hill's rights are being violated).

McGraw-Hill reserves the right to alter or modify the contents of the Product at any time.

This agreement is effective until terminated. The Agreement will terminate automatically without notice if you fail to comply with any provisions of this Agreement. In the event of termination by reason of your breach, you will destroy or erase all copies of the Product installed on any computer system or made for backup purposes and shall expunge the Product from your data storage facilities.

LIMITED WARRANTY

McGraw-Hill warrants the physical diskette(s) enclosed herein to be free of defects in materials and workmanship for a period of sixty days from the purchase date. If McGraw-Hill receives written notification within the warranty period of defects in materials or workmanship, and such notification is determined by McGraw-Hill to be correct, McGraw-Hill will replace the defective diskette(s). Send request to:

Customer Service
McGraw-Hill
Gahanna Industrial Park
860 Taylor Station Road
Blacklick, OH 43004-9615

The entire and exclusive liability and remedy for breach of this Limited Warranty shall be limited to replacement of defective diskette(s) and shall not include or extend to any claim for or right to cover any other damages, including but not limited to, loss of profit, data, or use of the software, or special, incidental, or consequential damages or other similar claims, even if McGraw-Hill has been specifically advised as to the possibility of such damages. In no event will McGraw-Hill's liability for any damages to you or any other person ever exceed the lower of suggested list price or actual price paid for the license to use the Product, regardless of any form of the claim.

THE MCGRAW-HILL COMPANIES, INC. SPECIFICALLY DISCLAIMS ALL OTHER WARRANTIES, EXPRESS OR IMPLIED, INCLUDING BUT NOT LIMITED TO, ANY IMPLIED WARRANTY OF MERCHANTABILITY OR FITNESS FOR A PARTICULAR PURPOSE. Specifically, McGraw-Hill makes no representation or warranty that the Product is fit for any particular purpose and any implied warranty of merchantability is limited to the sixty day duration of the Limited Warranty covering the physical diskette(s) only (and not the software or information) and is otherwise expressly and specifically disclaimed.

This Limited Warranty gives you specific legal rights; you may have others which may vary from state to state. Some states do not allow the exclusion of incidental or consequential damages, or the limitation on how long an implied warranty lasts, so some of the above may not apply to you.

This Agreement constitutes the entire agreement between the parties relating to use of the Product. The terms of any purchase order shall have no effect on the terms of this Agreement. Failure of McGraw-Hill to insist at any time on strict compliance with this Agreement shall not constitute a waiver of any rights under this Agreement. This Agreement shall be construed and governed in accordance with the laws of New York. If any provision of this Agreement is held to be contrary to law, that provision will be enforced to the maximum extent permissible and the remaining provisions will remain in force and effect.